THE MONS STAR

THE MONS STAR
The British Expeditionary Force
5 August–22 November 1918

DAVID ASCOLI

Birlinn

For
JOHN ALLAN, MM
formerly 'L' Battery, Royal Horse Artillery,
and last survivor of the action at Néry
on 1 September 1914

This edition published in 2001 by
Birlinn Limited
8 Canongate Venture
5 New Street
Edinburgh
EH8 8BH

www.birlinn.co.uk

First published in 1981 by
Harrap Limited, London

ISBN 1 84158 127 5

British Library Cataloguing-in-Publication Data
A catalogue record for this book is available from the British Library

Designed by Michael R. Carter
Printed and bound by The Bath Press, Bath

Contents

Illustrations

Acknowledgments

In a book such as this, which is a distillation of many minds and far-off memories, it is impossible to express my gratitude to everyone who has helped me. For example, over twenty years, since the subject first began to fascinate me, I must have spoken to, or corresponded with, at least five hundred old soldiers, for this is their story. Sadly, only a handful are left today. I have consulted dozens of regimental diaries and journals, not least *The Old Contemptible*, which only recently ceased publication. In the process I have taught myself, I hope, the difficult art of telling fact from fiction and distinguishing between the long bow and understatement. Old men forget – but with patience they can be encouraged to remember.

On another level, I can be more specific. I would like particularly to acknowledge the help of the following: David Smurthwaite and his library staff at the National Army Museum; Roderick Suddaby, David Nash and Michael Willis of the Imperial War Museum; the Department of Documents at the Imperial War Museum and Lady Patricia Kingsbury for permission to study, and quote from, Sir John French's unpublished diaries; Peter Liddle, for access to his unique private archive of the Great War at Sunderland Polytechnic; the curators of some thirty-six Regimental Museums; and the relatives of numerous members of the original British Expeditionary Force.

I would like to thank the following for their kind permission to reproduce the illustrations in this book: the National Army Museum (Plates 14, 16, 21); the Parker Gallery (Plate 12); the Trustees of the 43rd/52nd Light Infantry (Plate 37); and the Imperial War Museum for all other illustrations except for Plates 2, 3, 4, 9, 10, 13, 15, 23, 24 and 25, which are from my own collection.

Finally, I would like to thank my publishers for their patience and encouragement, and that is something which not every author can say. I know. I have been both publisher and author. Castor and Pollux? Jekyll and Hyde? Roy Minton, my editor, has ridden me on a properly tight rein, but always with kindness and understanding, and a wickedly accurate eye for my literary frailties. Any errors of omission or commission are mine, not his. The book, as it is here presented, is the work of designer Michael Carter. If it speaks for itself, it also speaks for his lively sense of visual narrative. And he would have had nothing to design without the immaculate typing of Alex Gracie.

I need hardly emphasize the extent of the literature dealing with all aspects of the Great War. I have done a thorough stint of research, and not least in French and German sources. I decided, however, after much consideration to omit a Bibliography, which must necessarily include much material difficult to obtain, and also much which is either inaccurate, self-justificatory or simply falsified. What has seemed to me the best – or most contentious – is referred to in the text or footnotes. My prime source, after all, has been the actors, the Old Contemptibles themselves.

Author's Note

Units and formations are distinguished in the text thus:

GERMAN
Italicized – i.e., *First Army, IX Corps, 48th Infantry Regiment*

FRENCH
Roman – i.e., Fifth Army, XVIII Corps, 84th Division. The unit and formation numbers happen not to coincide with those of the BEF

BRITISH
Roman – i.e., II Corps, 5th Division, 14th Infantry Brigade (Artillery distinguished thus, XV Brigade). Infantry battalions are shown at first mention as, for example, 1/Royal Berkshires and then abbreviated to 1/R. Berks (but see also Order of Battle, p. 245)

'The Mons Star'

The first campaign medal of the Great War – the 1914 Star – was struck in 1917. It was awarded to 'those who served in France and Belgium on the strength of a unit' or had 'service in either of those two countries' between 5 August and 30 November. It is not to be confused with the 1914–1915 Star awarded for subsequent service until the end of 1915, and which is identical in appearance except for the dates on the scrolls of the medal itself. No man could hold both medals.

The award of the 1914 Star was restricted to the Army and the Air Squadrons of the Royal Flying Corps who served in France and Flanders during the qualifying period. For some inexplicable reason, the Royal Navy and the Royal Marines – apart from the contingent sent to Antwerp in October – did not receive the medal. The safe passage of the BEF? Heligoland? Coronel and Falkland? The *Emden*? The Board of Admiralty did not protest.

In October 1919, by command of the King, a bar was awarded to all holders of the medal who 'had been under fire in France and Belgium during or between the qualifying dates', the words 'under fire' being further defined as 'within range of enemy mobile artillery'. This bar (marked by a silver rosette on the ribbon when worn without the medal) bears the inscription '5th Aug. – 22nd Nov.[1] 1914'. It is the proudest possession of the few remaining officers and men of that incomparable little Army, the last of a very special band of brothers; and it is the so-called 'Mons Star' (the name is unofficial, but long since hallowed by tradition) which is their badge of honour.

Fewer than 230,000 bars were awarded, and these went almost exclusively to the first three cavalry divisions, the first seven Regular infantry divisions, the 19th Infantry Brigade, the Antwerp force, four Yeomanry regiments, seven Territorial battalions, two Territorial companies of Royal Engineers and part of the Indian Corps.

By the end of November 1914 total British and Indian casualties were

---

[1] The choice of the final date has not been explained. It may either represent the notional 'end' of the first battle of Ypres or have been intended to coincide with the curiously belated declaration of war on Britain by Germany on 23 November.

89,864. 'The greater part of this loss had fallen on the infantry of the first seven divisions which originally numbered only 84,000.'[2]

This bare statistic conceals a terrible truth. For example: 1st (Guards) Brigade of 1st Division went to France 4,500 strong. By 12 November it had been reduced to: 1/Scots Guards – 1 officer and 69 men; 1/Black Watch – 1 officer and 109 men; 1/Camerons[3] – 3 officers and 140 men; 1/Coldstream Guards – *no* officers and 150 men. And again: by 5 November, 7th Division, which had landed on 7 October with an infantry strength of 12,000, had lost 356 officers out of 400, and 9,664 rank and file.

While these figures may not compare with the massive casualties of the later and greater battles of attrition, they have a particular significance of their own; for they represent the virtual destruction of 'the best-trained, best-organized and best-equipped British Army that ever went forth to war'. A hundred years earlier, before the battle of Fuentes de Oñoro, Wellington had said, 'Since this is the only Army Britain has, we must look after it.' By 22 November there was not much left to look after.

The Old Contemptibles had saved Britain, even Europe, by their example. Henceforth the pursuit of victory would fall, across four weary years, to the New Armies, to the volunteers and then – perilously late – the conscripts from field and factory. They fought famously and died gallantly. A Regular sergeant, who watched the Ulster Division's attack at Thiepval on the first morning of the Somme, recalls, 'I was in tears. I just had to turn away.' He was not alone.

But for these and many thousand others, there was no Mons Star. That was, is and always will be a singular epitaph to the first of the many. And this is their story.

---

[2] *Official History*, Vol. II, Note I.
[3] Early in September 1/Camerons had replaced 2/Royal Munster Fusiliers, which had virtually ceased to exist after the rearguard action at Etreux on 27 August.

Introduction

'My subject is War, and the pity of War'
Wilfred Owen

Hindsight is the first refuge of the historian. He is like a man standing on a bridge watching the debris of time long past flowing beneath him. He recognizes the debris, for he knows the course that the river has taken since the water was polluted by this flotsam; yet even from where he is standing some fragments on the surface are difficult to identify, others still defy explanation.

Far up-stream, out of sight though never out of mind, men are standing on other bridges. When first they came there the river below was clear. Each of them had – or believed he had – a certain knowledge of its course, although few could know the dangerous undercurrents or the rapids which lay ahead. All of them were, in greater or lesser degree, to add their own tithe to the debris. For while time flows on as a natural progression like a river, history – and its debris – is made by men.

In no human activity is this more true than in the conduct of war; and nowhere is it more clearly illustrated than during the first four critical months of what – regardless of every conflict before or since – remains, quite simply, the Great War. Those months were compounded of a series of 'ifs' unique in the history of military hypotheses.

If from the outset the Chief of the German General Staff had been the pragmatic Falkenhayn and not the mentally unstable Moltke; if the Schlieffen Plan had been scrupulously followed; if Kluck and Bülow had not become involved in a personal vendetta; and if Kluck, in defiance of orders, had not wheeled inward on 31 August . . . If the French Commander-in-Chief had not been the imperturbable Joffre, and the French Fifth Army had been originally commanded by Franchet d'Esperey rather than the petulant Lanrezac; if all six available Regular infantry divisions of the British Expeditionary Force[1] had been committed to battle at the outset; if they had been landed at Antwerp rather than, for reasons of political expediency, deployed in an untenable position on Lanrezac's left;

[1] In all communications, written or verbal, the French referred to *les Anglais* (or *nos Alliés*), for the good reason that their language has no word for 'the British'. In fact, the 54 infantry battalions of the original BEF were made up as follows: 36 English, 10 Scottish, 5 Irish, 3 Welsh. (See Order of Battle at p. 245.)

if they had been led by a man of greater military and moral stature than Sir John French. If . . .

We shall never know. But what we do know, from studying the debris in the river of time, is that wars may be fought by the led, but they are won and lost in the minds of the leaders. Thus in the drama that began to unfold on the Western Front in August 1914 the actors are the fighting troops, both officers and men; the directors are those set in high authority over them, both politicians and generals. Between them there was a gulf which was to grow ever wider as the action developed beyond the capacity of most of the directors to control events.

This is above all an account of the first British actors on the stage, and in a sense a requiem for the 'contemptible little army'. For them the first act of the play was to last for 110 days. As we shall see, few of them had the remotest idea of the plot or the scenario which the directors were struggling to present. For many of them, in their melancholy thousands, when the first curtain fell any explanation had become academic.

In relation to the vast conscript armies of the two great Continental powers which faced each other in the West on the outbreak of war (seventy-two German divisions[2] against sixty-eight French divisions), the BEF was very small; but by virtue of its long tradition, its strictly volunteer status and the extraordinary vision and reforming zeal of Richard Haldane, Secretary of State for War in the crucial years after the harsh lessons of South Africa, it was by far the most professional. It consisted initially (after long arguments to which we will return) of four infantry divisions, one hastily improvised infantry brigade and five cavalry brigades[3] (81,472 men and 30,000 horses), to which were added a fifth infantry division on 22 – 23 August, a sixth on 8 – 9 September and a seventh, together with another cavalry division, on 7 October, by which time the entire available home Regular Army strength had been committed to battle.[4]

At no time, up to the end of the first battle of Ypres, were there more than 250,000 British and Imperial troops in France and Flanders. Indeed, it is possible to read a library of French studies of the first weeks of the war without even being aware of a significant British presence on the battlefield (German accounts are properly more realistic, and in later years Kluck, whose early attitude to the BEF was one of contempt, wrote with admiration of its fighting qualities). An American historian,[5] while virtually dismissing the BEF's vital contribution at Mons and Le Cateau and enjoying the well-documented clashes of personality between Sir John French and Lanrezac, commander of the French Fifth Army (French would have clashed with anyone who was not a cavalryman or a member of Boodles), concedes that without the British presence, without British naval

[2] The full total, including so-called *Landwehr* and *Ersatz* divisions, was eighty-three.
[3] On 11 November 1918 the original BEF had grown to five Armies consisting of sixty-one infantry divisions, three cavalry divisions, and six tank brigades (*Official Digest of Statistics*).
[4] Further British Regular units reached France in late September from India; and also, on 14 September, the first Territorial battalion, the London Scottish, which entered the line at Messines on 30 October.
[5] Barbara Tuchman: *August 1914*.

supremacy, and without the heroic defence of the Ypres salient, the war would have been over by Christmas.

There are few moments more moving than Joffre's visit to French at Melun on 5 September:

> I cannot believe that the British Army will refuse to do its share in this supreme crisis . . . history would severely judge your absence.

And then, striking the table with his fist:

'Monsieur le Maréchal, the honour of England is at stake.' It took a French general to reduce the C-in-C of the BEF to tears; to precipitate the battle of the Marne; and so – in the longest of all possible views – to win the war.

Even though, by the end of December, the Western Front had become a static trench system stretching for over 350 miles from the Swiss border to the North Sea, it is possible to follow the fortunes of the BEF in virtual isolation from those of its neighbours. For this there are two main reasons – one, imposed upon it by the enemy; the other dictated by Kitchener's[6] uncompromising directive to his C-in-C in the field.

Committed on the extreme left of the line, with five French Armies to its right and nothing between it and the sea except four widely scattered French Territorial garrison divisions, the BEF stood directly in the path of Kluck's *First Army*, three times its size and the major instrument in the great enveloping movement designed to swing westward round Paris and crush the French armies against their own fortress defences in the south. Why the BEF was hazarded in this way is something we shall consider presently. But first it is important to put some essential facts in perspective.

The BEF did not go to Mons to *defend* the Franco-Belgian frontier. It went to provide an extension, on the extreme left wing, to the French *offensive* plan known as Plan XVII, which remains, in the shambles to which it was reduced within a week, as one of the unique monuments to military arrogance and stupidity. Indeed, it is a nice point (not often discussed by historians) what the British reaction would have been if France had been the first to violate Belgian neutrality.

At Mons the British line covered no more than twenty-one miles. Throughout the subsequent retreat, and during the advance to the Marne and then the Aisne, the British front was rarely wider than thirty miles. Even when the BEF was transferred to the Ypres sector after the stalemate on the Aisne, it covered a front of little more than thirty miles. It is this narrow – but vital – involvement which is the reason for so much French disparagement of the British war effort.

And here is another curious fact. Small as the British presence was in the

---

[6] Kitchener was appointed a reluctant Secretary of State for War on 6 August, the first and last serving soldier to hold that post. He owed this 'misfortune', as he described it, not to Asquith's advocacy (rather the reverse) but to his unique public esteem, shared only by the ageing Field Marshal Lord Roberts. As we shall see, he disliked politicians, strongly disapproved of the Franco-British plan, and distrusted Sir John French and above all French's Svengali, Henry Wilson. Alone, with Haig, he foresaw the main German strategy and the nature and duration of the war.

opening phase at Mons and during the days that followed, the full force of Kluck's *First Army* fell only on Smith-Dorrien's II Corps (which by 26 August consisted of three infantry divisions and one infantry brigade) and on three brigades of Allenby's Cavalry Division, while Bülow's *Second Army* (and to a lesser degree Hausen's *Third*[7]) was concentrated on Lanrezac's Fifth Army on the right.

Thus Haig's I Corps, on, so to speak, the 'inside' track, was scarcely involved in any fighting until 14 September on the Aisne.[8] It took no part in the battle of Mons, and during the retreat was engaged in little more than the greatly exaggerated affair at Landrecies on 26 August, the action at Etreux on 27 August and a rearguard action at Villers-Cotterêts six days later. Indeed, for much of the retreat – especially when Haig put the Sambre and then the Oise between himself and Smith-Dorrien – there was a gap of up to ten miles between the two corps of the BEF, and a similar gap between Haig and Lanrezac. But – and it is an important but – when, on 29 August, Joffre ordered Lanrezac to turn and fight Bülow's Army on the line Guise–St Quentin, Haig at once offered his full co-operation; and rightly so, for I Corps was in a position decisively to influence the course of the battle. Haig's request for permission to commit his troops was met by a categorical refusal from French (the acid exchanges between the C-in-C and his senior corps commander are striking evidence of the extent to which the directors were already distancing themselves from the actors and, indeed, from each other). Haig took no part in the battle of Guise. I Corps continued on its southerly retreat. And the distrust which the British had felt for Lanrezac after Mons was now entirely – and dangerously – mutual.

Yet in French's refusal to sanction Haig's plan lies the second reason for the comparative isolation of the BEF from the events around it.

Two days before French left London to take up his command, Kitchener gave him his instructions. They were very explicit, for Kitchener was under no illusions, least of all about French's shortcomings as a field commander. He did not care for the Franco-British plan, or for the sense of euphoria engendered in the C-in-C's mind by his Deputy Chief of Staff, Henry Wilson, who with Foch had been the architect of the joint offensive – 'a double miscalculation of force and place'[9] – to which the BEF was committed. Kitchener was likewise under no illusions about the Germans. He was the first to recognize the reason for the violation of Belgian neutrality and the weight and thrust of the German right-wing armies north and west of the Meuse. He alone foresaw the likely duration of the war, and therefore the need – and time – to raise and train an army comparable in size to those of the Continental powers. Unconsciously, perhaps, he remembered Wellington's words at Fuentes de Oñoro.

Therefore his directive to French was carefully designed to restrain the

---

[7] The German *Third Army* consisted of Saxons, and was therefore in the eyes of Moltke's staff unreliable. Hausen himself was more interested in good living and the *Almanach de Gotha* than in the stern realities of war. A more resolute commander would have converted Lanrezac's retreat into a rout.
[8] It was to be a very different story indeed when it reached Ypres two months later.
[9] Liddell Hart: *History of the First World War.*

latter (and through him Henry Wilson)[10] from confusing bravery with bravado, and from sacrificing British caution to Gallic *élan*. Thus his instructions opened with these words, with their strongly *defensive* implication:

> The special motive of the Force under your control is to support and *co-operate*[11] with the French Army in preventing *or repelling*[11] the invasion by Germany of French and Belgian territory and *eventually*[11] to restore the neutrality of Belgium. *These are the reasons*[11] which have induced His Majesty's Government to declare war, and these reasons constitute the primary objective you have before you.

Next, Kitchener underlined the vital need to 'look after' the very limited Regular Army committed to French's charge (the Territorial divisions created by Haldane were, in Kitchener's view, fit only for home defence, an attitude soon to be confounded by events). Thus he went on:

> . . . it will be obvious that the greatest care must be exercised towards a minimum of losses and wastage. . . . The gravest consideration will devolve upon you as to participation in forward movements where large bodies of French troops are not engaged and where your Force may be unduly exposed to attack.[12]

And then, donning his other, political mantle:

> In this connection I wish you distinctly to understand that your command is an entirely independent one, and that you will in no case come in any sense under the orders of any Allied General.

French, the archetypal cavalryman for whom war was still an occupation for gentlemen and the relief of Kimberley the summit of his military achievement, did not like the tone of Kitchener's instructions, peppered as they were with phrases like 'special motive', 'greatest care', 'gravest consideration', 'distinctly to understand'. He went forth to battle full of optimism, convinced of quick, decisive victory, scarcely aware of the size and nature of the challenge which confronted him. His self-assurance was no bad quality in a field commander; but one of his co-directors, Haig, knew his mercurial temperament (and temper) only too well (even to voicing his doubts to the King), and another, Smith-Dorrien, was to discover all too soon that Sir John French could be as dangerous an enemy as the Germans. Of all this the actors were unaware.

It did not take long for the euphoria to evaporate. On 21 August Lanrezac, repulsed by Bülow's *Second Army* at Charleroi on the Sambre and threatened by Hausen's *Third Army* at Dinant on the Meuse, started

---

[10] Kitchener's instructions, issued before the lengthy arguments of 12 August, still named *Amiens* as the concentration area.

[11] Author's italics.

[12] See p. 56.

withdrawing to the south without – if French is to be believed – informing his ally on his left. Suddenly the very situation which Kitchener had feared had become a reality; and equally suddenly French, fickle as a weathercock and convinced that he had been deserted by Lanrezac, ordered an immediate and general retreat.[13] Within forty-eight hours his initial enthusiasm had turned to something close to panic.

Now he took refuge behind Kitchener's directive; indeed, he went a good deal further. Whereas that directive had enjoined him 'to support and co-operate with the French Army', he chose rather the further instruction that 'your command is an entirely independent one'; and thus – even when Joffre was making his crucial decisions to return to the offensive – he continued his retreat towards the Seine, deaf to all advice except that of Henry Wilson. He thought at one time of withdrawing his entire force into some kind of armed camp at Le Havre, a proposal so insensate as to have justified his immediate removal from command. And on 30 August, the very day before Kluck committed his fatal blunder, he was even considering the evacuation of the entire BEF from France, an idea which brought Kitchener hastening to a meeting in Paris at which – although we have only French's highly suspect account – total disaster was averted.

The most charitable comment it is possible to make on the conduct of this flawed, volatile and unreliable man is that the BEF retreated so far and so fast, and the obsession with 'independence of command' was carried to such a point, that Kluck as he wheeled inward was convinced that the British had ceased to exist as a coherent fighting force and that the destruction of Lanrezac's Fifth Army was simply the *coup de grâce*. He may have written off the BEF. But he had not reckoned with Joffre; and he had certainly not reckoned with Galliéni, the Military Governor of Paris.

What Joffre really thought of French's conduct we shall never know. His memoirs are exquisitely reticent. French's account – not least his first Despatch dated 7 September, the crucial day of the battle of the Marne – is neither reticent nor accurate. At this distance in time it is only possible to admire Joffre's superhuman patience and his instinctive – even his historical – memory that, on the military stage, British actors are a great deal more reliable than British directors. Events were fully to justify his confidence.

We need not concern ourselves here with the political origins of the war (books on this subject in the French language alone occupy ten feet of shelf-space in the Bibliothèque Nationale); or with the Balkan campaign, which opened on 28 July; or (except in two vital respects) with the Russian offensive on the Eastern Front which – the phrase is apt – 'ground to a start' on 1 August. Our stage is smaller, and not unfamiliar to the ghosts of British soldiers long dead. The 9th Infantry Brigade spent its first night in France at Harfleur and, passing Agincourt and Crécy on its way to the

---

[13] Tom Fraser, a subaltern in the Suffolks, could not believe the order to retire. 'No one told us why. We thought we had done pretty well and were more than holding our own.' Luckily for him, no one told him about the true size of the enemy build-up to his front, or about the threat developing a few miles to his left. No one had told French either.

concentration area, bivouacked on 20 August on the field of Malplaquet. This probably meant little to the rank and file, but it appealed to the romantic taste of an officer in the Lincolns who noted in his diary, 'Next stop Waterloo!'

The stage was in fact set by the Germans, for it was here, on the Allied left, that the main assault was concentrated; it was here that the Schlieffen Plan had sought a swift and decisive victory; and it was here that the imponderables of war – ignored by Schlieffen – were to be vividly illustrated: moral cowardice, personal animosity, insubordination, physical exhaustion, resilient defence, even luck.

While we are not concerned with the political origins of the war, it is essential to summarize the military process which slowly but certainly made that war inevitable; for if Clausewitz's doctrine that war is an extension of policy is true, then it may fairly be claimed that the final decision was imposed upon the politicians by the generals. To understand why – and so to understand the involvement of the BEF – we must return to our river, and to another bridge where we can watch older and different debris floating past. We must go back to 1870.

In the summer of that year, before the emergence of the German Empire, Prussia (in the person of Bismarck) had provoked France (in the person of Napoleon III) to go to war.

The Franco-Prussian War was (if we except the Crimea and the battle of Sadowa) the first major European confrontation since the Napoleonic Wars. It ended in the total defeat and humiliation of France. The humiliation was to have greater consequences than the defeat.

The war started on 1 August and ended, for all practical purposes, thirty-three days later. It opened with a timid and grossly mismanaged French advance beyond the Moselle; it continued with a hasty withdrawal; and it reached its climax in a classic example of a battle of envelopment. Thereafter German and French military thinking was dominated by a single word: Sedan.

On the Prussian side, the instrument of victory was the elder Moltke, schooled in the doctrine of Clausewitz and in the theory that the essence of war is *battle*, and that the essence of battle is *concentration*.

On the French side, the instruments of defeat were an ailing Emperor; a commander (Bazaine) whose moral cowardice ('perfidy', said a later court of inquiry) was twice to turn the chance of success into irreversible failure; and a meddlesome Empress who was to send General MacMahon to his doom.

For France the ultimate humiliation was the loss of Alsace and Lorraine, and the recovery of the 'lost provinces' became a national article of faith; and given the growing ambitions of Imperial Germany, this meant war – and war on a hitherto unimaginable scale. Both sides had studied the lessons of August 1870; but in August 1914 these lessons were to be variously interpreted, and, in situations without prior model or parallel, variously misapplied. There is no schoolroom of war. The playground is the battlefield, and the players are soon distanced from the comfortable assumptions of war-games. 'Peace training tended towards solutions that were idealistic rather than realistic. For war, like politics, is a series of compromises.'[14] The next war was to be a very uncompromising affair.

'The prospect of a European War and of our being involved in it is horrible' wrote Edward Grey in a memorandum of February 1906. What he did not know – because he could not see beyond the river's bend – was that even then the prospect which he so dreaded had become a certainty. It was no longer a question of 'whether' but of 'when'. When Grey voiced his fear for the future the future was already determined and the end-game had begun: black – Germany and Austro-Hungary; white – France and Russia. Uncommitted and irresolute, Britain pondered her obligations, aware of her historic role, uneasy in her political conscience. In fact, the decision to enter a future European war had been taken for her long ago.[15] Thus does history offer its ironic hostages to fortune.

The military preparations for 1914 go back as far as 1891. In that year Moltke was succeeded as Chief of the German General Staff by Count Alfred von Schlieffen, a cold, intellectual Junker whose single-minded attitude to the war which he believed – indeed, wished – to be inevitable was indelibly stamped with the words 'Made in Prussia'. His recipe was unequivocal: total victory in the shortest possible time. But like all classic recipes, it needed the right ingredients, perfect timing, and precise attention to detail. When the time came, however, Schlieffen was no longer the cook. His successor – burdened with a legendary name – was to prove a disastrous *chef de cuisine*.

Schlieffen's plan was first conceived in 1895, two years after the Franco-Russian Dual Alliance which foreshadowed a war on two fronts for Germany and her Austrian ally. This plan was constantly refined until his retirement in 1906, a year after the Russo-Japanese War, and it was based on two historical precedents and on two fundamental imperatives. In both cases the ghost of Clausewitz was never far away.

The precedents were Cannae and Sedan, both of which obsessed his military thinking and both of which determined his strategic decision. He of all men had learned the lessons of 1870. He had absorbed the evidence of Gravelotte, where a series of suicidal frontal attacks by the Prussians had offered an opponent more resolute than Bazaine the chance of instant success; and he had seen how a battle of envelopment at Sedan two weeks later had brought instant victory.

The imperatives were those of scale and place. The whole resources of the German nation had to be mobilized, and to achieve his military objective he would need to conscript and train an army five times greater than any that had been put into the field before, sustained by massive industrial power and by a railway system capable of providing total flexibility of manœuvre.

[14] Liddell Hart: *History of the First World War.*
[15] Under the Treaty of London in 1839, the five Great Powers (Britain, France, Russia, Austria and Prussia) had guaranteed the neutrality of the then new sovereign state of Belgium 'in perpetuity'. This was to be the notorious 'scrap of paper'.

The choice of place was no problem – provided his military strategy was matched by political will. The common frontier with France ran for 150 miles from Switzerland to Luxembourg. Here the French had built a line of fortresses from Verdun to Belfort, buttressed by the natural barrier of the Vosges, while to the north of Verdun lay the difficult country of the Ardennes. Neither Hannibal nor Moltke would have gone that way, and Schlieffen was further aware that French obsession with the 'lost provinces' would allow their political hearts to rule their military heads.

The road was clear. It lay through Belgium, through Artois and Picardy, and so to the heart of France. To Schlieffen the violation of Belgian neutrality was simply a necessary means to a military end, and so his plan, cynically disregarding the Treaty of London, was based on a vast enveloping movement passing to the west of Paris and then, swinging eastward, destroying the French fortress system from the rear. Time was vital. Rightly calculating that Russian mobilization would be slow and inefficient, Schlieffen allowed exactly thirty-nine days for the defeat of France, leaving only ten divisions and the Austrians to defend the Eastern Front until the German armies in the West could be released to put the final seal on his grandiose concept.

For his Western offensive, Schlieffen created seven Armies. Two were to be deployed on the common frontier in the south to parry – indeed, invite – a French advance towards the Rhine. But to these Armies he allocated only one-eighth of his available strength. The remaining seven-eighths was concentrated farther north to check any French counter-offensive and to spearhead the great enveloping movement aimed at Paris. The right wing became an obsession with him – and in military affairs obsession can be a dangerous counsellor. For, even farther to his right, lay a small but potentially significant obstacle to his scheme.

In all his meticulous planning Schlieffen virtually discounted the possibility – or the effect – of British intervention. More seriously, since he was not interested in the views of the German naval staff, he recklessly ignored the influence of British sea-power. In the tremendous gamble which he had taken, he counted on the defeat of France before any outside agency could intervene, and with his eyes set firmly on the envelopment of Paris, he delivered himself of one of the great *obiter dicta* of military history: 'Let the right sleeve of the right-hand man brush the Channel.' It was a nice turn of phrase; but it did not happen, and the side doors to France were left open. Schlieffen, who died in 1913, cannot answer for a miscalculation that was to lose the war for Germany. [16]

We shall return to the British dilemma. But meanwhile in Berlin the joint politico-military view was that violation of Belgian neutrality would not necessarily force Britain to intervene. Indeed, the Kaiser's confidants were closer to the truth than they knew, for Britain, under a pacifist Liberal government, was not enchanted at the prospect of a continental war. Few people knew of the long discussions which had taken place in London and

[16] Even before Schlieffen's death, the younger Moltke had started to tamper with his plan by strengthening his left wing at the expense of his right.

Paris, or of the virtual commitment into which the military leaders, if not the politicians, had entered. The options were still open. The younger Moltke, nephew of the hero of 1870, and Schlieffen's successor in 1906, even expressed the view that it would be convenient to dispose of 160,000 or so British soldiers in the process of defeating the French.

When in August 1914 word went round that Britain was at war with Germany, James Taylor, then a lance-sergeant with the 9th Lancers at Tidworth, was astonished. 'Germany?' he said. 'I thought we were off for another go at the French.' The men of the old Regular Army had simple, if insular, prejudices. To them the French were effete, born losers who ate frogs' legs, kept mistresses, and were suitably associated in common parlance with contraceptives. The Germans were big and blond and beer-drinkers, who had produced Blücher and Bismarck. They also had a habit of winning wars. Sergeant Taylor felt he had more in common with such people. There was a note of good humour in the nickname 'Jerry' which was not echoed in the word 'Boche', and while men spoke of 'Kaiser Bill', no one knew or cared who was President of France. But as a professional soldier with seven years' service behind him, Sergeant Taylor was not concerned with politics. 'French or German, it was all the same to us. Whoever we were going to fight, we knew we would give a good account of ourselves. Anyone who took on the 9th would get more than they bargained for.' And so it proved. When, a month later, James Taylor had his first close encounter with the Germans it was to be short, sharp – and unique.

The French moved towards the inevitable confrontation by a different route which owed as much to temperament as to history.

While Schlieffen addressed himself to the prospect of the super-Cannae of his dreams, the French General Staff, too close to history for comfort, resolved that there would be no second Sedan. French military thinking throughout the 1890s remained passive and defensive, dominated by another dream: the recovery, in some vague future, of Alsace and Lorraine. The possibility that Paris itself might be the next Sedan was not considered. The road to Paris lay through Belgium, and Belgium's neutrality, after all, was guaranteed 'in perpetuity'. Thus French policy was designed to deter. Hence the Russian alliance, far more a marriage of convenience than of true minds; and the decision to build a fortress barrier along the common frontier – Verdun, Toul, Nancy, Epinal, Belfort – which would serve both as a shield and as a springboard against the day when France would redeem her honour and purge her humiliation. Schlieffen watched this conflict of conscience with interest. It suited his purpose very well.

But during the early years of the new century French military thinking, influenced by a generation of young officers to whom the doctrine of a defensive war was anathema, underwent a radical change. In part this was due to physical events – the evidence of Russia's military weakness in the war with Japan and the growing arrogance of Germany in her public utterances and her sabre-rattling demonstrations in Morocco; and a by-product was the start of tentative military consultations between London and Paris, initiated in 1905 (with an English sense of the ridiculous) by the military correspondent of *The Times*. [17]

The high priests of the new philosophy were Foch, commandant of the École Supérieure de Guerre, and Grandmaison, Director of Military Operations. This philosophy was quintessentially French, with its evocation of past glories and its obsession with *élan* and *attaque brusquée*, with bands and banners, even with the uniforms of a vanished age. It was irrelevant; and it was based on an absurd arithmetical error. It was as if 1870 had never happened.

The new philosophy can be summed up in the phrase *l'offensive à outrance*, and its component elements were the primacy of attack, the essence of battle (Clausewitz) and the equation of the moral to the material (Napoleon). The offensive spirit, argued Foch, was the true expression of the French temperament (by a terrible irony La Gloriette, the vast cemetery at Verdun, bears witness to the greatest *defensive* battle in the history of French arms), and thus the sole means of imposing the nation's will – the will to victory – on the enemy. But Foch had a head as well as a heart, and he understood, as Grandmaison did not, that war is as much about tactics as strategy, and that morale alone could not serve as a substitute for the basic principles of war. *Elan* and the famous French 75s were not enough.

But it was too late. With the offensive lobby in full cry, General Michel – appointed in 1911 as commander-in-chief designate – made one final, if hesitant, attempt to revive the old strategy of defence as a springboard for a counter-offensive, a policy not so much of 'wait and see' as of 'wait and act'. Michel was less concerned with history than with geography, and his eyes were fixed on Belgium. Indeed, in 1909 Schlieffen had obligingly published an article which, in all but precise detail, described his plan. But the tide was running too strongly, and so Michel – whose moral courage would certainly not have matched the coming confrontation – was jettisoned. In his place was appointed General Joffre.

Joffre was far from being an automatic selection (he was in fact third choice). He was, like the ill-fated Bazaine, an Engineer officer. But unlike Bazaine, he was without higher staff training, a man of few words, a good listener, slow to act but decisive in action, and above all confident in his own ability. If it was not given to him in the end to win the war, he can beyond argument be said to have ensured, by his brilliant improvisation at the gates of Paris, that the Germans would lose it. Years later Foch, not given to *arrière-pensées*, said of him, 'If we had not had him in 1914, I do not know what would have become of us.' We, standing on our bridge down-stream, know very well. The course of history would have been dramatically changed.

Joffre fully supported Foch and thus, the French General Staff tore up the sixteenth variation on the offensive theme and, twisting the facts to suit their theories, produced Plan XVII, which was formally adopted in March 1913.

[17] The revived Entente Cordiale of 1904 was a political instrument concerned primarily with colonial spheres of influence. It was not, as is often suggested, in any sense a military alliance. That was to come later, and even then in the form of an imprecise undertaking.

It is not possible, even with benefit of hindsight, to imagine a more arrogant or ill-conceived exercise in the art of modern warfare; and it is not without an element of irony that many of the senior officers who were responsible for this *folie de grandeur* were in the event to command the field armies required to put it into practice.

The plan was as follows. On the extreme right a task force (grandly called 'the Army of Alsace') was to secure the area where the French, German and Swiss borders meet; along the common frontier the First and Second Armies would strike north-east through Lorraine and the Saarland with their *general* objective (no specific objectives were laid down) the city of Mainz on the Rhine. There was no timetable. There were no reserves specifically allocated to reinforce success or protect against failure.

The Third and Fifth Armies were to attack eastward between Metz and Thionville or, if the Germans violated Belgian neutrality, north-east through Luxembourg and the Ardennes (terrain which was totally unsuited to an offensive, let alone *l'offensive à outrance*). The Fourth Army, consisting largely of Reserve divisions – and therefore, in the blinkered minds of French professionals, of no fighting value – was concentrated behind the forward armies with no specific role other than to march triumphantly through the gap created in the German centre by the assault divisions. The end-product – the date still unspecified – would be a *vin d'honneur* in Berlin.

Under Plan XVII the left flank of the French Fifth Army rested on Hirson, near the Franco-Belgian border and thirty-five miles from a small mining town called Mons. Between Hirson and the Channel ports – a distance of a hundred miles – there was a great gap, Schlieffen's chosen gap, where it was tacitly accepted that the British would provide at least a deterrent presence while the French armies, with traditional *élan*, disposed of the ancient enemy.

Even at the last hour the French General Staff, while accepting the possibility of a German violation of Belgian neutrality, remained convinced that the risk of British involvement and the affront to world opinion would limit an attack through Belgium to a modest infringement of territory east of the Meuse, and that the assessment by French intelligence of the German right-wing build-up was exaggerated and defeatist. When Joffre took over as C-in-C designate he found Michel's acute appreciation of German intentions in a safe. He did not even trouble to study it. Had he done so he might have saved himself much anguish, and France much blood. And again, even at the last hour, Castelnau – later to command the French Second Army at Nancy – on a visit to the military governor of Lille (who was voicing his concern at being exposed to a German envelopment) airily replied, 'So much the better! That will weaken their centre.'

Thus throughout the hot summer of 1914 the battle lines were drawn in the West. 'It must come to a war,' Schlieffen is said to have muttered on his death-bed. 'Only keep the right wing strong.' And it is there that our drama now unfolds. It is time to turn away from the main arena and consider what was happening in the wings.

CHAPTER 1

'If you wish for peace, prepare for war'

Of all the major European powers, Britain alone wished for peace; of all of them, she alone was slow (and reluctant) to prepare for war.

The reason lay far back in history. Britain is an island, sea-girt and thus reliant for her security and her prosperity upon the sea. From this improbable base she had built an empire, unique both in its size and in its authority, on her command of the seas – much of it, ironically, 'acquired' from the French. The Pax Britannica was buttressed by the Royal Navy and policed by a small and widely dispersed army which, exactly following the Roman imperial system, provided the hard core of locally recruited native levies.[1] Sometimes, as in the Indian Mutiny, the system came close to breaking down (the Romans had their mutinies too); but it was the Navy which was Britain's pride and her sure shield. When insolent foreigners challenged Britain's authority a Foreign Minister like Palmerston resorted not to sweet reason but to gunboat diplomacy. It worked like a charm.

After Waterloo, imperial Britain left Europe to the Europeans, although keeping a wary eye on shifting political alignments. Her single involvement – in the Crimea – proved singularly inept and even in that war it is conveniently forgotten that the French contribution in men and material outnumbered that of the British by two to one. Sixty years later, the disparity was to be ten to one in the opening phase.

The Crimean War (and, to a lesser extent, the Indian Mutiny) produced one vital side-effect. In 1868 Edward Cardwell, Secretary of State for War in Gladstone's first administration, was put to work to consider long-overdue reforms in an Army still little changed from the time of the Napoleonic Wars. The three main recommendations of his report were these: the reorganization of infantry regiments into units of two battalions (in some major centres of population there were to be three and even four battalions);[2] the introduction of short-service enlistment – seven years with the colours and five on the Reserve (but see p. 8); and the abolition of

---

[1] In the Indian Corps which reached France at the end of September 1914 each of the six infantry brigades contained one British battalion.
[2] At Mons on 23 August the first German attack fell on 4/Royal Fusiliers and 4/Middlesex.

the practice of commissions by purchase. Of these, the last was perhaps the most significant in the long term, for it provided the basis for a new and long-overdue professionalism; but given the British attitude to its Army, it was to take many years for this novel concept to work its way through the system. In one critical area, however, Cardwell dodged the issue, and that was the existing higher command and administrative structure. He would have been a brave man indeed to have suggested the replacement of the Commander-in-Chief, the Gilbertian Duke of Cambridge, by a proper General Staff on the Prussian model.

Behind his 'new' Regular Army Cardwell provided a second-line, home-defence Reserve in the old Militia and Yeomanry; and a third line in the Volunteers, a very British invention, somewhere between a social club and a private army, which against all the odds drew this comment from Wolseley in 1878:

> It is quite certain that the old prejudice against the soldier must soon die out altogether [*a pious hope*]. In fact, the Volunteer movement has popularized the Army [*an even more pious hope*][3]

This apparent state of grace in the Regular Army was soon to receive a rude rebuff in South Africa, where a great imperial power was taught a salutary lesson in the art of fire and movement by a determined and skilful army of amateur farmers who demonstrated that there is no substitute for expert marksmanship, and that in modern war the sole virtue of a horse is that of mobility. But above all, the war underlined the need for reform in that delicate but crucial area where Cardwell had feared to tread. South Africa was the graveyard of numerous military reputations which had been established in what have been described as 'Victoria's little wars'. Some generals who emerged with credit were to flatter only to deceive. Others, perhaps fortunately, would be too old when the greater crisis came. But one fact was clear, even to the most chauvinistic of military men. The romantic age of imperialism had died with the dawn of the new century. As the sound of distant thunder began to echo across Europe, Britain could no longer put her trust in naval supremacy alone. It was time to act.

The Boer War lasted two and a half years. In that time over 500,000 British and Imperial troops had been wastefully – and inefficiently – employed in reducing a guerrilla force which at no time numbered more than 40,000. What if the next adversary were to be a continental power, equipped and trained for a continental war? And what if the arithmetic of the opposing forces were to be reversed? One half of that equation was a matter for the politicians; the other half for the generals.

In 1903 a Royal Commission, appointed by Balfour's Tory government, published its report on the conduct of operations in South Africa. At least it avoided the laughable exercise in whitewashing which followed the Committee of Inquiry into the Crimean War, but its conclusions were

---

[3]The Volunteers prided themselves on their musketry skill. This slowly rubbed off on the Regular Army, and was to pay a priceless dividend in 1914.

evasive, unconstructive and irrelevant to the future. Among the witnesses who gave evidence were the new public hero, French, and his former chief staff officer, Haig. Both were cavalrymen. Both envisaged a major role for cavalry in any future war[4] although Haig, with a backward glance at the Boer Commandos, underlined the importance of greater emphasis on training in dismounted action.[5] He did not, however, advocate the idea of 'mounted infantry', which was anathema to him (the semantic arguments about 'dismounted cavalry' or 'mounted infantry' which continued for several years are testimony to the British genius for trivializing basic issues. The Germans came much nearer to the essential interdependence of combat troops by including *Jäger* battalions in their cavalry divisions, a practice repeated twenty-five years later by the presence of Panzer Grenadiers in armoured divisions.) War, like peace, is indivisible.

Yet Haig was wiser than he knew. When the Cavalry Division of the BEF went to France it was to prove its superiority in mounted combat from the very first contact with the enemy at Soignies on 22 August, but it also took with it the new short Lee-Enfield rifle with which it proved itself at least the equal of the infantry in its standards of musketry, and immeasurably superior to both the French and the Germans. Within two months of arriving in France the cavalry saw very little of their horses;[6] but there is no doubt that without his seven dismounted cavalry brigades in the line at Messines and in the salient, Sir John French might well have lost the first battle of Ypres. Paddy Byrne of the 9th Lancers reflects upon the fortunes of war:

> I suppose I'm one of the very few men who wore his spurs in a cavalry charge at Moncel in September and was still wearing them two months later in a trench at Hooge!

But there were more serious aspects of the Royal Commission's report. The military witnesses – with the notable exception of Ian Hamilton – disregarded the evidence of history, which proved beyond argument that the fire-power of modern weapons – above all the machine-gun ('the concentrated essence of infantry', in Liddell Hart's chilling phrase) – could dominate the battlefield and give the defence a formidable superiority over the attack (a lesson which the Germans, despite a four to one advantage in the canal salient at Mons, very soon learned). It was a lesson which all the combatants were to learn the hard way. The French answer was *élan*; but bullets are no respecters of *élan* if it is not supported by comparable fire-power and tactical skill. The German answer was sheer weight of numbers. The infantrymen of the 3rd British Division at Nimy

---

[4] In August 1914 the French and the Germans each put into the field ten cavalry divisions which caused as many problems to their own side as to the enemy, although the French Cavalry Corps of Sordet and Conneau were to play vital roles at three moments of crisis.

[5] In 1906 Haldane appointed Haig Director of Military Training at the War Office. During his tour of duty he made a vital contribution to the new concept not only of cavalry training, but of the whole Army.

[6] None the less, the horses absorbed a large number of effectives; and this, with escort and other duties, reduced a dismounted cavalry regiment to a rifle strength of little more than 400.

and Obourg on 23 August were astonished to see the Germans advancing upon them in close columns. 'It was an unbelievable sight,' says 'Pony' Moore of 4/Middlesex. 'You didn't need to aim. You just fired into the blue and they went down like flies, like a pheasant shoot without needing any beaters. After a bit, they retired in disorder. In a way, it was sickening to see all those men laying there.'

Artillery was another matter. In his evidence to the Royal Commission, Haig delivered himself of this remarkable statement: 'Artillery seems only likely to be effective against raw troops' – and this after a single experience, the campaign in South Africa in which the Boers had fewer than fifty effective artillery pieces and very little ammunition.

In the event, as Haig was presently to discover, the Great War was to be above all an artillery war. No reliable statistics are available, but on a reasonable estimate well over 700,000,000 shells were fired on the Western Front;[7] whether against raw or seasoned troops seems academic.

To talk to old soldiers of the BEF (and they could hardly be described as 'raw troops') is to understand the destructive and soul-destroying effect of constant shell-fire – 'like a long arm reaching out to find you, even when you were out of the line and having a well-earned kip.' 'We were in the courtyard of a farm near Wytschaete when a "Jack Johnson" arrived and wiped out all but four of my platoon.' Again and again, the same theme recurs: 'There was a road junction near Zandvoorde. A German shell arrived every eighteen seconds, bang on target. I couldn't find a runner who was ready to chance it. I don't wonder.'

For all Haig's comfortable assumption (and by July 1916 on the Somme he was making a much more dangerous assumption), the real German strength lay in their preponderance of heavy artillery, firing high-explosive shells. The French, despite their brilliantly versatile 75s, had no answer to this weight of German explosive in the early stages of the war; and this was even more true of the BEF, whose Horse and Field Artillery were issued only with shrapnel, and whose 'heavy', counter-battery capability consisted of just sixteen 60-pounders. When the official History describes the BEF as the 'best-equipped' Army ever to leave these shores it is in effect providing a damning commentary on years of political parsimony and complacent military thinking. Apart from a virtually total lack of heavy artillery and high-explosive shells, the BEF had only two machine-guns (water-cooled Vickers subject to nine different 'stoppages') to each infantry battalion; no short-range trench mortars; no close-range hand grenades; all of which were standard equipment (in quantity) of the German Army – a fact well known to, but disregarded by, the General Staff in London. Thus the BEF fought and survived its early battles by a mixture of training, discipline, good humour, courage, unique musketry skill and the brilliant use of divisional artillery. 'They were', said Zwehl of the German *Seventh Army*, 'very exceptional soldiers.'

The miracle is that a very professional lightweight, matched against a

---

[7] Between 23 August 1914 and 11 November 1918 the British total alone was 187,342,870 of all calibres (*Offical Digest of Statistics*).

scarcely less professional heavyweight, not only absorbed terrible punishment but finally won by a technical knock-out in the early rounds. Small wonder that the actors acquired a cynical attitude towards so many of their directors, who not only could not see the wood for the trees but stubbornly refused to recognize the trees for what they were.

The report of the Royal Commission was largely, but not entirely, pigeon-holed. No one, least of all the government, could pretend that the war in South Africa had been conducted with much distinction by the commanders and their staffs. And it was to this problem – the very one which Cardwell had funked – that Arnold-Forster, the Secretary of State, addressed himself by setting up on 6 November 1903 a Committee to examine 'the reconstitution of the War Office'. The Committee was chaired by Lord Esher and included Sir George Clarke, a soldier of no particular merit, and – with breath-taking nerve – Admiral Sir John Fisher, the peppery but dynamic First Sea Lord whose attitude to soldiers was that they were an expensive irrelevance, and who successfully resisted the creation of a Naval Staff throughout his time at the Admiralty. [8]

The 'triumvirate', as they were called, examined few witnesses, took no written evidence, and published no minutes. But they wasted no time, and the first part of their report, published on 1 February 1904, was to have a profound – and profoundly important – influence on the future structure of the British Army.

The Committee made three major recommendations: first, the abolition of the office of Commander-in-Chief (the last incumbent was Lord Roberts); second, the creation of a Committee of Defence, [9] chaired by the Prime Minister; third, the formation of an Army Council (this formally came into existence one week later) whose military head was the Chief of the General Staff, and which predictably included a civilian Finance Member to act as Treasury watchdog. On 9 August 1905 the Army Council fathered the embryo General Staff. The second part of the report, published on 26 February, proposed the establishment of seven Home Commands, which included Ireland.

All the Esher recommendations were duly adopted. Through all of them runs a single purpose, not often commented upon: they were based not on any aggressive intention but purely on creating properly integrated and administered machinery for home defence. In 1904 Britain, with only one distant (and largely forgotten) European commitment, resolutely maintained her historic policy of isolationism. But within a year the signs had begun to multiply. Wise men – and there were not many wise men – could read those signs, and from them recognize the revival of German imperialism. The Government averted its eyes, concerned only to ensure that in the event of war Britain would be secure from invasion. Repeatedly the Navy gave a guarantee of this security, but at the eleventh hour – and even beyond – the spectre continued to haunt the decision-makers, and

[8] When Churchill went to the Admiralty in 1911 he soon changed that.
[9] In 1908 it was renamed the Committee of *Imperial* Defence.

this obsession was materially to influence the eventual size and role of the original BEF.

In 1906 the British people voted into power, with a landslide majority, a party whose roots were strongly pacifist, anti-military, non-interventionist. In such a party there was no stampede of applicants for the hottest seat in the Liberal Cabinet. In the event it was occupied – in the best military tradition – by a volunteer. Richard Haldane was a lawyer, political scientist, educational pioneer, man of peace, with a passion for German philosophy and a deep distrust of German intentions. In his memoirs he recalls a meeting with Campbell-Bannerman. 'Nobody', said the Prime Minister, 'will touch the War Office with a pole.' 'Then give it to me,' said Haldane. It was as if Prospero was assuming the mantle of Minerva.

He was to become the greatest of all Secretaries of State for War. He had no illusions about the inevitability of the conflict to come, and so he set to work quietly, logically, although not without opposition, creating the highly tuned instrument which went to war eight years later; and just as Robert Peel had been the unlikely creator of the Metropolitan Police, so Richard Haldane became the improbable father of the BEF. For this he is little remembered to-day, because he was a very private man who sought no publicity. His task was to provide the generals – the professionals – with the best army that money could buy, and he had to do that as a member of a party – indeed, a country – which thought the world of its sailors but quibbled about its soldiers.

In the year in which Haldane took office the Army Estimates were approved – if that is the word – at £28,000,000 (less than the cost of a single armoured brigade to-day). The Estimates for the last year before the Great War were £28,220,000.[10] In other words, Haldane transformed a ramshackle organization into a modern fighting force strictly within his financial terms of reference. It was a remarkable achievement. He himself reflected later how much greater it could have been if soldiers had been better paid, and if money had been spent on the vital engines of war.

It took Haldane no more than a month to identify the basic problems and to marshal his proposals. His reasoning went like this.

What was the purpose and function of the British Army? First, since Britain was an imperial power, it must provide the military capacity to police its Empire (even Haldane, with his sceptical legal mind, assumed the historic role of the Navy). This left the question of the Regular Army at home, and of the various second- and third-line military and quasi-military institutions. If the purpose of the Regular Army was to provide a reservoir for imperial garrisons and a professional first line for home defence, then that would require a 'passive' answer to his first question. But the Navy had guaranteed the security of Britain from invasion, and therefore the Regular Army must be reformed so that it could be relieved of its passive function

---

[10] The Navy Estimates were subject to no such constraint. Jackie Fisher saw to that – and not even the most radical of Liberals would have crossed swords with Jackie Fisher.

and the responsibility for home defence transferred to an entirely separate but *interdependent* auxiliary force.

That was Haldane's first premise. He now asked himself a second – and logical – question. If the Regular Army was to be organized and equipped for an offensive role, where might it be required to fight? And in what kind of war might it be involved? Haldane did not need to consult any Delphic oracle. The battleground would be on the Continent, the enemy would be Germany, and the war would be on a hitherto unimaginable scale. [11]

Given the political – and indeed national – hostility to conscription in any form, Haldane had to work within very strict parameters. During his last two years as Commander-in-Chief (and long after that office was abolished) Lord Roberts campaigned strenuously for some form of compulsory national service, but not even his unique popularity and personal charisma could swing public opinion behind him. The hero of Kandahar was no match for Liberal pacifism and Treasury parsimony. Incredibly, it was not until 1916, after Kitchener's death, Lloyd George's arrival at the War Office, and the early disasters on the Somme that conscription was introduced, and then this was only justified by the moral, rather than military, premise of 'equality of sacrifice'.

In a sense, the volunteer system suited Haldane, for since he could not compete in terms of quantity with the great Continental powers, he could at least concentrate on quality. The political decisions about the nature of any British involvement in a future war – indeed, about any involvement at all – were matters for the Cabinet as a whole, and the Prime Minister and Foreign Secretary in particular. So far as the Army was concerned, it was for the directors – the General Staff – to decide, how, where *or whether* the actors would take their places on the stage.

Haldane's reforms were set in train in 1906 and virtually completed by the end of 1908. [12] It is neither possible nor necessary to analyse here the total revolution which he and his advisers achieved, but to understand that achievement, and its influence on the political options which were to face a reluctant Cabinet when it could no longer evade the issue, let us summarize the essential features of Haldane's grand design and add some footnotes, both quirky and illuminating.

1 The Regular Army at home was reconstituted as 'an expeditionary force' of six infantry divisions and one cavalry division, with a total projected strength of 165,000. The basis of service was Cardwell's Enlistment Act of 1870 but with some significant differences, due in part to the new 'expeditionary' role of the Army and to the introduction (on a very modest scale) of mechanical transport. The following table shows some apparently incongruous variations on the simple twelve-year system:

[11] When Haldane took office the only military contact with the French Government had been the curious exchanges between Repington of *The Times* and Huguet, the French attaché in London. In effect, this semantic discussion went no further than establishing the British posture in the event of a breach – from whatever side – of Belgian neutrality. Repington was to become something of a trouble-maker, inviting the epithet 'distasteful' from, of all people, the devious Henry Wilson.
[12] During this period the two key figures on the General Staff were Haig (Director of Military Training) and Grierson (Director of Military Operations) who were duly designated as the two Corps Commanders of the BEF. In the event, Grierson died on 17 August on his way to the forward area.

	With the Colours	With the Reserve
Infantry of the Line	7	5
Cavalry of the Line	7	5
R.H. and R.F. Artillery	6	6
Household Cavalry	8	4
Foot Guards	3	9
Royal Engineers	6	6
Drivers, RE	2	10
Army Service Corps	3	9
Drivers, ASC	2	10
Army Medical Corps	3	9

There is clear evidence of Haldane's logical mind in these figures, with the exception of the Household Cavalry (with a great deal of peacetime ceremonial) and the Foot Guards (who, alone of the infantry, did not serve 'East of Suez', and therefore were not required to provide a reservoir of overseas drafts).

With the ancillary services such as the Medical Corps the short period with the colours is a reflection of a small peacetime requirement which would be radically expanded on mobilization. Regiments of the Line converted their bandsmen into medical orderlies and stretcher-bearers when they went to France, but still managed to take with them, under various disguises, the means of making music. Notwithstanding, it was a Corporal Drummer of the 4th Dragoon Guards who is credited with firing the first shot on 22 August.

Men could, of course, sign on for their full '21'; but here is a revealing fact. When the BEF mobilized on 4 August there were, still serving with the colours at home, only 4,192 men with fifteen or more years of continuous service. In fact, because of the terms of service, it was a very young Army. Of those with the colours 46,291[13] had less than two years' service, and many of these were left at home because they were not considered to be adequately trained. It was not long before they were urgently required as reinforcements in France and Flanders.

At 1 October 1913 – the last applicable figure – the strength of the Regular Army at home and abroad was 247,250, needing 8,580 to complete establishment;[14] and when the BEF mobilized the average number of reservists recalled to the colours represented 61·8 per cent of the embodied strength of the BEF.[15]

2 With the 'expeditionary' role of the Regular Army established, Haldane turned next to the twin problems of its reinforcement and of home defence (not even his exceptional imagination could foresee the sheer scale and duration of the coming conflict, and therefore the immense resources in

---

[13] *Offical Digest of Statistics 1913/1914.*
[14] As an indication of the size of the Army's imperial commitment, on 4 August 12 out of the 28 cavalry regiments of the line were serving overseas.
[15] The war establishment of a cavalry regiment was 25 officers and 526 other ranks; and of an infantry battalion 30 officers and 992 other ranks.

PLATE 1. *'It was a very young Army'*

manpower which would eventually be required).

On mobilization the Regular Army Reserve would, under its terms of service, be recalled to the colours. Next in line stood the old Militia. This Haldane renamed the Special Reserve 'to indicate', in the words of the official History, 'what it had long been in practice – a depot for feeding the Regular Army'. In August 1914 this Reserve, considerably under strength, stood at 61,048 men, a figure totally inadequate to provide first-line reinforcements for an expeditionary force. To this problem Haldane addressed himself. The result – largely the work of the DMT, Haig – was the reorganization of the Yeomanry and the creation of the Territorial Army.

The old second-line Reserve had since 1859 been the Volunteers, a fact which, as we have seen, reflected the aversion of the British to compulsory service and their passion for playing games, whether in or out of uniform. The Volunteers had no military obligations, but many of them had served in South Africa, and had demonstrated an expertise in musketry greatly superior to that of the Regulars. Their strong local ties – even down to factory level[16] – gave Haldane the inspiration for his next reform.

The Territorial Army came into existence on 1 April 1908. Haldane, pursuing his policy of modernization and of 'rooting the army in the people', offered the Volunteers a simple alternative: join the new second-line force or cease to exist. They joined.

Haldane and Haig were extravagantly ambitious. The Territorial Army, as they originally envisaged it, was to consist of twenty-eight infantry divisions and twenty-eight Yeomanry brigades, organized on the exact model of equivalent Regular formations. There was no conceivable likelihood that the Cabinet or the Treasury would provide the money for so revolutionary an expansion. Haldane and Haig must have realized this. What they did, therefore, was to apply the old formula of wage negotiations: think of a number, double it, and then settle for the original figure. Thus when the Territorial Army eventually came into existence it was organized into fourteen infantry divisions and fourteen Yeomanry brigades, with a proposed establishment of about 312,000, administered by local County Associations, each formation commanded by a Regular Army general with a small permanent staff of Regulars. Within two years this second-line Reserve numbered 276,618 all ranks,[17] whose role in the event of war was primarily that of home defence. But when the Territorial Army was embodied on 4 August it at once volunteered for overseas service to a man. By the end of 1914 one division (the 42nd) had been sent to Egypt and three (the 43rd, 44th and 45th) to India to release Regular formations for service in Europe; and by December of that year there were seven Yeomanry regiments and twenty-two T.A. infantry battalions in France and Flanders (but see Order of Battle, p. 245).

[16] Many Volunteer units, after the fashion of social clubs, elected their officers – 'the guv'nor' in command, and so on, down the managerial scale.
[17] By 1914 this figure had declined sharply, but in any event the Territorial system was abandoned by Kitchener in favour of a 'national' recruiting campaign to raise 1,000,000 men – the 'New Armies' as they came to be called.

The transformation of the Regular Army into an expeditionary force involved a comparable change in every aspect of equipment and training. It is not possible here to deal in detail with the whole catalogue of reform, but a few examples will show the ingenuity of Haldane in working within his financial limits, the growing (if still imperfect) awareness of the General Staff – and of Haig in particular – of the nature of modern war, and the persistent British habit of combining innovation with absurdity. There were still plenty of Gilbert's 'modern major-generals' in high places. But at least these examples may explain how it was that, for all its lack of vital equipment, the BEF became so unique – and so professional – an instrument of war.

First, clothing. By 1908 the Army had adopted the familiar khaki service dress with the new webbing equipment ('too much brass and blanco' was one dry comment). In field service marching order an infantryman carried 61 lb of equipment (appreciably less than his French or German equivalent). A cavalry troop-horse[18] fared worse, for, 'looking for all the world like a Christmas tree', it carried something like eighteen stone. Apart from the normal horse furniture and arms, a cavalryman (and his horse) carried a remarkable array of spare horseshoes, two feed-bags (each with seven pounds of oats), waterproof cape, greatcoat, canvas bucket, haversack, thirty rounds of ammunition in a bandolier (a further sixty rounds in a bandolier slung round the horse's neck), knife, fork and spoon 'normally tucked jauntily into the top fold of his puttee'.[19] It was not the most comfortable set of accoutrements for a man likely to be involved in mounted combat.

But there was also, as Haldane knew, the Army's public image. So the off-duty Army walked out in smart and soldierly dress – blue, scarlet or rifle-green for the artillery and infantry, and eye-catching colour and variety for the cavalry. 'Church parade at Aldershot was a grand sight', recalls an old Hussar. 'I often wonder how many youngsters came, saw, and were conquered!' There is certainly no doubt that overalls, boots and jingling spurs were a powerful aid to recruiting, even if few ever achieved so romantic an ambition.

The new dress regulations included a pleasant example of good housekeeping, with a strong incentive element which bears Haldane's special hallmark. In Cardwell's time men were issued with new items of uniform at specified periods, irrespective of its condition. This produced, according to the individual soldier, 'the smart, the shoddy, and the scarecrow'. Haldane had a much better idea. From 1909 onward, each soldier was given a quarterly cash allowance equal to the value of a periodical issue of items of uniform. Out of this he purchased what was necessary to maintain himself 'in a smart and soldierly fashion', any unspent balance being paid to him *in cash*. The result was a quartermaster's dream and a *very* careful soldiery. By such simple means are worthy ends achieved.

---

[18] Cavalrymen still had the rank of 'private'. The word 'trooper' was not introduced until 1922.
[19] *History of the 5th Royal Inniskilling Dragoon Guards.*

Pay was another matter, for pay was under the scrutiny of sharp political and Treasury eyes. It was, as it always had been and would long remain, an insult to men with a sense of public service and – more seriously – a positive disincentive to recruiting both officers and other ranks from the best elements in society. It is a startling fact that an infantryman signing on in 1910 would have had to have served for *250 years* to earn the *annual* pay of a 1980 recruit.

The pay structure laid down in 1907–8 was so absurdly complicated that it is neither possible nor necessary to dwell on it in detail; but here are some of the general – and some of the more peculiar – features.

On enlistment an infantry private was paid 1s. a day plus (boy soldiers excepted) 3d. a day messing allowance, less the traditional deduction for 'barrack damages'. After six months' service daily pay was consolidated at 1s. 3d., plus 2d. a day 'kit allowance'; and after two years' service the daily rate was increased to 1s. 9d., at which figure it remained until the completion of twelve years without promotion. Such a man could at least console himself that he was being paid almost twice as much as a French *poilu*.

The new regulations then proceeded to confuse the issue, thus. First, they abolished Cardwell's system of 'good-conduct pay' and 'skill-at-arms pay' (both sensible incentives in an Army in which good conduct was often at a premium, and skill at arms a professional *sine qua non*). Instead, a proliferation of 'additional pay', ranging from 2d. to 2s. a day, was introduced: for instruction in gymnastics and signalling; clerical duties in the Orderly Room; for rough-riders, farriers and certain artillery grades. And on 1 October 1906 'proficiency pay' was authorized. It applied only to the cavalry, the artillery and the infantry. The minimum qualification was two years' service, a 3rd Class Education Certificate and a physical fitness test. The rates were 6d. a day, 1st Class, and 3d. a day 2nd Class. [20]

While Haldane was thus engaged in fashioning the expeditionary force and the new-style Reserves (and in the process inducing a wholly new attitude to the profession of arms) the generals addressed themselves to the questions of equipment and training.

Due largely to Haig's clear grasp of the relationship between equipment and tactics (or, put another way, the limitations imposed on tactics by inferior fire-power) a whole new generation of weapons was progressively introduced between 1906 and 1910. The quality was impressive, the quantity severely restricted by government parsimony. [21] And as we have seen, there were vital omissions which the Germans, long dedicated to the proposition of 'guns before butter', did not neglect.

By 1906 the infantry had been re-equipped with the new 'short' Lee-

---

[20] The pay regulations included two quirky details. A scale of fines for drunkenness was laid down, varying from 2s. 6d. to 10s. (in 1913 the Army Council smugly reported the lowest ever figure of 61 men in every 1,000). And finally, in the most literal sense, a soldier's funeral was met out of public funds at a cost of £1 15s. 0d.

[21] It was much the same story thirty years later. A corporal of the 3rd Hussars recalls a parade at Tidworth: 'We drove past the saluting-base in our new tanks – all six of them. The rest consisted of Austin mock-ups.'

Enfield rifle, a weapon of such outstanding quality that it was to remain standard equipment for forty years ('the butt was as good as the bayonet at close quarters' in the opinion of one old practitioner). By the same date each battalion had a section of two Vickers water-cooled machine-guns, much given to stoppages and over-heating. [22] In 1909 the Commandant of the School of Musketry at Hythe, Colonel W. N. Congreve, VC (later to command 18th Infantry Brigade), urged that the battalion MG sections should be increased from two to six guns, an 'extravagance' countered by the politicians by the simple expedient of a reduction in the Army Vote. [23] Congreve's reply was to concentrate on highly specialized training in musketry. The result was the legendary and, as it was to prove, decisive '15 rounds per minute' aimed rapid fire of the infantry (and cavalry) of the BEF. Some super-experts were even credited with 30 r.p.m. 'The best I ever managed', reflects Fred Dray of the East Lancs, 'was 24, but I'll let you into a secret. I shut my eyes, worked away at my bolt and clips, and finished up with a sore shoulder and a record number of "outers".' Still, it fooled the Germans. At Gheluvelt, even when they were reduced to 300 effectives, 1/Queens produced such a volume of rapid rifle fire that the official German account speaks of 'quantities of machine-guns' and of 'roads swept by machine-gun fire'.

By the end of 1909 the artillery had been re-equipped, the RHA with the 13-pdr, the RFA with the 18-pdr and 4·5 in howitzer, and the RGA with the 60-pdr. They were efficient weapons, superbly handled, but as we have seen, supplied almost exclusively with shrapnel rather than high-explosive ammunition; and there were not many of them. The total establishment of the original BEF was as follows:

RHA	30 × 13-pdrs
RFA	324 × 18-pdrs
	108 × 4·5 in howitzers
RGA	16 × 60-pdrs

To put these figures in perspective, it is worth recording that during the siege and reduction of Namur between 20 August and 25 August the Germans concentrated, on that single operation alone, more than 500 guns of all calibres.

The re-equipment of the cavalry was a reflection of the new doctrine for the employment of mounted troops which, in an Army largely dominated by the 'cavalry school', was a triumph of sense over sensibility. The chief evidence of this was the replacement of the ineffective carbine by the new Lee-Enfield rifle, and a standard of musketry comparable to that of the infantry. It was to prove a critical and in the event decisive departure from the traditional concept of mounted warfare, and one which neither the Germans nor the French – for all their massive cavalry resources –

[22] From the machine-gun instruction manual of 1908: 'A mule shall go between the shafts of the Maxim gun. When a mule is not available, an intelligent NCO shall take the shafts.'
[23] The additional cost would have been £104,000; the additional defensive capability in battle incalculable.

13

understood or practised.

It was not quite the end of the road for *l'arme blanche*; indeed, there were numerous clashes between French and German cavalry during the first encounters on the frontier; and between the eve of Mons and the crossing of the Aisne the British had the occasional opportunity to demonstrate their superiority in mounted combat.

With men like French and Haig in the saddle, so to speak, it was unthinkable that the old cavalry tradition – shock action with sword or lance [24] would be relegated to the history books. And this produced a classic example of the British genius for cracking nuts with sledge-hammers.

At the turn of the century the standard cavalry weapon was the sabre, a cutting sword which was largely ineffective against thick uniforms and leather equipment, and caused more damage to the horse than to the rider. In 1903 the first of three eight-man committees was set up to consider a new design. The mountain laboured for no less than three years and finally brought forth what became known as 'the 1908 Pattern Cavalry Sword, Mark I'. It was in fact a beautiful weapon: a pointing sword with a basket hilt and single-edged blade, thirty-five inches long, grooved, as drill instructors explained, 'to let the air in and the blood out'. The old hands did not take too kindly to it. Barney Waldron, a 'South Africa man' who went to France with the Greys, called it a 'toothpick'. 'It wasn't much use at close quarters, but we sharpened it up so that you could catch a man with a fair old swipe.' And catch a man he did in a rearguard action during the retreat. More seriously, many of the older cavalry reservists who rejoined on mobilization had never seen the new sword, let alone learned the new sword exercise, and many of them in fact went to France with the old pre-1908 sabre.

In one other area the re-equipment of the Army lagged behind the progress of the age, for it still depended almost entirely on horses (a fact which was to exercise the Staff greatly when it considered the arithmetic of mobilization [25]). Quite apart from the cavalry, an infantry division (with its field and garrison artillery) had some 5,500 horses, and even senior commanders of corps and divisions had to rely largely on an intrepid band of civilian volunteers who ran a kind of semi-official taxi service in the forward area. [26] It was not until the BEF had been transferred to Flanders that a motley variety of requisitioned vans and omnibuses and purpose-built motor-ambulances arrived to ferry troops back and forth and to evacuate casualties to clearing hospitals.

So gradually, and in a sense reluctantly, the British started to prepare for war. Haldane, within the limits imposed on him, had designed and built the little Army which would take the field, and the Reserves which would support and nourish it; the new General Staff, so far as the politicians would permit, had equipped and armed it for its task; but as yet no 'doctrine of

[24] Four of the six Lancer regiments of the Regular Army were included in the five cavalry brigades of the BEF. All drew blood.
[25] Frank Pusey, a battery clerk with 31st (Howitzer) Battery, went to France on 'a little round robin of a horse that had been pulling a milk float in Peckham a week before.'
[26] See Frederic Coleman: *From Mons to Ypres with French.*

war' existed, for the simple (if absurd) reason that so cerebral an exercise was considered unmilitary, and in any case what was wrong with the *Manual of Military Training*?

Haig thought otherwise, not least because each arm of the service had its own training manual which totally ignored the basic principle of modern warfare: that no man is an island, and that each arm of the service is dependent upon and responsible to the others. This situation he proceeded to rectify; and whatever criticisms may be levelled against him for his later conduct as a field commander – and they are many, and largely ill-founded – he should be remembered as the man who taught the British Army its job.

His doctrine of war was set out in *Field Service Regulations Part I (Operations)* and *Field Service Regulations Part II (War Administration and Organisation)*. Both volumes are still applicable – *mutatis mutandis* – to the art and science of war to-day, and both are required reading for students of the military history of a country which has long made a perverse virtue of the French shoulder-shrug: *On se débrouillera toujours!* ('We'll muddle through some-how!')

Haig's doctrine was simple: first, total attention to detail; second, close and constant co-operation between *all* arms. When in 1912 he was appointed to Aldershot Command (in effect, the garrison became I Corps of the BEF two years later) he galvanized every officer and man into an activity which few who served there have forgotten. 'No more dreary old "field days" and silly war games', recalls Bert Lloyd, then already an old soldier. 'We marched and marched and marched because, our officer told us, "When you go to war, you'll have to march and march and march". And we did! We spent days on the ranges, because, our officer told us, "There'll be a chap out there trying to kill you before you kill him." And he was right!' Aldershot buzzed. Haig was not popular with the diehards, but he earned the respect and admiration of his men, even if he was not a natural communicator, as one famous, if apocryphal, story suggests. Presenting the prizes at a Command athletics meeting, he announced, 'You have all run well. I hope you run as well in the presence of the enemy.'

So the well-tempered weapon was forged. The clock ticked on. The contemptible little Army polished its brass, mucked out its stables, and waited for the starter's pistol.

Meanwhile, things were afoot in another part of the forest.

Within a few months of taking office the new Cabinet authorized the start of informal talks between Grierson, Director of Military Operations, and the French General Staff. They were in fact 'informal' to the point of absurdity. They were also conducted with such secrecy that only the Prime Minister, Haldane and Asquith (Chancellor of the Exchequer) were kept informed. The Cabinet as a whole was kept in the dark. Even more remarkably, so was the Defence Committee. The reason, quite simply, was that, as so often in political and industrial affairs, they were little more than 'talks about talks'.

The French, not yet embarked upon the ultimate folly of Plan XVII, sought to establish the British attitude in the event of German aggression. They got no further than an assurance that in the event of war the Royal Navy would deny access by the German Fleet to the French Channel ports, which was no more than a simple act of self-preservation. The British played their hand with extreme caution. Haldane's 'expeditionary force' was still only an idea on the drawing-board, its precise role carefully undefined; and even if there was a tacit assumption that a British Army would fight alongside the French, it was clearly understood that there was no binding commitment. The key to the door was Belgium, for the only common ground between Germany, France and Britain was that all three were guarantors of Belgian neutrality; and it is one of the supreme ironies of history that in the very year in which the Anglo-French discussions began Schlieffen was putting the finishing touches to his plan to tear up the 'scrap of paper'.

But while London and Paris continued their desultory game of poker, history – not for the first time – played a joker. Henry Wilson, like so many men of influence in British military affairs, was an Irishman (commissioned in 1884 into the Royal Irish Regiment, whence he transferred to the Rifle Brigade). He had a sharp mind ('too sharp by half' was one verdict), a passion for intrigue, limitless ambition and, thanks to a French governess, a fluent command of the French language and an obsessive regard for all things French. That, in the Regular Army, was rare enough. And it was to have a profound – some might say disastrous – influence on events. For it is no exaggeration to say that, for all his comparatively junior rank, it was Henry Wilson who precipitated the battle of Mons and thereafter dominated the subsequent actions of Sir John French. [27]

In 1907 Wilson was appointed Commandant of the Staff College, and almost at once he paid the first of many visits to his opposite number at the École Supérieure de Guerre in Paris, Foch, architect of the new doctrine of *l'offensive à outrance* whence was born Plan XVII. The two men had everything in common except appearance – Wilson, tall and gangling 'with a face like a horse'; Foch, trim, small, with a face like a fox. Both men were natural extroverts. Both were exceedingly vain.

Wilson absorbed Foch's theories uncritically – although there was plenty in them to criticize – and back at Camberley he preached the gospel of the offensive spirit with evangelistic fervour. He even (and this was to prove a fatal error of judgment) accepted Foch's view that in the event of war the main enemy attack would be concentrated against the common frontier in the south, and that any breach of Belgian neutrality by the Germans would be a 'modest' affair *east* of the Meuse and aimed at Luxembourg and the Ardennes. It was as if neither of them had ever heard of Schlieffen or Sedan.

The course of history might have been very different if Wilson had moved on from the Staff College to a post in which there was little or no scope for his

---

[27] Wilson eventually became CIGS (in 1918), and was murdered by IRA gunmen outside his house in Belgravia in June 1922.

'political' appetite; but on 1 January 1910 – by when all Europe was set on a collision course – he was appointed Director of Military Operations. At last the college professor had achieved director status, and with his contempt for the pacifist lobby in the Liberal Party, he embarked on an extraordinary private crusade. This in essence was an undertaking – far beyond his terms of reference and his authority – to commit the British Government, in the event of war, to despatch an expeditionary force of six infantry divisions and one cavalry division to provide an extension to the left wing of the French Plan XVII. He knew perfectly well that he could not bind the Government to any such commitment; but his sharp Irish mind told him that he could drive the Government (which he despised) into a cul-de-sac from which there was no turning back. [28]

While Wilson was thus engaged in committing the BEF to 'Plan W' (the title was courteously provided by a French General Staff which needed no prompting in the art of political manœuvre), the Admiralty decided to play at soldiers. Jackie Fisher, unaware of (and certainly disinterested in) the Staff talks in Paris, proposed a sea-borne operation which would have made Gallipoli look like a beach party at Brighton. Studying his charts (though not his land maps), he discovered 'ten miles of sandy beaches on the Baltic coast of East Prussia' where the BEF could be landed, and there engage up to a million German troops. Remarkably, this lunatic idea was still a live issue when the Defence Committee met after the Agadir crisis in 1911, and it took a great deal of patient talk to persuade Fisher's successor, Sir Arthur Wilson, that it would be inadvisable for the Royal Navy and the BEF to commit joint suicide. Thereafter, not least because of Winston Churchill's arrival at the Admiralty, the Navy left the generals to work out their own salvation.

Henry Wilson, however, was not, as he has been described, simply a 'clever card-player'. He was an extremely able soldier; and he was well aware that it is not possible to send an expeditionary force overseas without meticulous planning; and, in these special circumstances, planning in two languages. Thus there came into existence the 'War Book', which laid down in extraordinary and explicit detail the organization, mobilization and movement of the BEF to France in the event of war. Nothing was overlooked. Every foreseeable contingency was taken into account. And when the day arrived the General Staff, so long derided, showed that Haldane's long years of patient endeavour had not been wasted. But before the button was finally pressed there was to be much heart-searching.

On the evening of 1 August Germany declared war on Russia. France immediately mobilized, [29] and on 3 August Germany, alleging an 'aerial bombing attack' (sic!) on Karlsruhe and Nuremberg, declared war on her.

The British Government held its hand. No one was aware of the extent to

---

[28] Wilson's proposal was to concentrate the BEF in the area of Maubeuge, a few miles from the Belgian frontier, ready to join in the French offensive on the fifteenth day after mobilization.
[29] Wilson's 'understanding' with the French General Staff was that Britain would mobilize on the same day. In fact, she did not mobilize until three days later, and it is fascinating to speculate what would have happened if the BEF had reached the forward area that much earlier.

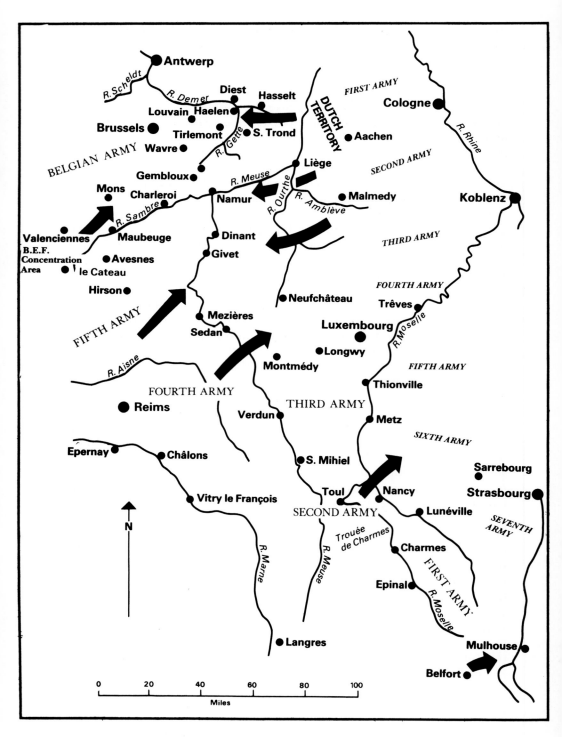

MAP 1. *The Western Front, August 1914*

which Henry Wilson had morally committed the BEF, or indeed of the French operational plan. On 1 August the Government's sole obligation was to Belgium. Wilson's diary reflects his fear that Albion would again prove perfidious.

On 3 August Edward Grey, the Foreign Secretary, met a tense House of Commons, mindful of Northcliffe's thunderous opposition to military intervention in any form. In a long speech he rehearsed the course of events since Sarajevo, and the crisis of conscience which now faced the country. It was a sad speech, delivered by a sad and disillusioned man; but he carried the House with him, except for the Radical wing of his own party and Keir Hardie, the Labour pacifist, who declared that he 'would raise the working-class against the war'. Not for the only time, a Labour politician greatly misconceived the temper of the British people. The rows of silent headstones are a mark of Hardie's shame, and a tribute to the national spirit which he so grossly impugned.

On 4 August Grey requested a final assurance from the German Government that it would respect Belgian neutrality. He received no reply. Indeed, he was already too late, for in the early hours of that morning the German *First* and *Second Armies* had invaded Belgium. At 4.30 p.m. the British Government issued mobilization orders to the BEF, the Special Reserve and the Territorial Army; and at 11 p.m., London time, it declared war on Germany.

At 4 p.m. on the afternoon of 5 August a hastily convened Council of War met at Downing Street. It was a very curious gathering indeed, and in a sense a dress-rehearsal for the drama which was now about to begin; for there were assembled together for the first time all the directors: Asquith, Grey, Churchill and Haldane on the civilian side; on the naval and military side, the Chiefs of Staff and their heads of departments; for the BEF, Sir John French (C-in-C designate), Haig and Grierson (respectively commanders of I and II Corps), Murray, who was French's un-distinguished choice as Chief of Staff, and (inevitably) Henry Wilson, the Sub-Chief of Staff; and finally, for no good reason other than sentiment, the venerable Lord Roberts. This left one empty chair. It was occupied by the formidable figure of Lord Kitchener, intercepted that morning at Dover on his way to resume his proconsular role in Egypt, and now persuaded to accept the office of Secretary of State for War. [30]

'What', asks John Terraine, [31] 'were they all wanted for? The answer is: to decide what to do.' It is remarkable, but it is true. All Haldane's work, all the meticulous preparation for a national emergency, can now be seen to have been conducted in a political and military vacuum. Only one man at that table, Henry Wilson, knew the French plan and the extent to which he had committed the Government to become involved in that plan. These details he now revealed in a long, impassioned and enthusiastic apologia.

[30] Two days earlier Haig had written to Haldane urging him – without success – to return to the War Office which he had done so much to create.
[31] John Terraine: *Douglas Haig.*

He was not one whit abashed; but then, he was an Irishman.

History does not record the long silence that must have fallen on the Cabinet Room. Presently Sir John French intervened with the suggestion that it might be more effective to land the BEF at Antwerp to bolster Belgian resistance and provide a threat to the German right flank (it did not occur to him that Antwerp was incapable of absorbing a force even as small as the BEF, or that the Germans might, without deviating from the Schlieffen Plan,· eliminate the British Army, as a secondary by-product to the destruction of the French). In the event Churchill vetoed the idea, because it would involve trespassing on Dutch territorial waters and the Navy could not guarantee protection of BEF transports in the open waters of the North Sea (what price now Jackie Fisher's absurd Baltic extravaganza?).

Kitchener listened and brooded. Wilson fumed and fretted. The Cabinet Ministers, mindful of their political skins, accepted *an* involvement but hedged their bets with the old bogey of a possible German invasion. And so the meeting ended on a note of indecision. It was agreed that an expeditionary force of *four* infantry divisions [32] and five cavalry brigades should commence embarkation for France on 12 August to take its place alongside the French Army. But where?

Kitchener had grave misgivings about the French Plan XVII, as well he might; but he could not influence it. He was even more concerned at the intention to concentrate the BEF as far forward as Maubeuge. He had his reasons.

First, he knew too much about Sir John French. Second, he deeply suspected Henry Wilson's excessive optimism. Third, he foresaw, with uncanny instinct, the weight and direction of the German thrust north and west of the Meuse. Fourth – and most importantly – he envisaged a *long* and bitter war against the major military power in Europe; and in this he was (with Haig) alone.

So he argued that the BEF should concentrate no farther forward than Amiens. That at least would provide time, and a chance to influence (perhaps decisively) the Schlieffen strategy without the risk of disaster by exposing the BEF on the Belgian frontier. But he was too late. Wilson had worked on French, and the French had worked on Wilson. It was Plan XVII or nothing, and it was Plan XVII that won in the end. Kitchener finally gave way on 12 August, and the BEF went to Maubeuge, at what cost in lives and equipment we shall never know. The directors have much to answer for to the actors.

---

[32] 1st, 2nd, 3rd and 5th. The 4th Division, stationed in Eastern Command, would be held back, as would the 6th Division, split between Ireland and York.

CHAPTER 2

The Play Begins

'I fired my first shot in anger about eleven o'clock of the morning of 23 August near St Ghislain on the Mons Canal,' recalls Harry Bell of the Royal West Kents. [1] 'When the final whistle went four years and a bit later, where do you think I was? Two hundred yards from where I started!'

In those few words, marvellously understated, one old soldier illuminates the futility, the pity, even – in a black sense – the absurdity of the Great War. In the intervening years much had happened to Harry Bell: twice wounded, once left for dead, the sole survivor of his original platoon, promoted to sergeant, shifted from unit to unit. Yet his last impression is one of amused surprise. Harry Bell was lucky. He survived, so to speak, by two hundred yards. For thousands of others who were not so lucky, two inches might have made all the difference.

Harry Bell was very typical of the men of the old Regular Army, and the composition of that Army is as much a commentary on the social as on the military climate of the time. In his case, he simply wanted to be a soldier.

Not many did. As Haldane had discovered, the Army – except in times of crisis – had long been held in almost universal public disesteem, and never more so than in the years immediately following the Boer War. There are still veterans of that time who remember notices in public-houses which said 'NO DOGS! NO SOLDIERS!' in that order (a caveat which owed as much to empty pockets as to a reputation for rough-housing).

Nor was the volunteer an object of pride, let alone envy, among his family and friends (secretly, perhaps, when he came home in his tightly tailored walking-out dress?). On the contrary, he was looked upon, in terms of working-class solidarity, as a deserter who in removing himself from home had also removed a necessary contribution to the meagre household budget. To 'go for a soldier' was to invite a standard witches' curse: 'Now that you've made your bed, you must lie on it!'

One mother at least had cause to eat her words. In 1877 a Mrs Robertson wrote scathingly to her son who had left a job in private service to join the 16th Lancers: 'What cause have you for such a Low Life? The Army is a

[1] 13th Brigade, 5th Infantry Division.

PLATE 2. *Brothers-in-arms: the Pusey family.* L. to r.: *Ambrose (1/West Yorks); Frank (31st Bty, RFA); Edwin (1/West Yorks); Stuart (4/RF).* Seated: *Father Thomas (ex-P.O. Volunteer Rifles) and mother*

refuge for all Idle people. I would rather Bury you than see you in a red coat.' Mrs Robertson did less than justice to her 'Wully', for he was to become Quartermaster-General of the BEF, Chief of the Imperial General Staff, and the only man ever to have risen from private soldier to Field Marshal.

A few – surprisingly few – joined because they came from families with strong military ties. For example, George Cox of the Rifle Brigade had a soldier father and no fewer than eight soldier uncles; and once in the Army, family links were perpetuated by the practice of 'claiming', by which a man could 'claim' a younger brother from another regiment into his own.[2] In 1903 Bert (robustly christened Ethelbert) Wheeler enlisted in the Middlesex Regiment. Within four years he – and two more Wheelers – had been claimed into the 20th Hussars by their eldest brother; and in 1914 all four duly went to war together.

But by far the largest number of those men who were to make up the BEF enlisted for other reasons: unemployment (the Edwardian age was by no means as golden as it has been represented); boredom; a taste for adventure; an escape from the drab cul-de-sac of slums to romantic corners

[2]The practice has survived to our own day.

22

PLATE 3. *The glamour of uniforms. Pte Henry Fletcher in parade dress, 5th Dragoon Guards, 1912*

of Empire (Kipling, the soldiers' friend, was also the greatest of all recruiting officers); the glamour of uniforms; an emergency exit from sexual indiscretions or from the law; even, unfashionable as it may now seem, a real sense of service and patriotism. 'I remember', recalls an old 19th Hussar, 'that there were lots of pictures of old battles on my schoolroom walls – *The Charge of the Light Brigade* and one called *Aliwal* – and I thought that if it wasn't for the likes of them, there wouldn't be the likes of me.'

Some men, like Fred Milton, a farm worker at South Brent, walked innocently into a baited trap. 'One Saturday a friend and I went into Newton Abbot to see the bright lights and with never a thought of joining up. About four o'clock we were spied by a recruiting sergeant, and within a couple of hours we found ourselves in the Devons. And there I stayed for twenty-two years.'

Others went in by the wrong door. Bert Turp, born in a public-house in South Ockenden ('my mother was there at the time'), had always set his heart on the cavalry. 'They showed me a list and there at the top was the 1st King's Dragoon Guards. Top of the list was good enough for me, so I said "1st Dragoons" – and of course finished up in the Royals.'

But whatever the reason, however improbable the impulse, these men all shared one priceless virtue in common. All of them were volunteers (they would not even have understood what the Kaiser meant when he described them as 'mercenaries'). Thus while in Continental armies men were fed into the machine on a continuous belt system, processed according to differing terms of service, and then returned as it were to store, the Regular Army was always chronically short of men serving on the home establishment (units overseas were maintained at full strength by drafts from parent or sister battalions and regiments).[3] This throws up some interesting sidelights on the British genius for improvisation. Many men when applying to join the regiment of their choice were told that it was 'closed' or 'full up'. With the exception of Household regiments (and perhaps half a dozen others), this was never true – and never has been.

For instance. A sample of fifty men who enlisted in the cavalry between 1908 and 1912 shows that forty-one came from towns and cities and only nine were, as might have been expected, countrymen (the cynical explanation is that the latter knew far too much about horses for their comfort). A similar sample of men applying to join the infantry shows that only twelve out of fifty were accepted into their own county regiments. An old RSM of the Manchester Regiment recalls that four out of five men in his battalion were unemployed Irishmen from Liverpool. Similarly, in many Scottish regiments there were as many Cockneys in kilts as there were Jocks. And men who had set their hearts on the Royal Horse Artillery were posted to the 'RH and RFA' without option. And taking another sample, forty-two out of fifty men enlisted at least six months under the proper age of eighteen.

[3] When 4/Royal Fusiliers mobilized on 4 August 1914 they required to embody 734 reservists to bring them up to full war establishment of 992.

The reason was not insensitivity or guile on the part of the Adjutant-General's department, but simply a means of spreading a small amount of butter evenly on a large loaf of bread. For obvious reasons the practice did not – because it could not – apply to Yeomanry and Territorial units. And when during the creation of the New Armies Kitchener agreed, much against his will, to allow the formation of 'Pals' Battalions' in the industrial cities of the north, a terrible price, in terms of stricken communities, was paid on the Somme.

A great deal of uninformed nonsense has been talked about the old Army, projecting it as a typical example of the British obsession with class. Any social historian who insists that the British Army of the Edwardian years is a ripe field for a thesis on the divisive effect of British class-consciousness should first study the French Army, the German Army and – above all – the Russian Army of the period. All were conscript armies. All were *ruthlessly* disciplined armies. All, when the crisis came, suffered in greater or lesser degree from the inbuilt attitudes of a class structure so much more rigid than that of the British that the whole system began to break down. During the crucial day of the attack on Gheluvelt on 31 October when the British line had been broken the German assault infantry faltered and stopped simply because the 'system' did not delegate decision-making by the leaders to the led. On the same day at least four British battalions found themselves commanded – and the word is explicit – by warrant officers or NCOs.

Much has been written about the legendary British sense of humour, and it was – all the way from Mons to Ypres – to be both exemplary and anodyne. What other army could march to battle on this sardonic note?

I don't want to be a soldier,
I don't want to go to war.
I'd rather hang around
Piccadilly Underground
And live on the earnings of a high-born lady.

The French, with a language marvellously suited to great flights of military rhetoric, urged their soldiers to revive the noble examples of Austerlitz and Jena ('I never wish to hear the words *la gloire* again', said one exasperated Député). Officers called their men *mes enfants* – and treated them not so much as children as delinquents; and their marching song *Sambre et Meuse* was soon to have a very hollow ring.

The Germans, mindful of the great Frederick's *Hunde, wollt' Ihr ewig leben?* ('Dogs, do you wish to live for ever?') evolved a less drastic philosophy in the phrase *Maul halten ist aushalten!* (or roughly translated, 'Shut up and bear up!'). As they marched they also sang – 'always', said a Belgian, 'the Germans sang' – but the songs were as heavy as their boots and as humourless as their national character. Very occasionally they let the mask slip. Here is a rare, and rather daring, example:

Herunter mit den Hosen,
Herauf mit dem Rock,
Herein mit dem kleinen Pomerän'schen Stock. [4]

The British Regular soldier, long an artist in the use of the four-letter vernacular, freely spiced with Urdu and Arabic infelicities, wasted few words – and quickly invented his own versions. He took to France the musical-hall ditties of the day, including the improbable *Tipperary*, but soon devised rude variations on the conventional themes; and with his ear for a short, sharp rhyme, he was delighted to discover that his chief German opponent was called Kluck. Occasionally this sense of fun had unexpected results. When 4/Royal Fusiliers landed at Le Havre they came ashore whistling the *Marseillaise*. The population was enchanted. The men then sang 'Hold your hand out, you naughty boy!' – and the locals, convinced that this was their national anthem, reverently uncovered and stood to attention. It is not to be wondered at that the British lose their battles, but win their wars.

But though, in Laurence Binyon's words, 'they went with songs to the battle', life in the Regular Army was real and life was earnest.

Discipline was strict, but not, as in the bovine German system, brutal; for while the British soldier may have been simple, he was not a simpleton. The game – and all British institutions are, in one sense or other, games – was played according to a set of unwritten rules. Holy Writ itself was called King's Regulations, and part of the game – brought to a fine art by the wily old soldier – was to discover the loopholes. Officers and NCOs resorted to cheating by the use of phrases like 'dumb insolence' and 'conduct prejudicial to good order and military discipline' [5] which literally covered a multitude of sins.

The Victorian barracks in which the soldiery was housed – seemingly all designed by the same architect – were spartan, but no more so than many of the homes the men had left behind them. Food was plain, monotonous, cooked with a fearsome disregard for digestion, and invariably cold by the time it reached the barrack-room. Drunkenness was widespread, with beer at a 1½d. a pint, and venereal disease so great a threat to military efficiency that to contract it was treated as a disciplinary offence. But it was in other respects a healthy life, with unlimited opportunities for sport and recreation (neither of them a routine feature in the French and German armies), and the serving soldier of the pre-war period was hard, fit and persuaded that cleanliness came first and godliness a bad second. [6]

Non-conformists and misfits were disposed of not by tedious recourse to the Orderly Room but by a process known in Aldershot and other garrison

[4] 'Down with the trousers,
 Up with the skirt,
 In with the little Pomeranian stick.'
[5] Section 40, Army Act.
[6] The problem of fitness – especially in the infantry – was a major cause for concern when reservists rejoined their units from 'soft' civilian life on mobilization.

towns as 'helping them over the wall'. Persistent offenders – and many of these were to prove themselves the bravest and most resilient men when the moment of truth came – were either despatched to the 'glasshouse' to cool off or were confined to barracks for varying periods. 'I once was given seven days C.B.,' says Tom Kyte of the 13th Hussars. 'It suited me very well. I spent my time cleaning saddlery for my mates and finished up two quid to the good.' Holy Writ apart, there was one ultimate crime, that of stealing from a fellow-soldier; yet even here there was an unwritten code of honour. It is impossible to find a French or German translation for 'no names, no pack-drill'.

This whole system revolved around a unique breed, the long-service warrant officer and NCO. Certainly there were men who revelled in their rank or abused their authority (there were also stupid subalterns and crass colonels); but the picture of the swaggering sadist, bullying the cowed rankers into submission, is simply untrue. Men do not follow sadistic leaders. The mainsprings of the old Regular NCOs were professional competence and devotion to duty, and their sole weapon a withering sarcasm which fooled no one but rather endeared them to their flock.

So it was in the relationship between NCO and young officer. A subaltern writing to his father in 1910 said of one of his sergeants: 'At the risk of sounding blasphemous, I can honestly say that with his stripes I am often healed.' And there is the celebrated – and not, perhaps, entirely apocryphal – story of the tongue-tied subaltern marching his platoon towards a cliff's edge while his sergeant pleaded, 'For God's sake say something, sir, even if it's only good-bye!'

This almost paternalistic attitude was to carry the BEF through many moments of crisis. A letter written to the mother of Captain T. H. Preston, killed near Ypres in October 1914, is only one of many similar expressions of the special relationship which existed between officers and their men (a relationship constantly and touchingly illustrated in Preston's own letters home before his death):

> Dear Madam,
> On behalf of myself and men who served under your son, beg to offer our deepest sympathy in your great sorrow. Being in charge of the detachment taken to France by Captain Preston and being with him from then up to the 21st October, I became very intimate with almost everything he done. No officer could have had more respect or confidence from his men . . . ever kind and cheerful, in the fiercest fighting he was always cool, cheering up his men, without thought for his own safety . . .
> Yours truly,
> E. H. Thomas,
> Sergeant,
> 1st Bn., East Lancashire Regt. [7]

It is a tribute from one gentleman to another.

[7] 11th Brigade, 4th Infantry Division.

The social caste – as opposed to class – system in the Army reflected the Army's social priorities. Cavalrymen, word-perfect in *Debrett*, expected their officers to be noble, rich, eccentric, brewer's sons, or better still all four. The Guards were always rather special, with a curious ritual by which a guardsman could only address an officer through his NCO ('with all that whisky on his breath', said a Grenadier, 'I'm not surprised.') 'Chippy' Carpenter of the Coldstream, whom we shall meet again at Ypres, remembers an occasion in London at which the commanding officer took leave of his men. The battalion was paraded on the barrack square, and the Colonel, riding up to the saluting-base, addressed them thus: 'In all my service I have never known a battalion so low in literacy and so high in venereal disease. I bid you good-day.' And turning his horse, he rode away. 'And do you know,' says Chippy, 'he was absolutely right?'

In the county regiments and in the gunners, engineers and in the other services, mess bills were smaller[8] and there was less scope for eccentricity. But there was an equally fierce pride in regimental tradition and a deep family feeling which was to carry these officers and men through the ordeal by fire which they were presently to face.

Such then were the actors, marshalled upon the stage by Haldane's patience and purpose. When the strange dress-rehearsal took place on the afternoon of 5 August, he was present, but only as an adviser, not as a director. Lord Chancellors do not deploy armies. Seely, his successor, had gone four months earlier, and only that morning Kitchener had returned from Dover to occupy the chair which Asquith, to his lasting discredit, had for so long left empty at the War Office at this critical time. Almost alone among those present at the meeting, Haldane saw in Kitchener the Cromwellian qualities necessary to match the hour. As we have seen, it did not take long for this austere but prescient man to impose his will – in all but one vital respect – on his co-directors, who, when they did not openly show their resentment, privately expressed their anxiety. Kitchener's judgment – like Churchill's a quarter of a century later – was not always secure, but the greatest single criticism of him is that he did not demand the dismissal of Sir John French until December 1915.

Thus, with the new directors installed, the curtain rises on the prologue. The scene is Southampton.

'It was generally felt', wrote Sir John French some years later,[9] 'that we were under *some obligation*[10] to send as strong an army as we could. . . . As to the exact number, it did not appear we were under any definite obligation. . . .' That, from the man who resigned as CIGS after the Curragh 'mutiny' in March 1914 and notwithstanding was appointed C-in-C designate of the BEF in the following July, is an extraordinary observation. It is all the more

[8]In 1914 a subaltern's pay was 7s. 6d. a day. (*Pay Warrant, Art. 228.*)
[9]French: *1914.*
[10]Author's italics.

extraordinary because it is true. When the War Council staged its dress-rehearsal on 5 August it is no exaggeration to say that no one present – not even French or Asquith or Grey – knew the extent of Britain's military commitment, with the exception of Henry Wilson. During one of his numerous meetings with Foch, Wilson had asked what was the minimum number of men that would provide an effective extension to the French left wing under Plan XVII. 'A single soldier will do,' replied Foch. 'And we will make certain that he is killed.' Wilson took the hint and, without consultation or authority, promised the whole of Haldane's 'expeditionary force'.

We know that, for quite different reasons, the Government and Kitchener decided to hold back two infantry divisions. [11] Thus the BEF which began to assemble at Southampton in accordance with the detailed and impeccably efficient procedures laid down in the War Book was as follows:

I Corps (Haig)
    1st Infantry Division (Lomax)
    2nd Infantry Division (Monro)
II Corps (Grierson)
    3rd Infantry Division (Hubert Hamilton)
    5th Infantry Division (Fergusson) [12]
Five unallotted infantry battalions for L. of C. duties [13]
Cavalry Division (Allenby) [12]
One (5th) independent cavalry brigade (Chetwode)

The general location of these formations on mobilization is of interest, for it shows a high degree of staff organization and planning to have brought so many scattered elements and ancillary services to a single point of embarkation in such sequence that they would sail for France over a six-day period not piecemeal but in correct order of battle. (For example, the Cavalry Division was scattered through five Home Commands, yet, with the exception of 3rd Cavalry Brigade, sailed on 15 August as a complete formation.)

I Corps, with the exception of two Guards battalions in London District, was tidily stationed and ready for war in Aldershot Command.

II Corps did not exist as such until mobilization (Grierson was then GOC Eastern Command). 3rd Infantry Division was located in Southern Command (chiefly in Tidworth and Bulford), and 5th Infantry Division was in Ireland.

1st Cavalry Brigade was in Aldershot; 2nd Cavalry Brigade in Tidworth; 3rd Cavalry Brigade in Ireland (less 16th Lancers at Aldershot); 4th Cavalry Brigade divided between Eastern Command at Colchester and

---

[11] By 9 September both these divisions had been sent to France – also for quite different reasons.
[12] 5th Infantry Division and 3rd Cavalry Brigade embarked for France direct from Dublin and Cork.
[13] On 22 August four of these battalions were formed into 19th Infantry Brigade (Drummond) at Valenciennes and attached to II Corps.

London District; 5th Cavalry Brigade in Eastern Command and Northern Command (York).

Except for the formations in Ireland, this Expeditionary Force was transported from Southampton[14] to France (Le Havre, Rouen and Boulogne) between 12 August and 17 August smoothly, efficiently and in extraordinary secrecy. Even when an official Press statement announced at 9.45 p.m. on Monday 17 August that 'the Expeditionary Force as detailed for Foreign Service has been safely landed on French soil', the Germans seem to have paid little attention; for on 20 August, when the BEF had *completed* its concentration in the Le Cateau – Maubeuge area, Moltke informed Kluck, whose *First Army* was then starting to move south and west of Brussels, that 'a landing of British troops is reported at Boulogne: their advance from about Lille must be reckoned with. *It is believed that a disembarkation of British troops on a large scale has not yet taken place.*'

Never had so large an Expeditionary Force been assembled in these islands;[15] never before, indeed, had the British Army mobilized for war. But the procedure laid down in the War Book had been carefully rehearsed, and when the order was issued on the afternoon of 4 August (the previous day had been a Bank Holiday, which may well have been a contributory factor in delaying the decision) the machine clicked into gear with surprising efficiency, although not without some inevitable – and not so inevitable – problems.

The recall of nearly 70,000 reservists proved a quartermaster's nightmare. 1/Wiltshires reported a total shortage of size 10 and 11 boots; 40th Battery RFA was deficient in dial sights; there were plenty of uniforms, but not always in the right size in the right place. Filling up non-commissioned ranks with suitable men caused difficulties, and 12th Lancers reported that they had fourteen farriers 'supernumerary to war establishment'. Perhaps the greatest problem of all was the shortage of horses, despite a careful register made during the previous year (Wilson's diary is peppered with querulous asides about the failure to provide adequate numbers of suitable animals). Draught horses, in a country still geared to horse-power, were available in quantity; but cavalry and artillery remounts were a different matter.[16] 'It took twice as long to train a troop-horse as it did to train a cavalry recruit', in the view of Albert Whitelock of the Bays. And horses were soon to become a melancholy, though anonymous, element in the growing casualty list. 'On September 15', says Frank Pusey, 'we had our first bad day, and the Battery was shaken at the loss of so many old friends. One gun team of black horses – the pride of No. 1 Section – which were used for funerals at Woolwich, were all killed whilst standing with the gun limber on the flank of the Battery.'

In all the sad, silent cemeteries of the Western Front, there are no

[14] Transport and stores were largely shipped from Newhaven, Avonmouth and Liverpool.
[15] The official History makes the interesting point that II Corps, which was to fight the battle of Mons, numbered 'just under 36,000', while the strength of the British Army at Waterloo was 31,485.
[16] 'Despite the relatively small number of British cavalry, forage was the largest item of supplies sent overseas, exceeding even ammunition.' Liddell Hart: *History of the First World War.*

[*This paper is to be considered by each soldier as confidential, and to be kept in his Active Service Pay Book.*]

You are ordered abroad as a soldier of the King to help our French comrades against the invasion of a common Enemy. You have to perform a task which will need your courage, your energy, your patience. Remember that the honour of the British Army depends on your individual conduct. It will be your duty not only to set an example of discipline and perfect steadiness under fire but also to maintain the most friendly relations with those whom you are helping in this struggle. The operations in which you are engaged will, for the most part, take place in a friendly country, and you can do your own country no better service than in showing yourself in France and Belgium in the true character of a British soldier.

Be invariably courteous, considerate and kind. Never do anything likely to injure or destroy property,

II W V

2

and always look upon looting as a disgraceful act. You are sure to meet with a welcome and to be trusted; your conduct must justify that welcome and that trust. Your duty cannot be done unless your health is sound. So keep constantly on your guard against any excesses. In this new experience you may find temptations both in wine and women. You must entirely resist both temptations, and, while treating all women with perfect courtesy, you should avoid any intimacy.

Do your duty bravely.
Fear God.
Honour the King.

KITCHENER,
Field-Marshal.

PLATE 4. *Kitchener's order to the BEF, issued to every soldier on 10 August 1914*

memorials to these patient, uncomprehending creatures. They deserved better.

The whole process of mobilization went ahead in a spirit of cheerful optimism, and in an atmosphere of tight security. It was a hundred years since the British Army had set foot on the Continent. It had been there before, and over the centuries it had acquired a reputation for great bravery in action, and stupendous misbehaviour when not so engaged. [17] To this historical truth Kitchener at once addressed himself. And in each man's pay-book was inserted a personal order signed by the Secretary of State. It was, for some curious reason, marked 'Confidential', and beyond the normal exhortation to the military virtues, it warned the soldier against the temptations of wine and women. The Lord Protector would have greatly approved. The soldiers – or those who troubled to read it – survived the perils of wine and had no time to enjoy the pleasures of women. They were to be involved all too soon in the more important problem of survival.

'We reached Southampton on the evening of 13 August and embarked the next morning for Le Havre. No one told us where we were going and none of us much cared. We were off to war, we knew we were good, and we were sure it would all be over pretty quick.' That was the view of George Lovett of the KRRC. It was a view shared by virtually every officer and man who sailed from Southampton.

Standing on our bridge and looking up-stream, it is very difficult to understand to-day why the BEF went forth to war with so little comprehension of the test of strength which lay ahead. Even twenty-five years later it is possible, from personal recollection, to wonder at the same

[17] In 1798 an anonymous observer wrote, 'The army went to Flanders and swore horribly.' Wellington's views are well known.

sense of euphoria which possessed another, even more vulnerable, BEF.

The answer lies in the splendid insularity of the island race. None of these men, and very few of their officers, had even set foot in France. None had ever seen a German soldier. They had chased the Boers around the Transvaal; they had played dangerous games with Pathans on the Frontier; they had lived the life of Reilly in Abbassiya; most had not got beyond the Rose and Crown. But if anyone had mentioned to them Spicheren or Wörth or Mars-la-Tour or Mukden they would have probably assumed that they were the names of indifferent selling-platers on which they had wisely saved their tanners.

The letters and diaries of those who now assembled at Southampton are a touching and revealing commentary on the innocence of the contemptible little Army.

Corporal Snelling of the 12th Lancers, who had never seen the sea before, wrote home on 10 August 'They say [*a phrase which was to become very commonplace*] that we are going to Southampton. Everyone is very kind and buys us drinks. I feel quite a bit of a hero.' A week later he was writing about the French countryside ('just like Wiltshire') and the cheering crowds which greeted them at every stop. On 21 August he recorded in his diary 'We received orders to march at 6 a.m. next day, rest on Sunday [*the day of Mons*], reach the firing line on Monday. We are to support three French Cav. Bdes who are in pursuit of a German Army Corps.' He was sadly wrong. And, more sadly, six weeks later he was dead.

Captain Henry Dillon ('Rabbit' to his men) of 2/Oxford and Bucks L.I. recorded the same feeling of euphoria, although at a different level. Writing home on 10 August, he said, 'On 4 August we had 22 officers and 486 men. By 8 August – *mirabile dictu* – we had 27 officers and 1,198 men![18] Problems. Problems.' He then went on to speculate. 'They say we are going first to Paris (which sounds amusing) and then to Brussels.' And the day before his battalion embarked at Southampton, he wrote thus to his brother: 'Could you give orders for the *Times* and the *Mail* to be sent over daily?'

So, as if on its way to annual manœuvres, cheerful, confident, happily concerned with creature comforts, the BEF went to war.

The weather was perfect, the sea like glass, which was just as well for the men packed in the transports, and particularly for the thousands of horses. Away to the east, out of sight of the soldiers, the sailors were silently keeping vigil and sealing off the Channel from prying German eyes. In the five days during which the BEF was moved to France 1,800 special trains were run (Southampton Docks handled 80 on the busiest day) and the transport ships shuttled to and fro to the three ports of disembarkation. It is a measure of what we call progress that such an operation would not be possible to-day.

The men were in high spirits. The local inhabitants turned out in force to give them a rapturous welcome. Both sides discovered that the word

---

[18]Of these there remained, on 11 November 1918, one officer and twenty-eight NCOs and ORs who had served continuously throughout the war with the battalion.

THE
SCRAP OF PAPER
Prussia's Perfidy—Britain's Bond.

The Treaty of 1839 (which the German Chancellor tore up, remarking that it was only "a scrap of paper") said:

> "BELGIUM.... SHALL FORM AN INDEPENDENT AND PERPETUALLY NEUTRAL STATE. IT SHALL BE BOUND TO OBSERVE SUCH NEUTRALITY TOWARDS ALL OTHER STATES."

These are the Seals and Signatures of the Six Nations who guaranteed Belgian Independence and Neutrality

GREAT BRITAIN - Palmerston
BELGIUM - Sylvain Van De Weyer
AUSTRIA - Senfft
FRANCE - H. Sebastiani
GERMANY - Bülow
RUSSIA - Pozzo Di Borgo

Germany has trampled on the Treaty she signed.

CAN BRITONS STAND BY WHILE GERMANY CRUSHES AN INNOCENT PEOPLE?
ENLIST TO-DAY

PUBLISHED BY THE PARLIAMENTARY RECRUITING COMMITTEE, LONDON.   Poster No. 7   4921-14   HANBURY, TOMSETT & CO. LONDON, N.W.

PLATE 5. *A rare, and early, recruiting poster, showing the 'scrap of paper'* 'souvenir' was common language, and soon cap badges and buttons were changing hands in return for croissants and kisses. 'An old girl gave my horse a huge bun', said Fred Elphick of the 4th Dragoon Guards, 'and he bravely swallowed it.' John Allan, landing at Le Havre with 'L' Battery, RHA, made his first contribution to the *entente* by answering the call of nature. 'I was very surprised when a woman attendant carefully wiped the seat for me. That's something I'd never seen in Glasgow.' James Mostyn, an officer in the Royal Engineers, recorded in his diary 'Landed safely. Kissed by two girls. Embraced by a priest. After all this, the Germans should be quite a relief!'

As they landed the units of the BEF moved into bivouac, sorted themselves out, and prepared for the train journey to the concentration area, the one which Wilson had agreed with the French General Staff and which Kitchener considered tactically unwise and strategically hazardous.

It is worth digressing briefly to consider what might have been the outcome if Kitchener had won the argument and concentrated the BEF in the area of Amiens some sixty miles south-west of the Belgian frontier. He would certainly have gained time. But time for what? The whole weight of Kluck's *First Army* which fell – 'stumbled' would be nearer the truth – upon the BEF at Mons could have been concentrated on the left flank of Lanrezac's Fifth Army, and we know how close Lanrezac came to disaster without that additional and surely decisive blow. Even if Kluck had continued his march on Paris in accordance with Schlieffen, he would have passed well to the east of Amiens, and with a strong flank guard could have contained the BEF if it attempted a sortie. We know how much Sir John French relied on Henry Wilson's advice, and we also know the terms of Kitchener's instructions to him. Wilson, like a spoiled child deprived of his favourite toy, would have sulked; and Murray, French's Chief of Staff, was not the man to have proposed any major offensive action against an enemy whose overwhelming strength would by then have been apparent. In all probability the outcome would have been another Dunkirk, and long before the eventual counterstroke on the Marne, France would have been defeated. So – and one can only speculate – the verdict of history might well be that Henry Wilson was right for the wrong reasons and Kitchener wrong for the right reasons. It is, in the light of history, even possible to make out a case for French's Antwerp alternative.

The concentration area was a narrow strip twenty-five miles long by about ten miles wide running from Maubeuge in the north-east, some four miles from the frontier, to Le Cateau to the south-west and occupied in, so to speak, descending order by the Cavalry Division, II Corps and I Corps, with the five infantry battalions assigned to L. of C. duties training up to Valenciennes west of Maubeuge. On its right was XVIII Corps of the French Fifth Army, and on its immediate left the French 84th Territorial Division. [19] It had not taken long for the reservists to feel the effects of the

---

[19] As the BEF moved forward on 21 August, part of Sordet's Cavalry Corps (which had been reconnoitring beyond Charleroi and Namur) was transferred to the British left flank, a complicated manœuvre which caused considerable confusion on the line of march.

August heat, new boots and loaded packs. Some could not even manage the short climb out of Boulogne to the bivouac on the same cliffs where Napoleon had stood a century before, and more than one infantry officer recorded his concern, little knowing what lay ahead on the dusty cobbled roads not of Belgium and then Germany, but of Picardy and beyond. 'We marched and marched and marched because, our officer told us, ''You'll have to march and march and march''.' Too true.

But not yet. The BEF moved up by train, if not in comfort, at least neatly labelled *hommes 40, chevaux 8*. It was roses all the way. At every stop – and there were many – the inhabitants turned out to cheer. The kilted Scots were special objects of wonder. Jim Strachan of the Black Watch 'felt quite coy as all the lassies gathered round'. So did the lassies. Coffee (something new to the British soldier) was provided everywhere; John Allan was reprimanding men for scrounging tomatoes; at Wassigny an old man pressed a small puppy on Ernest Smith of the Queen's, which regretfully he had to decline; the war seemed very far away. Yet at Amiens there occurred a small, but graphic, example of our earlier metaphor of the current of events. As his train was leaving Gunner Sayre (later to win two Military Medals) was looking out of his carriage. 'I noticed we were passing over a river and I asked an officer what it was called. ''The Somme'', he said. Didn't mean a thing to me.' In less than two years the Somme was going to mean a very great deal to Gunner Sayre.

By the evening of 20 August the BEF was safely in its billets. Chippy Carpenter was having a decent mug of tea; Corporal Snelling was detailed for outpost duty, and was grumbling because his horse had cast a shoe; Jim

PLATE 6. *On the way to the concentration area.* Hommes *40,* chevaux *8*

Strachan was pleased to take his kilt off for a wee while. It had been a very hot day. Of the enemy there was neither sign nor news; and the same was true on the other side of the hill.

On 14 August the executive directors arrived at the theatre. On that day Sir John French crossed to France with his chief staff officers. After spending the night at Amiens, he sent Robertson, the Quartermaster-General, and the various departmental chiefs ahead to set up GHQ at Le Cateau, while he himself set off on a round of visits, taking with him Murray, his Chief of Staff; [20] Wilson, his Sub-Chief; Colonel Huguet, now seconded to him as Liaison Officer; and Colonel Fitzgerald, his Private Secretary (significantly, he did not take his chief Intelligence Officer, Macdonogh). The next three days were to have a crucial bearing upon events.

French's first call was in Paris, where he met among others Poincaré and Messimy, the War Minister. It was not an encouraging start. French, despite Wilson's careful coaching, kept his cards close to his chest. He had no experience of dealing with foreigners whose language he could not speak, and for all Wilson's injections of adrenalin, he was conscious not only of his rank but of his instruction that 'you will in no case come in any sense under the orders of any Allied General'. Poincaré instinctively disliked French. Messimy was horrified when he was told that the BEF would not be ready for action until 24 August – i.e., in nine days' time.

French was in no particular hurry, or, more accurately, he was not going to be hurried to suit his ally's convenience. On 15 August the French First and Second Armies were still making progress in the south; Liège was resisting the German battering-ram; there seemed as yet no sign of any significant threat to the French left flank, although Intelligence was beginning to piece together a jigsaw puzzle with formidable implications. It did not matter. Plan XVII had taken account of everything; the incompetent Germans would conveniently walk into a baited trap; if the facts suggested otherwise, then the facts were wrong.

If French kept his thoughts to himself it did not mean any lessening in his conviction of swift, decisive victory, carefully fostered by Wilson. This state of optimism was to last for just eight more days, although before then it was to be severely – and in the event crucially – tested.

Writing of French on that Saturday in Paris, Barbara Tuchman says, 'The immediate purpose for which the BEF had come to France – to prevent her being crushed by Germany – appeared to escape him.' [21] This is simply not true. The BEF had come to France to join with the French in the liberation of Belgium and the defeat of German imperialism – no more, no less. For no other reason would Asquith's Government have agreed to a British involvement in Europe. It cannot be reiterated too often that this, and this alone, was the reason for Britain's entry into the Great

[20] Micky Lay, of 2/Oxford and Bucks L.I., notes, 'Sir Archibald Murray was the most detested General in Aldershot Command. We were very pleased when he was replaced as our Divisional Commander by General Monro.'
[21] Tuchman: *August 1914.*

War. That this decision was to lead to other and more sombre conclusions is not the fault of Sir John French.

From Paris, French went on the next day to Joffre's headquarters at Vitry-le-François, a small town on a river which would very soon have cause to be remembered: the Marne. Here the atmosphere was different, for Joffre was still riding high on the crest of Plan XVII. Between them Wilson and Huguet had alerted GQG [22] to French's unpredictable temperament, and he was duly received with the courtesy due to his rank and the tact necessary to ensure his fullest co-operation. Joffre, who had ensured that no politician would influence his military decisions, was aware that French was not a free agent, but answerable to Kitchener and a Cabinet of doubting Thomases, and he handled his visitor with great skill.

French was impressed by the air of efficiency and optimism at GQG, though not by the social graces of many of the senior officers ('a low lot', he later called them). He was fully briefed on the situation, and on the assured success of Plan XVII. 'From information I received', he wrote in his first despatch dated 7 September, 'I understood that little more than one, or at most two, of the enemy's Army Corps, with perhaps one Cavalry Division, were in front of my position; and I was aware of no outflanking movement by the enemy.' It has been suggested that Joffre thus deliberately deceived French, but on 16 August this was indeed GQG's airy appreciation of the situation. [23] Thus encouraged, French agreed to do his utmost to have the BEF ready to conform with a general advance on 21 August. This made nonsense of his forecast to Messimy the previous day, and was to be the first of many subsequent and often inexplicable changes of both heart and mind. Henry Wilson must have felt that it had been a day well spent.

Not so the next day. On 17 August French travelled on to the headquarters of Lanrezac's Fifth Army at Rethel. It was to be a disastrous confrontation. Edward Spears, then a lieutenant attached to Lanrezac's headquarters as Liaison Officer, has given a classic account of what transpired. [24]

The tone was set by Lanrezac's Chief of Staff, Hely d'Oissel, who delivered to Huguet on his arrival what was as much an alibi as a broadside. Lanrezac then appeared, showing signs of strain, for this apostle of *l'offensive à outrance* was acutely aware that the Germans were hourly providing evidence of their true intentions, and that Plan XVII was already seriously compromised. To his daily representations to Joffre he had received nothing but dusty answers. He was now in no mood to accommodate the Commander-in-Chief of an ally he disliked and an army he despised.

The two men retired alone for half an hour. Since neither spoke the other's language – and neither revealed what passed between them – it

---

[22] Grand Quartier Général, the designation of French GHQ. The German equivalent was OHL, Oberste Heeresleitung.
[23] In fact, the BEF was faced by the whole of Kluck's *First Army* consisting of *four* active Corps (*II, III, IV* and *IX*); *three* Reserve Corps (*III, IV* and *IX*), two of which were detached to contain the Belgian Field Army in Antwerp; and *three* Cavalry Divisions (*2nd, 4th* and *9th*); together with three second-line brigades. A total of over 320,000 men.
[24] Spears: *Liaison 1914.*

PLATE 7. *A GALLERY OF DIRECTORS*

French

Wilson

Robertson

Macready

Haig

Smith-Dorrien

Pulteney

Allenby

must have been a curious conversation. When they emerged French walked over to a wall-map and, pointing to the Belgian town of Huy on the Meuse, asked (in schoolboy French prompted by Wilson) whether the Germans were crossing the river at that point. It was a very fair question, for if it were true, then it demonstrated clearly that the Germans were embarked upon a gigantic right hook. 'Tell him', said Lanrezac, with all the sarcasm of which the French language is uniquely capable, 'that I think the Germans have come to the river to fish.' Wisely, Wilson reduced this caustic reply to something harmless in translation. But French, always quick to take offence, had noted Lanrezac's tone, and the damage had been done. It was never really to be repaired. [25]

That evening French returned to his headquarters at Le Cateau, there to be greeted with the stunning news that earlier in the day Grierson, commander of II Corps, had died of a heart attack in the train on his way to the concentration area. It was a serious loss, for Grierson was an able soldier, an expert in German military affairs, and a close associate and friend of both French and Haig. French at once telegraphed Kitchener and asked that he be replaced by Sir Hubert Plumer, then GOC Northern Command. Kitchener did not even reply. Instead, on 19 August, he sent Sir Horace Smith-Dorrien ('Smith-Doreen' as every old soldier remembers and reveres him).

Kitchener's decision was to put the seal on a fateful day. Why he chose Smith-Dorrien is a matter for conjecture. The two men had not served together since Omdurman (where – for such are the fortunes of war – Haig had also been involved). It is a reasonable assumption that he decided that he would take this early opportunity of imposing his authority as Secretary of State on French. What he succeeded in doing was to create a deep sense of animosity among the directors which, combined with French's unfortunate experience at Rethel, served only to add an unnecessary dimension to the purely military problems which lay ahead. It is only fortunate for the BEF that a similar clash of personalities was now taking place on the other side of the hill.

Before we take stock of the general situation on the Western Front on 20 August (when the BEF had arrived in its concentration area, and was preparing to join in the general advance into Belgium) [26] it is interesting to consider a decision which had also been taken on 19 August, and one which has been neither discussed nor explained.

On that date Kitchener informed GHQ that he was despatching the 4th Infantry Division to France.

---

[25] A very strange man, Sir John French. At least four men who were present that morning at Rethel have confirmed what happened. Yet this is French's own account as recorded that evening in his private diary: 'General Lanrezac appears a very capable soldier and struck me very much by his sense (?) and decision of character. We fully discussed the situation and arrived at a mutual understanding.'

[26] 'We shall take up an area North of the Sambre: on Thursday the heads of our columns should be on the line Mons–Givet with the Cavalry on the outer flank. Should the German attack develop in the manner expected, we shall advance on the general line Thuin – Dinant [*i.e. north-east*] to meet it.' Such was the extraordinary entry by French in his diary on Tuesday, 18 August. Perhaps it is the voice of Henry Wilson to which we are really listening. Either way, it is the voice of unreason.

Why? French, although later to complain that his Expeditionary Force had not included his 'III Corps' (Despatch of 7 September), did not request any such reinforcement (indeed, Joffre's estimate of the German strength facing him would not have caused him to call for help). On 19 August all was sweetness and light at GHQ. Henry Wilson was busily dispensing optimism, and the men of the BEF were sewing on new buttons, and learning the dozen words of French which got them most of what they needed except that which Lord Kitchener's severe (but not universally respected) admonition had proscribed. 'It was a lovely day,' remembers Jack Armstrong. 'I sat outside a little house and a small girl climbed on my knee and took the whistle out of my tunic pocket and blew and blew. It was the first time I felt real homesick.'

But on 19 August GHQ was writing its orders for the advance into Belgium. Why then the despatch of 4th Infantry Division? Certainly by then the invasion threat had ceased to haunt the corridors of Whitehall. Was this really an *amende honorable* and a realization that if the BEF were to march into Germany, it might as well do so with five rather than four divisions? That is one, if very improbable, answer. What is much more likely is that Kitchener – who alone had measured the true purpose and size of the German invasion of Belgium – sent the 4th Division to bolster the left wing of the BEF. Such a decision would be in keeping with his instruction to French, and a slap in the face for those who had opposed his 'Amiens' strategy. In the event, he was right. How right he could not have guessed on 19 August.

Between 3 August and 20 August – in other words, the period from Germany's declaration of war on France to the concentration of the BEF – much had happened, not least the first clear indications of cracks in the Schlieffen Plan, and of the disintegration of Plan XVII. So it is important to set the scene as it was on the morning of the British advance to battle.

First on the French side. Plan XVII in its final form, issued by Joffre on 14 February 1914, started with these words:

> From a careful study of information obtained, it is probable that a great part of the German forces will be concentrated on the common frontier [*i.e., between Thionville and Belfort*]. Whatever the circumstances, it is the C-in-C's intention to advance with all forces united to the attack of the German Armies.

The inaccurate conclusion in the first sentence (totally controverted by the evidence in August) made dangerous nonsense of the second. '*Whatever* the circumstances'? At least Joffre remained consistent.

On 8 August General Bonneau's task force on the extreme right advanced into Alsace and captured Mulhausen. By 10 August he was back where he started; and the next day he was dismissed, the first of twenty-eight generals to be (as the French put it) *limogés* by the first week in

September. On 14 August General Pau repeated the exercise with a larger force and more success.

On that same day the French First Army (Dubail) and the Second (Castelnau) struck north-east into Lorraine (they were still moving forward when French went to visit Joffre at Vitry). But on 20 August they were violently counter-attacked by the German *Sixth* and *Seventh Armies*, defeated in the battles of Sarrebourg and Morhange, and driven back on their fortress defences.

'*Whatever* the circumstances'? But certainly. Joffre now started a complicated series of lateral movements of formations and, belatedly, the introduction of Reserve divisions into the line. More significantly, despite the circumstances, he put into operation the contingency element of Plan XVII by committing the Fourth Army, his main reserve, to a joint offensive with the Third Army into the Ardennes. It was to prove an expensive disaster.

The effect of Joffre's decision to strike immediately at the German centre [27] with two Armies meant that Lanrezac's Fifth Army, on the French left, poised to deliver a flank attack against the German right – that 'modest violation of Belgian territory' which Foch had so complacently prophesied – now found itself threatened in turn by three German Armies totalling nearly 700,000 men, and already embarked upon Schlieffen's great enveloping movement north and west of the Meuse. Leaving one corps to defend the river-crossings between Dinant and Givet, he moved the rest of his Army – much altered by additions and subtractions – into a dangerous salient formed by the junction of the Sambre and Meuse between Namur and Charleroi; and there, filled with foreboding, he awaited the outcome of the battle in the Ardennes and the arrival of the BEF on his left. The 'veritable lion' had been brought to bay; and Joffre did not care for the signs of disobedience or the growls of dissent with which his orders were now greeted. Already Lanrezac had booked his ticket to Limoges.

Moltke had his problems too. First, he was incompetent. He owed his position as Chief of Staff to his name and to his social standing at the Imperial Court. Of this the professional soldiers at Supreme Headquarters were very well aware. Second, he was not in any true sense the Commander-in-Chief. That nominal position was occupied by the Kaiser himself as Supreme War Lord, and the Kaiser wished only to be fed a diet of victory upon victory. With this his cronies obliged him regardless of the truth (of which, let it be said, his key Army commanders were themselves often unaware). Under the increasing strain Moltke's nerve broke, and it was to be a signal – indeed, the only – stroke of fortune for the Allies that he was not dismissed until the tide had turned on the Marne.

Moltke never understood the basic premise of Schlieffen's plan, largely

---

[27] French Intelligence had no proper knowledge of the strength or location of the German *Fourth* and *Fifth Armies*: Plan XVII had assumed that the centre of the German line would be the weakest point. One did not argue with Plan XVII.

because he allowed himself to be influenced by the fact that two of his left-wing Army Commanders – the Crown Prince and Prince Rupprecht of Bavaria – were his social superiors. Thus one of his errors during the critical first fortnight was to allow the *Sixth* and *Seventh Armies* to pursue the French back across the frontier (and so behind their fortress defences), instead of enticing them farther into Schlieffen's 'mousetrap' in Lorraine. Only because of this was Joffre able to transfer northwards those vital divisions which were to form the basis of Maunoury's Sixth Army and so convert imminent defeat into improbable victory.

Moltke's next error was not his fault, for it was a political rather than a military decision. Schlieffen had planned that to facilitate the by-passing of Liège, the invasion of Belgium should also include a crossing of the 'Maastricht Appendix', that small part of Holland which separates the German and Belgian frontiers. In the event the Germans baulked at this double violation of neutrality, and this was to have an important effect on Moltke's timetable.

But the most significant error of all was simply one of German arrogance, shared equally by Schlieffen and Moltke. It was the assumption that the Belgians would stand aside and allow the Germans to walk over them; and that the British would not, at the eleventh hour, honour their pledge to go to war in defence of Belgium's neutrality. It was one of the greatest errors of judgment in military history; and certainly one of the costliest. Total casualties in the Great War are conservatively put at 8,020,780 killed and 21,228,813 wounded – a bloody price to pay for a scrap of paper.

The German invasion of Belgium can be summarized shortly; and it is proper to record that the resistance of the Belgian Army – six infantry divisions and one cavalry division – and the fortitude of the Liège and Namur garrisons had an incalculable influence on the German offensive plan. It also called down upon the heads of the Belgian people the full savagery of a very savage military machine. The Germans had not expected any resistance. They responded with such brutality that even Moltke was shocked by his armies' excesses.[28] Let there be no doubt about German atrocities. They were in every sense atrocious.

Early in the morning of Tuesday, 4 August, patrols of Marwitz's *Cavalry Corps* crossed the frontier and pushed cautiously forward towards the Meuse at Visé, probing the Belgian positions and masking the concentration behind them of Kluck's *First Army*. On the same day a special task force of Bülow's *Second Army* (the equivalent of two divisions in strength) deployed for the attack on Liège, the great fortress which stood in the path of the German right-wing armies.

The first assault – a night attack on 5 August – was repulsed with heavy losses. The following day a second attack was launched by Ludendorff (a name to be conjured with in the later stages of the war), who found the town unoccupied, the Belgians having withdrawn their 3rd Division to a new defensive line behind the river Gette, midway between Brussels and the

---

[28] Moltke: *Erinnerungen, Briefe, Dokumente, 1877–1916.*

German frontier.[29] The twelve outlying forts of Liège, long considered impregnable, were now isolated, and over a period of ten days were pulverized by German (and – hastily borrowed for the occasion – Austrian) siege howitzers of unexampled calibre, the last fort surrendering on the morning of 16 August. The Germans never forgave the defenders of Liège. In strict 'Schlieffen' terms, the delay to their right-wing timetable was small – perhaps two days. But consider what those two days might have meant. The Belgians could well have been eliminated on the Gette and Antwerp sealed off or even occupied. Kluck's leading columns would have been across the Mons – Condé canal by 20 August, and the BEF caught in the open, marching northward to a fatal rendezvous.

Two entries in Sir John French's private diary show his total incomprehension of the true situation in Belgium. On Tuesday, 18 August, he recorded:

> A wire from British Minister in Brussels saying the King of the Belgians was anxious to see me and pressing me to go to his HQ at Louvain. I have wired to ask if a Special train can be sent to meet me at Mons or Ath.

The following day he noted:

> There is no answer from the King as to my request for a Special train.

And very fortunate too; for on 18 August King Albert had started to withdraw his army into the fortress of Antwerp and had moved his HQ to Malines. The following day, 19 August, the Germans entered Louvain, so that French's 'Special train' would have steamed into the station to an unexpected reception. Since he would have arrived in company with Murray or Wilson, we are left to speculate what the fortunes of the BEF might then have been.

Meanwhile, not all was well on the German side. While the final destruction of the Liège forts was taking place Kluck's *First Army* was pouring into Belgium to the north of the city, Bülow's *Second Army* to the south, and Hausen's *Third Army* through the Ardennes towards Dinant and Givet.

Since Kluck on the outside of the great swinging arc had the farthest to travel, Moltke decided on 17 August to create an Army Group under Bülow to control the pace and alignment of the right wing. Hausen presented no problem. He was a Saxon, much concerned with good living, and conscious that his role was in a sense subsidiary. He was very happy for someone to give him orders while he looked around for elegant châteaux in which to establish his HQ. Not so Kluck. He was an abrasive character, who disliked Bülow and considered himself (not unjustifiably) as the *Schwerpunkt* of the

---

[29]The remaining division of the Belgian Field Army was then at Namur, whence it was skilfully withdrawn on 23 August to join the Antwerp garrison.

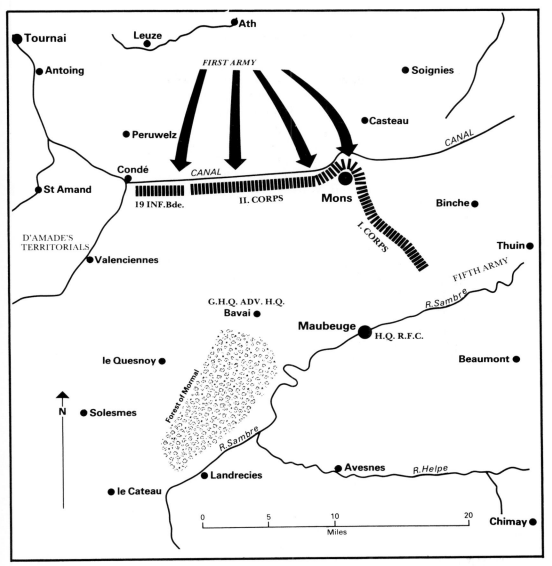

MAP 2. *The British Sector, 20–26 August*

Schlieffen Plan. His immediate answer to Moltke's directive was to ignore all orders from Bülow, and this was to have an important bearing on events.[30]

So we come to the morning of 20 August. By noon on that day the Belgian Field Army had withdrawn into the perimeter of Antwerp, and this, as we shall see, was to have an unexpected influence on the future conduct of operations on the Western Front. To contain this Army, Kluck detached his *III* and *IX Reserve Corps*, a decision which was to cost the Germans the

[30]On 27 August, after the battle of Le Cateau, Moltke rescinded his order. The result was to prove the salvation of the BEF.

battle of the Marne. That morning Kluck's advance columns of cavalry (Marwitz) occupied Brussels. An ecstatic Kaiser issued a special Order of the Day.

Farther south Bülow had crossed the Meuse in strength at Huy and was moving on Namur on both sides of the river. The siege of Belgium's last southern stronghold began on 20 August, supported by the great guns released by the fall of Liège. By 25 August it was over. The road to Paris was open.

At 1 p.m. on 20 August Sir John French issued Operation Order No.5, signed by his Chief of Staff, Murray.[31] It was the order to advance 'north of the River Sambre', and appended to it were detailed march tables for 21, 22 and 23 August. In the words of the official History 'the intention still was that the British Army should take the offensive'.

French's Order started with the words 'Information regarding the enemy and allied troops will be communicated separately.' No such information was communicated, for the good reason that no accurate intelligence was available.[32] Joffre was still busily presiding over the collapse of Plan XVII, blind to the overwhelming evidence of German intentions, of the growing threat to his left flank (and to the BEF), of the withdrawal of the Belgian Field Army into the Antwerp fortress, deaf to Lanrezac's warnings of the danger to his Army in the Namur – Charleroi salient, and the appearance of Hausen's *Third Army* at Dinant on the Meuse. At Vitry the spirit of Pangloss reigned supreme. All was for the best in the best of all possible worlds. Within forty-eight hours Pangloss's world had collapsed.

Thus the directors rang up the curtain. And what of the actors?

'That Friday was a very hot day' recalls Bob Barnard. 'We marched up along a straight cobbled road and it was hard going. No-one had told us anything and when I asked my officer, Mr Steele, where we were bound for, he didn't know no more than me. "Belgium", he said. A pal of mine who was a signaller thought we were going to Brussels and said that the Belgian army was giving the Germans a rough old time. During the afternoon we saw some French cavalry in breastplates and helmets and I thought they looked a bit shabby. Later there was a trickle of civvies coming the other way and I saw little carts being pulled by dogs. My feet were hurting and I thought it was a funny sort of war.'

So the BEF advanced to battle, and to a very unfunny sort of war.

[31] Murray had a disconcerting habit of referring to I Corps and II Corps as 'First Army' and 'Second Army', while Corps Commanders used Arabic rather than Roman numerals: viz, 1 Corps and 2 Corps.
[32] The following evening, 21 August, an Order was sent to the Cavalry Division. It started thus: 'The information which you have acquired and conveyed to the C-in-C appears to be somewhat exaggerated.' It was signed, predictably, by Henry Wilson.

CHAPTER 3

Mons

It stands, like many medieval towns, on a small eminence, a few miles inside the Belgian border midway between the rivers Sambre and Scheldt, which are connected by a canal. It has not changed greatly, for whereas in 1914 it was a major centre of communications, to-day it is by-passed to the west by the Paris-Brussels *autoroute* which branches east to Liège, just north of the town. But in 1914 all roads led to Mons: from Brussels in the north, Charleroi in the east, Maubeuge in the south and Lille/Valenciennes in the west by the Paris – Brussels *autoroute* which branches east to Liège, just north Mons, small, not greatly celebrated, was at the crossroads of Flanders and Picardy, Artois and the Ardennes. Its name, a battle honour of sixty-two British regiments, [1] commemorates an action which lasted for forty-eight hours, just three times the span of Waterloo which lies twenty-five miles to the north-east. One hundred years separates the two battlefields. They have nothing else in common.

It was not the best of places to fight an encounter battle with the weapons and numerical resources of a twentieth-century army, but then it was not the chosen battleground either of Sir John French (whose first objective lay farther north beyond the Sambre) or of Kluck, who was not even aware that he was confronted by the BEF as he moved south-west from Brussels. [2]

French's entry in his diary for Friday, 21 August, notes:

> Lanrezac says that 8 German Army Corps and 3 Cavalry Divisions are now north of the Meuse. I doubt if there are more than 6: but time will show.

It did; for on that date there were in fact *ten* (including Bülow's *Second Army*).

This entry is significant for two reasons. First, it shows that Lanrezac had

---

[1] Emblazoned on the colours of thirty-nine of these.
[2] Reports from his cavalry patrols on 22 August confused the presence of the French 88th Territorial Division in Tournai with the imagined arrival there of the BEF. As a result Kluck halted his *IV Corps* for two hours, and thus crucially delayed its arrival on the Mons battlefield.

correctly appreciated the enemy's true intentions, if not yet their true magnitude, which Joffre stubbornly continued to discount despite the evidence; and this, taken in conjunction with events on the southern and central fronts, meant only one thing: Plan XVII had started to disintegrate on the very day on which the C-in-C had ordered 'an advance with all forces united to the attack of the German Armies'. By that afternoon four of his own Armies were in retreat. The fifth, Lanrezac's, heavily engaged on the Sambre and threatened farther south on the Meuse, was about to follow suit.

French's diary tells us something else, for it gives us an important clue as to why the battle of Mons – the battle which should never have happened – took place two days later. Since the meeting at Rethel on 17 August, French had in a sense broken off diplomatic relations with Lanrezac, and his doubts – soon to be translated (not without reason) into profound distrust – were daily allayed by his Svengali, Wilson, to whom an anxious Spears came on the afternoon of the 21st with news of impending disaster on the Sambre. Even though he was an inexperienced subaltern, Spears could see that the BEF was embarked on a highly dangerous collision course. Wilson, despite GHQ's own air reconnaissance reports, could not – or would not – accept what had now become an incontrovertible fact. Spears returned to Lanrezac's HQ feeling as if he were another Nolan at a second Balaklava. Hence French's laconic comment. Hence the battle of Mons.

Events move rapidly in war. So do the thoughts and actions of volatile generals. To illustrate this it is necessary to anticipate the course of the next two days. French's diary entry for Sunday, 23 August (the day of the battle of Mons itself), shows a curious sense of detachment, his optimism draining away, and an apparent unawareness of the situation on his front. It is almost as if he had abdicated all responsibility to Smith-Dorrien, commander of II Corps:

> We live from hour to hour. The most contradictory reports are circulated [*French spent much of the day at Valenciennes, remote from the battle and from reports*]. The fog of war hangs heavily over us.

And then:

> According to Joffre we may *tomorrow*[3] be attacked in our present forward positions by 2½ Army Corps and 1 Cav. Div. Aeroplane reconnaissances do not tally with this.

In fact, since that very morning he was already being attacked by three Army Corps,[4] with a fourth entering the battle,[5] and with two cavalry divisions ranging far – and dangerously – to his left. To this precarious situation we shall return.

---

[3] Author's italics.
[4] From the British right to left: *IX, III* and *IV Corps.*
[5] *II Corps.*

The terrain which the BEF occupied in its march to battle was difficult and depressing. During his many bicycle trips to France before the war, Henry Wilson had studied it carefully, but he had never considered it as a battlefield. Plan XVII was concerned with a more distant and decisive frontier a hundred miles to the east.

Mons lies at the centre of an industrial and mining area stretching from Charleroi to Lille and traversed for much of its way by the Condé canal which, running south-west from the Sambre, forms a loop at the villages of Obourg and Nimy, skirts round the north of Mons and thence straight west for sixteen miles to its junction with the Scheldt (see Map 2). The canal ran – as it still does – through a continuous belt of pit-heads, slag-heaps and mining villages, broken – chiefly to the east of Mons – by open ground and wooded slopes, and to the west by a network of ditches and water-courses. By a curious fluke, it was to be occupied along its length almost entirely by infantry battalions from counties where the landscape was one of cornfields rather than collieries. [6]

'I took one look at it,' said Jim Cannon, born and bred in Suffolk, 'and thought what a bloody place to live. I took a second look and thought what a bloody place to fight.' Most of the men who arrived on the battlefield of Mons had done their soldiering in India or Egypt, in Long Valley or on Salisbury Plain. No one could remember manoeuvres in Barnsley or the Black Country, and firing among slag-heaps and round miners' cottages was a novel problem for which Haig's training regulations had not accounted.

The gunners, with happy memories of Okehampton and Larkhill, were not amused. 'My F.O.O. looked at the slag-heaps,' said Walter Pursey, 'and thought they were God's gift to an observation officer. We set off to climb one and within a couple of minutes our boots were sizzling, and down we came. No more slag-heaps, and precious little observation.'

The cavalry were disappointed too, although during the advance their area of operation took them to the east of Mons and into more open country, if not the kind of ground to invite the enemy to test their quality in mounted action. 'The cobbled roads were a proper bugger', said Arthur Newton, a farrier with the 5th Lancers.

> I seemed to spend my whole time shoeing horses, and it was even worse during the retreat. It would have been better if we had ridden across country, but the orders were that we weren't to damage standing crops. I never want to see another field of sugar-beet again!

So, in stifling August heat and in a curious air of unreality, the gap narrowed. Away to the north-east the sound of the distant gunfire warned the advance guards of the BEF that the cheerful preliminaries were over. So, more vividly, did the steady stream of refugees who now cluttered the roads leading south from Mons. The stream would soon become a flood.

---

[6] Middlesex, Royal Fusiliers, Royal Scots Fusiliers, Northumberland Fusiliers, Royal West Kents, KOSB, KOYLI, East Surreys, DCLI.

Even Henry Wilson must have begun to wonder. This was not the scenario for success.

In the light of subsequent events, French's Order of the 20th with its march tables for the three following days and its implied intention to deploy facing north-east along the general line Binche – Lens (eight miles north of Mons, and not to be confused with the town of the same name near Arras) seems inexplicable until it is remembered that under Plan XVII Lanrezac had been given this instruction:

> In the case of the enemy violation of neutral territory, the Fifth Army will move north-eastwards for an advance into Belgian Luxembourg [i.e., *east* of the Meuse].

The advance of the BEF accordingly conformed to this movement as an extension of Lanrezac's left, and the march tables (cavalry leading, followed by II Corps and, in rear, I Corps) merely reflect the inability – or refusal – of GHQ to recognize the true extent and direction of the German threat far to the west of the Meuse.

On the 21st, French issued Operation Order No. 6 (signed this time 'G. M. Harper, Colonel, G.S. for C.G.S.')[7] which, totally ignoring Lanrezac's belated realignment into the Meuse – Sambre salient, spoke vaguely of 'a column of all arms (reported) moving on Mons from Brussels'. It was a formidable 'column', for it consisted of three Army Corps and one cavalry division of Kluck's *First Army*. Yet the Order of the 21st simply confirmed the march tables set out the previous day, with only slight variations to the location of outposts and an instruction to the Cavalry Division to move west to the area of Thulin as a flank guard as soon as the infantry was in position. It is not surprising that Lt Spears returned that evening to Lanrezac's HQ with a heavy heart.

'Let the right sleeve of the right-hand man brush the Channel.' Kluck was word-perfect in Schlieffen, which Moltke was not. Moreover, Moltke was beginning to lose control of his generals. And his generals were beginning to question the competence of Moltke. If Joffre had his problems at Vitry, so – increasingly – did Moltke at Koblenz, where German Supreme HQ had now taken up residence.

Kluck was concerned about the BEF (and also about the Belgian Army lying over his right shoulder in Antwerp). Where were the British? And in what strength? He was convinced that the BEF had landed at Ostend, Dunkirk and Calais, for no better reason than that that was the view of Supreme HQ. Thus his first instinct was to move west from Brussels to intercept any threat from the Channel ports – in other words, an accurate interpretation of Schlieffen.[8]

---

[7] Between 11.55 p.m. on 21 August and 8.25 p.m. on 24 August, *no* written Orders were issued by GHQ. The battle of Mons was fought by Smith-Dorrien and Allenby.
[8] On 22 August the great gap between Valenciennes and the sea was occupied by General d'Amade's incomplete and semi-trained Territorial divisions, thus: 84th at Douai; 82nd at Arras; 81st at St Omer; 88th at Lille.

PLATE 8. *The earliest surviving air reconnaissance report. 22 August 1914, Area Soignies – Enghien*

But, as we have seen, on 17 August Kluck had been put under Bülow's command, by no means the first of Moltke's errors of judgment. Bülow, worried about the growing gap between his *Second Army* and Kluck's *First*, ordered him to turn south-west and leave the coastal area to Marwitz's cavalry. Kluck protested. Bülow insisted – 'otherwise the *First Army* might get too far away and not be able to support the *Second Army*'. Kluck protested loudly to Supreme HQ. Moltke ordered him to conform. And so it was that a British aerial reconnaissance[9] on 22 August reported that a massive German column marching on Ninove had wheeled south-west in the direction of Mons.

It is 22 August, the last day of speculation, for by the next morning the arguments were at an end, the errors committed, the battle joined. So

[9] Four Squadrons of the new Royal Flying Corps were based at Maubeuge from 18 August. Had GHQ listened to the reports of their commander, General Henderson, there would have been no battle of Mons.

before history takes over, let speculation have one final fling.

Liddell Hart has said that the attack of Bülow's *Second Army* on Lanrezac at Charleroi was premature. He is right, and for reasons which Bülow later admitted; for if Moltke had not interfered, if Kluck had been left to march westward in the direction of Amiens before turning towards Paris, the BEF would certainly have continued its innocent advance into Belgium. By delaying his forcing of the Sambre crossings by one day, Bülow would have then lured French into a trap from which it is difficult to envisage any escape. But Bülow was as unaware of the exact location and size of the BEF as Kluck, and it was Lanrezac's retreat in the face of a double threat on the Sambre and on the Meuse – not any subtlety on Bülow's part – which caused French to stop his own advance. This in turn explains the curious alignment of the BEF on the morning of 23 August, with I Corps facing east and II Corps north, for it halted thus while in the process of wheeling to bring its left flank into line facing north-east between Binche and Lens. So, in a sense, it was Lanrezac who inadvertently saved the BEF from the folly of its General Staff.

The morning of Saturday, 22 August, was fine and clear. During the night 2nd Cavalry Brigade had pushed forward patrols to the north of Obourg and Nimy, but without making contact with the enemy. None the less, local inhabitants and refugees spoke of the roads leading south from Brussels filled with marching columns – intelligence which, we have seen, was dismissed by Wilson as being 'somewhat exaggerated'.

At dawn on the 22nd, 'C' Squadron of the 4th Dragoon Guards, under the legendary Tom Bridges, had occupied an outpost position at Casteau, north of Mons, keeping two troops mounted and two ready for dismounted action. About 7 a.m. – the exact time has been a matter of argument – some movement was observed to the north-east, and Corporal Drummer Thomas fired at a mounted figure. He went to his grave years later persuaded that he had scored a hit. There is no dispute that he fired the first British shot of the Great War. That the honour fell to a bandsman is not so generally known.

An hour later a group of five horsemen [10] appeared moving cautiously down the main road. Two or three hundred yards short of Bridges's concealed squadron they stopped and turned back. Bridges at once released his two mounted troops under Capt. Hornby, and they set off in hot pursuit. Ted Worrell takes up the story: [11]

> We drew swords and galloped at full pelt down the road. As the German patrol reached the rest of their squadron, the whole lot turned and bolted. I suppose the chase went on for a mile but we were better mounted and caught up with them on the outskirts of Soignies and

[10] *4th Cuirassiers, 9th Cavalry Division.*
[11] The regimental history of the *4th Cuirassiers* dismisses the affair with the words 'Contact was made with an enemy patrol.'

there was a proper old mêlée. Captain Hornby ran his sword through one Jerry and Sgt. Major Sharpe got another. I got a poke at a man but I don't know what happened to him. There was a fair old noise what with the clatter of hooves and a lot of shouting. The Jerries couldn't manage their long lances at close quarters and several threw them away and tried to surrender but we weren't in no mood to take prisoners and we downed a lot of them before they managed to break it off and gallop away. Our horses were pretty blown so Capt. Hornby decided not to give chase. I suppose it was all over in five minutes but we certainly showed them that the 4th were hot stuff.

Fred Bulmer also took part in the fight:

It was a wide cobbled road with tramlines and a couple of our horses lost their footing and came down. I remember that we galloped past a racing stable (we later found that the owner was an Englishman and he gave us a good old cheer!). Then we were into the Germans. I'd say they were two to our one, but numbers didn't count for much in such a confined space and their clumsy lances were no match for our swords. I saw Captain Hornby stick one man and down he gone. I got a big Jerry in the bridle arm and he turned and bolted. Then it was all over. We hadn't lost a single man but we had a couple of horses killed and one or two slightly wounded. I don't know how many Jerries were killed and wounded – I'd say fifteen or twenty – but we rounded up eight prisoners and as many horses and collected quite a stack of lances and loaded the prisoners into a farm cart and set off back the way we come.

It had been a heartening first encounter, and 'C' Sqn returned to a heroes' welcome from the 2nd Cavalry Brigade and a special message of congratulation from its commander, General de Lisle.

The 4th DG was not the only cavalry regiment to distinguish itself on the 22nd. Farther east, the 5th Cavalry Brigade covering the approach march of I Corps was reconnoitring in the direction of Binche, and shortly before noon the Greys encountered a strong force of all arms moving south-west from La Louvière.[12] The Greys dismounted two squadrons and met the advance guards of this force with so withering a fire that the Germans not only hastily withdrew, but reported that they were opposed by 'at least one cavalry brigade'. George Scorey of the Greys[13] enjoyed his first taste of action.

They started to shell us but couldn't get the range at all. When we opened up, I wouldn't say they actually turned and ran, but they retired pretty sharpish.

[12] *13th Division* of *VII Corps* and part of Richthofen's *I Cavalry Corps (Second Army)*.
[13] George Scorey was later to earn some kind of immortality as 'the policeman on the white horse' at the Wembley Cup Final of 1923.

Next it was the turn of the 16th Lancers sent up from the 3rd Cavalry Brigade to support the Greys. A troop of 'A' Sqn, coming upon two companies of *Jägers* in the open, charged them with the lance, and turning, came back for a second bite at this inviting cherry. Pte Betts had not expected so early a chance to try his skill at arms:

> There were several corn-stooks in the field and the Germans tried to take cover behind them, but we were going a fair gallop and they didn't have much chance. To give them credit they stood their ground, though they hadn't any time to make a run for it and we speared quite a number on the way through and some more on the way back. Funny thing, but I don't remember the sound of any firing, though three or four of our lads were brought down. As we came at them the second time, I aimed at a Jerry but he dodged me and my point went into the ground. Luckily the lance-shaft broke or I would have been fetched out of the saddle.

The cavalry had cause to be pleased with their day's work. The Germans, unable to penetrate the covering screen, were none the wiser about what lay behind it or where, and in what strength the main British force was being deployed.

Throughout the 22nd the BEF was moving steadily north in accordance with the original march tables, still committed to the alignment from which the joint offensive with Lanrezac would be launched two days later. GHQ was at Le Cateau, with Advanced HQ at Bavai. A few miles farther north Smith-Dorrien, arrived from England the previous day, had set up II Corps HQ in a remote and inaccessible house at Sars-la-Bruyère.

There is no record of any conversation between Kitchener and Smith-Dorrien before the latter left to take up his command, nor does Smith-Dorrien's subsequent account of events refer to any discussion. It is reasonable to think, however, that Kitchener would have warned him of Wilson's dangerous optimism, of his influence over French, and of his own view of German intentions. And the new corps commander needed only to study the Operation Order of 20 August to have serious doubts about the frontage he was expected to cover with just two infantry divisions, and the possible threat to his exposed left flank.[14] Unknown to him, Haig had similar doubts. But not GHQ – not, that is to say, until midnight on that Saturday; and in the few hours left to him Smith-Dorrien hastily reconnoitred a second, less extended position some three miles south of the Mons canal – just in case. In war it is better to be safe than sorry.

Before describing the final positions occupied by the BEF before dawn on the 23rd, we must turn to the events of the previous day. In a sense that day was to belong to Lt Spears, for there can surely be no other instance in war of a subaltern saving the skin of his C-in-C. Spears was too late to stop the

[14] 19th Infantry Brigade did not yet exist, and Allenby's Cavalry Division was still concentrated on the BEF's right.

battle of Mons, but not too late to avert inevitable disaster. It is a pity that his more senior counterpart at GHQ, Col. Huguet, was to prove in the critical days ahead so devious and disloyal a counsellor. With friends like Huguet, no one – not even Henry Wilson – needed enemies.[15]

Wilson, the great hedger of bets, had already listened to Spears's account of the situation on the Sambre and on the Meuse. Now, early on the 22nd, he persuaded French to visit Lanrezac. Only an Irishman of his wit and charm could have bridged the gap left by the unhappy meeting at Rethel five days earlier. Together they set off for Fifth Army HQ at Chimay. By one of those extraordinary chances by which history is made, they met Spears on the road and learned from him that Lanrezac had gone forward to the HQ of his embattled X Corps at Mettet, twelve miles south-east of Charleroi. They also learned from him of the growing crisis on the Sambre, and the implications which this crisis held for the BEF. French listened but did not comment, and despite Spears's urgent request, he decided – perhaps wisely, since he needed little excuse to avoid a meeting he had not sought – to return to Le Cateau. If by so doing he thought he could distance himself from difficult decisions, he was soon to learn otherwise.

That afternoon Spears attended a meeting at Lanrezac's HQ, where he was shaken to learn that the planned offensive would not take place, and that in the face of German pressure, the Fifth Army would start withdrawing *in conformity with the Fourth Army on its right*. The BEF was not mentioned. More seriously, he was given by the Intelligence Staff a chilling appreciation of the true size and direction of the great enveloping movement of Kluck's *First Army*. It was a moment that Spears would long remember.

He set off immediately for Le Cateau on a nightmare journey across roads jammed with transport and with a growing flood of refugees; and four hours later he reached GHQ. The directors were at dinner. The innocent actors were already taking their places on the stage twenty-five miles away. For them a very different dinner-table was being set. It was 8 p.m.

Fortunately for Spears, he was met by Col. Macdonogh, the able but grossly underrated Chief Intelligence Officer, who listened – without surprise – to what he had to report. Around them the chief staff officers of I and II Corps and the Cavalry Division were busily engaged in finalizing details for the great advance into Belgium on the following day. It was, as Spears was later to tell a friend, as if Aristophanes was trying to rewrite Aeschylus.

Presently Sir John French appeared with Murray. Spears made his report. French and Murray' withdrew to an adjoining room, and the cheerful *gaudeamus igitur* continued round the mess-table. Away to the north the actors, wearied by long marches under a scorching sun, tumbled into their billets, neither knowing nor much caring what fate was being prepared for them in a smoke-filled room back in Le Cateau. 'Come to think of it', says Fred Northey,

---

[15] It is interesting that the English edition of Huguet's book, published after the war, is called *Britain and the War: A French Indictment*.

we had no idea where we were and certainly didn't know where the French were. I remember there was a big hill in front of us [Bois la Haut?] and we dug some shallow trenches and the mess-cart came up with some stew and we settled down for the night.

Back at Le Cateau no one settled down for the night. About 9 p.m. Murray appeared, to summon the eager planners to French's presence. It was to be a moment of supreme anticlimax. There would be no advance the following morning. Instead there would be adjustments to the outpost lines held by I and II Corps, and the Cavalry Division would move to the area of Thulin – Elouges to protect the left flank of II Corps. There would be no questions. Officers would report back.

No questions? But history is not so easily dismissed. And even while Lt Spears was making his weary way back to Chimay,[16] a staff officer from Lanrezac's HQ arrived at 11 p.m. at Le Cateau with a request that French would launch an immediate attack against the right flank of Bülow's advancing *Second Army*.

It was a very curious request, for at 3 p.m. that same afternoon Lanrezac had reported somewhat petulantly to Joffre that the BEF was still 'in echelon' behind him. This was not true. In fact the BEF was already some nine miles *forward* of the retreating Fifth Army, and separated by a gap of ten miles from the French XVIII Corps, which in turn had scarcely been involved in any fighting. The only explanation is that Lanrezac was already looking for scapegoats, and that his eleventh-hour 'request' was a cynical attempt further to discredit Sir John French.

If this is so the attempt unexpectedly backfired, for French, while declining to order an attack on Bülow's flank, agreed to hold his present position for twenty-four hours, or in other words to put the entire BEF at risk with both its flanks in the air. 'After that', he noted in his diary, 'I must consider whether the movement against my front [*sic*] and the French retreat did not render it necessary for me to retire again to the ''Maubeuge'' position.'

It is never easy to explain the actions of Sir John French. If it was his intention to up-stage Lanrezac, then he was taking a reckless gamble. If he felt he was following one part of Kitchener's instructions, then he was flagrantly disobeying another. In his memoirs he wrote: 'In view of the German Army commander's palpable intention to effect a great turning movement round my left flank, it is very difficult to realize what was in Lanrezac's mind when he made such a request to me.' It is equally difficult to realize what was in French's mind when he wrote those words. He could not have referred back to his own diary (see p. 85), or even to the second section of his first Despatch of 7 September. The answer is largely academic. The BEF was on its own, and would so remain for the next fourteen days. The actors must now pay for the indiscretions of the directors.

[16] For all his exceptional conduct during this critical period, Edward Spears did not even rate a 'mention' in French's first Despatch of 7 September.

The revised deployment of the BEF at dawn on 23 August, the day of the battle of Mons, was as follows (see Map 3).

Halted in the process of wheeling to the north-east, the line – if it can be so described – resembled a shepherd's crook. I Corps, with 5th Cavalry Brigade, faced east in accordance with the original plan, its right flank resting on Grand Reng eight miles north-east of Maubeuge and its general line following a ten-mile curve through Peissant, Haulchin, Harmignies to the southern edge of the Bois la Haut, a dominating feature at the base of the canal salient. This position was held by 1st Division on the right and by 2nd Division on the left, which closed up to make contact with II Corps at the Bois la Haut. Since I Corps was to take virtually no part in the forthcoming battle, we need not concern ourselves with the detailed location of its various units.[17]

II Corps held the canal salient and the line of the canal itself (some twenty-one miles, and including eighteen road and rail bridges) from Obourg to Le Petit Crepin in the west, whence the line was extended as far as Condé by 4th Cavalry Brigade until the afternoon of the 23rd, when it was relieved by two battalions of 19th Infantry Brigade (which as it came into action was put under Allenby's command).

It was no sort of defensive position, running for the most part, as we have seen, through a long straggle of mining villages and then through a dreary tract of water-courses and osier-beds. Fields of fire were restricted, artillery positions in any conventional sense non-existent, and the salient formed by the loop of the canal round Mons a potential death-trap. It was Smith-Dorrien's good fortune that Kluck (and, indeed, Bülow) had no idea where this line began and ended, or – more importantly – that it was held by little more than infantry outposts. To Kluck we will return, for on 23 August he showed – not for the last time – his serious shortcomings as a field commander. History has been too kind to Kluck. It is time the record was put straight.

II Corps was deployed with 3rd Division on the right and 5th Division on the left. Since the battle of Mons has a special significance in the annals of the British Army, it is proper that the reader should be reminded who were the first of the many (but see also Order of Battle, p. 245):

3rd Division *(right to left)*

8th Infantry Brigade
    2/Royal Scots   Bois la Haut – thence to Obourg
    1/Gordon Highlanders   } and along the canal to Nimy
    4/Middlesex
    2/Royal Irish Regt   in reserve in the salient

---

[17] It had been the C-in-C's intention to push the left of I Corps still farther north to the Mons canal, but battle was joined before this move could be effected.

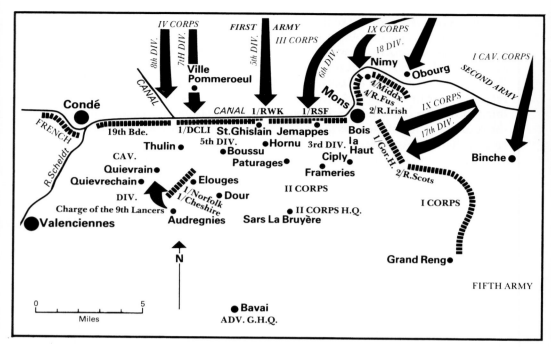

MAP 3. *Mons*

9th Infantry Brigade
    4/Royal Fusiliers   from Nimy to Ghlin
    1/Royal Scots Fusiliers   from Ghlin to Jemappes
    1/Northumberland Fusiliers   two companies from Jemappes to
                                           Mariette

    1/Northumberland Fusiliers   ⎫
       (two companies)   ⎬ in reserve
    1/Lincolns   ⎭

7th Infantry Brigade
    3/Worcesters   ⎫
    2/South Lancs   ⎬ Divisional Reserve at Ciply,
    1/Wiltshires   south of Mons
    2/Royal Irish Rifles   ⎭

5th Division *(right to left)*

13th Infantry Brigade
    1/Royal West Kents   at St Ghislain
· 2/King's Own Scottish   from St Ghislain to Les Herbières
      Borderers
    2/Duke of Wellington's   ⎫
    2/King's Own Yorkshire Light ⎬in reserve
      Infantry   ⎭

14th Infantry Brigade
 1/East Surreys
 1/Duke of Cornwall's Light
  Infantry

from railway bridge at Les
Herbières, thence to road bridge at
Pommerœul

 2/Suffolks
 2/Manchesters
} in reserve

15th Infantry Brigade
 1/Norfolks
 1/Bedfordshires
 1/Cheshires
 1/Dorsets
} Divisional Reserve

By dawn on 23 August the Cavalry Division had moved across the rear of II Corps and was concentrated in the area Thulin – Elouges – Audregnies, with 4th Cavalry Brigade on the canal. At 3 p.m. this Brigade was relieved by 1/Middlesex and 1/Cameronians of 19th Infantry Brigade, with 2/Royal Welsh Fusiliers and 2/Argylls in reserve.

Thus for most of the first day of Mons there were 9½ battalions of II Corps holding the forward position, with outposts on the north bank of the canal. Against this thin khaki line were to be launched – piecemeal, as it happened – six German infantry *divisions*. Even a David so uniquely expert with his sling must have retreated from so daunting a Goliath; but not before he had scored some very palpable hits.

At 5.30 a.m. on 23 August, French called a conference at Smith-Dorrien's HQ at Sars-la-Bruyère, to which were summoned Haig and Allenby. According to Smith-Dorrien, the C-in-C 'was in excellent form and told us to move forward, or to fight where we were', an order which as a statement of decisive intention left something to be desired. In answer to a question about the enemy's position and strength, French replied, 'Little more than one, or two, enemy Corps with perhaps a cavalry division.'

It is not possible to understand how, despite the evidence of his cavalry patrols, of his air reconnaissance reports, or Spears's warning, French still clung to the fantasy which he had so readily accepted at Vitry a week before. In fact, only five hours earlier, after the visit of Lanrezac's emissary, he had written in his diary: 'Macdonogh at the same time informed me that the Intelligence Dep. believed there are 3 German A.C. marching on us, the West Corps being as far as Ath!' [*itself an underestimate*], and that he had decided '*in view of this last information*[18] that I would retain my present forward position for 24 hours'. It must have come as a severe shock when 'about 5 p.m. I received a most unexpected message from General Joffre telling me that at least three German Corps were moving on my position in front and that their *II Corps* was engaged in a turning movement from the

[18] Author's italics.

direction of Tournai. [19] The truth was out. It was also very out of date.

Smith-Dorrien (towards whom French's attitude was cold, if not actually hostile) then asked what were his orders 'as soon as things got hot'. He pointed out his proposed – and shortened – second line of defence, and it seemed that he (French) 'approved my action'. With that the C-in-C set off for Valenciennes and removed himself from any further involvement in the battle of Mons. It was 9 a.m., and the first German shells were already falling on 8th Infantry Brigade in the canal salient.

Throughout the night of 22/23 August the forward battalions of II Corps were occupied with their defensive preparations on both sides of the canal while the artillery hunted around for suitable positions in the wilderness of pit-heads and slag-heaps (120th Battery even brought four guns as far forward as the towpath at St Ghislain). Strung out along their extended front, the infantry concentrated on the protection of the many road and rail bridges, and on the approaches to these from the northern side. No one – not even the two Divisional commanders, Hubert Hamilton and Charles Fergusson – had any knowledge of what was happening on the other side of the hill. Perhaps it was just as well.

Tom Bradley and Bill Cleave of 4/Middlesex were a short distance from the machine-gun section at the Obourg bridge. 'We dug little pits for ourselves – rabbit-scrapes really – lit a fag, and wondered what the Germans would look like when they arrived. There were a lot of fir-trees about 400 yards away across the canal and then some higher ground beyond. Were they up there watching us?' 'And then', recalls Pte Bradley, 'I suddenly remembered it was my birthday. And no one had sent me a birthday-cake!' He was soon to have a memorable present instead.

Kluck, still smarting under the indignity of being subordinated to Bülow, and resenting the instruction to close inward on *Second Army*, was moving south-west of Brussels towards Mons. He assumed that the full Expeditionary Force of six infantry divisions lay somewhere to his front, but it did not occur to him – perhaps because of his personal obsession with the idea of envelopment – that the natural location of the BEF would be an extension of Lanrezac's line on the Sambre from Namur and Charleroi. He was a stubborn, arrogant man, not readily disposed to accept Bülow's orders. There are none so blind as those who will not see, and none so deaf as those who will not listen. Sir John French, a not dissimilar man, was in the event more fortunate.

Kluck's Operation Order for 23 August, issued at 8.30 p.m. on the 22nd, merely mentioned the patrol clash with the 4th DG at Soignies (which should have told him something), and the shooting down of a British aeroplane 'coming from Maubeuge' (which should have told him even more). 'It was thus', says the official History, 'in complete ignorance of the strength of the British that Kluck advanced to the Canal, believing that

---

[19] *First Despatch, 7 September.* But see also diary entry on p. 85.

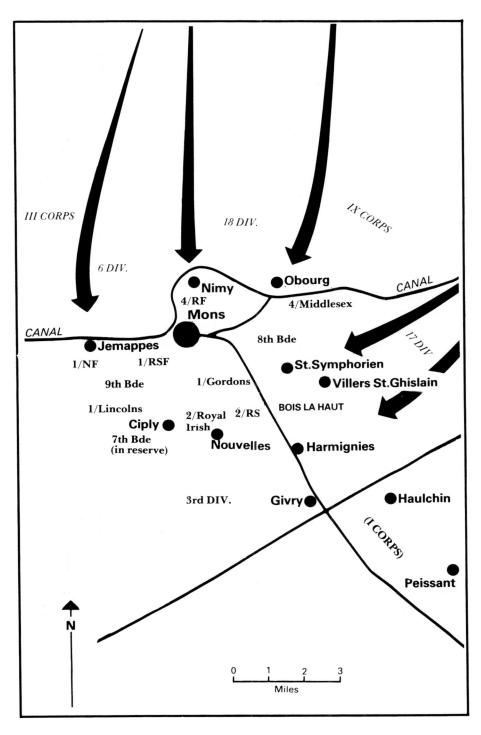

DIAGRAM A. *Mons: the Salient*

there might have been only cavalry in front of him.' So the great wheeling mass of the German *First Army* stumbled into battle – on its left *IX Corps*, then *III Corps, IV Corps* and, a day's march to the west, *II Corps*. It was the first of Kluck's cardinal errors of generalship, for if concentration is the essence of battle, then he ignored that imperative, and with it lost the chance of a decisive victory.

With his Army moving south-west in echelon, and with no knowledge of the BEF's position (even a man of modest intelligence might have guessed from his map that it was based on Mons and the line of the canal), Kluck did not wait to deploy his full available strength (six infantry divisions and one cavalry division, all within striking distance of the canal); but feeling his way cautiously with patrols of *9th Cavalry Division*, he at once committed *IX Corps*,[20] which happened to be the leading formation and fortuitously opposite the dangerously exposed canal salient held by Hamilton's 3rd Division.

In Mons and the surrounding villages it was just another summer Sunday as people made their way to Mass and trains carried August holiday-makers about their normal occasions. It was a very strange scenario. Pte Godley of 4/RF – who was to win the Victoria Cross that day for his gallantry in covering the withdrawal of his battalion at the Ghlin bridge – was entertained to breakfast at his machine-gun post by two hospitable children, while towards noon men of the Northumberland Fusiliers at Mariette, to the west of Mons, were astonished to see a party of small girls innocently walking down the main road towards the bridge, regardless of the fire-fight raging round them. But as the battle grew in intensity and spread, the reality struck home, and by afternoon the roads to the south – particularly the main *chaussée* to Maubeuge – were filled by a growing stream of refugees, the old and the young with their few movable possessions piled on carts and in prams, going they knew not where but seeking only safety from the storm which had burst upon them.

It was a misty morning, soon giving way to hot sunshine. By dawn the guns of *IX Corps* had started to search the perimeter of the salient from the high ground to the north of the canal. Pte Bradley had not long to wait for his birthday present. By 9 a.m. the German infantry[21] were pressing forward, first towards the Middlesex position at Obourg and then farther west against the Royal Fusiliers at the Nimy and Ghlin bridges. So began an unequal contest, eight battalions matched against four companies. For both sides it was the first taste of action, for *IX Corps* had not been involved against the Belgians on the Gette; and because of its peculiar, episodic nature Mons was one of the very few 'infantry' battles of the Great War. The ground on both sides of the canal provided few opportunities for the proper deployment of artillery, and as the battle spread westward during the day the forward troops were soon so closely involved that the gunners –

---

[20] *17th* and *18th Infantry Divisions.*
[21] *18th Division.*

certainly on the British side – resorted to moving to positions from which, often with single guns, they could engage the enemy over open sights. 'It was crazy', said Gunner Pursey, he of the sizzling boots, 'but we spent an hour actually in front of the leading company of Royal Scots Fusiliers.' Three days later, at Le Cateau, the pattern had already begun to change.

Pte Bradley and his friend had wondered what the enemy would look like. Now, at Obourg, they discovered. The first infantry attacks against the salient were launched at a range of 500 yards, and in close column. They were met by so great a volume of rifle and machine-gun fire that, in Bradley's words, 'they went down like ninepins until all we could see in front of us was a regular wall of dead and wounded. Above the noise of rifle fire, you could hear a strange wailing sound and they turned and ran for the cover of the fir trees.' It was reminiscent of the attack of the Prussian Guard at St Privat forty-four years earlier; and the result was the same.

Why should this have been so? Not only were the weapons of 1914 – not least the machine-gun – immeasurably more lethal and accurate than those of 1870, but all German tactical training had long been based on a single premise: 'Hold the front, seek the flanks.' There are three likely answers. First, that Kluck struck blindly at the first target within his reach; second, that he – and his subordinate commanders – ignored their own tactical premise and, with an arrogance born of numerical superiority, blundered into a frontal battle when a pause of less than twenty-four hours would have presented them with *two* exposed flanks to attack; third, that he had not reckoned with the quality of his opponents, or their unique expertise in the use of infantry weapons. It is worth repeating Zwehl's estimate of the BEF: 'They were very exceptional soldiers.'

'The first taste of action'; a conventional phrase, but a by no means conventional experience.

The men of the BEF – and their equally professional opponents of *First Army* – were highly trained in the *theory* of battle. But what of their reaction to the *practice* of war? Many of them – as their letters and diaries tell us – had no idea what it would be like to be on the receiving end of an arsenal of destruction. This was not bravado. It was the simple reaction of simple men to the ultimate purpose of their profession. It has often been said that the Victoria Cross is won by men with no imagination. This is not true. It is won by men with an exceptional ability to control fear – one of the two basic instincts of all animals, be they rabbit, recruit or RSM. What then was it like in the canal salient on the morning of Mons? Listen to Pte Jack of 4/Middlesex.

'When the firing began, I was frightened by the noise. I'd never heard anything like it. Most of the shells were bursting well behind us, but there was also a strange whistling sound as the bullets came over. I felt a bit excited but not really afraid. There were four of us in a rifle-pit and our officer walked over to us and I remember thinking: "Get *down*, you silly bugger." Later on I heard the poor man was killed.'

'Then the man next to me was hit. I was firing away and suddenly he give a sort of grunt and lay still. I'd never seen a dead man before, but I was to see a few more before it was all over. Sometimes killed clean. Sometimes bits and pieces. I just got used to it. You do. But do you know, to this day it turns my stomach over to see a cat or a dog killed by a car?'

It is a strange fact that while men accepted the prospect of death without, so to speak, quantifying its impact, they came very soon to treat it with an odd sort of contempt. Here is Lt Arthur Talbot Rice of the 5th Lancers in a letter home at the end of August:

> One soon gets accustomed to the most extraordinary sights. Two days ago I came across eight German gun limbers and three dead horses in a heap in a sunken road, and it seemed quite natural.

Casualties were accepted with a kind of stolid resignation and small show of emotion.[22] But it was a war which cruelly disabused men of any complacency. On the day of Mons the casualties in 2/Manchesters, one of the reserve battalions of 14th Infantry Brigade, were only 18 killed and wounded. Three days later at Le Cateau, the battalion's casualties were 14 officers and 339 other ranks; and meanwhile those of Pte Jack's battalion in the canal salient were 15 officers and 353 rank and file.

As the first mass attacks on the apex of the salient between Obourg and Ghlin foundered in the face of concentrated rifle and machine-gun fire, the German infantry withdrew to the cover of the fir plantations. There was a brief lull, while the defenders licked their own wounds and the enemy kept up a desultory and largely ineffective artillery bombardment to which 107th Battery replied with enthusiasm from a position just east of Hyon.

Half an hour later the Germans resumed their attack in even greater strength, but now in extended order and over a much wider front. Thus at last the infantry of the *17th Division*, working round the salient, found – though it seems not to have realized it – the open flank of 3rd Division, and the two battalions of 8th Infantry Brigade facing east. At this stage neither Kluck nor Bülow seem to have had any idea of the disposition of Haig's I Corps. It is clear from their subsequent accounts of the battles of Mons and Charleroi that Bülow considered the BEF to be Kluck's responsibility, and that Kluck either ignored or disobeyed any orders given to him on 23 August. Precisely the same personal vendetta was continued over the next two days, when Kluck refused to become involved in the investment and capture of Maubeuge even though it lay directly in the path of his *IX Corps*. That Bülow was thus obliged to detach his own *VII Corps* to do Kluck's job for him was to have a crucial effect two weeks later. All this was greatly to the relief of Haig, whose entire I Corps suffered fewer than forty casualties

[22] In his memoirs *Annals of an Active Life,* General Macready, Adjutant-General of the BEF, makes the interesting point that casualties in Territorial units were a cause of greater sense of loss than in the old Regular Army because of the closer sense of personal involvement among men from small, local communities.

PLATE 9. *The Mons canal: the bridge at Nimy today*

in the battle of Mons; and by implication, this conflict of personality on the German side also gave Lanrezac the opportunity to fend off his pursuer, and by the evening of 24 August his Fifth Army, much battered, had reached the line Givet – Avesnes, fifteen miles to the south of the BEF and with a ten-mile gap and the river Sambre between it and Haig's I Corps.

No such comfortable options presented themselves to Smith-Dorrien, now faced by an enemy superiority of at least three to one. He accepted the situation with an equanimity worthy of Joffre; and he was also, in a sense, lucky. Sir John French had removed himself to Valenciennes, whence he could not interfere in a difficult and delicate operation, while, at his HQ at Hal, Kluck had lost all control of a battle which he had simply allowed to 'occur', and which he assumed to be no more than a brief embarrassment to the great *Vormarsch* on Paris. OHL, still remotely located at Koblenz, was out of contact with the right-wing Armies. During these crucial hours not one senior officer was sent forward to the battle area. The ghosts of the elder Moltke and Schlieffen must have shuddered.

As the morning wore on the situation in the canal salient became increasingly ominous. On the north-west face the Royal Fusiliers, despite losing virtually every officer of the two forward companies defending the bridges, and in the face of repeated attacks in overwhelming strength, continued the 'stubborn resistance' which they had been ordered to maintain. It was a justly famous passage of arms. And it was at Nimy that Lt Maurice Dease, the battalion machine-gun officer, though repeatedly wounded, continued to hold at bay an estimated two battalions of German infantry. His posthumous award of the Victoria Cross was the first of the Great War,[23] soon to be followed by that of Sidney Godley, also severely

[23] Between August 1914 and November 1918, 628 Victoria Crosses had been awarded.

wounded and taken prisoner, although not before a final Cockney gesture of smashing his gun and throwing it into the canal.

To the east the position was still more critical, for here the loop in the canal exposed 8th Infantry Brigade to both infiltration and flank attack. 4/Middlesex, holding a front twice as extended as that of the Royal Fusiliers to the Obourg bridge and thence south towards the Bois la Haut, had dealt severely with the first attack by *18th Division*; but by 10 a.m. infantry of *17th Division* supported by *IX Corps* artillery began to penetrate the thinly held line on either side of Obourg and to probe the eastern flank in the direction of the high ground where 1/Gordons and 2/Royal Scots had dug themselves in with wide fields of fire commanding the approaches from St Symphorien and Villers St Ghislain.

Tom Bradley again:

> It was like sitting in a sack not knowing what was going on outside except that, whatever it was, it was noisy and dangerous. The place was swarming with Germans and by mid-morning they had even got round behind us but not in any great numbers. At times you didn't know if you were firing at friend or foe. But in spite of our casualties, we managed to hang on. By noon we had lost all but one of our company officers. I remember feeling very hungry, and wished I was back home.

About 10.30 a.m. the machine-guns of 2/Royal Irish, the reserve battalion of 8th Infantry Brigade, were sent up to support the Middlesex as they slowly fell back from the canal; and at 12.30 p.m. all four companies of the battalion were ordered into Tom Bradley's 'sack'. Their task was a daunting one – to keep the neck of that sack open, and so allow the brigade to retire to Smith-Dorrien's second defensive line roughly three miles south of Mons and running north-west from Frameries through Paturages and Wasmes to Hornu.

Farther east, strong German attempts to turn the flank of 8th Infantry Brigade, and so close the sack, were met by stubborn resistance from the Gordons and the Royal Scots around the dominating Bois la Haut feature; and here, with the only good observation and fields of fire along the whole of II Corps' front, the gunners had their chance. XL Brigade (6th, 23rd and 49th Batteries) caught the German infantry in the open and did considerable execution. Despite repeated and costly attacks, *17th Division* could make no headway, and by early afternoon there was a lull in the fighting along the right flank. The sack remained open – but at great and growing cost.

Meanwhile west of the salient, because of Kluck's haphazard deployment of his Army, the encounter battle did not begin in earnest until 11 a.m., and then spread like a slow fuse along the straight length of the canal.

The British line, with its absurdly extended battalion frontages, was

PLATE 10. *The Mons salient: Bois la Haut – the German view*

properly concentrated on the several road and rail bridges, with outposts thrown across to the north bank of the canal to cover the approaches. All bridges were prepared for demolition during the night, but were not to be blown except on Divisional orders. [24] Here the right of the line was held by 1/Royal Scots Fusiliers at Jemappes and two companies of 1/Northumberland Fusiliers at Mariette, both of 9th Infantry Brigade. From Mariette westward the line was extended by 13th and 14th Infantry Brigades (5th Division), and then, from 3 p.m., by 19th Infantry Brigade (see p. 59).

The first attack on the straight canal line was made by *6th Division* of *III Corps* against the bridges at Jemappes and Mariette. Plainly word had not got around of the warm reception given to *18th Division* earlier in the day north of Mons, for the enemy infantry once more advanced in close formation – the official History speaks of 'a column of infantry in fours swinging down a country lane east of Mariette' where it was cut down by the concentrated fire of a company of 1/NF – and soon the Germans paused to reflect upon the unwisdom of such tactics while their artillery, faced by the same problems as their British counterparts, searched blindly for invisible targets. By noon 1/RSF and 1/NF had withdrawn their outposts across the canal. They had suffered few casualties, and were still securely holding their bridges.

By noon also, 1/Royal West Kents was briskly engaged with the

[24] When the time came to withdraw several bridges were left intact due to a shortage of exploders. The likely reason is that an army advancing to take the offensive – and on 22 August the BEF had been such an army – is not concerned with *demolishing* bridges. Likewise with maps. By 22 August all maps of France had been handed in, leaving only those of Belgium – and beyond. As a result one battalion commander was obliged to conduct the retreat with the sole aid of a small school atlas.

PLATE 11. *A pontoon bridge over the canal at Jemappes after the withdrawal of 9th Infantry Brigade*

PLATE 12. *1/Royal Scots Fusiliers at Jemappes Bridge, Mons Canal, 23 August 1914*

Brandenburg Grenadiers of *5th Division*. The battalion had pushed a company as far forward as Tertre, a mile north of the canal, and 'A' Sqn, 19th Hussars,[25] showing considerably more enterprise than the German cavalry, was reconnoitring still farther to the north-west in the direction of Hautrage. It was here that Harry Bell fired his first shot in anger:

> They came forward in a solid mass. And in a solid mass down they went. Things were pretty hot, however, and soon we began to retire towards the canal. Our casualties were quite stiff (Lt Anderson and my platoon sergeant were killed early on and I had two close shaves myself), but the rest of us got back across the bridge safely.

What Harry Bell did not know was that his single company had been opposed to three German battalions and a machine-gun company which were stopped in their tracks as they debouched on either side of Tertre by the combined fire of the Royal West Kents, a company of 2/KOSB, the machine-gun section of 2/KOYLI and the four guns of 120th Battery on the tow-path of the canal. A German account speaks of major casualties: 'In our company alone we lost five officers and half our men . . . Our first battle is a heavy, unheard-of heavy defeat, and against the English, the English we laughed at.' By the end of that day German laughter had turned to healthy respect.

An hour later the infantry of *III Corps* attacked farther west against the remaining companies of 2/KOSB and 1/East Surreys (14th Infantry Brigade) at the road and rail bridges at Les Herbières – and with little cover, soon experienced in their turn the quality of British rifle-fire. After a short pause two battalions of the *52nd Regiment* resumed the attack at 1.30 p.m. against the East Surreys. George Roupell,[26] a platoon commander whose diary provides one of the most vivid, revealing – and often humorous – accounts of Mons and the weeks that followed, made this entry:

> KOSB on our right, DCLI on our left . . . We got into a position on the embankment and as the enemy came through the wood about 200 yards in front, they presented a magnificent target, and we opened rapid fire. The men were very excited as this was their first 'shot in anger'. Despite the short range a number of them were firing high but I found it hard to control the fire as there was so much noise. Eventually I drew my sword and walked along the line beating the men on the backside and, as I got their attention, telling them to fire low. So much for all our beautiful fire orders taught in peace time!

It is perfectly clear from Kluck's memoirs that he had not the slightest idea of the progress of the battle on his immediate front. Nor had Bülow, whose

[25] One squadron of cavalry was allotted to each infantry division for reconnaissance purposes (see Order of Battle at p. 245).
[26] Lt (later Brigadier) Roupell was to win the Victoria Cross on St George's Day, 1915, at Hill 60. It is a melancholy commentary on the sacrifice of the old Army that by 13 November 1914 only five of the original officers of his battalion were still left.

excessive caution had already offered Lanrezac a golden chance to counterattack the *Guard Corps* west of Dinant. The eager Franchet d'Esperey (I Corps) had asked in vain to deliver a destructive blow at the open flank which Bülow had presented to him. Too late. The spirit of offensive, the very spirit of *élan*, had been drained away from Lanrezac at Charleroi. Both had been replaced by one idea: survival.

Caution had become the order of the day; and caution was long to remain the order of the day. Commanders, well schooled in military theory, now found themselves faced by realities for which the text-books had not catered. It is not easy for men trained to deal in thousands to grasp the complexities of handling much vaster numbers. Sir John French, remote from the battle, was still under the dangerous spell of Wilson's optimism. [27] Lanrezac was at total odds with Joffre, who still was clinging to the shattered remnants of Plan XVII. Moltke, believing what he was told, preferred not to tell what he believed. On the crucial German right flank a curious situation developed as Bülow tried, by force of gravity as it were, to stop Kluck from swinging back into his original orbit, and also to instil into Hausen on his left some of the determination which he himself so signally lacked. But despite a succession of blunders and lost opportunities, the German flood-tide was growing hourly more irresistible.

We left Fergusson's 5th Division still firmly holding its own on the canal, and it was not until mid-afternoon that Kluck's *IV Corps*, two hours behind schedule, approached the positions held by 1/DCLI and 19th Infantry Brigade between the bridge at Pommerœul and Condé, wearied by marching and too late to influence the battle. Kluck at last could congratulate himself. He had found the left flank of the BEF. That knowledge – if indeed he realized it – was his sole justification for a day ill-spent and expensively protracted. Not one German soldier had crossed the canal between Mons and Condé. Four divisions had been defied by fewer than ten battalions. Napoleon, with his equation of the moral to the material, would have greatly approved.

But it was, as Smith-Dorrien had long realized, a lost cause. The fatal weakness lay in the salient. Given time – and time is a precious commodity in war – he would never have so exposed 3rd Division, French and Wilson notwithstanding. So he ordered the withdrawal from this death-trap, and his decision to do so meant that his stalwart 5th Division must inevitably conform. Thus, early in the afternoon of 23 August, II Corps began to retire on its second, and shortened, line three miles south of the canal.

It is not necessary to describe here in detail how 8th and 9th Infantry Brigades fell back from Tom Bradley's sack, the machine-gun sections of the Royal Fusiliers, the Middlesex and the Royal Irish killed or captured, firing to the last. Nor how the Gordons and Royal Scots extricated the 23rd

---

[27] Even on *24 August*, Wilson was, in his own words, 'drafting orders for an attack to-morrow by cavalry division, 19th Bgde and IInd Corps, to NE, pivoted on Mons'. Pivoted on *Mons*? On 24 August, Mons was in German hands.

Battery from the Bois la Haut position in a brief and bitter hand-to-hand fight.

The withdrawal from the salient started at 2 p.m. as the Royal Fusiliers, covered by Pte Godley's machine-gun, began retiring through Mons and then towards Ciply and Nouvelles through barricades set up by 1/Lincolns, the reserve battalion of 9th Infantry Brigade, on the three roads leading south of the town. The Germans made no attempt to follow up the Fusiliers, who, in the words of the official History, 'withdrew, the supporting companies covering the retirement of the advanced companies with peacetime precision'. 'I never saw a single German all afternoon,' recalls Bob Barnard. 'It was stifling hot and my feet were still hurting!' It is quite evident that the enemy were in no mind to invite any more lethal doses of rifle-fire, even though, despite Pte Godley and the gallant efforts of 57th Field Company RE, they had succeeded in capturing the bridges at Nimy and Ghlin.[28]

At 3 p.m. the left-hand battalions of 9th Infantry Brigade also began an orderly retirement on Frameries, three miles south of the canal. First 1/RSF evacuated Jemappes, and here L/Cpl Charles Jarvis worked single-handed under intense fire for 1½ hours to destroy the vital bridge at Lock 2. Three miles farther west at Mariette, covered by the two companies of 1/NF, who refused the order to withdraw until 4 p.m., Capt. Theodore Wright, adjutant of 3rd Divisional RE, although twice wounded made repeated but unsuccessful attempts to blow the road bridge.[29] By that evening only two out of eight bridges in the 3rd Division sector had been destroyed (see footnote to p. 67).

Thus by 5 p.m. the whole of 9th Infantry Brigade had been withdrawn to the Frameries position. The Germans – partly because of their own severe casualties and partly through lack of co-ordination between the commanders of *IX Corps* and *III Corps* – did not follow up their success.

In the salient, however, it was another story, for here as the afternoon wore on the fighting became increasingly bitter and the situation increasingly confused. The German infantry – now across the canal in considerable strength – pushed forward to Hyon in an attempt to outflank 8th Infantry Brigade from both the east and west. The key to what had become a quite separate battle was the Bois la Haut feature, for so long as this was in British hands the escape route from the sack remained open. Through this gap the Middlesex withdrew, losing some sixty men in a final and defiant rearguard action on the outskirts of Hyon – 'I was dead lucky to get away, if you know what I mean,' said a thoughtful Tom Bradley – and by dusk the remnants of the battalion had reached their new position at Nouvelles, where throughout the hours of darkness they were rejoined by scattered parties and even individual men who had been cut off in the general confusion of battle.

[28] For graphic accounts of the exploits of this Company north and west of Mons, see 'Demolitions at Mons', *RE Journal* March 1932, pp. 26 *et seq.*, and *History of the Corps of Royal Engineers*, Vol V, p. 178 *et seq.*
[29] Capt. Wright and L/Cpl Jarvis were awarded the Victoria Cross. Wright was killed in action at Vailly on the Aisne on 14 September.

It was now the turn of the Royal Irish, the two battalions defending the eastern perimeter of the sack, and the three batteries of XL Brigade. The former, having lost nearly half their number in covering the withdrawal of the Middlesex, found their own line of retreat blocked, and were obliged to make good their escape by means of a long and hazardous detour round the north and east faces of the Bois la Haut.

Shortly after 7 p.m. the Germans made one final attack on the line held by the Gordons and the Royal Scots along the Harmignies – Mons road which skirts the eastern slope of the Bois la Haut. It was brave, desperate and very costly. [30] The Gordons and the Royal Scots, well entrenched and with excellent fields of fire, showed once more the quality of musketry which throughout the day had proved that numerical superiority alone was not enough. It was a lesson which was to have a significant effect on Kluck's tactical approach, for when three days later the BEF turned to fight again at Le Cateau, it was treated to the full weight of the artillery of *First Army*.

At 9 p.m. the enemy had had enough. General Doran, commander of 8th Infantry Brigade, ordered the withdrawal from Bois la Haut and – not without some critical exchanges – the right wing of 3rd Division fell back on the Nouvelles position. 'It was all done without fuss or bother', recalls Arthur Rose of 6th Battery.

> We come down from the hill, hooked in, and trotted off while the Gordons covered us. 23rd Battery had a nasty moment, but they got away too. We didn't lose a gun.

At midnight the only sound was that of German bugles blowing the 'cease fire'.

At midnight, I Corps was still deployed in virtually the same positions which it had occupied throughout the day of the battle. Beyond some desultory shelling, it had not been attacked, and was not even aware of the situation in the salient and along the canal, or for that matter the crisis developing farther east, where Lanrezac was already in full retreat. Why the Germans applied so little pressure to I Corps we shall presently see.

The withdrawal of 3rd Division from the salient to Smith-Dorrien's second position meant that 5th Division, and beyond it 19th Infantry Brigade, had also to evacuate the canal line which they had so successfully defended throughout the day. Casualties here had been slight, and indeed 19th Brigade had not been in action at all until 5 p.m., when Kluck's *IV Corps* (*7th* and *8th Divisions*) belatedly reached the battlefield. [31] By the early hours of the 24th the BEF had completed its retirement, and now lay south of Mons on the higher ground which had been Kluck's objective for the previous day. Thus French's decision to stand and fight for twenty-four hours in his perilously exposed forward position seriously – perhaps

---

[30] The *7th (Bremen) Regiment* of *17th Division* alone lost 5 officers and 376 men (official History).
[31] The following day this Corps was to find itself matched against 5th Division and Allenby's cavalry in the first major attempt at envelopment of the BEF's left flank.

decisively – upset the German timetable. Joffre was quick to acknowledge this fact. Not so Lanrezac, intent only on distancing himself from the attentions of Bülow and Hausen. There is now no doubt that he owed the survival of his Fifth Army to the determined resistance of that small but resolute ally of which, even after the war, he spoke only with contempt. Lanrezac was later to receive the Grand Cordon of the Legion of Honour. Of no other of the directors on the Western Front can it more truly be said that his honour rooted in dishonour stood.

At dawn on 24 August the BEF – perhaps wisely left in peace throughout the night by an enemy sharply reminded that numbers alone are no answer to professional skill – lay facing slightly inclined to the north-east, [32] thus:

I Corps	Broadly in its original position, but with three battalions of 5th Infantry Brigade filling a temporary gap in II Corps' front

II Corps	
3rd Division	Nouvelles – Ciply – Frameries
5th Division	Paturages – Wasmes – Hornu
19th Brigade	Thulin – Elouges
Cavalry Division	Thulin – Elouges – Audregnies – Quievrain

The front had thus been reduced to seventeen miles. Both flanks remained in the air, for Lanrezac's Army was fifteen miles to the south, and on the left d'Amade's 84th Territorial Division was already retiring through Valenciennes towards Cambrai.

And what of the first day of action? It had not been particularly victorious, in the same sense that Dunkirk was not a victory. Casualties totalled 1,642,[33] of which more than half had been incurred by the Royal Fusiliers, the Middlesex and the Royal Irish in the canal salient (a figure which would soon be considered the daily small change of trench warfare).

But if Mons was not a British victory (and even Wilson's two 'absent' divisions would not have made it so), it was for the Germans a limited and very expensive success. There is no reliable record of enemy casualties on that day, but from personal accounts and from the official monograph on the battle – 'murderous fire . . . the casualties increased . . . the whole advance stopped . . . with bloody losses, the attack gradually came to an end' – it is clear that they were very considerable.[34] The infantry soldier of Kluck's *First Army* was brave and, at regimental level, bravely, if blindly,

[32] This alignment seems to have convinced Kluck that the BEF would continue its retirement to the west – i.e., on Amiens. On this day his conviction was shared by Sir John French.
[33] The most serious loss was among regimental officers, 'brave even to the point of foolhardiness', said one eye-witness.
[34] A private German opinion puts the figure at at least 6,000 and possibly as high as 10,000.

led. That not one such soldier crossed the canal west of Mons until after dusk on the 23rd is a tribute to the training, the discipline and above all the incomparable musketry of the BEF. To have fought at Mons is a distinction as great as that of Henry V's band of brothers at Agincourt.

The battle had other, far-reaching effects, as the events of the next three days were to prove, for the 'murderous fire' of the British infantry persuaded Kluck of the folly of frontal attack (a folly, admittedly, forced upon him by Bülow's timorous attitude to the exploitation of the initial success on the German right wing). He now reverted to his – and Schlieffen's – original obsession: the envelopment of the Allied left flank, irrespective of what Bülow wished. By the evening of the 23rd Bülow gave up the unequal struggle with Kluck and left him to his own devices. Earlier it has been said that in war obsession can be a dangerous counsellor. We shall now see how, in the mind of a commander of Kluck's limited ability, that counsel can lead to disaster.

Thus the official German monograph:

> After the stubborn defence of the enemy, especially opposite *III Corps* [*i.e., along the canal west of Mons*], Kluck expected that the British would offer energetic resistance the next day [*24 August*] on the high ground south of Mons. He therefore resolved to continue the attack next day enveloping the left flank, with the intention of cutting off the enemy's retreat to the west.

In a grandiose gesture, Kluck despatched all three divisions of Marwitz's *II Cavalry Corps* into the wide-open spaces occupied by d'Amade's divisions. It was a curious decision, for his orders for 24 August announced: 'The attack will be so directed as to force the enemy into Maubeuge.' With Marwitz in his proper role, this might well have happened. But it did not.

Tired, hungry, but content with their performance, the actors sorted themselves out among the slag-heaps and consoled themselves with such sleep as they could get. Ted Golden of 2/KOSB was given a bowl of soup by an elderly lady with a Gallic passion for Scotsmen. 'I believe if we had had a spare rifle, she would have joined us there and then. I couldn't understand her speech, but I had an idea she didn't like Germans.' All along the line it was much the same; and so it must have been when the soldiers of Marlborough and Wellington passed this way. 'The discipline and restraint of the men after their ordeal was exemplary,' reported Sir Nevil Macready, the Adjutant-General, adding (in a letter to a friend some years later), 'They didn't much care for wine anyway!' Meanwhile, what of the directors?

Haig spent a quiet day contemplating the landscape and seemingly unconcerned about the dramatic events taking place to the north and west, or the growing crisis east of the Sambre. There is no record of any communication with II Corps except for a call for assistance from Hubert Hamilton about 3 p.m. as he began to extricate 3rd Division from the salient.

It is now clear that there were two reasons for what a Guards officer described in his diary as I Corps' 'rest day'. First, the stubborn resistance of 3rd Division absorbed the full resources of *IX Corps*, leaving Kluck with no reserves on his left (the few shells which fell within the I Corps area were fired at long range by the artillery of Bülow's *VII Corps*). Secondly, Kluck's decision during the day to envelop the British left and force the BEF back into Maubeuge meant that the longer he could persuade Haig to hold his present ground the better. In fact it was not until after midnight that I Corps was ordered to cover the right flank of II Corps by a slow withdrawal to what French had called his 'Maubeuge' position,[35] and at dawn, after a spirited artillery demonstration, the troops marched off. The enemy made no immediate attempt to follow.

Smith-Dorrien spent a very different kind of day. He had inherited two problems: a frontage more suited to two corps than two divisions, and a wide-open left flank protected only by Allenby's Cavalry Division, and beyond that, by d'Amade's scattered Territorials.[36] As we have seen, the full weight of *First Army* fell on II Corps, and throughout 23 August and the following day[37] Smith-Dorrien fought a brilliant, single-handed battle. He himself gave the credit to his subordinate commanders[38] and to his resolute men. They in turn trusted him implicitly, and without trust – as Lanrezac learned to his cost – a general is a figurehead and not a leader. 'I saw Smith-Doreen only twice', recalls Bert Aldous. 'He was quite a little man, but very spick and span with boots you could have shaved in. He talked to as many men as he could, quiet and serious but cheering us up and saying how well we had done.'

'A single-handed battle'? It is a fair claim, for GHQ took no part in it. French, as we know, had gone to Valenciennes at 9 a.m. 'I left Murray to make a provisional arrangement in case a retreat became necessary,' he noted vaguely in his diary. He did not return to Bavai until 5 p.m., by when Smith-Dorrien had been obliged to make his own urgent arrangements.[39]

Lest the reader may think that criticism of French is unjustified, it is necessary only to refer to two passages in his first Despatch written just two weeks later:

> About 3 p.m. on Sunday, the 23rd, reports began coming in to the effect that the enemy was commencing [*sic!*] an attack on the Mons line, apparently in some strength.

And again:

> The right of the 3rd Division, under General Hamilton, was at

---

[35] The position in fact lay to the west of Maubeuge, roughly following the main road to Valenciennes thus, right to left: Feignies – la Longueville – Bavai – St Waast – Wargnies – Jenlain, a front of ten miles.
[36] In fact, as the 84th Territorial Division fell back south-west from Condé through Valenciennes, it was followed by the German *II Corps*, perhaps the most signal of all Kluck's blunders. Had this Corps been directed *south*, 5th Division would surely have been cut off.
[37] On the 24th, Allenby's cavalry played a significant part.
[38] One, General Hamilton (3rd Division), was killed in action on 14 October.
[39] No orders were issued to II Corps on 23 August.

Mons,[40] which formed a dangerous salient; and I directed the Commander of the Second Corps to be careful not to keep the troops on this salient too long, but, if threatened seriously, to draw back the centre behind Mons.

This is not only meaningless but untrue. The second line – i.e., the Frameries–Paturages position – had already been reconnoitred by Smith-Dorrien, and it was his decision, and his alone, to withdraw 3rd Division from the salient (it was French's Order of 20 August that put it there in the first place) and then to evacuate 5th Division from the canal.

The truth is more simple. Murray was incompetent, and, in the absence of his C-in-C, incapable of making any critical decision. Wilson, having made 'a careful calculation', decided, in spite of Macdonogh's intelligence reports, that the BEF was *still* faced by no more than two German corps and was busy planning a resumption of the original offensive.[41] Alone among the executive directors at GHQ, Sir William Robertson, Quartermaster-General and a canny Scot, foresaw the true implications of the battle on the 23rd and made his plans for sustaining a long and arduous retreat.

It was left to Joffre to bring GHQ momentarily to its senses. On his return from exchanging pleasantries at Valenciennes, French 'received a most unexpected message telling me that at least three German Corps . . . were moving on my position in front and that their *II Corps* was engaged in a turning movement from the direction of Tournay. He also informed me that . . . the 5th French Army on my right was retiring . . . the Germans having gained possession of the passages of the Sambre between Charleroi and Namur.'

An unexpected message? Smith-Dorrien had already been anticipating Joffre by several hours in his reports. So had Macdonogh. So had the Royal Flying Corps. So – for days rather than hours – had Lt Spears. At this point 'GHQ had, to a large extent, lost its head'.[42]

24 August was a day of mixed fortunes. It belonged, on the British side, to 5th Division and the Cavalry Division. For Kluck, it was another day of indecision and of missed opportunity. At GHQ several different battles were being fought – in every sense. French felt that a limited retreat was necessary, but mindful of the fate of Bazaine in Metz in 1870, he was determined not to get trapped in Maubeuge. Wilson was not thinking of Maubeuge. His mind was still incomprehensibly fixed on distant horizons and victorious offensives. By the morning of the 24th he must have been the only man in France who still believed in the primacy of Plan XVII.[43] As for Murray, he was already working himself into a state of collapse, unable or

---

[40] Not so. The *left* of 3rd Division was at Mons.
[41] See footnote to p. 70.
[42] Terraine: *Mons*.
[43] But see French's diary entry on p. 85. It is difficult to know whether to believe French, Wilson – or either.

unwilling to act as honest broker between French and Wilson. It did not occur to anyone to ask the opinion of Smith-Dorrien.

Joffre's 'unexpected' bombshell convinced French of two things. First, that he must act, and act soon. Secondly, that he must seriously contemplate a much more drastic course. And once again it was Lanrezac who took the decision for him. At 10 p.m. on the night of the 23rd Spears, in his now routine role of Messenger in a Greek tragedy, arrived at Le Cateau with the news that Fifth Army had started a further withdrawal which would carry it far to the south of the BEF. French reacted at once. How close he came to over-reacting we shall presently see. He sent Spears back the next morning to Lanrezac with a brusque message that in view of his (Lanrezac's) unilateral action, he considered himself under no further obligation to co-operate, should his own left flank be compromised. Lanrezac did not reply, but passed French's message on to Joffre. Joffre's problem was that he had no authority to give orders to French; but tactful suggestion can be as effective as abrupt commands, and ever since their first meeting, Joffre had the measure of French's temperament. This, as will presently be apparent, was very fortunate indeed.

At 1 a.m. French, instead of issuing immediate orders to his subordinate commanders, summoned their chief staff officers to Le Cateau, a time-consuming procedure which contributed directly to Smith-Dorrien's problems during the day. French's decision was to withdraw the BEF immediately to the Maubeuge position as a temporary expedient while he made plans for a general and potentially hazardous retreat.[44] The sole virtues of the Maubeuge position were that it was only eight miles behind the existing front, and that it continued the process of shortening the original line. With a now typical lack of authority, French left his two corps commanders to settle the actual order of retirement in consultation, merely indicating that I Corps was to occupy the new line from Feignies to Bavai, and as has been indicated, to cover the retirement of II Corps. None of the roads converging on Maubeuge was to be used.

On stage the actors awaited first light in expectation of renewed attacks on the 3rd and 5th Divisions. The order to retire reached Haig some hours before Smith-Dorrien,[45] and at 4 a.m. 1st Division moved off, followed forty-five minutes later by 2nd Division. Whether deliberately or not, no orders were given to *IX Corps* to pursue Haig until 8 a.m., by when I Corps had effectively broken off contact and was too far to the west to be engaged closely, and so driven into the Maubeuge defensive perimeter. It was the first of several escapes that day.

Smith-Dorrien was less fortunate. Had the order to retire reached him earlier there is little doubt that he too could have slipped away from Frameries, and even from the whole II Corps position. GHQ's lack of

---

[44] These plans were incorporated in Operation Order No 7 timed and dated 8.25 p.m., 24 Aug, 1914. It was French's way of conforming with Joffre's 'suggestion', but totally controverted by Operation Order No. 8 issued the following afternoon (*q.v.* p. 89).
[45] It was not until noon that the two corps commanders were able to meet and, belatedly, co-ordinate their movements.

urgency at this critical time drew one of the very few expressions of anger from Smith-Dorrien in his later account of events.

The men of II Corps felt confident of their ability to hold the enemy on their new line. Except in the salient – and no way could the salient have been defended – the day had gone well. The Germans had been taught a salutary lesson, and were in no mood to repeat the experience. Indeed, one battalion commander, whose unit had suffered over six hundred casualties opposite St Ghislain, spent a nervous night in expectation of a British counter-attack ('If they had known, they would have walked over us.').

This partly explains the German decision to break off the action at midnight. The more important reason – as the events of 24 August were to show – was Kluck's change of mind, or, more precisely, his refusal to listen any longer to Bülow. He now had a very rough idea of the strength and disposition of the BEF (he still believed that *six* infantry divisions were somewhere in front of *First Army*), and accordingly he reverted to the wide enveloping movement round the British left from which he had been deflected in turn by Moltke and Bülow. If he could hold Smith-Dorrien's centre with his *III Corps*, then in theory he had a mass of manœuvre for his flank attack more than adequate to eliminate the BEF. [46] In practice he had already compromised his chances, and was further to compound his initial error during the next twenty-four hours.

Among the slag-heaps and mining villages the men of II Corps waited, unaware that Lanrezac had left them out on a limb, unaware that Kluck was now planning to lead with his left before delivering a massive right hook, unaware that time was running out for Sir John French, and therefore for them.

When at 4.30 a.m. the order to withdraw reached the brigades of 3rd Division it was greeted with disbelief. It is difficult to find a single surviving veteran of that first encounter who does not recall the sense of dismay, 'a feeling', described by Harry Pratt of the Northumberland Fusiliers, 'that we'd simply wasted our time on the canal'. This feeling of frustration was even stronger in 5th Division, which had given the enemy a bloody nose at small cost to itself and was awaiting the second round of the contest with lively anticipation. [47] Lt Roupell, a mild man, was very angry. 'I hope', he wrote, 'they know what they're doing.'

'They' were not yet sure what they might be compelled to do. The fighting-men knew nothing of the conflict of opinion at Le Cateau, for this was not the scenario which they had rehearsed. But they trusted Smith-Dorrien and their own commanders, and grumbling (as was their historic privilege) they started the delicate task of disengaging. At least Bob Barnard had some satisfaction. His feet had stopped hurting – and that was fortunate. For the BEF was now embarked on a long, long trail which was to take it, during the next two weeks, 160 miles south to the gates of Paris.

[46] *IV Corps, II Corps, II Cavalry Corps,* and – a day's march to the north – *IV Reserve Corps.* This latter corps was to enter the battle on the 26th.
[47] 5th Division was to find the second round a very different affair. Its performance on the 24th, faced by three German divisions, was to be a notable, if largely forgotten, passage of arms.

Smith-Dorrien's first problem was to clear the roads of unit transport which had been pushed forward in expectation of Wilson's triumphal advance into Belgium. It was not an easy operation, and made more difficult by the stream of refugees escaping from the battle area and the limited number of roads available; but – and this is a timely reminder of the efficiency of the much maligned divisional staff officers – the operation was conducted with great skill and without enemy interference.

Smith-Dorrien's next problem was one which would have been difficult to solve on peacetime manœuvres, let alone in the middle of a pitched battle. This was to switch positions between 3rd and 5th Divisions, partly to allow the 3rd, which had suffered much more severely on the previous day, to slip away first and partly to shorten the distance which the 5th had to cover when it withdrew from the left flank. This delicate manœuvre was in the event carried out so smoothly over the next two days that the two divisions crossed tracks without even seeing each other.

The first German attack started before dawn with a heavy bombardment against Ciply and Frameries, and this extended westward within an hour along the whole front of II Corps as far as Wasmes and Hornu. Plainly the Germans had learned their lesson and were not this time committing their infantry without artillery preparation. In fact the bombardment was largely ineffective in the built-up area now occupied by II Corps, and it was not long before a massed infantry attack was launched on Frameries by *6th Division* of *III Corps*.[48] It was driven back with heavy loss by 7th Infantry Brigade (the divisional reserve on the previous day) and four guns of 109th Battery, and in the lull that followed 8th Infantry Brigade began its retirement southward from Nouvelles, unmolested by the enemy. Even as they marched off a second massed attack was made on Frameries. It was repulsed once more with even heavier losses by 1/Lincolns and 2/South Lancs. Alf Tebbutt of the Lincolns (9th Infantry Brigade reserve) had a busy time. 'I just kept firing away at the mass of Germans in front of me until my rifle was almost too hot to hold. At 400 yards you couldn't miss and I never thought to see so many dead and wounded men in such a small space.' At 9 a.m. the 9th Brigade made an orderly withdrawal through Frameries and marched off to Sars-la-Bruyère, there to be greeted by a proud and happy Smith-Dorrien. 'They were desperately tired and battle-scarred,' he wrote later, 'but they came in singing.'

It was now the turn of 7th Brigade, the rearguard at Ciply. They delayed their withdrawal a little too long, and 2/South Lancs, enfiladed by machine-guns from the slag-heaps about Frameries, lost nearly 300 men before the brigade struck south towards Genly. The official History comments: 'The Germans made no attempt to press them; indeed, they handled 3rd Division on this day with singular respect. It had, in fact, inflicted on them very heavy losses at a cost to themselves of 550 men.' It was not until noon that the enemy cautiously entered Frameries and found no defenders there. A German account has this to say: 'Up to all the tricks of the trade from their

<hr>

[48] The orders given to *III Corps* this day were to hold the British centre while Kluck prepared his attack on the open left flank.

experience of small wars [*very few men of the BEF had fought in any small wars*], the English veterans brilliantly understood how to slip off at the last moment.'

So, its right flank covered by I Corps, 3rd Division made good its escape.

Farther west, the situation was more critical. The gap between Frameries and Paturages had been filled by three battalions of 5th Infantry Brigade, hastily borrowed from 2nd Division. In the event these battalions were not required, and returned to I Corps during the morning without having fired a shot or seen the enemy.[49] About 10 a.m. the German attack[50] developed against 5th Division's line running north-west from Paturages to Hornu.

There followed a running fight which took place over the next two hours among the pit-heads and villages of this desolate landscape. Once again the main blow fell upon those battalions which had been in reserve on the 23rd – 2/Duke of Wellington's of 13th Infantry Brigade and 1/Bedfords and 1/Dorsets of 15th Infantry Brigade – the former at Paturages and the latter at Hornu.[51]

Throughout this morning the Germans were clearly intent on pinning down 5th Division rather than overrunning it. The main achievement of their artillery was the very efficient shelling of their own *Brandenburg Grenadier Regiment*, which seems to have been virtually wiped out on the approaches to Hornu. No record of casualties for this regiment on the 24th are to be found in the official lists. It had already been severely handled by the Royal West Kents on the canal the previous day.

The gunners of 5th Division did rather better, as they improvised a cat-and-mouse game among the slag-heaps. Pte Kennedy of the Dorsets was astonished to find three howitzers of 37th Battery parked alongside his company and 'firing away at close range as if they were machine-guns'. Neither side had any experience of combat in such a landscape, where commanders had little control and men had to invent their own tactics. At this the British infantry were both ingenious and brave; and the British artillery brave and highly effective.

About 11 a.m. Fergusson started to withdraw his 13th and 14th Infantry Brigades. Only at Wasmes was there a minor disaster, when 2/Duke of Wellington's did not receive the order to retire, and were badly cut up. 'They suffered nearly 400 casualties, but they had held at bay a whole German brigade of six battalions.'[52]

The crisis on the left flank came shortly before noon, for here 19th Infantry Brigade and the Cavalry Division had already retired, undisturbed, at about 9 a.m. Two hours later Fergusson also received the order to withdraw 5th Division to its position on the new line west of Bavai,

[49] Micky Lay of 2/Oxford and Bucks L.I. was very disappointed. 'I wondered if we were ever going to get into action.' He need not have worried. There would be plenty of time in the months and years ahead; and a DCM and two MMs to prove it.
[50] *5th Division* and part of *6th Division* of *III Corps*.
[51] The reserve battalions of 15th Brigade were at Dour with 119th Battery. Their hour was soon to come.
[52] Terraine: *Mons*.

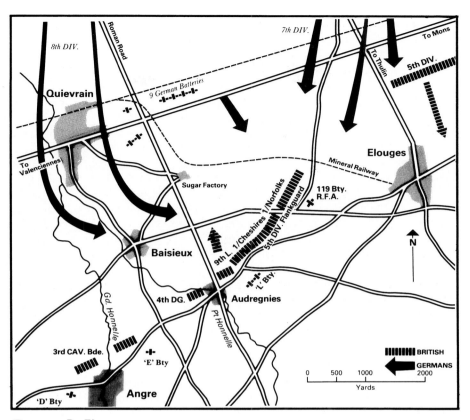

DIAGRAM B. *Elouges*

and at 11.30 a.m. the 13th and 14th Infantry Brigades had marched off towards Eth, six miles to the south.

They had scarcely set out when the entire artillery of *IV Corps* opened up from positions north of the main Valenciennes road and from the direction of Quievrain. Kluck's right hook, inexplicably delayed, was about to begin in earnest.

There now began an extraordinary battle in which the entire *IV Corps*[53] was launched against *two* British infantry battalions, part of two cavalry brigades, and four batteries of artillery. The official History describes it as 'the flank guard action at Elouges' – a masterpiece of understatement. It was not only a full-scale battle but a crucial one, for against all the odds (and they were immense) Fergusson's and Allenby's men effectively stopped Kluck's attempt at envelopment in its tracks.[54] They did more than that. They caused Kluck to lose another vital day, and in due course to take leave of his senses.

The Elouges arena was a rough rectangle three miles wide and two miles deep, bounded on the north by the Mons–Valenciennes road, thence south

---

[53] *7th* and *8th Divisions* (twenty-four battalions and nine batteries of artillery).
[54] Throughout this unequal battle the British artillery – 119th Bty and 'D', 'E' and 'L' Btys, RHA – lost not a single gun. The infantry were less fortunate.

PLATE 13. *The Elouges ridge looking north-west to Quievrain. It was across this field that the 9th Lancers made their charge*

to Elouges, and south-west to Audregnies. The western boundary followed the shallow valley of the Honnelle stream to Quievrain. (See Diagram B.)

At noon, realizing the danger to his flank, Fergusson called on Allenby for assistance, and at once he sent up 2nd Cavalry Brigade to Audregnies, and 3rd Cavalry Brigade to Angre to cover the approaches from Baisieux. At the same time Fergusson despatched what to-day would be called a 'task force' consisting of his two remaining reserve battalions, 1/Norfolks and 1/Cheshires of 15th Infantry Brigade, and 119th Battery, under Colonel Ballard of the Norfolks, to fill the gap between Elouges and Audregnies. Tom Lawrence of the Norfolks remembers the scene well. 'We were on a little ridge, Cheshires on our left, 119th on our right, and a clear field of fire across cornfields to the north-west. Might have been back home in Norfolk! We hadn't any time to dig in and so were sitting ducks for their gunners, but they weren't much good.' The infantry waited.

But first it was the turn of the cavalry. At 12.45 p.m. the German infantry began to advance in two columns from Quievrain and Baisieux. To check this movement General de Lisle ordered the 9th Lancers and a squadron of the 4th DG to take the German infantry in flank, 'if necessary by a mounted attack northwards'. With benefit of hindsight, this order invited a modern version of Balaklava, for it meant charging at least six battalions of infantry and six batteries of guns across 2,000 yards of open ground. The result was not dissimilar.

As the 4th DG debouched to the north-west, Colonel Campbell led two squadrons of the 9th at the gallop towards Quievrain under a hail of fire. Crossing the Roman road, the 9th were brought to an abrupt halt by a wire

82

fence. 'We simply galloped about like rabbits in front of a line of guns,' wrote Francis Grenfell. [55] 'Men and horses falling in all directions. Most of one's time was spent in dodging the horses.' The survivors of the charge wheeled to their right and took cover behind a sugar factory and some slag-heaps. It was not until mid-afternoon that the scattered elements of 2nd Cavalry Brigade were able to reassemble at Ruesnes, eight miles south of Audregnies. Casualties, despite the confusion of the charge, were surprisingly light – 250 men and 300 horses. It had been a brave affair in the best or, as Wellington would have felt, the worst British cavalry tradition, and the check to the advance of *IV Corps* was short-lived. When the attack was resumed it was the turn of the Germans to be on the receiving end.

At 1 p.m. 'L' Battery came into action. The German infantry pressing forward from Quievrain across the open ground in their turn presented an uniquely inviting target at 2,000 yards range and, in the words of the official History, the 13-pounders of the RHA, firing low-burst shrapnel, 'literally mowed down the advancing masses'. The enemy ran back to cover, and when they bravely tried again they received the same treatment.

Tom Bridges of the 4th DG remembers seeing the six guns of the battery drawn up behind the railway embankment north-east of Audregnies, firing 'according to the drill-book as if they were on range practice'. John Allan was too occupied to watch the results. 'Bombardier Perrett and I were busy bringing up ammunition and it was a very hot day in every sense. [56] I don't know how long the action lasted [*approximately three hours*] but I remember a staff-officer galloping up and shouting: "Good old 'L'!"' [*This was the Brigade-Major of 2nd Cavalry Brigade sent to order Major Sclater-Booth to retire. It was then 4 p.m.*] 'On our way back a farrier who was an old South Africa man told me we had fired more shells in one afternoon than during the whole Boer War!' The battery total was in fact less than 450 rounds, of which very few were wasted. When, two years later, John Allan was in action at Gommecourt on the Somme the allocation was 1,000 rounds *per gun* – and the effect significantly less decisive.

At 3 p.m., long after 3rd Division on the right of the line, protected by the I Corps rearguard, had begun its orderly retirement on Bavai, Fergusson's situation on the left was, by every canon of war, beyond redemption. It is worth describing the position again.

5th Division flank guard had now been reduced to two infantry battalions, 'L' Battery, and 119th Battery, occupying the two-mile ridge between Elouges and Audregnies, with a covering party of 3rd Cavalry Division and two RHA batteries at Angre. Against this tiny force the Germans had committed their entire *IV Corps*, *7th Division* attacking south from Thulin and *8th Division* first from Quievrain and, as the hours passed, farther west from Quarouble. The German superiority was of the order of six to one.

[55] Two hours later Captain Grenfell was to win the Victoria Cross in company with Major Alexander of 119th Bty in helping to manhandle their guns to safety from Elouges.
[56] No fewer than four German batteries tried to silence 'L', but their shooting was poor and the total casualties on the British side were fewer than a dozen, and caused by a single shell.

'When it comes to it,' said Tom Lawrence, 'numbers aren't everything in battle.' Too true. It is the volume and accuracy of fire that counts; and discipline; and sheer guts. And this once again the Germans discovered. They were no less brave. A veteran of the *36th Regiment* [57] remembers what it was like: 'They fired like devils. Simply to move was to invite destruction. In our first attack we lost nearly a whole battalion.'

But it could not last. At 4 p.m. 'L' Battery and 119th Battery had been pulled back. An hour later Colonel Ballard ordered the retirement of his two battered battalions. The Norfolks managed to extricate themselves and join the main body of 15th Infantry Brigade at Wargnies. The Cheshires on their left were sent three orders to retire. None reached them. They stayed, fought and died. When, later that night, the roll was called only 200 out of 1,000 answered. And by midnight, hungry and tired to the point of collapse, the BEF had safely reached its new position.

So ended the battle of Mons. It leaves many questions unanswered; but it also answers many questions. On the British side, it had been an exceptional vindication of professionalism, discipline and training – above all, of expert musketry and the kind of gunnery that was born of the British passion for field sports. The BEF should have been killed stone dead on the canal. It was not. It survived because of its conviction of its own superiority; and because in Smith-Dorrien II Corps was led by a very exceptional soldier.

The casualties on the 24th were greater than those on the first day: over 2,000, of which 1,650 had been suffered this time by 5th Division. Such are the fortunes of war. The total casualties on the two days of the battle of Mons were still significantly less than those at Waterloo a hundred years earlier.

And what of the Germans? The records, official and personal, are unreliable and often contradictory. We now know the size and composition of Kluck's available force on both the 23rd and 24th, a superiority of at least three to one in infantry and an even greater preponderance in artillery. Yet throughout these two days Kluck had little idea of the substance of the BEF, only of its shadow. His conduct of the battle of Mons was marked by a total lack of enterprise and by his obsession with the tactics of envelopment. The German account of the 24th speaks of 'the pursuit of the beaten enemy'. This is quite untrue. Inexplicably, *IV Corps* halted in the afternoon and bivouacked for the night on the line Elouges–Baisieux–Quiverechain. In other words, throughout that day *7th* and *8th Divisions* had only managed an advance of little more than three miles. The BEF then lay eight miles farther south.

It has been said that Kluck's fatal mistake was his inward wheel a week later. It is arguable that the root of his error lay in his failure to win the battle of Elouges.

[57] *8th Division, IV Corps.*

CHAPTER 4

The Retreat Begins

On 25 August, as the reality of war began to dispel the fog of illusion, three men – each for different reasons – took a decision of critical importance.

By that morning French, convinced that he had been deserted by Lanrezac and persuaded at last that he was confronted by an enemy in formidable and growing numbers, abandoned all thought of offensive action. To Kitchener he proposed, without precise commitment, 'to retire on my lines of communication', even to withdraw the BEF into some kind of fortified encampment at Le Havre (the same idea was to occur to him in another form during the first crisis at Ypres two months later).

What he intended to do when he reached the coast he did not suggest, although his real purpose is now clear. How he intended to get there does not even bear speculation. I Corps on his right was disengaging, and in retiring south of Maubeuge had virtually lost touch with Lanrezac, whose main force was already a full day's march farther to his rear. Smith-Dorrien's II Corps, wearied by two days' fighting, was withdrawing in the face of strong enemy pressure. Between the two Corps lay the Forest of Mormal. To reach Le Havre would have meant marching the BEF – now reinforced by 4th Infantry Division[1] – across the front of four German Army Corps and three cavalry divisions. It requires no more than a glance at the map to realize what would have happened.

Kitchener gave French a short, sharp answer. So, more tactfully, did Henry Wilson, even if he was later to insist that had all six divisions of the BEF been sent to France at the outset 'this retreat would have been an advance and defeat would have been a victory'. With directors capable of such fantasies, what hope was there for the suffering actors?

None the less, on this critical day Wilson used his influence to dissuade French from an act of criminal folly; and it is a measure of French's capacity for self-deception that there is no mention in his diary of the extraordinary manœuvre which he had proposed. Instead, his entry for 25 August reads as follows:

> Wilson said he was sure they intended to turn our left: in which case we should be cut off from our base. Murray was uncertain. I disagreed

---

[1] 4th Division, less some of its artillery and services, had reached the Le Cateau area on 24 August.

entirely with Wilson's views but rather preferred retirement in view of uncertainty as to French plan of operation. I decided to retire toward St. Quentin and Noyon and *if necessary*[2] to get behind the line of the Oise to re-organize and re-fit.

Let the reader make of that what he will. Within a few hours – and without explanation – the evacuation of France had become the retreat to the Seine.[3]

What French's diary tells us – apart from its startling revelation of his mental confusion – is that from now on his mind was obsessed with a single word: retreat. How far or for how long was not of immediate importance. That Wilson's reading of Kluck's intention was only too accurate he must have accepted, even if his diary entry tries to suggest that he was himself master of events. His men, who had taught Kluck's Army a salutary lesson, did not understand. No one told them. 'It had been pretty rough,' said Jack Downie, 'and we were tired. But each time the Germans came at us, we gave them a bellyful and they didn't like it. We could have kept it up.' The cavalry had done well, the unfortunate affair at Audregnies notwithstanding. The artillery, incredibly, had lost only the two guns of 120th Battery on the canal towpath.

But it is part of the pity of war that the actors have to play out their roles with little knowledge of what is happening in the wings or behind the scenes; and Jack Downie, firing away across the footlights, would have been surprised if he had known the true size of his hostile audience.

If French had lost confidence in Lanrezac he had also, more seriously, lost confidence in himself. Now his sole object – not, in the circumstances, an unworthy one – was to preserve his small Army from being sacrificed in the interests of an ally whose defeat seemed to him inevitable. Yet within twenty-four hours there occurred a major crisis which in the event was to prove that the actors were made of sterner stuff than some of their directors. It was to be the day of Le Cateau.

On 25 August Moltke in Koblenz made a very different decision. On the previous day his seven Army commanders had reported crushing victories all along the front. Namur had fallen. Kluck, not yet even aware of the true size and location of the BEF, was announcing 'the continued pursuit of the beaten enemy'. Bülow spoke of 'disintegrating resistance'. Supreme Headquarters had yet to learn that generals are liable to confuse fact with fiction. Even to the end – and he had not long to go – Moltke had his doubts, for there is a world of difference between tactical success and strategic victory; and while there was evidence of the one, there was little of the other. Where were the prisoners, the captured guns, the abandoned booty, which distinguish rout from retreat? And what of his own casualties, carefully concealed from him – so carefully that no first-line reinforcements were provided for the right-wing Armies until 8 September?

[2] Author's italics.
[3] But see p. 89.

It did not matter. The Kaiser, in what Moltke called his 'shout-hurrah' mood, issued a Special Order of the Day which somewhat prematurely claimed that the war in the West had been won. And on 25 August Moltke ordered the movement of Bülow's *Guard Reserve Corps* and Hausen's *XI Corps* to the Russian front, where they conveniently arrived two days after Hindenburg had already won a famous victory at Tannenberg. Two Corps of Kluck's Army had earlier been detached to watch Antwerp.[4] On 26 August the equivalent of two more corps were to be detailed to contain the unimportant fortresses of Givet and Maubeuge – 'truly a bad investment', in the words of Liddell Hart. By then the original seventeen Army Corps (cavalry excluded) of the three right-wing Armies had been effectively reduced to eleven, and in so doing Moltke had driven a coach and horses through the Schlieffen Plan. There were to be other coaches and several more horses as this second-rate courtier played out his last three weeks as German executive director.

On 25 August Joffre also made a decision. With all his five Armies in retreat and Plan XVII in ruins, he began to piece together a new disposition of his forces to meet the growing threat to his left wing. It is a measure of this imperturbable man that at no time did he contemplate the possibility of defeat. His new plan was designed to buy time, to contain the enemy, and to create the conditions for a return to the offensive.

By now the main German strategy was clear to him, and his mind was fixed on his increasingly vulnerable left flank. On this critical day, he did not know of Moltke's decision to discard the basic imperative of the Schlieffen Plan, or of French's sudden flirtation with the idea of recreating a Torres Vedras at Le Havre. It has been suggested uncharitably that he was as much concerned with keeping the BEF in the line as with keeping the Germans out, but this is not true. Joffre was an uncomplicated soldier who believed that the essence of war is battle, and that for such a moment of crisis the French had coined a sovereign phrase: *reculer pour mieux sauter*. He had only to compare the performance of the BEF at Mons with Lanrezac's spineless reaction to the battle of Charleroi. He was profoundly impressed by the courage and determination of the British in the face of Kluck's Army, and although he never said as much, he must have wished that he had a few Smith-Dorriens. Fortunately, he did have one, Franchet d'Esperey, commander of Lanrezac's I Corps, and presently he was to make good use of this lively little man. With Lanrezac he would deal later.

In the great gap between the BEF and the sea there were General d'Amade's four Territorial divisions and, by 25 August, Sordet's overworked but resilient Cavalry Corps. Facing this ill-equipped and scattered force were two German Army Corps and two of Marwitz's cavalry divisions. Here, in Picardy, where as yet unknown to either side the

---

[4] The previous day, 24 August, the Belgian Army made a sortie in strength from Antwerp designed to support the French and British on the Sambre and on the Mons canal. But it was too late, and on 26 August the Belgians retired behind their fortress defences. None the less, their action sowed a seed of doubt at OHL which was to grow in direct proportion to the extension of the German lines of communication.

decisive battles of the Great War would later be fought, Joffre began to improvise what was in effect 'Plan XVIII'.

Like every great commander, he took a calculated risk. With his only reserve, the Fourth Army, fatally committed in the Ardennes offensive he decided to create a new mass of manœuvre on his left; and his first step was to detach the 61st and 62nd Reserve Divisions from the Paris garrison and send them to join d'Amade in Arras. His reasoning was simple. The defence of Paris was a secondary consideration to the halting of Kluck's advance. If he could not parry the thrust, the thrust would destroy him. So – *tout le monde à la bataille!*

Joffre now went further. Confident – and, as it proved, rightly – that Dubail and Castelnau could hold the Germans on the fortress line in the south, he decided to use d'Amade's divisions as the nucleus of a new Sixth Army on his left flank under General Maunoury, then commanding a task force facing Metz. And to this Army he assigned first his VII Corps and then his IV Corps from the right wing. [5] It was a magnificent gamble. And it was to save France, although on that Tuesday in August Joffre could not have known that his professional opponents, Moltke, Kluck and Bülow, were between them to commit a series of blunders which were to cost Germany the war. And curiously the unwitting agent of this extraordinary reversal of fortune was to be Sir John French.

The Maubeuge position which the BEF had reached on the evening of the 24th was in no way suitable for prolonged defence, let alone a springboard for the offensive which Wilson was still busily planning. Its sole advantages were that it avoided the trap which Kluck was trying to set, and that it significantly shortened the BEF's line. That nature now intervened where Kluck had failed was not, as we shall see, the C-in-C's fault.

French spent the day motoring around his eastern flank visiting Haig at I Corps HQ, Sordet at Avesnes twelve miles south of Maubeuge, and then went to General Snow's recently arrived 4th Division near Le Cateau. Significantly, he did not call on Smith-Dorrien. Later that afternoon he returned to his Advanced HQ. His diary entry reads:

> It was a very critical hour whilst I was at Bavai. Murray was just splendid and issued the necessary orders with the utmost promptitude. [6] I left most unwillingly [for Le Cateau] at 7.20 [p.m.].

Operation Order No. 7, to which we have already referred, opens with these vague words: 'The Army will move tomorrow, 25th inst, to a position in the neighbourhood of Le Cateau, exact positions will be pointed out on the ground tomorrow.'

This Order was in fact French's response to Joffre's 'suggestion' not to

---

[5] When to these he added the 55th and 56th Reserve Divisions and the crack 45th Algerian Division the Allied left wing briefly found itself with a unique superiority of two to one.
[6] No orders were issued until 8.25 p.m., an hour after French had left for Le Cateau.

leave a potentially fatal gap of twenty miles between Lanrezac's XVIII Corps and d'Amade's troops at Cambrai. What then are we to make of the following extracts from Operation Order No. 8, issued twenty-four hours later on the 25th (the time of issue on the GHQ Order was defaced)?

> It is the intention of the C-in-C to continue the retirement tomorrow (the 26th) *with a view to covering his advanced base (Amiens) and protect his L. of C.*[7] . . . The retirement will be carried out from left to right. *The 4th Division will fall back in the general direction of Péronne*[7] . . . I Corps will start at 5.30 a.m. and march to the area of *Busigny.*[7]

Whose words are these? French's? Wilson's? Certainly not Murray's, who signed them. We shall never know. 26 August was not to be a day of dangerous retreat. It was to be a day of desperate battle.

The Order for the 25th meant a minimum twenty-mile march 'to the neighbourhood of Le Cateau' by men already wearied beyond ordinary endurance. So far it had been possible to get some sort of rations forward to the fighting troops. From now on it would be a matter of brilliant improvisation by the Quartermaster-General, Robertson, who, rightly reading the portents, began stock-piling essential supplies on roads leading to the *south*, not the west. Not all the directors were intent on fighting a losing battle.

Charlie Watts, a reservist with 1/Hampshires of 4th Division, whose passion in life had been to join the cavalry when he enlisted in 1904 – 'I tried for the Carbineers but they were closed' – remembers ration dumps at every crossroads during the retreat. 'Sides of beef, stacks of bacon and bully, jam, tea. But there wasn't time to hang around cooking a four-course meal. I'd say our main diet during the retreat was German blood and French apples.' Bardolph and Pistol could not have put it better.

The withdrawal to the Le Cateau position involved a difficult decision. Immediately to the south of Bavai (the junction between I and II Corps) lay the Forest of Mormal, ten miles long and five miles wide and traversed by two roads running west to east but with only rough tracks from north to south which were incapable of accommodating large marching columns.[8] GHQ accordingly allocated all roads west of the forest to II Corps, and those on the east to I Corps, the intention being that the two formations should re-establish contact that evening at Le Cateau.[9] This decision meant that I Corps had to cross the Sambre and, unexpectedly, share its roads with two French Reserve divisions retreating from Maubeuge. More seriously, it created a ten-mile gap between the two British corps which was to have fateful consequences. It was not until eight days later that they were to see each other again.

---

[7] Author's italics.
[7] Author's italics.
[8] None the less, John Allan clearly remembers 'L' Battery following one such track, its guns and limbers bearing white markers to distinguish them in the dark.
[9] This intention, as incorporated in the march Order, took no account of any enemy intervention.

Kluck's orders for the 25th were based on another of his false assumptions. Convinced that French would stand and fight on the Maubeuge–Valenciennes line, he decided to spring his trap: *IX Corps* would attack Haig at Bavai, *III Corps* Smith-Dorrien at Wargnies, *IV Corps* would envelop the British left, and *II Cavalry Corps*, recalled from chasing shadows, would take the British rear.[10] With *II Corps* following up from Condé and *IV Reserve Corps* half a day's march away, 'the envelopment of the British Army, provided it stood, seemed certain'.

'Provided it stood.' But it did not stand. By 5.00 a.m. it had slipped away, for neither the first nor the last time; and Kluck, faced by confused and contradictory air reports, was driven to improvisation. To switch the direction of large bodies of troops on an indifferent road system takes time; and time was now a precious commodity for the BEF. Of Kluck's several odd decisions on the 25th, the halting of *IX Corps* to join in the investment of Maubeuge is the most curious;[11] and when, the following morning, the collision came on the Le Cateau–Cambrai road, the disposition of *First Army* had been, as we shall see, significantly changed (see Map 4), and for a very singular reason.

Meanwhile the BEF continued on its divergent march on Le Cateau, while GHQ prudently departed to St Quentin, twenty-five miles to the south. Leslie Carswell was a clerk in the QMG's office. 'I don't know how often we moved house during the retreat,[12] but we got pretty good at it, scarcely bothering to unpack wherever we stopped.'

5th Division on the Roman road west of the forest was not disturbed by the enemy though greatly taxed by the sweltering heat, which took its toll as more and more stragglers fell out on the line of march (most of these managed to reach Le Cateau during the night). Towards evening a violent thunderstorm broke. 'I never thought I would welcome being soaked to the bone,' recalls Jack Downie. 'Good as a bath and twice as refreshing.'

3rd Division, now on the left of II Corps, was less fortunate, for it was this flank on which Kluck was trying, with remarkable lack of enterprise, to bring – in every sense – his heavy guns to bear. Throughout this day the Germans showed little determination in pursuit and a reluctance to engage the British rearguards closely. There are several possible reasons for this. By now Kluck's infantry were as weary as their opponents, and had suffered severely in the fighting of the two previous days. *II Corps* continued to press on the heels of d'Amade's 84th Division as it retired on Cambrai, instead of swinging south. *IV Corps* seems to have been marking time in order to let *IV Reserve Corps* close up. Marwitz's cavalry was still north and west of Cambrai. The more likely truth is that Kluck, having earlier convinced himself that the BEF was withdrawing in the general direction of Amiens, reacted more slowly and with greater caution than his orders suggest to the growing evidence that the British were in fact retiring almost due south. 'For want of a nail, the shoe was lost . . .'

---

[10] Kluck was unaware of the arrival of 4th Infantry Division.
[11] But see p. 92.
[12] Six times. St Quentin–Noyon–Compiègne–Dammartin–Lagny–Melun.

On this flank there were skirmishes and rearguard actions, first at Le Quesnoy where 1st and 3rd Cavalry Brigades put up a spirited fight, and then, more critically, at Solesmes, where there was considerable confusion and a traffic congestion made all the greater by the streams of refugees crowding into the narrow streets. Here the presence of Marwitz's cavalry and greater boldness by *IV Corps* might have proved decisive. Instead, 2/South Lancs and 1/Wiltshires of 7th Infantry Brigade held the fort to the north of the town while two brigades of 4th Division, sent forward that morning, occupied a strong position on the high ground to the south. By late afternoon Solesmes was sufficiently clear for 7th Infantry Brigade to fall back to its position near Caudry south of the Le Cateau–Cambrai road, followed by 19th Infantry Brigade and a much scattered Cavalry Division. But it was not until the early hours of the 26th that Smith-Dorrien learned that the three brigades of 4th Division had reached their position on his left in the area Haucourt–Esnes. The Germans made no attempt to maintain contact but bivouacked for the night in and around Solesmes; for by then Kluck had come to two conclusions, both incorrect and both based on pure guesswork: first, that the BEF had taken up a defensive position facing *east*, [13] and secondly that the position was occupied 'by the whole British Army of six [*sic*] divisions and a cavalry division'. Thus he envisaged the miniature Cannae of his dreams on the morrow, with the BEF finally caught in the grip of an unbreakable vice.

Smith-Dorrien, however, was under no illusions. He had 'lost' I Corps beyond the Forest of Mormal and the Sambre; he had a shrewd idea of the enemy strength in front of him (although the appearance of *IV Reserve Corps* on his left late during the afternoon of the 26th was an unwelcome surprise); above all, his own men, who had carried the burden of fighting during the past three days, had been pushed to the limit. The arrival of 4th Division had been providential, but his own formations were disorganized and in need of rest. During the afternoon he received a private note from Wilson anticipating French's Operation Order No. 8 with its intention of continuing the retreat next day in the general direction of Péronne – i.e., to the *south-west*. As the hours passed the conviction grew on Smith-Dorrien that he had two options, one of which, an immediate continuation of the retreat, was an invitation to disaster. By midnight he had therefore taken a brave and – as it was to prove – controversial decision.

By midnight a very different situation had developed on the right flank. The day had not gone according to plan.

Haig's line of retirement had presented problems from the outset, since not only did he have to go, so to speak, the long way round, but the shortage of roads necessitated three separate crossings of the Sambre. [14] Moreover, as we have seen, these roads were shared by crowds of refugees, by two French Reserve divisions, and by the tail of Sordet's Cavalry Corps as it

---

[13] Kluck's Operation Order for the 26th, issued at 11.50 p.m. on the 25th, instructed '*IV Corps* to envelop the northern, *III Corps* the southern flank of the position'.
[14] During this day Haig was unwell, which may explain his uncharacteristic behaviour at Landrecies that night.

crossed over to the left flank of II Corps. And there was another interested party: the enemy. Throughout the day I Corps averaged little more than two miles an hour. 'It was hot, tiring, and very frustrating,' said Chippy Carpenter, Colonel's bugler of 1/Coldstream Guards, standing every bit of five feet six in his socks. 'There were a lot of false alarms but we never saw the enemy', and by evening 1st Division, on the outside track, well to the east of the Sambre, had struggled along the cluttered roads to the area of Marbaix and Dompierre, where, to the ill-concealed annoyance of the local inhabitants, it went into billets.

By 5 p.m. 2nd Division had also reached its billets after an uneventful but equally tiring march. It is now clear that Kluck was as unaware of the whereabouts of Haig's I Corps as he had been during the battle of Mons. Had he sent *IX Corps* in pursuit the following day, Haig would have had a very rough passage. In his memoirs Kluck insisted – with the hindsight of unsuccessful generals – that it was Bülow's decision to detain this Corps at Maubeuge.[15] That may be. What is certain is that by now Kluck and Bülow had achieved a relationship about as warm and cordial as that between French and Lanrezac.

Thus undisturbed, 2nd Division went into billets: 4th Guards Brigade with, interestingly, Corps HQ at Landrecies, eight miles east of Smith-Dorrien's 5th Division at Le Cateau; 6th Infantry Brigade to the east at Maroilles; 5th Infantry Brigade and 5th Cavalry Brigade covering the division at Leval. The unnatural calm was soon to be broken.

At the southern end of the Forest of Mormal there were two crossings of the Sambre – one, two miles from Maroilles, the other at Landrecies. In these two villages the 6th and 4th (Guards) Brigades halted for the night after their long march. Neither brigade had any knowledge that the enemy was close at hand. The enemy was no wiser. 'According to the statements of German officers, they seem to have been equally unaware of our presence at Landrecies and Maroilles.'[16] It was still that kind of war. Indeed, the *14th Regiment* of *IV Corps* had been ordered to Landrecies to billet there for the night, ready for the flank attack on Le Cateau the next morning. General Scott-Kerr, commander of the 4th (Guards) Brigade, commented later: 'It was like musical chairs. There was only room for one, and luckily we got there first.' We will return to see not only how this game was played, but how, from a small pond, great ripples of anxiety spread out to GHQ at St Quentin.

Farther east, 6th Infantry Brigade settled down at Maroilles. The Divisional cavalry ('B' Sqn, 15th Hussars) was engaged by German outposts[17] at the river bridge at 6 p.m., and there was a lively little battle. Ted Fowler recalls: 'We dismounted and sent our horses back. We could see the Germans creeping across the bridge and we fired away at them but they kept coming. Close enough for me to see a man with big Kaiser

---

[15] On 25 August Koblenz had no knowledge of the whereabouts of its right-wing Armies. OHL had issued no orders to Bülow since *18 August.*
[16] *Official History*, Vol I, p. 124n.
[17] *48th Infantry Regiment, III Corps.*

moustaches. He came running forward and I was sort of sorry when I shot him down. Then the Berkshires came up and we went back.'

It was 7 p.m. when 1/Royal Berkshires were sent forward. The approaches to the Sambre bridge were across marshy ground. Alfred Green was one of the leading company.

> We had to make our way along a kind of stone causeway. So did the Germans, and there was a rare old hand-to-hand fight, bayonet and butt, and as our other companies came up, the Germans fell back to the bridge. We had lost quite a few – fifty or sixty – and in the dark we dursn't go on. I had some blood on my bayonet and a hole in my ammunition pouch, so I suppose I was lucky.

By midnight the Germans were in control of the Maroilles bridge. There they stayed.

Meanwhile about 5.30 p.m. there were rumours of large enemy forces approaching Landrecies. These proved to be unfounded, but a picquet consisting of No. 3 Company, 3/Coldstream, and two machine-guns was sent out to the fork-road half a mile to the north, while the rest of the brigade put the town in a state of defence. With Haig and his Corps staff also within the perimeter, the situation was not unlike that of a small frigate with an admiral on the bridge.

Shortly after dark the outlying picquet heard the sound of an approaching column. The sentry's challenge was answered in French,[18] and at once the two leading platoons of the Coldstream were charged. Thus there began a confused mêlée which, like most night actions, seemed to those involved like a pitched battle on a grand scale. In fact, no more than a single battalion was engaged on either side, and the 'artillery' consisted of one German field gun, duly silenced by a British howitzer of 60th Battery which scored a direct hit with its third round, killing (according to the German account) three officers and sixteen men. The fight continued until after midnight, when the enemy withdrew into the southern edge of the forest, little knowing what would be the consequences of their chance encounter.

First, Haig, quite contrary to his nature, panicked. Since his Corps had not previously been in action, it was hardly encouraging for the future that he should now lose his head over what was no more than a skirmish (he should never have been in Landrecies in the first place). At 1.35 a.m. he telephoned GHQ to say that he was under 'heavy attack' and called for help as the situation was 'very critical'.[19] It requires little imagination to realize the effect these portents of doom had at St Quentin, where even the ebullient Wilson was now filled with foreboding. French's diary echoes the general air of gloom:

---

[18] Some accounts speak of the leading German troops being dressed in French uniforms. This is highly unlikely. The Germans were not expecting any opposition.
[19] Casualties at Landrecies were: 3/Coldstream – 126; 2/Grenadiers – 7; Germans – 127. Writing to Kitchener on the 27th, French put enemy casualties at 'no less than 800 to 900'.

At 2 a.m. Wilson came into my room. [*There follows a garbled account of the affair at Landrecies.*] Wilson said he thought there was a great chance of the enemy getting between our two Corps.

Smith-Dorrien was asked [*at 3.50 a.m.*] if he could help Haig but professed himself unable to make a move.

No sooner had anxiety on Haig's account ceased than trouble re-occurred with S-D.   S-D says he cannot retire.

French, who seems to have been incapable of grasping the full implications of the German movements on the 25th, now forgot about the threat to his left flank in his conviction that the true danger lay on his right. He duly ordered Haig to withdraw I Corps, not south-west to Busigny (see extracts from Operation Order No. 8 on p. 89) but due *south* to Guise. The effect of this was significantly to widen the gap between I and II Corps (a gap which was already causing Wilson concern), and to put not only the Sambre but also the Oise between Haig and Smith-Dorrien.

At 5 a.m. French asked Huguet to send an extraordinary message to Lanrezac, of all people, telling him that Haig had been 'violently attacked', that I Corps was retiring on Guise or, if necessary, *south-east*, that the general retreat would continue the following day in the direction of Péronne – i.e., *south-west* – and asking for assistance. Lanrezac may be forgiven for thinking that the British C-in-C had gone mad.

Such was the unexpected achievement of a single German battalion at Landrecies. It had also done something more immediately important. Smith-Dorrien was now on his own, with both his flanks in the air, and a major encounter battle about to begin.

CHAPTER 5
Le Cateau

26 August, the 568th anniversary of the battle of Crécy. There is little doubt that Sir John French would have wished himself and his Army that morning on Edward III's old battleground away to the west near Abbeville on the Somme, with the English Channel invitingly close at hand.

French's order to continue the retreat in the direction of Péronne was passed to the formations of II Corps at 10.15 p.m. the previous evening and to the Cavalry Division at 11 p.m. (General Snow, unaware of the C-in-C's intention, had already ordered 4th Division some hours earlier to prepare a defensive position on the left of II Corps south of the Le Cateau–Cambrai road. Two of his brigades, it should be remembered, had spent the 25th covering the retirement from Solesmes.)

The events which now were to lead to the forthcoming battle are of special importance, since they illustrate clearly the extent to which both sides were groping in the dark, and how the imponderables of war can influence the actions of commanders.

Kluck, as we have seen, had wrongly interpreted the true axis of the British line of retreat, but his assumption that its direction would be to the south-west was a fair reading of French's mind.

French, despite Wilson's warning, had reverted to his original intention, and his eyes were fixed on Amiens (what price Kitchener's earlier argument now?) and on the coast beyond. He had only the vaguest idea of where *First Army* lay (his Order opened with the words 'The enemy followed our movement this morning (the 25th) and is also passing troops of all arms to the West and South.' [*sic*]). From Joffre he had received disturbing news of the true German strength facing him – disturbing enough for a wiser man to reconsider his plans for the 26th.

Haig's progress round the Forest of Mormal to make contact with the right flank of II Corps (and thence south-west to Busigny) had been rudely interrupted by the unexpected appearance of the enemy at Maroilles and Landrecies.

Smith-Dorrien, who alone could feel Kluck's *First Army* breathing down his neck, obediently accepted French's order for the continuation of the retreat, but as darkness fell, so his doubts increased; and with a degree of prudence singularly lacking at GHQ he began to think in terms of fighting rather than retreating – 'a stopping blow,' he later wrote, '*under cover of which we could retire*.[1] At no stage did he consider a prolonged defensive battle, despite French's subsequent accusation. (In considering his alternative plan Smith-Dorrien reasonably assumed that I Corps would cover his right flank. It was not until 3.50 a.m. on the 26th that he first heard of Haig's defection. By then it was too late to alter his mind again.)

Smith-Dorrien's decision was forced upon him by the condition of his men as they reached their billets during the evening and night of 25/26 August (2/Royal Irish Rifles did not arrive at Caudry until 9 a.m. the following morning after an adventurous march). Jack Tyrrell of 1/DCLI[2] sums it up: 'I've never been so tired, and that went for the rest of us. We had been on the go for what already seemed like weeks. There had been quite a few casualties and some of the older ones had fallen out on the line of march. But especially I remember being hungry and thirsty. I don't think we had had a square meal for two days and just when we got to Lee Catoo[3] and thought we were in for a rest and some grub, we were sent on to a ridge across the river [*the Selle*] with some of the East Surreys. There I sat down and in no time at all I was asleep.'

Smith-Dorrien watched and noted a thousand other Tyrrells. His Corps was in the process of sorting itself out after a day of confused fighting and hard marching. For all their fatigue the men were in good heart, but not, in Smith-Dorrien's view, in any condition to embark upon a hazardous continuation of the retreat early the next morning. He was not alone in thinking this.

At 2 a.m. Allenby came to Smith-Dorrien's HQ at Bertry. He reported that his four brigades were widely scattered – how scattered he did not then know – and that both men and horses were 'pretty well played out'. Unless he could get away at once, he would be forced to fight at daylight. Smith-Dorrien immediately sent for General Hamilton, commander of 3rd Division, whose HQ was close by. Could his troops move off at once? Hamilton was adamant. He could not possibly continue the retreat until 9 a.m. at the earliest – and both men knew that that would be too late; and that what was true for Hamilton would be even more certain for Fergusson's 5th Division in the congested area around Le Cateau, and for Drummond's 19th Infantry Brigade, now under command of II Corps near Reumont on the Roman road farther south.

Smith-Dorrien, well aware that he was disobeying orders, made his mind up. He asked Allenby if he would co-operate. Allenby readily agreed. 'Very well, gentlemen,' said Smith-Dorrien, 'we will fight, and I will ask General Snow to act under me as well.' It was a brave decision. There is no doubt now that, despite the cost, it saved the BEF but in the end – because Sir John French was a man incapable of recognizing true leadership when he saw it[4] – Smith-Dorrien was made to pay a heavy price. The one criticism

[1] Author's italics.
[2] 14th Infantry Brigade, 5th Division.
[3] As every Old Contemptible refers to it.
[4] But see p. 111 for the most classic example of French's capacity for saying one thing and thinking another.

of him is that he delayed his decision too long; for by the time the new orders to stand and fight reached his scattered brigades there was little opportunity to make anything other than the most elementary defensive preparations; some units, in the general confusion, were already acting on earlier orders to retire; and by dawn Haig's I Corps was marching south towards Guise and away from the scene of battle. At 6 a.m. the German guns opened up.

The battlefield of Le Cateau was in striking contrast to the battlefield of Mons. One veteran who fought there has accurately described it as 'Salisbury Plain without the trees'.

From Le Cateau a road runs straight north-west for fifteen miles to Cambrai. On either side of this road there is rolling countryside unbroken by hedges and dotted with villages which, after the fashion of those days of open warfare, were to be defensive lynch-pins and a magnet for German artillery. The ground, baked by an August sun, made any effective digging impossible, and when accounts speak of 'entrenched infantry' the reader must not imagine anything remotely comparable to the deep and elaborate systems of later and greater battles. 'The thing was', said Fred Petch of 2/Suffolks, 'to throw up a sort of parapet and to keep your head and your bum down.'

The battle of the 26th is referred to in the official History (though not by the Germans) as the battle of Le Cateau. In fact, the small town of Le Cateau, lying in a hollow in the valley of the Selle, was a death-trap which Smith-Dorrien wisely avoided. If the day's action is to be rightly described it should be called the battle of Caudry, which lay almost exactly at the centre of the British line.

PLATE 14. *Le Cateau: 'entrenched' infantry*

But before following the course of the battle we must first return to Smith-Dorrien's HQ at Bertry.

Having made his decision to stand and fight, he sent a detailed explanation of his plan by car to St Quentin, where it was received at 5 a.m. French's diary records only the briefest of comments (see p. 94), but in view of his subsequent contributions to a distasteful controversy, his formal reply should be recorded:

> If you can hold your ground the situation appears likely to improve. [5] Fourth Division must cooperate. French troops are taking offensive on right of I Corps [*they were not*]. Although you are given a free hand as to method this telegram is not intended to convey the impression that I am not anxious for you to carry out the retirement, and you must make every endeavour to do so.

'This reply', wrote Smith-Dorrien later, 'cheered me up.' He rightly assumed – since it had never been his intention to sacrifice II Corps in a heroic last stand – that the C-in-C approved his decision. He did not know Sir John French very well; and he was too busy to read the small print which French had written into this telegram. Smith-Dorrien was about to fight a critical battle. French was taking out a personal insurance policy.

The British position at Le Cateau may be likened to a flattened horseshoe with – at least in the early stages – a small nail sticking out at its right-hand corner (this was formed by 1/DCLI, which, with two companies of 1/East Surreys, had been sent the previous evening to the high ground east of Le Cateau, there to link up with I Corps. For reasons we have seen, that contact was never made).

The line of II Corps and 4th Division ran for about ten miles east to west, with 19th Infantry Brigade in Corps reserve on the right at Reumont, 1st, 2nd and 3rd Cavalry Brigades to the right rear, and 4th Cavalry Brigade behind the left centre at Ligny (see Map 4).

The right was held by 5th Division with 14th Brigade in an arc just south of Le Cateau, 13th Brigade west of the Roman road, and 15th Brigade at Troisvilles.

In the centre – and not subjected to great pressure during the battle – was 3rd Division, with 9th Brigade at Inchy, 8th Brigade at Audencourt, and 7th Brigade at Caudry.

The left flank was occupied by 4th Division, with 11th Brigade at Fontaine-au-Pire, 12th Brigade around Longsart, and 10th Brigade at Haucourt and Esnes, with the Warnelle ravine running laterally behind the two forward brigades.

Throughout the day the infantry was subjected to a tremendous pounding, and despite considerable losses, nowhere was the line broken. But Le Cateau was above all an artillery battle, and the performance of the

---

[5] There can have been no conceivable grounds for this burst of optimism.

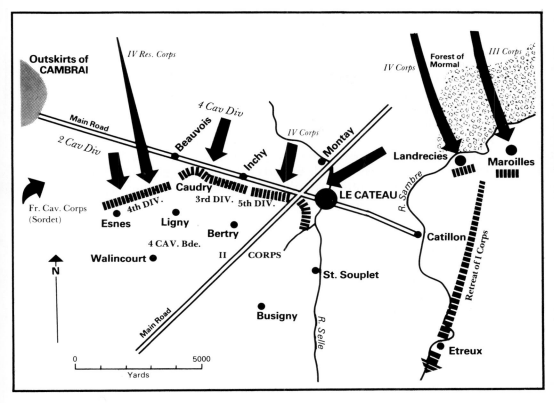

MAP 4. *Le Cateau*

Royal Regiment (a total of 228 guns matched against at least 550 on the German side) remains among its greatest feats of arms. Only 38 guns were lost (27 of these in 5th Division's sector), although losses among men and horses were much more severe. It does not reflect too highly on the quality of the enemy gunnery, and indeed the German records are strangely silent about their own casualties at Le Cateau. The figures have never been published.

Against Smith-Dorrien, Kluck committed, from left to right, *III Corps* (*5th* and *6th Divisions*), *IV Corps* (*7th* and *8th Divisions*), *II Cavalry Corps* (*2nd*, *4th* and *9th Divisions* and – by early afternoon – the entire artillery and at least one division of *IV Reserve Corps*.[6] It should have been more than enough to achieve a crushing defeat. It was not. The BEF survived, dealt the enemy another smashing blow, and so lived to fight another day.

The fighting on the 26th followed a very different pattern from the opening encounter three days earlier, and for this there are three main reasons. First, the battlefield – open, undulating country marked by ridges and spurs – was quite unlike that of Mons; secondly, the British were concentrated on a much shorter line; thirdly, the German plan was to

99

achieve a double and simultaneous envelopment.

The battle itself fell into two distinct halves. Until noon, except on the two extreme flanks, it took the form of a long and unequal artillery duel. Clearly the Germans had learned their lesson at Mons, and here, with little or no cover for their infantry other than that provided by the natural contours of the ground, they spent most of the morning bombarding the British positions on the open ridges south of the Le Cateau–Cambrai road, with the clear intention of holding the centre while developing their two flank attacks.

Throughout this first phase, which chiefly involved 13th and 14th Brigades of 5th Division, 19th Brigade, the three brigades of 4th Division and the whole of Smith-Dorrien's artillery, the British line, despite very heavy casualties, not only held firm but exacted an even heavier retribution. Many years later a German officer who fought with *7th Division* of *IV Corps* recalled the stubborn resistance of 2/Suffolks and 2/KOYLI on the ridge to the south of Le Cateau:

> I did not think it possible that flesh and blood could survive so great an onslaught. Our men attacked with the utmost determination, but again and again they were driven back by those incomparable soldiers. Regardless of loss, the English artillery came forward to protect their infantrymen and in full view of our own guns kept up a devastating fire.

Lt (later Col) Rory Macleod of 80th Battery, XV Brigade, whose description of the battle on the right flank[7] is one of the most vivid and authentic accounts of the action, recalls not only the gallantry of the Suffolks and the KOYLI, but the exceptional conduct of his own men when, at the height of the battle, they were engaging the enemy at ranges down to 1,200 yards: 'The drill throughout was admirable. All the men, in spite of the shelling and casualties, were as calm, quiet and steady as if on a gun drill parade.' Tom Bridges had recorded the same impression of 'L' Battery at Audregnies two days earlier. At Le Cateau the story was repeated by the gunners all along the hard-pressed line. And to the crucial right flank we will return.

The second phase of the battle of Le Cateau began around 2 p.m. By then Kluck had committed five infantry divisions and three cavalry divisions with no significant success. But the moment had come for Smith-Dorrien to begin the delicate task of disengaging, for by then Fergusson on his right had reported that in the face of overwhelming pressure his men had started 'dribbling away'. II Corps and 4th Division had delivered the 'stopping blow'. It was now time to go; and once again the BEF slipped away. Not, as we shall see, unscathed, for as with the Cheshires at Elouges, the order to retire never reached some battalions and scattered parties of men, and nightfall brought one major – and, in more than one view, unnecessary –

---

[6] *II Corps* was also available at Cambrai, six miles to the west.
[7] Col. R. Macleod, *An Artillery Officer in the First World War* (unpublished MS).

disaster. But by 7 p.m. Smith-Dorrien's men had marched off, watching with surprise – and some derision – Kluck's artillery still pounding the positions that they had earlier left.

Le Cateau deserves a book to itself, not only because it was the last old-style encounter battle in which the BEF was to be involved, but because it exemplifies, within a comparatively small compass, all the exceptional qualities of the old Regular Army – steadiness, discipline and the virtue of true professionalism. The battle was not fought by grizzled veterans, but by men whose average age was no more than twenty-five. Not all were equal to the test. Not all, by any means, were heroes. Shortly before noon one company commander had to force his men back into the line at pistol-point. But they did go back. And fought. And died.

The day-long action of the 26th may be most concisely described in theatrical terms as 'a play in two acts, with an epilogue'; each act divided into two scenes set 'stage right and stage left, the forenoon and the afternoon of a single day'. The epilogue is played, as it were, after curtain-fall. *Exeunt omnes*.

By a strange irony, this metaphor exactly reflects, on the British side (and to an extent on the German) the confused entrances and exits of the actors.

When Smith-Dorrien decided to stand and fight there was no time to ensure that his order could everywhere be communicated to brigade level – and 'brigade level' on 26 August meant what would later be called 'the front line'. [8] Thus before dawn 19th Infantry Brigade had already marched off from Le Cateau. Halted at Reumont, it became Smith-Dorrien's sole Corps reserve. On the right, 1/DCLI and the East Surreys and 2/Suffolks had fallen in at 5 a.m. ready to move, as had 1/King's Own and 2/Lancashire Fusiliers on the extreme left. After the thunderstorm on the previous evening, there was a thick mist. The curtain did not rise on the first act until 6 a.m.

The map on p. 99 shows how the stage was then set. The narrative provides a shorthand account of the progress of the action. But the following table may help the reader to appreciate the comparative strength of the German formations committed against the British brigades, and the time-scale of this commitment. The sequence of brigades reads from right to left:

	BRITISH	GERMAN
RIGHT	14th Brigade	*7th Division*
	13th Brigade (part)	*72nd I.R. (8th Division)*
	19th Brigade (part)	*5th Division* (p.m.)
	3rd Cav. Brigade	*6th Division* (late p.m.)

[8] At 6 a.m. on the 26th, Smith-Dorrien's HQ was at Bertry, only 4,000 yards south of the Cambrai road; Hamilton's 3rd Division HQ was beside him; Fergusson's 5th Division HQ was at Reumont, 4,000 yards from Le Cateau; and Snow's 4th Division HQ *less than a mile* from the enemy. It was still a very 'small' war.

CENTRE	13th Brigade (part)	
	15th Brigade	*8th Division*
	9th Brigade	*4th Cav. Division*
	8th Brigade	*9th Cav. Division* (part)
	7th Brigade	
LEFT	11th Brigade	*9th Cav. Division* (part)
	12th Brigade	*2nd Cav. Division*
	10th Brigade	*7th Reserve Division* (p.m.)

DIAGRAM C. *Le Cateau: the Ridge*

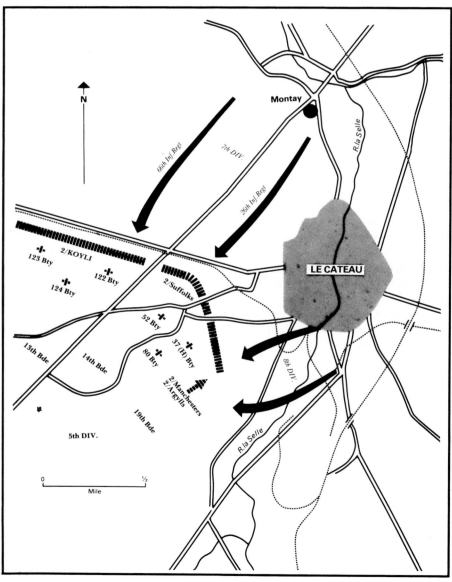

About 6 a.m. DCLI[9] and East Surreys, fallen in and ready to march off, were surprised at close range by infantry of *IV Corps* which had worked its way through Le Cateau under cover of the morning mist. There was a sharp action, but with the support of 3rd Cavalry Brigade, the column, after suffering some 200 casualties, succeeded in fighting its way back along the valley of the Selle, where, covered by the ubiquitous 'L' Battery, RHA, it rejoined the main body of 14th Brigade around noon in the area of Honnechy and Maurois on the Roman road. The German infantry did not attempt to pursue, and when, belatedly, *27th* and *165th Regiments* of *III Corps* reached Honnechy late that evening the birds had flown. Jack Tyrrell, wounded in the arm during the first exchanges, could not believe his luck: 'I wasn't badly hurt, but I couldn't use my rifle. If the Germans had really come after us, they would have eaten us alive. Why, when we got back to the main road, we even had time for a proper meal before marching off again!'

None the less, this withdrawal uncovered Smith-Dorrien's right flank, and, with the Germans in possession of the high ground to the east of Le Cateau, 5th Division faced the prospect of imminent envelopment and destruction. It is impossible to explain why this did not happen. Perhaps the only answers are that once again Kluck failed to make use of his immense numerical superiority (the infantry of *III Corps*, within easy reach of Le Cateau, did not enter the battle until the afternoon), and that the German officer quoted above accurately described the quite exceptional bravery and determination of the small British force which on this flank stood between Kluck and victory.

During the early forenoon of the 26th, this force consisted of 2/Suffolks and 2/KOYLI on the ridge immediately south-west of Le Cateau astride the Roman road, supported by XV Brigade RFA (11th, 52nd, 80th and 37th (Howitzer) Btys), XXVIII Brigade RFA (122nd, 123rd and 124th Btys) and – near Reumont – 108th Heavy Bty, RGA.

On this killing-ground, 2,000 yards square and innocent of any cover, the Germans concentrated first a great weight of artillery and then, as the day progressed, nine infantry battalions and five machine-gun companies. The terrain today, over sixty years later, is exactly as it then was. To visit it is a sobering and chilling experience, for by 11 a.m. it was overlooked from the north, enfiladed from both east and west, and swept by machine-guns concealed in the dead ground near the Le Cateau cross-roads. A major break-through here, and the road to St Quentin was open.

There was no break-through. Not only did the right flank hold, but the two infantry battalions, the forty-two field guns and the single Heavy Battery of the artillery matched everything that *IV Corps* could throw against them. In his account of the action Lt Macleod noted that German shrapnel proved comparatively ineffective, and that most of the damage to

---

[9] By sheer chance, the main casualties on 26 August were suffered by battalions (and artillery units) which had emerged relatively unscathed from the fighting around Mons: 1/DCLI, 2/Suffolks, 2/KOYLI, 2/Manchesters, 2/Argylls, 1/Gordons, 2/R. Scots; and from 4th Division, 1/King's Own, 2/Lancashire Fusiliers, 2/Royal Inniskillings, 1/Royal Warwicks.

PLATE 15. *Le Cateau:* (Above) '*It was a misty morning.*' *The cross-roads seen from the Suffolks' ridge.*
On the left of the Roman Road, the position held by 2/KOYLI
(Below) *the position held by 2/Suffolks as seen from the cross-roads on the Roman Road*

guns and casualties to gun-crews was caused by direct hits; and the infantry experienced greater losses from machine-guns than from artillery. Charlie Mitchell, a driver with 124th Battery in close support of the KOYLI – so close that gunners and infantrymen found time to exchange ruderies – watched as each of his six guns was successively put out of action. Farther to the right, it was much the same story with 52nd Battery.

At 11 a.m. the Manchesters and two companies of the Argylls were sent forward to help the Suffolks, but, enfiladed from the right, they suffered very heavy casualties and could make little progress. And about the same time, Fred Petch of the Suffolks, having successfully kept his head and his bum down for five hours, was knocked out:

> I was firing away at some Germans trying to creep up a little gully to my right when I was hit by two machine-gun bullets. One ricocheted off the stock of my rifle but the other went through my left hip and out through my right leg, which left me pretty well paralysed. There was no way anyone could move me, and I was picked up later that evening by the Germans. [10]

It was now noon; and, on the right, the end of the first act. George Reynolds of the KOYLI (who had taken a terrible hammering), noted wryly: 'It was as if the referee had blown his whistle. We lay there and wondered what the second half would be like.' Of such men was the BEF made.

In the centre of the line – that is, from the extreme left of 5th Division to the left of 3rd Division at Caudry – the forenoon had passed without great incident. *8th Division* of *IV Corps* and Marwitz's *4th Cavalry Division* had made no great effort to attack this sector, beyond persistent and ineffective bombardment and the occupation – and subsequent loss – of Inchy on the main road. British casualties here during this period were fewer than 200, so we may pass farther left to the 4th Division, where Kluck's right-hand pincer was being prepared.

4th Division at least had not been exhausted by the marching and counter-marching of the first week of the campaign. It lay now, at dawn on the 26th, as a refused flank on Smith-Dorrien's left, facing north-west. Between it and Hamilton's 7th Brigade at Caudry there was a gap of one mile. To its left, six miles away, lay Cambrai, now occupied by d'Amade's 84th Division, and this gap was filled by Sordet's Cavalry Corps. 4th Division's genial commander, General Snow, was not informed until 5 a.m. that he was to stand and fight under Smith-Dorrien's orders. 'I should have done so in any case,' he said later.

Snow was lucky. First, Kluck did not know that he was there. Secondly – for that reason – Kluck did not order his *II Corps* to turn south-east

---

[10] Pte Petch, a quiet man, had no great respect for the treatment which he received at the hands of his captors.

instead of chasing shadows on the road to Amiens. Thirdly, the left flank was protected by a natural hazard – the Warnelle ravine – which ran behind Snow's forward brigades and thus gave him a strong reserve position. And fourthly, the initial attack on 4th Division was made by *2nd Cavalry Division* and part of *9th Cavalry Division*, neither of which was too much enchanted by being employed in a dismounted infantry role, and the former of which was described that afternoon by an officer of *IV Reserve Division* as 'cowering behind buildings' in Cattanières at a decent remove from the enemy.

None the less, the first act opened on the left with a setback. 4th Division was disposed thus at dawn: on the right 11th Infantry Brigade about Fontaine-au-Pire, 12th Infantry Brigade north of Longsart and thence to Esnes, with 10th Infantry Brigade in reserve at Haucourt south of the ravine.

Without his Divisional cavalry squadron (not yet arrived), Snow had no eyes and ears, and thus no knowledge of the strength and location of the enemy. So it was that as 1/King's Own of 12th Brigade was forming up at dawn to move on to its new position it was caught in the open by heavy machine-gun and artillery fire[11] and suffered more than 400 casualties before it could be extricated, first by the concentrated rifle-fire of 1/Hampshires on its right ('range 1,000 yards and hardly a round wasted', was Charlie Watts's comment) and then by a bold, if costly, intervention by two companies of 1/Royal Warwicks from the Divisional reserve, in which a young subaltern named Bernard Montgomery distinguished himself.

The Germans now turned their attention to the left-hand battalions of 12th Brigade (2/Lancashire Fusiliers and 2/Royal Inniskilling Fusiliers) in an attempt to outflank the British position and capture Esnes. In this narrow area they concentrated the dismounted regiments of *2nd Cavalry Division*, two *Jäger* battalions, five artillery batteries and (according to their own records) twenty-one machine-guns. But with a clear and uninterrupted field of fire and (belatedly) the support of XIV Brigade, RFA, the two British battalions held firm – though not without severe losses – for nearly two hours. Indeed, during a lull in the fighting, a company commander of the Inniskillings casually walked forward and counted forty-seven dead *Jägers* within a hundred yards of his position. By 10 a.m. 12th Infantry Brigade had, in the words of the official History, 'fought *2nd Cavalry Division* to a standstill'.

There followed a period of comparative calm, broken by artillery exchanges and ineffective attempts by the enemy to work round the left flank of 12th Infantry Brigade at Esnes. What General Snow did not know was that during the morning the artillery of *IV Reserve Corps* had been hurriedly pushed forward, and that *7th Reserve Division* was about to enter the battle after a forced march from Valenciennes. None the less, he decided about noon to withdraw first 12th Brigade and then 11th Brigade south of the Warnelle ravine. It was a wise move.

---

[11] *4th* and *7th Jäger Battalions* and two Horse Artillery batteries of *2nd Cavalry Division* south of Cattanières and Wambaix.

The 'second half', for which George Reynolds had been waiting on the shell-torn ridge south of Le Cateau, may be said to have started about 1.30 p.m., for it was then that Smith-Dorrien judged that the moment had come to begin his withdrawal. All along the line his troops were in close contact with an enemy in great and growing strength, and the exercise on which he was about to embark was in many ways an unprecedented one. In the short account which follows it is possible to mention only the main incidents and some of the leading actors involved. For an excellent blow-by-blow précis of the whole operation the reader is referred to a small pamphlet based on official sources and published by the Historical Section of the War Office. [12]

The main threat to Smith-Dorrien lay on his unprotected right flank, and by early afternoon the situation there had become extremely critical as *5th Division* of *III Corps* entered the battle and began working up the valley of the Selle. By now the embattled infantry – Suffolks, KOYLI, Manchesters and Argylls – and XV and XXVIII Brigades RFA were being subjected to the artillery fire of three entire German divisions and to frontal and flank attacks by at least twelve infantry battalions. There was no way in which they could be reinforced, and little likelihood that the survivors could be extricated.

It is necessary to comment briefly here on a factor which had already led to avoidable losses, and which was now to have even more serious consequences: the breakdown of communications. Signal companies (still a branch of the Royal Engineers) had, of course, no wireless; telephone lines were in short supply, and in many cases cut by shell-fire. Most orders, therefore, had inevitably to be transmitted by word of mouth, and by no means every staff officer or other messenger succeeded in running the gauntlet of the bullet-swept battlefield. One such runner, Charlie Mitten, was wounded four times in an attempt to reach 15th Brigade HQ. Thus Smith-Dorrien's order to retire, issued at 1.40 p.m., did not reach 5th Division until 2 p.m. The order in turn did not reach forward units until 3 p.m., and some battalions – notably 2/KOYLI – never received it at all. This 'lost hour' – and the confusion which proceeded from it – was to prove expensive. And even after the final curtain fell towards dusk, there was a melancholy epilogue on the road from Audencourt to Bertry in 3rd Division's sector.

Smith-Dorrien's order to his divisions was to retire in succession from right to left. 5th Division – apart from those battalions and batteries cornered on the Le Cateau ridge – slipped away without much difficulty, 15th Brigade and three battalions of 13th Brigade reaching the DCLI and East Surreys of 14th Brigade in some disorder but with few casualties south of Reumont on the Roman road, where they were covered by 19th Brigade and 1st and 3rd Cavalry Brigades. There was no pursuit, for Kluck's *III Corps* was still engaged by the rearguard at Le Cateau, and its *6th Division*

---

[12] *The Battle of Le Cateau* (War Office, March 1925).

PLATE 16. *Driver Frederick Luke, VC, and 37th (Howitzer) Battery at Le Cateau, 26 August 1914*

had not yet reached the battlefield. Kluck himself was still convinced that Smith-Dorrien was facing east and retiring on Péronne, even though *First Army* had by then been involved in a north-south battle for eight hours.

The critical problem remained. Could the rearguard of 14th and 13th Brigades be saved? The first to go were the gunners. They had suffered tremendous punishment, and not one of the seven batteries on the ridge was any longer capable of sustained action. Gun by gun they came away. Among the last to leave was 37th (Howitzer) Battery, which had been attached to XV Brigade; and for their outstanding gallantry during this final episode Capt. Reynolds and Drivers Luke and Drain were awarded the Victoria Cross. Here, without any heroics (he was only twenty-one at the time), is Frederick Luke describing the action, exactly sixty-six years to the day later:

> After the action of 23 August at Mons, we had to fall back in line with other troop movements. We came into action a few times during the next two days of retirement. Most of our men and horses were feeling a bit tired and we camped just outside Le Cateau for the night 25/26.
>
> At about 3 a.m. on 26 August we were aroused and was told that we were moving on and going into action. With the rest of the Brigade we moved into a cornfield and opened fire at about 4 a.m. on the German gun positions [*in fact, some two hours later*]. Heavy German fire was causing some heavy casualties among Gunners and Horses and the gun-teams had to move further to the rear.
>
> At about 3 p.m. we had orders to bring the guns out. Owing to Casualties among the Horses, we could only get back with 4 guns out of the six. These 4 were taken to the rear.

It was here that Capt. Reynolds called for volunteers to go back to try and rescue the other 2 guns. Along with Drain and Coby I volunteered to go back with one other team. We walked the horses with limbers along the road to the Guns. As we reached to within 300 yards we started the Gallop. The Germans who were by this time only 100 yards away, opened fire as soon as they saw what we were after. One team of horses was shot down but our team managed to come through with only Driver Coby being killed, and a few flesh wounds. After sorting ourselves out, we continued our Retreat towards St. Quentin.

As the scattered units of 5th Division retired to the Roman road south of Reumont, there was a great deal of 'sorting out' to do.

The withdrawal sealed the fate of Fergusson's rearguard. The remnants of the Suffolks, Manchesters and Argylls managed to fight their way back, and in so doing checked every attempt by the newly arrived *5th Division* of *III Corps* to work round the open flank. Once more Kluck blundered, for he was convinced that the entire BEF lay before him, and, unaware of the great gap between Smith-Dorrien and Haig, made no attempt to exploit a situation to which Fergusson would have had no answer. Indeed, *6th Division* of *III Corps* never entered the battle on the 26th, although by noon it was within easy striking distance.

2/KOYLI was now isolated. The order to retire never reached it, and by 4 p.m. the forward companies were surrounded and overwhelmed. The survivors numbered 8 officers and fewer than 300 men – including George Reynolds, who would long have cause to remember the 'second half'. But the sacrifice was not in vain. It was not until 7 p.m. that *7th Division* reached Reumont, and *5th Division* Honnechy. By then Fergusson's men and 19th Infantry Brigade had marched away in a drizzle of rain, units inextricably mixed up but without disorder or panic. Smith-Dorrien watched them go. 'It was a wonderful sight, the men . . . apparently quite unconcerned . . . walking steadily down the road – no formation of any sort. I likened it at the time to a crowd coming away from a race meeting.' By 9.30 p.m. they had reached Estrées, ten miles to the south.

There was no pursuit. The Germans had suffered severely (how severely we shall never know, for no casualties for 26 August were published). They bivouacked that night about Honnechy and Maurois, and when the advance was resumed at 4 a.m. the following morning Kluck had given Smith-Dorrien a twelve-hour start. And as the BEF marched south, Kluck resumed his pursuit of shadows south-west towards Péronne and Bapaume. At last the pressure was off.

3rd Division, holding the centre of the line, had nowhere experienced the same weight of attack as the two divisions on either flank. Indeed, the Germans (*8th Division, 4th Cavalry Division* and part of *9th Cavalry Division*) seem to have concentrated on pinning Hamilton's men to the ground by intensive artillery bombardment, while the flank attacks were developed. Early in the afternoon, however, the artillery bombardment was intensified, and an infantry attack succeeded in capturing the northern outskirts of Caudry. A similar attack on Audencourt farther east was repulsed with heavy losses.

At 3.30 p.m. Hamilton gave the order for the withdrawal to begin from right to left, covered by 8th Infantry Brigade at Audencourt. 9th Brigade and 7th Brigade retired without interference through Bertry and Montigny, followed an hour later by 8th Brigade. But here again there was a breakdown in communications, and this, as we shall see, was to have tragic consequences. By nightfall the whole Division – except for 1,000 men – was on its way to Beaurevoir, thirteen miles south-west of Le Cateau. Again there was no pursuit.

4th Division experienced greater difficulty on the left, for by early afternoon *2nd Cavalry Division* had been replaced by *7th Reserve Division* of *IV Reserve Corps*, and in the face of massed infantry attacks, 11th Brigade fell back across the ravine to Ligny. The enemy came forward in great strength but was driven back by the rearguard, 1/Rifle Brigade, and the guns of XIV and XXIX Brigades. Rfm. George Cox was in the thick of things: 'They came at us in what looked like their thousands but despite losing a lot of men, we managed to hold them off and our gunners, catching them in the open, gave them a real pasting.' The Germans made two more determined attempts to capture Ligny. Twice more they were driven off with heavy losses.

About 4.30 p.m. *7th Reserve Division* turned its attention to 12th Brigade on the extreme left at Esnes, and might here have won a major success had it not been for the timely intervention of Sordet's Cavalry Corps, which broke up repeated attempts by the infantry of *IV Reserve Corps* to work round the British flank. Soon after 5 p.m. 12th Brigade began its withdrawal to the south, covered by 2/Seaforths of 10th Brigade. 11th Brigade followed an hour later from Ligny, covered by XXIX Brigade and 4th Cavalry Brigade, and by nightfall 4th Division had disengaged and was marching south on Vendhuille and Le Catelet, although compelled to leave most of their wounded on the battlefield.[13] Once more there was no attempt at pursuit. During the afternoon *II Cavalry Corps* had inexplicably been withdrawn into bivouac two miles north-east of Cambrai, whence they could no longer influence the battle; and *IV Reserve Corps*, exhausted by its long march from Valenciennes and severely handled in its repeated attacks on Ligny and Esnes, was too weary for any further effort. *II Corps*, Kluck's potential trump card, was fully occupied by Sordet and by d'Amade's 84th Division at Cambrai.

So ended the battle of Le Cateau; but not quite. There was an epilogue to follow. Just as the day had started with minor disasters, so now it ended with a major one.

At Audencourt in the centre of 3rd Division's line the order to retire never reached the rearguard of 8th Infantry Brigade, consisting of 1/Gordons,

---

[13] As noted earlier, 4th Division's Field Ambulances did not reach the forward area by 26 August.

two companies of 2/Royal Irish and a party of 2/Royal Scots,[14] – by a strange irony the same three units which, by holding the Bois la Haut position south of Mons, had made possible the escape of 8th Brigade on 23 August.

Now, isolated from all help, they withstood repeated attacks by the massed artillery and two regiments of *8th Infantry Division* for six hours, and in so doing undoubtedly gave General Hamilton breathing-space in which to disengage the remainder of his division. At 12.30 a.m. the following morning this defiant rearguard started to retire, but just north of Bertry it was intercepted by the enemy. After a brief resistance, all but 200 men of the group were killed or captured. To all intents and purposes, 1/Gordons ceased to exist.[15]

While the actors had thus been fighting for their lives, and in so doing. frustrating once again Kluck's attempts at a decisive envelopment, the directors were fighting a very different battle at St Quentin.

The day had not started well, with Haig's despairing cries for help at Landrecies. At 5 a.m. Smith-Dorrien's message arrived from Bertry. And later that afternoon Murray suddenly collapsed at his desk.[16] Ever since the advance to Mons he had been grossly overworked, while French contributed little more than his own mental confusion and Wilson cheerfully planned the demise of the BEF. Haig had not been alone in doubting Murray's capacity to handle two men as temperamentally incompatible as his C-in-C and his Sub-Chief, but the war was less than one week old and it was ominously early for the strain to show. The actors had fortunately demonstrated much greater mental and physical stamina. Murray recovered quite quickly, but the damage had been done, and he was never the same man again.

Unaware of the crisis at GHQ, Joffre now announced his intention of visiting Sir John French, and, after instructing Lanrezac and d'Amade to join him there, he set off early for St Quentin. It was a rendezvous full of interesting possibilities. Joffre, still denied the authority to issue any direct orders to French, was soon to discover that the Germans were by no means his only problem.[17]

Lanrezac came only under strong pressure from his own Chief of Staff, for he had reached the point of open contempt for GQG and did not relish a confrontation with Joffre. Nor had his attitude towards the BEF changed since the first meeting at Rethel: too small, too unreliable, and led by a man both incompetent and untrustworthy. It was as if the battle of Mons had never taken place, while the battle of Le Cateau had only just begun.

Joffre had not come to St Quentin to read the Riot Act, but to explain his new plan for countering the growing threat to the Allied left and to

---

[14] In all, a total of about 1,000 men.
[15] A week later the battalion was replaced in 8th Infantry Brigade by 1/Devons.
[16] This not unimportant incident is not mentioned by French in his diary entry for that day.
[17] This meeting on 26 August cast a long shadow forward to another conference at Doullens in April 1918, where in the face of an even greater crisis the decision was at last taken to appoint Foch as Generalissimo of the Allied Armies in the west.

co-ordinate the retreat while his Sixth Army was being assembled on the Somme. He was greeted by a very different British C-in-C from the one he had met at Vitry only ten days earlier. French at once launched into a diatribe against Lanrezac, accompanied by accusations of infamy, cowardice and gross dereliction of duty. Lanrezac listened impassively. Joffre, unable to follow this flood of English invective, simply noted 'the Field Marshal's rather excited tone'. He turned to Lanrezac. Would Fifth Army act in support of the BEF? Yes, said Lanrezac without precise commitment, it would, little knowing that three days later he would be obliged to honour that undertaking in extraordinary circumstances, with Joffre sitting at his elbow and silently watching his conduct of what was to be the vital battle of Guise.

There was a long pause. Joffre turned now to French. Would the Field Marshal agree to the plan set out in his General Instruction No 2 of 25 August? There was an even longer pause. French expressed ignorance of any such instruction. Murray, preoccupied with other matters, had not seen it. Wilson, the linguist, said that it was still being translated. Since the whole future conduct of the war depended on General Instruction No. 2, it is remarkable that Joffre did not lose his temper. Instead, 'in his flat, level tones' he rehearsed his proposal to withdraw to the line Laon–La Fère–St Quentin (running south-east to north-west), and to hold the Germans on that line while his new Sixth Army was being formed on the Somme, whence it would resume the offensive against the German right flank.

French, now ready to put the most sinister interpretation on any suggestion for co-ordinated action, would have none of it. He agreed 'to retreat deliberately' (whatever that meant, since half his Army was then engaged in a battle for survival). Beyond that he would not commit himself. The meeting broke up, and Joffre returned to GQG convinced of two things: Lanrezac had become a dangerous liability; and there was a growing possibility that Sir John French would become an even greater one.

Fortunately for Joffre, there were similar liabilities on the German side; and fortunately for the Allies, they had Joffre. Meanwhile, while one battle was raging at St Quentin, another had now ended at Le Cateau.

The battle of Le Cateau was precisely what Smith-Dorrien had intended it to be – 'a stopping blow'. It is also a classic example of one of the most difficult and hazardous military manœuvres – a withdrawal in broad daylight from close contact with greatly superior enemy forces. So successful was this manœuvre – and so contrary to all probability – that Kluck was entirely deceived. When on the morning of the 27th he was at last officially released from Bülow's tenuous command he directed *First Army* to pursue south-west towards Amiens, or, in other words, virtually in the opposite direction to the BEF's axis of retreat. [18]

---

[18] By pure chance Kluck's wild-goose chase succeeded in disrupting Joffre's preparations for the assembly of his new Sixth Army, an improvisation of which Kluck was totally unaware.

Thus the BEF made its weary way south for five days undisturbed by anything more than the occasional enemy cavalry patrol. It was not until the early morning of 1 September that *First Army* again stumbled upon the BEF at Néry and Villers-Cotterêts south-east of Compiègne; but that is anticipating events.

Le Cateau was not without its price. Since Kluck had aimed at a double envelopment, most of the casualties were incurred by the two flank divisions, 5th and 4th. 3rd Division in the centre had a relatively quiet day, and 4th Division's losses would have been lighter if it had not been without its field ambulances. The final figure – arrived at in the official History after taking account of stragglers rejoining, and some adventurous escapes by determined men who managed to reach home by way of Boulogne and Antwerp[19] – was 7,812 men and 38 guns.[20] Repeatedly, French referred to Smith-Dorrien's force as 'shattered', in order to justify his subsequent decision to retire, if necessary, to the west of Paris and even to St Nazaire, and thence to a safe haven beyond the Channel. At no stage was Smith-Dorrien's force shattered. Severely mauled, but not shattered. At 8 p.m. on the 26th Huguet reflected the mood at GHQ, now removed to Noyon, in a telegram to Joffre: 'Battle lost by the English Army which appears to have lost cohesion.' The English Army was presently to prove Huguet wrong.

Ever since the battle of Le Cateau, there has been much argument over the subsequent relationship between French and Smith-Dorrien. Smith-Dorrien disobeyed a direct order. Of that there is no doubt. So did Nelson. Disobedience is not of itself a virtue; but since it takes two sides to fight a battle, it is often involuntary.

When he came to write his first Despatch on 7 September (the date is important, for the immediate crisis was then over), French said:

> I cannot close the brief account of this glorious stand of the British troops without putting on record my deep appreciation of the valuable services rendered by General Sir Horace Smith-Dorrien.
>
> I say without hesitation that the saving of the left wing of the Army under my command on the morning of the 26th August could never have been accomplished unless a commander of rare and unusual coolness, intrepidity, and determination had been present to personally conduct the operation.

It is scarcely possible to imagine a more glowing – or better deserved – tribute; but then we are dealing with a very strange man indeed, who seems not to have paused to reflect that the qualities he was praising in Smith-Dorrien were precisely those which he himself so singularly lacked.

When five years later French published his memoirs, rather than let the

---

[19] Some men, it must be recorded, were less than resolute.

[20] Long afterwards, by which time he had access to the true figures, French still wrote 'At least 14,000 officers and men, about 80 guns, numbers of machine-guns as well as quantities of ammunition, war material and baggage.'

record stand, he tried to disclaim his earlier view – 'completed, of necessity, very hurriedly, and before there had been time or opportunity to give thorough study to the reports . . .' What reports? By 7 September French knew exactly what had happened at Le Cateau. His 'shattered' II Corps was then advancing towards the Petit Morin. His presence in the line, his ability to play a significant part in the battle of the Marne, was due entirely to 'a commander of rare and unusual coolness, intrepidity and determination'.

Here are some of French's *arrière-pensées* about Le Cateau:

> The effect upon the British Army was to render the subsequent conduct of the retreat more difficult and arduous.

In fact, Smith-Dorrien's stand made that retreat possible. If anyone compromised it, it was Haig with his precipitate retirement to Guise.

> II Corps was saved by Allenby, Sordet and d'Amade.

This is nonsense, and deliberate nonsense. In his own later account, Smith-Dorrien paid proper tribute to Sordet and d'Amade for their part in protecting his left flank and inviting the attention of Kluck's *II Corps* at Cambrai (Kluck's error and Smith-Dorrien's good fortune). Allenby made no claim to a decisive part in the battle, for the good reason that his Cavalry Division was so widely scattered that it could only provide limited support.

> In more than one of the accounts of the retreat from Mons, it is alleged that some tacit consent at least was given at Headquarters at St. Quentin to the decision taken by the commander of the 2nd Corps. . . . There is not a semblance of truth in this statement.

Really? Then see French's telegram to Smith-Dorrien on p. 98. If that is not 'tacit consent', then French is guilty of both double-think and double-talk.

So, while the directors played with words, the actors marched off along the dusty August roads of France. Desperately tired they may have been. Shattered they were not.

CHAPTER 6

Towards the Turning Tide

In all the literature – and mythology – of the Great War, there are few profound or profoundly true statements of opinion. Here is one: 'If Joffre stood the test of early failure, the German commanders did not stand the test of early success.'[1] The ten days that followed Le Cateau were to prove this in a vivid and dramatic way.

Few men can ever have carried a greater burden than Joffre. Although technically answerable to his Government in a political sense, he had already assumed complete authority – and with it, responsibility – for the conduct of the war. At any time Poincaré could have dismissed him or decided, as some of his Cabinet urged, to run up the white flag. Fortunately, Poincaré believed in Joffre, as Joffre believed in France; and when on 2 September the Government left the capital for Bordeaux, Joffre and the indomitable Galliéni, Military Governor of Paris, became in effect the sole arbiters of their country's fate. As Millerand, the new War Minister, took his leave of Galliéni, he instructed him that Paris was to be defended à outrance. It was.

The flight of the Government freed Joffre of any remaining political shackles. He could now concentrate, in the little time that was left, on devising a military solution. To achieve this he needed an iron will, brilliant improvisation and a blundering opponent. The first he had never lacked; to the second he now addressed himself; and the third – partly the product of the second – was to prove his unexpected salvation.

This was Joffre's situation on the morning of 27 August as the BEF marched away to a rendezvous somewhere south of the Oise. He had under his own command the equivalent of six Armies; and – holding a critical place in the line – an independent allied force of five infantry divisions and one cavalry division, to which he could not issue direct orders. On his right two of his Armies were strongly resisting heavy German attacks on the Moselle. The crisis here was yet to come. In the centre there were serious, although not insuperable, problems. Third Army had been pushed back to

[1] Maurice: *Forty Days in 1914.*

the heights of the Meuse, and was in some disarray.[2] Fourth Army, under de Langle de Cary, was fighting stubbornly near Reims, when Joffre on a visit found its commander calm, confident and 'perfectly master of himself'.

The growing danger was on the left, where Lanrezac, seeming to have lost the will to fight and by now mutinously critical of Joffre and GQG, was certainly no longer master of himself; and beyond Lanrezac was the bruised but resolute BEF, led by a man of fickle temperament, trusting no longer in his ally, scarcely trusting any longer in himself. French in this mood provided Joffre with a problem, at once military and diplomatic, which was to be his daily concern in the sea of troubles on which he was now launched.

Fortunately for Joffre, however, the British C-in-C was not, like him, a free agent. He was responsible to his political masters, and in particular to Kitchener, soldier first and politician very much second. There is little doubt that but for Kitchener's intervention on 1 September French would have quit the field and shipped the BEF home.[3] That he could not have done this by way of his original ports of entry was due to several factors, of which his earlier indecision was one and Kluck was another.

And beyond the BEF? Here lay the road to Paris, barred only by d'Amade's second-line divisions and Sordet's weary cavalry. This was Schlieffen's killing-ground, as it should also have been Kluck's. Indeed, when OHL on the 28th issued its first orders in ten days to its right-wing commanders, *First Army* was instructed to continue its enveloping march north and then west of Paris, Bülow to attack and occupy the capital itself, and Hausen to advance south-east to the Seine. Within two days, as we shall see, a mixture of arrogance, excessive caution and plain disobedience threw Schlieffen into the discard and OHL into disorder.

Between the first clashes on the frontier and the end of August, French casualties were of the order of 212,000, a staggering 20 per cent of mobilized strength and 40 per cent of Regular officers and NCOs.[4] It was a figure which would have daunted a lesser man than Joffre. But Joffre was no *catastrophard*. His Armies were neither destroyed nor even routed. The spirit – *his* spirit – remained, and now he began to build a dam to stem the tide which threatened to engulf his open flank. His General Instruction No 2, issued on the 25th, had proposed that this dam should cover à great arc from Amiens through Reims to Verdun, and that the Germans should be held on the general line of the Somme. Other things being equal – and they were not – the counter-offensive would begin on 2 September, ironically or perhaps deliberately the anniversary of Sedan.

From the morning of the 27th until the hour of decision ten days later, this extraordinary man in his De Dion car, piloted by a former racing-driver

---

[2]On 30 August its commander, General Ruffey, a man with all the qualities and defects of Lanrezac, was replaced by General Sarrail.
[3]Macready remembers Henry Wilson, whimsical as ever, walking up and down a school-room in GHQ at Noyon and chanting: 'We shall never get there.' 'Where, Henri?', asked Macready. 'To the sea, to the sea!' replied Wilson.
[4]From 23 August to 27 August inclusive, the casualties of the BEF were 14,811, a not dissimilar percentage. 'The British losses at Waterloo were 8,458.' (*Official History*.)

with a panache of which Murat would have been proud, toured the front ordering here, creating there, improvising, brooding, planning only for the turn of the tide. His stamina, in a man not given to physical exercise, was phenomenal; his routine exquisitely French. Joffre enjoyed his food. However critical the situation, nothing – but *nothing* – stood between the Commander-in-Chief and large and leisurely meals. Only twice, during these difficult days, did he lose his temper, once with Lanrezac and once with French; and on both occasions rightly so. We will leave him now – although he will not leave us – and turn again to the BEF.

By the afternoon of the 26th GHQ had given Smith-Dorrien up for lost, and during the rest of that day no orders or indeed communication of any sort reached Bertry. Thus the withdrawal from Le Cateau was conducted by Smith-Dorrien's staff, and by midnight his weary men had reached a line fifteen miles south of the Cambrai road as follows: 5th Division and 19th Brigade on the Roman road at Estrées; 3rd Division at Beaurevoir; 4th Division at Le Catelet and Vendhuille; all covered by the Cavalry Division. On this line II Corps and 4th Division halted, for no better reason than that the men were incapable of marching farther; and here began the process of sorting out units which had become inextricably mixed up in the confusion of the day's fighting.

Meanwhile Smith-Dorrien went on ahead to St Quentin, only to find that GHQ had left there at midday and had moved twenty miles farther south to Noyon on the Oise. There Smith-Dorrien arrived at 1 a.m. on the 27th, to find the staff comfortably asleep and seemingly convinced that at least half the Expeditionary Force had ceased to exist. It was even rumoured that the Cavalry Division had been destroyed. On 26 August the casualties in the Cavalry Division totalled fourteen.

French was duly roused, and Smith-Dorrien – who could have done with some sleep himself – made his report. Instead of expressing relief and pleasure at the outcome of Le Cateau, French lost his temper and accused Smith-Dorrien of excessive optimism and, it may be suspected (although Smith-Dorrien never said as much), of gross disobedience. There was no mention of the earlier – and not irrelevant – meeting with Joffre and Lanrezac. None the less, before returning to St Quentin, Smith-Dorrien agreed new lines for his withdrawal on the 27th with Wilson: 5th Division and 19th Brigade to a position just south of St Quentin; 3rd Division to Ham and 4th Division to Voyennes on the Somme; the west flank to be covered by the Cavalry Division. The effect of these adjustments would be to bring the axis of the retreat due south. It also meant some long, hard marching under a burning August sun. Throughout the next ten days the BEF sweltered under a cloudless sky.

By dusk on the 26th Kluck decided that, having won a major victory, he would rest on his laurels for the night. There is no doubt that if he had followed up at once with the uncommitted divisions of III Corps and IV Reserve Corps, and if he had not withdrawn II Cavalry Corps from his right flank, he would have confirmed the worst fears of Sir John French. He counted his prisoners ('several thousands', he reported to OHL, when the true figure was 2,600), his captured guns (only 38), and surveyed the debris of the battlefield. But he did not pursue.

By now the reader will be well aware of the reasons. First, he himself had suffered extremely heavy casualties which he did *not* report. Secondly, he was at serious odds with Bülow. But most importantly, he still clung to the belief that the BEF was retiring south-west, and thus he determined either to cut off this retreat or to force the British back to the Channel ports (an elaboration of the Schlieffen Plan for which Schlieffen had not allowed). Thus, while the greater part of his Army bivouacked for the night around its camp-fires, and to the sound of its regimental bands on the line of Smith-Dorrien's defensive position from Honnechy to Esnes, Kluck ordered his *II Corps* and *II Cavalry Corps* to resume the pursuit of the BEF on the 27th towards Péronne and Bapaume. This movement, followed by the rest of his Army, carried him farther and farther away from a now exasperated Bülow. But by pure chance it also carried him into the concentration area of the new Army which Joffre was creating on his left flank. This was gratifying for Sir John French. It was less gratifying for Joffre.

We last left I Corps retreating in some confusion from the minor affairs at Maroilles and Landrecies. Throughout the 26th Haig marched southward on the road to Guise, widening the already dangerous gap in the BEF's line.[5] To the north-west he could hear the sound of battle; and he had Smith-Dorrien on his conscience, as well he might. The only incident to mar an otherwise uneventful day was the ambushing of 2/Connaught Rangers, the rearguard of 5th Infantry Brigade, by troops of *X Reserve Corps* and *1st Guard Cavalry Brigade* at le Grand Fayt. Once again an order to retire failed to reach the battalion, and in the ensuing fight the Connaughts lost 300 officers and men.

The affair at le Grand Fayt was the first involvement of British troops with Bülow's *Second Army*; and this is a convenient point to describe how and why both sides moved as they did between the battles of Charleroi and Mons and the first climax on 30 August.

After the opening encounters the BEF and Lanrezac's Fifth Army retreated south-west, a direction dictated as much by natural features such as the Sambre, the Forest of Mormal and the Scheldt as by any concerted enemy pressure. The reader will recall that as early as 20 August Bülow was constantly pulling Kluck inward towards his own right flank, while Kluck, when he was not planning to force French into Maubeuge, was seeking to envelop the left of the BEF.

On 26 and 27 August the picture altered, at first slowly and then dramatically. First Lanrezac changed direction south and east of south

---

[5]The gap between I Corps and II Corps reached a maximum of eighteen miles on 28 August. That the enemy did not exploit this potentially decisive opportunity is a measure of Kluck's stubborn folly. In fact, his reports to OHL on the 27th and 28th suggest that he had convinced himself that the BEF had virtually ceased to exist.

towards Vervins, chiefly because of a widening gap between him and de Langle's Fourth Army on his right. Likewise Haig, instead of retiring south-west on Busigny, was directed due south to Guise, and this brought his rearguards into contact with Bülow's right wing; and this in turn caused GHQ to pull Smith-Dorrien inward on the 27th from the Somme to the Oise.

The maverick was Kluck, his freedom of action restored to him on the 27th. Convinced that Smith-Dorrien was retreating in disorder towards Amiens, he launched the whole of *First Army* south-west, having first summoned *18th Division* of *IX Corps* to follow up his advance from Maubeuge, where it had been wasting its time since the 25th.[6] But by the 28th Smith-Dorrien was on or behind the Oise and Kluck had lost all contact with him (on this day he reported to OHL that *First Army* 'had defeated the British Army'). Instead Kluck stumbled upon d'Amade's two Reserve divisions at Péronne on their way south from Arras to join Maunoury's new Sixth Army, then beginning to form between Amiens and Roye. The effect of this collision was fortuitous, for it put paid to Joffre's proposal to launch his counter-offensive on the Somme and he was obliged to improvise a new concentration area for Maunoury farther south. Thus, as he pressed forward, Kluck set in train a series of miscalculations which were to culminate in a stupendous blunder. He had mentally disposed of the BEF; he neither knew nor cared about the reception that Joffre was preparing for him farther south (indeed, it suited Joffre to pull his left back closer to Paris, provided that Lanrezac could hold Bülow in check *and provided that French was prepared to co-operate by holding the centre*); and he had greatly embarrassed Bülow, a fact which seems to have given him some pleasure.

Bülow had cause for concern. The farther west Kluck marched, the greater the gap between *First* and *Second Army*. By 28 August this had increased to fourteen miles, and just as Bülow had kept pulling Kluck inward, so Kluck's advance now dragged Bülow outward towards St Quentin and Ham. By the evening of 28 August *Second Army* was marching across Lanrezac's front. This was the first moment for which Joffre had been waiting. To his reaction, and to those of Lanrezac and Bülow, Haig and French, and above all Kluck, we shall presently return.

By the 27th, II Corps was across the Somme and in accordance with French's Operation Order No. 9, signed by Wilson and timed 8.30 p.m., was heading for Noyon and the left bank of the Oise. Wilson gratuitously added an instruction to both Corps Commanders to throw away all 'unnecessary' ammunition and equipment and 'to load up your lame ducks and hustle along'. This was the language of defeat. It was duly countermanded by Smith-Dorrien and torn up by Haig's Chief of Staff. No one came forward to see for himself, least of all Wilson. He would have been greatly surprised – as was his C-in-C the following day – to discover that

---

[6] *17th Division, 13th Division* (*VII Corps*) and part of *VII Reserve Corps* were left behind to invest Maubeuge, which did not surrender until 7 September.

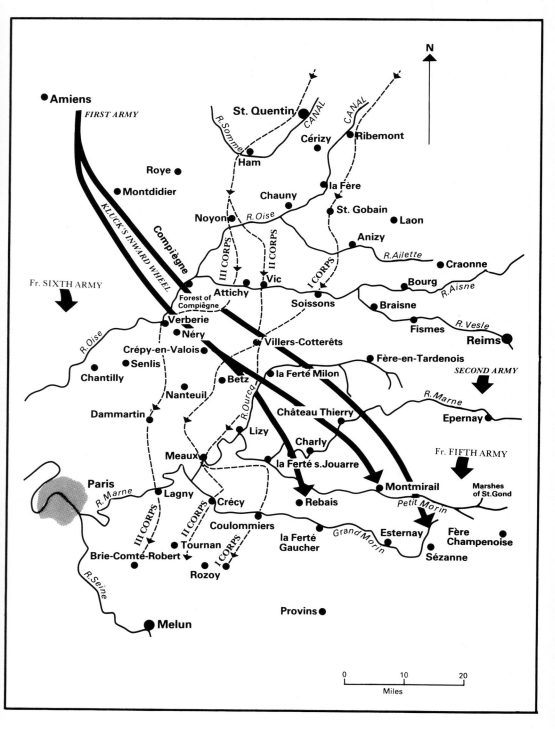

MAP 5. *The retreat, 27 August – 4 September*

the 'shattered' II Corps was plodding along in good heart, rearguards facing about, and covered with expert skill by a Cavalry Division which, far from being decimated, had learned, by long training and exceptional horse-mastership, how to conduct an ordered retreat.

None the less, it was hard going. The one memory of all the men is of indescribable weariness and a sense of not knowing where they were going, or why. This was not the fault of their officers, who knew no more than they. It is the essence of a retreating army that while it may march towards a sunset, it may not know when to expect the next sunrise. Or care.

The letters, diaries and reminiscences of the men who took part in the long retreat are very much of a pattern. Fred Steel of the Royal Scots, who had survived Bois la Haut and Audencourt, is typical:

> I was an old soldier, at least I thought I was with ten years service. I didn't drink much, hadn't gone for promotion, and liked the life. Above all, I kept myself very fit and this was to stand me in good stead with all the marching and fighting. I think I preferred the fighting. At least it took the weight off your feet.
>
> It was certainly a long slog back, very hot and dusty, and when we halted by the roadside, we dropped off like logs and it took a big effort to get us moving again. Some men's feet were in a terrible state and I don't know how they kept going. The worst ones we put on our transport wagons and even on the guns and limbers of some artillery that was following behind us. We managed an occasional wash in streams and ponds but no one dared take his boots off. There's nothing an old soldier dislikes more than being dirty and scruffy, and we were certainly that.
>
> At times like those you lose all idea of time and distance, but when we reached Ham on the 27th we must have covered thirty miles since the previous evening, and the march to Noyon the next day was another fifteen. [7]

On the 28th, with Kluck moving steadily south-west, French took the wise precaution of closing his advanced base at Amiens; and the following day he started to transfer his main bases at Rouen and Le Havre to St Nazaire on the Loire, with a new advanced base at Le Mans, a decision which caused startled concern in Whitehall. [8]

And on the 28th, French, seeming at last to have recovered his composure, noted that the day was 'so quiet' that he felt able to motor north from his new HQ at Compiègne to visit his troops near Noyon. French was at his best among his soldiers, for with them he felt at home, insulated from the world of critical decisions, bickering foreigners and intrusive politicians. The men, remote from the world in which their directors were

[7] A French cavalry officer recorded this in his unit diary: 'We crossed the route of an English battalion retiring after having suffered very heavy losses. It moved in touching order: at the head, imperturbable, a party of wounded. I ordered a salute to be given to these brave men.'

[8] For a fascinating exchange of telegrams between French and Kitchener at this time, see *Official History*, Vol I, Appendix 22.

living, liked French too, his stocky figure and rubicund face reflecting an air of sturdy reliability and bulldog tenacity. History had thrust him into a role for which he was not equipped. It is difficult to envisage a better commander of a cavalry regiment.

He spent that day talking to his men and passing on to them the warm congratulations of Joffre, which he had received by telegram earlier in the morning. And on his return to Compiègne that evening he made the following rather sad entry in his diary – sad, because once again it is counter to everything that he was saying to Joffre and to Kitchener, and counter to everything that he was to do and say during the days which followed:

> I had a most agreeable surprise. I met the men and talked to them as they were lying around resting. ½ million of these would walk over Europe. The 5. Division has quite recovered and its units are re-organized and in perfect trim, but with terrible gaps in the ranks.

In every dramatic situation there is always room – indeed, opportunity – for a side-show; and one such now took place. That it was the brain-child of Winston Churchill should be no cause for surprise.

Ever since the War Council meeting on 5 August there had been a 'Belgian lobby' which pressed for a landing on the coast; not, curiously, to take the pressure off the French, but rather to give physical support to the Belgians. Churchill (one of this lobby), with his acute appreciation of the relation between sea-power and military strategy, decided to play games. On 27 August, when the BEF was retreating to the south, he despatched a brigade of Royal Marines under General Aston to Ostend. [9]

The landing of 3,000 Marines had no very precise objective. They were intended to join up with elements of the Belgian Army in the area, to make their presence widely known, and, in the words of George Durrant, one of their number, 'to cheer the locals up'. In fact, the operation had no immediate effect, and the Marines were withdrawn on 31 August.

What the Marines did not know – what Churchill did not know – was that this modest exercise caused great ripples of anxiety at OHL in Koblenz. Moltke had always been concerned about the possibility of a major British intervention on his extreme right flank (for a brief moment Kitchener had actually considered landing his 6th Infantry Division there). Liddell Hart has expressed his surprise that Kluck made no attempt to secure the Channel ports when they lay at his mercy. The answer is a matter of arithmetic. Vast as was the German military machine, massive as was its *mobilized* strength, by 27 August growing casualties and Moltke's persistent tinkering with his right wing meant that there were no troops available to 'brush the Channel with their right sleeves'. Did Kitchener know this? What might have happened if he had used his 6th Infantry Division and his Territorials to convert Churchill's 'promenaders' into a major threat to the

---

[9] General Aston's Royal Marines did not qualify for the Mons Star. That distinction was to be reserved for the much larger combined operation six weeks later.

PLATE 17. *'A long way to Tipperary.' The retreat*

Germans' lengthening lines of communication? For by 29 August the wildest rumours were circulating at OHL – General Aston's 3,000 Marines had grown to 40,000, and there were excited stories of the landing of 80,000 Russians. Indeed, that afternoon Moltke came very close to withdrawing his right-wing Armies to the Belgian border. Another week was to pass before his imagined fears were to become harsh realities; but at the gates of Paris, not on the beaches of Ostend.

We left I Corps marching south to Guise and thence to la Fère, at the junction of the Oise and the Serre. The two divisions had joined up at Oisy, where they were obliged to share a single road. On the 27th, 2nd Division was leading the way, followed by 1st Division, with 5th Cavalry Brigade guarding the high ground to the north-west of the Oise near the village of Etreux, which was a Corps supply-point.

North of Etreux the rearguard was found by 2/Royal Munster Fusiliers of 1st (Guards) Brigade, a section (2 guns) of 118th Battery RFA, and two troops of 'C' Sqn 15th Hussars. This small force was now to be involved in an epic action.

Early on the 27th Bülow was pushing the right flank of *Second Army* south-west towards St Quentin – not with any intention of bringing Haig to battle (he had no idea of the presence of I Corps on the road to Guise) but rather of keeping contact with Kluck. Thus it was by pure chance that his leading troops (*Guard Cavalry Division* of *I Cavalry Corps* and *X Reserve Corps*) stumbled upon the British rearguard facing north-east in the villages four miles from Etreux. The first contact was made at 9 a.m., and throughout the next two hours there was some desultory skirmishing while the enemy sought to discover the strength and location of the British force. About 11 a.m. the Germans launched the first of several attacks in strength from the north-east, but these were easily repelled by the Munsters, supported by the two guns of 118th Battery.

Shortly after noon the main body of 1st Division was clear of Etreux and well on its way to Guise. And at 1 p.m. orders were despatched to all units of 1st (Guards) Brigade to 'retire at once'. This message, although sent through two channels, failed to reach the Munsters. The story of the Cheshires at Elouges and the Gordons at Audencourt was about to be repeated.

Throughout the afternoon the Munsters held off German attacks in great strength from three sides – almost the last message received from the commanding officer, Major Charrier, reported: 'Am holding on to position north of Fesmy village, being attacked by force of all arms. Getting on well. The Germans are driving cattle in front of them up to us for cover . . .' – but the odds were too great; and at 5.30 p.m. the battalion began to fight its way out. It was too late. By then the Germans had cut the main road just north of Etreux and had brought up a battery of artillery to within 1,000 yards. In quick succession the two guns of 118th Battery were knocked out, and shortly before 9 p.m. the remnants of the battalion, under the only remaining officer, Lt Gower, were overwhelmed. The sole survivors were two platoons of 'A' Company which were saved by a troop of the 15th Hussars.[10]

For nearly twelve hours the Munsters[11] had fought against impossible odds – at least nine battalions of *X Reserve Corps* and four batteries of artillery. Their sacrifice, once more the price of an avoidable error, ensured that Haig could continue unmolested on his way. Except for occasional cavalry clashes (12th Lancers had an hour of glory on the 28th at Cérizy), I Corps saw no more of Bülow. When, on 1 September, it was in action again its opponent was Kluck, for by then something very unexpected had happened.

On the 27th, Joffre decided to act – 'a necessary adjustment', he called it, with some degree of understatement. He was fighting for time. On his left Maunoury was retiring in the face of Kluck's advance while the main body of his Sixth Army was beginning to move out from Paris to join him. There was not much room for manœuvre left here *if* Kluck maintained his direction to the north and west of the capital. In the centre, French was wedded to one idea: retreat. It seemed to Joffre that the only way he could persuade – even shame – French into keeping his place in the line was to create a major diversion, even perhaps win a tactical victory. He therefore addressed himself to Lanrezac.

On this day Fifth Army was still retiring south, not greatly molested by the cautious and worried Bülow, and even less by Hausen, whose much

[10] For his gallantry and initiative that afternoon Sergeant Papworth was awarded the Victoria Cross.
[11] 2/Royal Munster Fusiliers were replaced in 1st (Guards) Brigade by 1/Queen's Own Cameron Highlanders on 5 September.

attenuated *Third Army* was dragging its feet and marching south-east away from *Second Army*. Here, on Bülow's left flank, there was already a gap of fourteen miles. Moltke, with no knowledge of the situation on his right other than daily reports of a victorious offensive and crumbling resistance, turned his back on Schlieffen and dreamed the impossible dream – a comparable series of hammer blows against the French Armies in the south, the capture of Nancy and a decisive super-Cannae. The prospect greatly appealed to the Kaiser. The decision greatly relieved Joffre.

Since the battle of Charleroi, Lanrezac had refused to stand and fight. Joffre now decided to relieve him of any such option. On the 27th, he ordered him to turn on his pursuers. 'You have expressed to me your intention of throwing back by a counter-offensive the troops which are following you.' The moment was now ripe for such a blow. Joffre's order ended with the words 'Do not take into account what the English are doing on your left.' It has been suggested that this was a sarcastic afterthought. Joffre was in no mood for sarcasm. What he was saying was this: 'Do not use the British as an excuse for inaction on your part. Fight *your* battle. Leave Sir John French to me.'

Predictably, Lanrezac protested. He was very foolish to do so. On the 28th Joffre decided to visit Lanrezac at his HQ at Marle (that evening it moved south to Laon). He was a very angry man. In any less critical circumstances he would certainly have put Lanrezac on the first train to Limoges. Now, in his first public display of temper, he gave Lanrezac an unequivocal order. The following day Fifth Army would wheel to face north-west – admittedly a difficult and complicated manœuvre – and attack the German flank on the line Guise – St Quentin. Lanrezac sullenly agreed. Impertinently he asked that the order be put in writing. It was.

While these acid exchanges were taking place at Marle, Haig had brought I Corps south of la Fère on the Oise, and in so doing had begun to narrow the gap between him and Smith-Dorrien. Now, on the 28th, he received reports from air reconnaissance that the enemy was moving from east to west across the front of Fifth Army and I Corps. It was a golden opportunity, and at once Haig, unaware of Joffre's peremptory order, sent word to Lanrezac that he would readily co-operate in an attack on this inviting flank. Lanrezac, surprised and gratified at this unsolicited offer of support from the British, expressed his appreciation. There was only one snag. Haig explained that he must first obtain the consent of his Commander-in-Chief.

Of all the decisions taken by French in those difficult days, his categorical refusal to permit the involvement of I Corps in the battle of Guise was perhaps the most unfortunate. Ever since Mons his constant complaint had been that Lanrezac had repeatedly left him to carry the heat and burden of the day (not strictly true, but true enough to justify a deep sense of grievance and distrust). Now one of his own Corps Commanders – not the suspect 'peasant' on his right – saw the chance of delivering not a 'stopping blow' but an attack which could produce, in concert with Lanrezac, the first great tactical victory since the encounter battles on the Sambre and on the Canal. Moreover, Haig's Corps was not shattered, as French believed Smith-Dorrien's to be. Apart from the affairs at Landrecies, le Grand Fayt and Etreux, it had scarcely seen the enemy. By the morning of the 28th, its total casualties were 1,636, almost all of which had been incurred in three rearguard actions. The men were tired; but so were the Germans.

If it is the function of an army to fight, then it is difficult to understand why French acted as he did. If he had agreed to Haig's request he would not in any way have disobeyed Kitchener's original instructions; indeed, he would have been following them precisely – 'every effort must be made to coincide most sympathetically with the plans and wishes of our Ally'. But those instructions were already two weeks old – and two weeks is a long time in a military campaign. The answer is very simple. By now French had opted out of battle. He was heading for the exit door; and he could not get there fast enough.

29 August was a day of some importance. Not only did it bring the first taste of success for Lanrezac's Fifth Army, but by nightfall the course of events had tempted Kluck, far to the west, to make a fateful decision. Yet during this day, as on no other throughout the war, the Allied directors were at total odds with each other.

Relations between Joffre and Lanrezac had reached breaking-point, while Lanrezac's anger at what he felt, with some justification, to be his 'betrayal' by French was passionate. Haig not only resented French's interference in what he believed to be a matter of personal honour but also his refusal to grasp the opportunity provided by Bülow. French, determined not to fight, neither trusted nor believed Lanrezac any longer, and felt that Haig had usurped his authority. [12] For once no one seems to have been angry with Smith-Dorrien. II Corps was enjoying a rest-day south of the Oise between Noyon and la Fère.

The tension generated between Haig and French on this day is well illustrated by these extracts from the exchanges which took place between them.

French's reply to Haig ran thus: 'Commander-in-Chief does not approve of any active operations on the part of our First Corps tomorrow (29th) and has already ordered a halt for one day's rest.' When Haig then suggested at least some modest artillery support he received precisely the same dusty answer.

There the matter might have rested; but French was a bully, and early on the 29th Haig received this message from GHQ: 'Please be good enough to inform C-in-C how it was that any confidential promise of support by First Corps was made to General Lanrezac or why any official exchange of ideas was initiated without authority from Headquarters.'

Haig was having a taste of Smith-Dorrien's medicine, and liked it no

[12] Tucked away in French's long diary entry for the 29th is this revealing sentence. Referring to reports of Lanrezac's success at Guise, he wrote: 'I am sorry I have ordered the retirement tomorrow, but it can't be altered now.'

more than he. 'I do not understand what you mean,' he replied. 'I have initiated no "official exchanges of ideas".' He went on to remind French of the course of events since leaving the area of Maubeuge and the part played by I Corps in protecting Lanrezac's left, adding for good measure: 'The extrication of this Corps *from the false position in which it was placed*[13] still demands the greatest exertion from us all.' And then one final sally: 'I therefore beg you will not give credit to such allegations as the one under reference without first ascertaining whether it is true or not.'

The wheel came full circle later that day. After his dramatic appearance at Laon (where we will return), Joffre took his indispensable lunch at the station buffet and drove on to see French at Compiègne. It was not a comfortable meeting. It was too late to involve the British in the critical battle of Guise, but not perhaps too late to stop a further withdrawal which would uncover Lanrezac's left. Joffre did his best, but his best was not enough. He records seeing Murray tugging at French's tunic when it seemed that the C-in-C was about to be persuaded by the logic of the situation. Joffre departed, in his own words, *de très mauvaise humeur*. In fact, he had lost his temper. French's diary explains why:

> Joffre was anxious to know how soon I could cooperate. I told him not before Tuesday Sept. 1st. This seemed to disappoint him. He then left.

So, while the sound of battle echoed down from the north-east, the BEF rested. It had earned that rest; but its day of inactivity had seriously compromised Joffre's master-plan.[14]

When word reached Lanrezac that I Corps would not co-operate in the forthcoming attack he was beside himself with rage and, in the words of an embarrassed Spears, 'said terrible, unpardonable things about Sir John French and the British Army'. He had reason to be angry. Haig's two divisions and above all his 150 guns would almost certainly have had a decisive influence on the opening phase of the battle. Joffre was wiser than he knew when he told – warned? – Lanrezac 'not to take into account what the English are doing on your left'. In fact the English spent a quiet day five miles away resting in the peace and quiet of the Forest of Gobain.

The battle of Guise opened with an attack north-west in the direction of St Quentin. It had hardly begun when Joffre arrived at Fifth Army HQ at Laon. It was an extraordinary thing to do, for it was tantamount to suggesting that the C-in-C had no confidence in the ability or willingness of one of his Army Commanders to carry out an order; and it is a measure of Lanrezac's strange character that he put a very different construction on

---

[13] Author's italics.
[14] On 29 August Joffre introduced a new director. This was Foch, commander of XX Corps, whose *Détachement* (created by subtractions from Fourth Army and Third Army) was designed to fill the gap between Lanrezac and de Langle. On 5 September this Detachment was formally designated Ninth Army.

Joffre's appearance. If Joffre wished to watch the battle from a seat in the stalls, then Joffre could assume responsibility for its success or failure, and for any consequences that might flow from it.

In fact, Joffre found Lanrezac much more composed. His conduct that day is a sad reflection on what might have been if his undoubted qualities had not been submerged by his temperamental defects ever since the first collision at Charleroi. Joffre did not interfere. He stayed at Laon for three hours and, seemingly satisfied with Lanrezac's command of the situation, went off to lunch, and then to try out his powers of persuasion on Sir John French at Compiègne. His route took him by way of Soissons, and therefore south of the Forest of Gobain. He would not have been greatly enchanted if he had driven through the area occupied by Haig's unemployed divisions.

The attack towards St Quentin soon ran into difficulties, and little progress was possible here; but the direction of this advance at once presented an open flank to Bülow, whose *Second Army* [15] was bearing down on the Oise on either side of Guise. Against this threat Lanrezac could muster I Corps, X Corps and III Corps, while holding the Germans on his left with XVIII Corps and two Reserve divisions.

Lanrezac fought a brilliant battle. As Bülow pressed forward he met stubborn resistance on the river and, judging the moment exactly, Lanrezac switched Franchet d'Esperey's I Corps to the centre and drove the *Guard Corps* and *X Corps* northward in great confusion. For the first time since 21 August the enemy was in full retreat. Franchet had earlier shown his qualities of leadership in his counter-attack against Hausen at Dinant. Now he demonstrated that the spirit of *élan* was not dead, and it was a special matter of pride for him that the first Germans to show their backs to Fifth Army were the famous — some might say infamous — *Guard Corps*. Joffre, despite all his other preoccupations, did not misread the signs. He needed men like Franchet; and it was not long before he was to put him to work on a much more crucial assignment.

Bülow, cautious in advance, now proved craven in retreat. During the late afternoon he called on Kluck for help. Kluck declined the invitation. He had in fact come to a decision that day, at once arrogant and ambitious, but for the moment he was not interested in saving Bülow's skin. Nor need he have worried. The battle of Guise was a victory for Lanrezac, but a victory which contained the seeds of disaster.

By midnight Lanrezac realized that Fifth Army's success had left him isolated, with Fourth Army a day's march to his right rear and the BEF twenty-five miles behind his left. Since Joffre had ordered the attack, he reasoned, Joffre alone must order the retreat. Such are the follies which proceed not from the clash of arms but from the clash of personalities. Truly it may be said again that while wars are fought by the led, they are won and lost in the hearts and minds of the leaders.

Joffre had already perceived the danger, but by yet another of those now

[15] Left to right: *Guards Corps, X Corps, X Reserve Corps, VII Corps* (part). His *Guard Reserve Corps* was already on its way to the Eastern Front.

PLATE 18. *Bridge over the Oise north of Villers-Cotterêts, destroyed during the retreat*

familiar strokes of fate, his order to Lanrezac to start withdrawing did not reach Laon until 7 a.m. on the morning of 30 August. Fortunately, Bülow, although reporting his usual 'victory' to OHL, was in neither the mood nor the condition to pursue Lanrezac. Fifth Army thus began its retirement without interference towards the south-east. And Joffre moved his HQ from Vitry to Bar-sur-Aube thirty miles farther south. The stage was being set for the climax of the first act.

French's diary entry for Sunday, 30 August, includes this passage:

> I have told the General (Joffre) *emphatically* that I cannot fill the gap between Compiègne–la Fère. I have decided to retire behind the Seine to the west of Paris, if possible in the neighbourhood of St. Germain. *The march will occupy at least 10 days.* [16]

Luckily, he did not convey the latter part of this decision to Joffre. Luckily, he did inform Kitchener of his extraordinary intention.

French's Operation Order No. 11, dated 29 August, and timed 9 p.m. (i.e., covering the movement of the BEF on the 30th), laid down a new line running roughly east to west from Soissons to Compiègne, while GHQ departed to Dammartin, only a short day's march from Paris. The men had had a full day's rest while Lanrezac was occupied with Bülow at Guise. While they were glad of the refreshment, they were mystified by the decision to continue the retreat. John Morris of 2/Royal Sussex, 2nd Infantry Brigade, who had not yet fired a single round or even seen more than a distant enemy cavalry patrol, was perplexed. 'We had spent a good day, getting ourselves cleaned up and hoping for a bit of action. We could hear some firing away to our right, but we couldn't understand why we had to go on retreating when there weren't no enemy in sight.'

As John Morris marched away towards Soissons he could not have guessed that some two weeks later he would be back again travelling in the opposite direction and very much involved with the business of battle.

[16] Author's italics.

CHAPTER 7

The Great Blunder

During the morning of 30 August, Bülow sent a message to Kluck reporting that his Army was 'exhausted by the battle of Guise and unable to pursue'. It was the moment for which Kluck had been waiting.

Kluck, as we know, was a convinced disciple of Schlieffen, and the instructions he had received from OHL on the 28th were in accordance with the master's plan, although the right wing was a little behind schedule. There was, however, one significant difference. Where Schlieffen had based his whole strategy on overwhelming numerical superiority on the right, Moltke had repeatedly eroded that superiority. For this he and Kluck were now about to pay the price.

Kluck was not greatly concerned about counting heads. As he daily reported to OHL, the battle was as good as won. On his immediate front, Maunoury had been 'driven in disorder' across the Avre, which runs south from Amiens. The British had disappeared since their 'defeat' at Le Cateau, and it was a reasonable assumption that they had ceased to exist as a cohesive force (the exact words which Huguet, the doom-monger, also used in his report to Joffre that day). In both these assumptions, as so often before, Kluck was wrong. Victory can be a heady wine. The certainty that he had won a crushing victory now went to Kluck's head.

With the enemy in headlong flight, why, he reasoned, was it any longer necessary to continue what was no more than a symbolic victory parade to the north and west of Paris? The time had come to finish the argument and destroy the broken remnants of Lanrezac's Army. Just before 6 p.m. that evening he received another message from Bülow asking him to wheel inward in order to complete the destruction of the French Fifth Army. Kluck needed no further prompting. Calling upon his troops for 'further forced marches', he gave as his objectives for the 31st Noyon and Compiègne to the south-east, leaving *IV Reserve Corps* to watch his right flank. It was the final nail in Schlieffen's coffin. The great blunder had been made.

In all the later arguments, one thing is certain. The decision to wheel south-east across the face of Paris was made by Kluck; indeed, he did not inform OHL[1] until the following day. Moltke, with little alternative, agreed to what was already a *fait accompli*. When, five days later, he attempted to impose his will on Kluck (and by then it was too late) his order to *First* and *Second Armies* was so remote from reality that it would have required Kluck to perform what Liddell Hart has neatly described as 'a sort of backward somersault'.

While Kluck was marching towards a false dawn, much was happening on the Allied side. Suddenly Maunoury, retiring towards the general line Beauvais–Creil–Senlis north-west of and uncomfortably close to Paris and unaware of the inward wheel of *First Army*, found himself opposed by little more than the occasional patrol. At last he had the breathing-space for which he had been fighting desperately since the earlier engagements south and west of Péronne.

French was equally unaware of Kluck's wheel, and concerned only with continuing his retreat. On the 30th[2] he sent a message to Kitchener saying that he had 'decided to make a prolonged and definite retreat due south, passing to the west or east of Paris', a proposal which drew from a mystified Kitchener the reasonable question 'What is the meaning of this?' If it meant anything, the implication was that French had decided to take the BEF out of the line as far and as fast as possible. On the following day French despatched an even more incomprehensible telegram which contrived on one sheet of paper to report: a major success for Fifth Army at Guise; a direct lie – 'I should like to have assumed a vigorous offensive at once'; a more precise statement of intent – 'I have decided to begin [*sic*] my retirement tomorrow in the morning [*1 September*] behind the Seine, in a south-westerly direction west of Paris'; and a denial of any intention of making a 'prolonged and definite retreat'. Kitchener may be forgiven for thinking that Sir John French had become mentally unbalanced. There was only one thing for it. He decided to visit the C-in-C immediately.

Meanwhile Lanrezac was in trouble; he would have been even more shaken had he known that Kluck was bearing down on him in great strength from the north-west. The BEF was now a day's march to his rear, and on his right there was a gap of twenty miles between him and de Langle. Fortunately, Joffre kept his nerve. His two main problems were time and Sir John French. On the 30th and 31st he also had no firm evidence of Kluck's wheel, although there were growing indications of a change of plan, if not yet of exact direction. His determination to return to the offensive at the first appropriate moment remained unshaken. Meanwhile in order to straighten his line he ordered a further withdrawal of Fourth and Fifth Armies and of Foch's Detachment towards the Seine.

French's Operation Order No. 12, issued at 6.15 p.m. on 30 August,

---

[1] On 30 August, OHL moved from Koblenz to Luxembourg, still far removed from the battlefield and with little knowledge of the situation at the front.
[2] On this day French formed III Corps on his left flank. It consisted of 4th Division and 19th Infantry Brigade, under General Pulteney.

ordered a continuation of the retreat south[3] of the Aisne, and while GHQ moved to Dammartin, the order for the following day, the 31st, brought the BEF on a line running east to west from Villers-Cotterêts through Crépy to Verberie on the Oise south of Compiègne. It also brought I Corps and II Corps together for the first time since the seemingly distant days of the 'Maubeuge' position on the 25th.

On reaching Dammartin French found Huguet waiting for him. His diary entry reads: 'Gen. Joffre has appealed very strongly to me to remain in the fighting line, but I have told him it is impossible to do so until my force has been re-organized and re-fitted.' Two letters that day, one from Kitchener and one from Poincaré, received the same obdurate reply. French even added another bit of grit to the ill-oiled machinery. 'It appears now that *Lanrezac* [his italics] is throwing back his left flank and thus widening the gap.'[4]

And what of the actors? By now the men were becoming increasingly disheartened. The rest-day on the 29th had done much to revive their spirits. A decent sleep, a hot meal and a relief from constant marching had made them, if not fighting fit, at least ready and willing for action. Since crossing the Oise, the Cavalry Division apart, they had seen little or nothing of the enemy. They could not understand, therefore, why they must now continue the retreat. George Macklin of the Wiltshires is an example:

> We had lost count of the days. All we knew was that we had come to France to fight. Now for no reason we were told the retreat would go on. Just that. No one told us why. We had lost a lot of our pals, but we hadn't expected a tea-party. It was back to the road and the dust and the heat and never a German in sight. No wonder we felt bloody-minded.

Pte Macklin raises an interesting point. Throughout the retreat, and indeed long after, the men lived and moved in a kind of vacuum, both isolated and insulated from what was happening around them. And the same was true of their officers. Theirs not to reason why? Perhaps. But men respond readily to the truth, however distasteful or however daunting. Phrases like 'tactical withdrawal' or 'necessary re-alignment' invite four-letter answers, and the soldiers of the BEF were in a four-letter mood.[5]

The real truth is that GHQ knew very little more than the men, and what it did know it did not like. It therefore seems to have taken refuge behind a conspiracy of silence; and that is a negation of leadership. This strange kind of military boycott (GHQ Operation Orders during these days gave the minimum information about the enemy or about the French on either flank) extended downward to the three Corps Commanders. The effect was

---

[3] The original second paragraph inexplicably ran: 'The Army will move *west* tomorrow.' This was altered in pencil to: 'Order changed later and Army moved south.'
[4] French's second Despatch dated 17 September presents a very different picture.
[5] In his diary for 28 August Capt. Needham, a Special Reserve officer with 1/Northamptons, of 2nd Infantry Brigade, who to that date had not fired a single round, recorded: 'My sergeant asked me why we were still retreating. I said it was a "strategic retirement". He looked blank. I felt a fool.'

PLATE 19. *Néry, from the German position*

contagious, as divisional and brigade war diaries show. It was left to Kluck, by chance and not by intention, to remind George Macklin and his friends that war is real and war is earnest.

The morning of 1 September dawned misty. By now the BEF was south of the Forest of Compiègne on either side of the Oise. Lack of contact with the enemy may have induced a relaxation in arranging proper outposts. Of the main body of *First Army* there had been no sign since Le Cateau.

1st Cavalry Brigade (the Bays, 5th DG and 11th Hussars) and 'L' Battery, RHA had bivouacked for the night in the small village of Néry, midway between Crépy and Verberie on the Oise. It lay in a valley with a ridge some 600 yards to the east. The brigade was disposed thus: 5th DG at the northern edge of the village, the Bays and 11th Hussars in farm buildings around the centre, and 'L' Battery in an orchard a little farther south.

At 4.30 a.m. orders were given for the brigade to saddle up, ready to move off, but because of the thick mist this order was temporarily postponed. 5th DG and the Bays sent out patrols north and south, but these returned without any contact to report. 'L' Battery accordingly let their poles down and began watering their horses by sub-sections at the near-by sugar factory. It was then 5.30 a.m. – another typical beginning to the now daily routine of the retreat.

But not for long. As the mist began to thin a patrol of the 11th Hussars galloped in after encountering a large body of dismounted German cavalry on the ridge to the east of the village. [6] Almost immediately a shell burst over the middle of the village, followed by heavy rifle and machine-gun fire from the ridge; this was the signal for the start of an intense artillery bombardment by three four-gun batteries. The fire was concentrated on the Bays and 'L' Battery, now clearly visible at short range on the southern edge of the village.

[6] *4th Cavalry Division* of Marwitz's *II Cavalry Corps*, the leading formation of Kluck's inward wheel. Kluck's later account confirms that he had no knowledge of a British presence in this area.

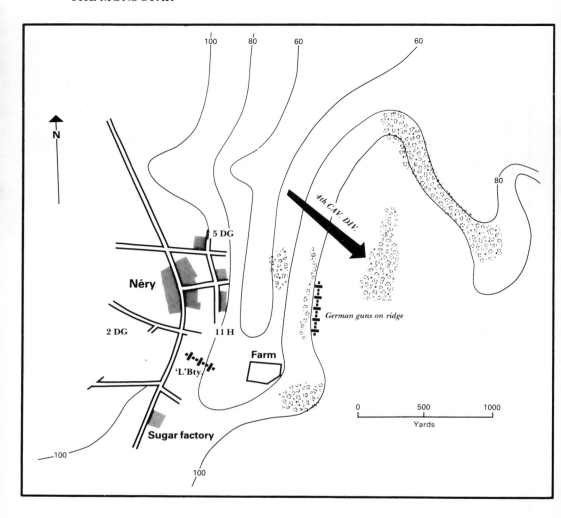

DIAGRAM D. *Néry*

There were immediate casualties, and many of the terrified horses of the Bays bolted. Three guns of 'L' Battery were quickly put out of action, but Capt. Bradbury rallied the survivors, and ran to man the three remaining guns. One of these was knocked out at once by a direct hit which killed a sergeant and a gunner and severely wounded Lt Giffard. A second, gallantly served, kept up a sustained and accurate fire on the German batteries until – with Lt Campbell killed, and every member of the crew dead or wounded – it was in turn silenced.

There remained only the single gun of F sub-section. For nearly an hour this gun bore a charmed life,[7] and despite the concentrated fire of the German batteries on the ridge, it remained in action – how effectively was

[7] It stands today in the Rotunda at Woolwich as a proud memorial to the officers and men of 'L' Battery.

PLATE 20. 'L' Battery at Néry. 'F' Sub-section gun: Capt. Bradbury, BSM Dorrell and Sgt Nelson

to be discovered later that morning. But so unequal a contest could have only one end. Shortly before 8 a.m. there remained only Capt. Bradbury, BSM Dorrell and Sgt Nelson. Returning for the last time to fetch ammunition, Bradbury was mortally wounded by a shell which severed both his legs; and at 8.10 a.m. 'L' Battery fired its last round. For their outstanding gallantry Bradbury, Dorrell and Nelson were awarded the Victoria Cross. The battery's casualties were three officers and twenty men killed and two officers and twenty-nine men wounded. For all purposes it had ceased to exist as an effective unit. [8]

'L' Battery's action undoubtedly saved 1st Cavalry Brigade. It also resulted in a humiliating defeat for Marwitz's *4th Cavalry Division*. Under cover of its fire, the three regiments in Néry were able to work round the German flanks and by dismounted action pin the enemy to the high ground. Shortly before Dorrell and Nelson fired their last round, 4th Cavalry Brigade and 'I' Battery, RHA reached the scene, followed by part of 10th Infantry Brigade and 1/Middlesex. These reinforcements subjected the Germans, now exposed on the ridge, to such a devastating fire that they retreated in disorder. [9] When, shortly after noon, 1/Middlesex occupied the high ground they found eight of the enemy's guns abandoned. The remaining four were found the following day in the near-by forest. It was a fitting reward for 'L' Battery.

Néry was not the only action on 1 September, for that morning Kluck was across the Aisne in some strength, although marching south-east at an oblique angle to the BEF's line of retreat. He was pursuing a different prey, and his main objective was Château Thierry and the Marne crossings. So

[8] After Néry it was withdrawn to the advanced base at Le Mans and replaced by 'H' Battery, RHA.
[9] So great was the damage caused to *4th Cavalry Division* at Néry that it was withdrawn from Marwitz's Corps and sent back to join *IV Reserve Corps* as part of Kluck's flank guard.

135

obsessed was he with the destruction of Lanrezac that he ignored the existence of the BEF, even when the rough handling of *4th Cavalry Division* at Néry must have told him that the despised British were still a force very much to be reckoned with. During the day he received two more sharp reminders.

About 10 a.m. near Crépy, a few miles east of Néry, 13th Infantry Brigade was attacked by the five *Jäger* battalions of Marwitz's *Cavalry Corps*. As at Néry, it was a chance encounter, and the attack was not pressed. By noon the enemy drew off, leaving the rearguard of Royal West Kents to follow the main body of 5th Division to the south. The Germans made no attempt to maintain contact.

At the same hour the most serious action of the day was fought in and around Villers-Cotterêts ten miles east of Crépy. Here I Corps, having at last closed in on Smith-Dorrien's right flank, was retiring through the forest. The right rearguard provided by 4th (Guards) Brigade of 2nd Division was holding the northern edge of the forest when during the forenoon it was attacked by a large force of all arms. [10] The forest here was crossed by a number of wide rides which provided natural lines of fire for machine-guns, and there followed a bitter and confused battle in the woods. The main brunt of the early fighting fell on 2/Coldstream and on the Irish Guards, the first major action in which this regiment – at that time the youngest in the Brigade – had taken part. Here too Col. Morris, the redoubtable commanding officer of the Irish Guards, was killed by a burst of machine-gun fire. General Scott-Kerr, the brigade commander, who was seriously wounded during the action, later noted in his diary:

> My impression of the German attack was that the infantry were doped. [11] One saw groups of men walking up to our line mooning along with their rifles at the trail, as if stupified. I believe they used their infantry at that period as a screen behind which they brought up their machine-guns, and when the latter appeared you had to look out for squalls. They were horribly efficient.

So, supported by the 9th and 17th Batteries, the Guards fought their way slowly back. Two platoons of Grenadiers, surrounded by the enemy, refused to surrender, and were killed to a man. By early evening the fighting died away and 4th (Guards) Brigade retired towards Betz. Its casualties amounted to over 300 officers and men; 6th Infantry Brigade (which covered its withdrawal) lost 160. As for the enemy, the official History records: 'Some weeks later it was ascertained . . . that the Germans had suffered very heavily in this affair, having lost all sense of direction and fired on each other.'

By 10 p.m. the BEF had reached a line running east to west from la Ferté Milon through Nanteuil towards Senlis, on which it billeted for the night.

---

[10] Advance guards of *III Corps* and of *2nd* and *9th Cavalry Divisions*.
[11] A more probable explanation is that they were drunk (see p. 141).

While these rearguard actions were taking place on 1 September, there was a very different confrontation 40 miles away in Paris.

The previous day the War Cabinet, profoundly concerned by the implications of French's apparent intention to retire completely from the line, agreed that Kitchener should pay an immediate visit to France. The purpose of this visit was to discover the true overall situation, and if necessary to order French to conform with the general movements of his ally.

The meeting took place at the British Embassy in Paris; and since Kitchener did not survive to give his own account, we have only French's version. Not to put too fine a point upon it, the atmosphere was less than cordial. In his memoirs, French spoke of his resentment at what he felt to be political interference with his 'executive command and authority'. But the real reason for his boorishness is explained by his diary entry for that day:

> K. arrived dressed in khaki as a F.M.! He said he wanted to visit Joffre and the troops. The Ambassador objected strongly to this and so did I. We had rather a disagreeable time!

It was a perfectly reasonable request, and Kitchener was entirely entitled to wear uniform (French does not seem to have resented later visits to the troops by the King in Field Marshal's uniform). As War Minister, his responsibility was above and beyond that of Sir John French, and a visit to Haig and Smith-Dorrien and to the troops might have been illuminating as well as encouraging – in both directions. As a Field Marshal (senior to French) he was still a serving soldier, and habitually wore uniform at his War Office desk. He had no intention of up-staging French, but he was aware that in the event of a meeting with Joffre and Poincaré his appearance in khaki rather than a frock-coat would not pass unnoticed. But French, always quick to take offence, was very angry indeed.

In the event Kitchener did not meet Joffre, nor did he visit the troops. He returned to London that evening, having reached a compromise. In no circumstances would the BEF evacuate France without written Cabinet approval. Meanwhile French was authorized to continue his withdrawal on the clear understanding that he was to conform closely with Joffre's plans. Before leaving Paris, Kitchener summed up the situation in the following telegram to the Cabinet:

> French's troops are now engaged in the fighting line, where he will remain conforming to the movements of the French army, though at the same time acting with caution to avoid being in any way unsupported on his flanks.

During the next four crucial days, French was to interpret the last proviso very literally – to the despair of Joffre, Galliéni, Franchet d'Esperey and Maunoury. And his own troops.

For Joffre the picture was becoming clearer and the options narrower. British and French air reconnaissance confirmed that Kluck's change of direction was beginning to take shape, which was more than could be said of the Allied front.

On Joffre's right Lanrezac was across the Aisne, but in some disorder and moving south-east under pressure from Bülow, widening the gap between the Fifth Army and the BEF. [12] By now Joffre had made a decision: 'the most painful of my life', he said later. Wherever and whenever the moment came to turn upon his pursuers he could no longer rely on Lanrezac. If the coming offensive – the last chance of saving France – were to be decisive, the men needed not a dispirited, defeatist commander but a leader capable of inspiring them to a supreme effort. Such a man was at hand; but Joffre was not yet ready.

In the centre, the BEF was continuing its retreat, a day's march ahead of Lanrezac. After his meeting with Kitchener, French went so far as to propose a defensive position on the Marne, and it must have been with some relief that he received a courteous reply from Joffre telling him that the pressure on Lanrezac was such that the Seine seemed a more suitable line from which to launch the counter-offensive. Accordingly French ordered a withdrawal the following day to a narrower frontage from Meaux on the Marne to Dammartin; and at 10 p.m. GHQ moved fifteen miles south to Lagny. The day had been full of alarms and rumours of strong penetration of the BEF's position, but in fact 'the large bodies of enemy cavalry' were scattered parties of *4th Cavalry Division* which had fled in confusion after the affair at Néry, and now found themselves cut off. Their activities were inoffensive, and Cpl Crawte and three men of the 4th Hussars on patrol had the satisfaction of rounding up twenty Uhlans who said they were hungry and seemed happy to be protected from a crowd of enraged villagers.

On the left, Maunoury's Sixth Army covered an arc from Beauvais to Senlis on either side of the Oise. Since the previous evening – for reasons which were then not yet clear – it had not been greatly molested, and the battered 61st and 62nd Reserve Divisions had been withdrawn to recover in the area of Pontoise, no more than fifteen miles from Paris. We now know that Kluck had discounted any threat from this quarter as he wheeled inward, and had left *IV Reserve Corps* at Quinquempoix to watch his right flank. What Kluck did not know, but OHL had begun to suspect, was that Joffre's IV Corps and three other divisions were being railed up from the south and were due to reach Maunoury within two days. The great blunder was gathering momentum.

Much else happened on this critical day, 1 September. The Germans were within two days' march of Paris – if, indeed, Paris was their objective. The political confusion, the Gallic frenzy, of that day has been marvellously described elsewhere. [13] We are concerned here only with the

---

[12] This gap was filled the following day by a new Cavalry Corps under General Conneau formed by transferring 2nd and 10th Cavalry Divisions from Nancy.
[13] Tuchman, *op. cit.*

pity of war; and that pity has nothing to do with politics. At this moment, another director entered the theatre.

Galliéni had been Joffre's superior before the war, and indeed had recommended him for the post of commander-in-chief of the field armies. How wise a choice it was we now know. Galliéni was not interested in appearances. Not for him the *chic* of the officer corps. 'The art of war', he said to a colleague, 'lies in the head, not in the headdress.' Spears loved him. Wilson – perhaps envious? – did not. He is best summed up by his chief-of-staff, General Clergerie, who was called to a meeting on the evening of 3 September – 'one of those long conferences he holds on grave issues. They usually last from two to five minutes.'

Galliéni was Military Governor of Paris, in normal times a prestigious post reserved for senior generals who had rendered outstanding service to the State. But the times were not normal. Galliéni found himself required to defend 'the Entrenched Camp of Paris' without an army. Furthermore, the reinforcements allocated to Sixth Army had to pass through the capital, and thus through Galliéni's area of responsibility. On 1 September, after urgent representations – and Galliéni was a formidable advocate – he persuaded Joffre to break with precedent and put Maunoury under his command, while himself remaining subordinate to the C-in-C. Thus there came into existence what was to be called – by Galliéni, if by no one else – 'the Army of Paris'. And armed with this weapon, it was to be Galliéni, more than any other single man, who recognized Kluck's blunder for what it was, and so rang up the curtain on the battle of the Marne.

On this same day Joffre issued his General Instruction No. 4. It was a very cautious document, as the first paragraph shows:

> . . . the outflanking movement against the left of the forces, insufficiently arrested by the British Army and the Sixth Army, constrains the forces as a whole to pivot on our right.
> As soon as the Fifth Army has escaped the menace of envelopment, the Armies will resume the offensive.

There followed directions for a general retirement behind the Seine and the Aube 'which may be regarded as the limit of the retirement, without any implication that this limit must necessarily be reached'. There was no indication of any kind that Kluck had wheeled inward. Joffre was beginning to sound a little like Sir John French. But his Instruction ended thus:

> If circumstances permit, portions of the First and Second Armies [*on the Moselle*] will be brought at an opportune moment to take part in the offensive. Finally the mobile troops of the Entrenched Camp of Paris may likewise be able to participate in the general action.

Reading these words, it is difficult to believe that Joffre was within four days of taking a decision which would change the course of the war. But within hours of the issue of General Instruction No. 4 a bag was found on the body of a German cavalry officer. It contained papers and a map which showed in detail the direction to be followed by each corps of *First Army* and the daily objectives to be reached. The map also showed that the flank guard would consist only of *IV Reserve Corps* and the battered *4th Cavalry Division*. The main thrust was south-east from the Oise to the Ourcq, and then to the Marne. This meant only one thing. The target was no longer Paris. It was Lanrezac's Fifth Army. When, on 3 September, an air reconnaissance report confirmed this movement beyond argument to the eager Galliéni, his chief staff officers, watching the changing pattern on the operations map, could scarcely contain their excitement. 'They offer us their flank!' they cried.

Bob Barnard was still going strong.

After the first couple of days at Mons, we seem to have spent our time just marching and crossing rivers.[14] Since we left Caudry we hadn't seen a single German nor fired a single round. It had been very hot and very tiring but most of us had become hard and fit. I still marvel at how the cavalry kept going because they were fighting rearguard actions most of the time but the horses, although tired, looked in good condition, which is more than you could say of the French horses we saw. Some of our battalion were certainly in a bad way with their feet worn raw. Most of these were carried on the transport and I believe the worst cases were taken back by train to the base hospital. We didn't know where we were going no more than fly, but I remember the day was September 1st when we saw the first signpost which said 'Paris'. I was quite pleased at that, as I had never been to Paris.

Bob Barnard was going to be out of luck.

By the morning of 3 September the BEF was across the Marne on a line from la Ferté-sous-Jouarre to just south of Lagny (that day GHQ moved, for the last time, to Melun on the Seine). Here, abreast of Paris and facing due north, it halted and spent that and the following day resting.[15] And here it should have stayed, having at last disengaged itself from the enemy. Why, on 5 September, it was ordered to make another – and final – march fifteen miles to the south we shall presently see.

On the night of 2 September Moltke, far away in Luxembourg, had compounded Kluck's original blunder by issuing the following order to his right-wing commanders: 'The French are to be forced away from Paris in a south-easterly direction. The *First Army* will follow in échelon behind the *Second Army*, and will be responsible henceforward for the flank protection of

---

[14] Between 20 August and the end of the retreat 4/Royal Fusiliers covered 237 miles. In the process (leaving aside small streams) it crossed the Somme, Oise, Aisne, Marne and the Grand Morin.
[15] The 4th of September was literally a red-letter day for Bob Barnard and many others, for they then received their first mail and parcels from home since 12 August.

the force. [16] Had Moltke troubled to establish the true situation he would have been surprised to learn that *First Army*, far from being in échelon behind *Second Army*, was already a day's march *ahead* of it. Kluck, never disposed to play second fiddle to Bülow, simply ignored OHL's instructions and pressed on across the Marne at and on either side of Château Thierry. In so doing he was driving his men to the limit of endurance. One of his officers wrote: 'It is the delirium of victory which sustains our men, and in order that their bodies may be as intoxicated as their souls, they drink to excess, but this drunkenness helps to keep them going. . . . Abnormal stimulants are necessary to make abnormal fatigue endurable. [17]

On 4 September Moltke lost his nerve and finally tore up the Schlieffen Plan. He decided to seek a decision in the centre and on his left, with *Fourth* and *Fifth Armies* attacking south-east and *Sixth* and *Seventh Armies* striking south-westward through the French fortress line, the jaws thus closing inward on either side of Verdun. Meantime his right wing, Schlieffen's instrument of victory, was ordered to turn outward and, facing west, hold off any counter-move which the French might attempt from the area of Paris. 'The movement to face west', he added vaguely, 'might be made at leisure.' It was a lunatic manœuvre and, given the relative positions of *First* and *Second Armies* (Hausen's *Third Army* was already trailing far behind), an impossible one. Predictably Kluck ignored it and drove forward in his pursuit of Lanrezac. Small wonder that Galliéni's staff watched with excitement as the great blunder began to reach its climax.

On 3 September Joffre set off for Fifth Army HQ at Sézanne, twenty-five miles south of the Marne. During the morning the Army had fallen back across the river, but had failed to destroy the bridges in its sector; and by evening Kluck, in defiance of Moltke's orders, had also pushed part of *IX Corps*, and the heads of *III* and *IV Corps*, across in continued pursuit.

Joffre's mission was difficult and distasteful. Its purpose was to relieve Lanrezac of his command, a hard decision at any time but doubly so at this critical moment. His successor was no problem. On the way to Sézanne, Joffre arranged a brief meeting with Franchet d'Esperey, commander of I Corps, who alone had demonstrated a true offensive spirit and a proper resolution, first at Dinant and again during the battle of Guise. Did he feel capable of commanding an Army? asked Joffre. Franchet shrugged. But certainly, he replied. He was the kind of man who would have accepted the ultimate military responsibility as if it was the most natural thing in the world. When Joffre gave him his new command, however, Franchet kept his own counsel. He had no intention of retiring behind the Seine. [18] He was determined to turn and fight – and the sooner the better.

An hour later Joffre arrived at Fifth Army HQ. There are two versions of what happened there. Joffre later wrote that he had, with infinite regret,

---

[16] Neither in this nor in his subsequent order did Moltke even mention the BEF. For had it not, according to Kluck, ceased to exist?
[17] 'Undoubtedly, it was the influence of alcohol that caused the Germans to commit many of their acts of vandalism and brutality of which there is more than sufficient evidence.' Terraine: *Mons.*
[18] On 4 September he did go so far as to move his HQ from Sézanne to Romilly-sur-Seine.

told Lanrezac that he was 'used up and undecided' and that he would have to go, to which Lanrezac, after a moment's reflection, replied, 'General, you are right.' Lanrezac's account is very different. He protested strongly, and insisted that his present predicament was entirely due to GQG (and so, by implication, Joffre), who had refused to listen to his warnings before and after the battle of Charleroi. The fact that, in a sense, both Joffre *and* Lanrezac were right was now academic. By midnight Franchet was in the saddle at Sézanne. His arrival had much the same effect as a violent electrical storm, which left his staff and commanders in a salutary state of shock.

The 4th of September was the day of decision. While Kluck marched steadily on across the Petit Morin, French decided to visit his troops, now enjoying a well-deserved rest. He was absent from Melun until that evening, and this was to prove unfortunate. His diary included three entries, to the last and most important of which we will return in proper sequence.

First he noted, with just a touch of malice:

> Lanrezac has been put in arrest with 4 other generals and is to be tried, it is said, by Court-Martial.

Then he wrote:

> Smith-Dorrien came in whilst I was with Haig. He tells me that in his Corps *discipline* is suffering. The shortage of officers demoralizes the men.[19] A great deal of looting and irregularity is going on[20] – particularly in the 5th Division. . . . This is very unfortunate but it is a characteristic of War.

None the less, French was heartened by the general condition of his men, though II Corps, on which had fallen the brunt of the fighting, was seriously under strength, and without a significant part of its divisional artillery. Yet there is no evidence that the C-in-C gave any indication to his Corps Commanders, let alone his troops, that great events were impending. The truth is that even now French's eyes were still fixed on the Seine and not on an immediate return to the offensive. In fairness, the same was true of Joffre, although for different reasons. But by the morning of the 4th Joffre had caught three tigers by the tail – Galliéni, Franchet and Foch. Between them they were to decide the issue for him.

First Galliéni. By 4 September he had pulled Maunoury back almost to the outer defences of the capital, and already reinforcements from IV Corps were beginning to reach the Army of Paris. This movement was not an act of desperation but a deliberate withdrawal *pour mieux sauter*. And air

---

[19] On this day, the first reinforcements reached the BEF via St Nazaire.
[20] Smith-Dorrien's diary confirms this, although in much less exaggerated terms.

reconnaissance early that morning showed *IV Reserve Corps*, Kluck's flank guard, marching straight across his front towards Lizy on the Ourcq and Meaux on the Marne. Instinctively Galliéni realized that if he himself acted without delay he could light the fuse to which Joffre hesitated to put a match. It was a curious trick of fate which brought these very different two men together at this moment: Joffre, the field commander, with six Armies and the future of France in his hands, aware that the wrong decision at the wrong time and in the wrong place would bring disaster; Galliéni, his former superior, with only an improvised army, thinking like a Military Governor of Paris but persuaded that the enemy had dealt him a trump card. Both men knew that the key lay in the hands of an unreliable, temperamental Englishman at Melun.

Throughout the morning Galliéni tried to contact Joffre, and throughout the morning Joffre avoided him (later Galliéni with dry humour recorded that the battle of the Marne was the result not of a *coup de main* but of *coups de téléphone*).

At 1 p.m. Galliéni set off with Maunoury to see French and explain his plan for a concerted attack on Kluck's flank and rear – on 6 September if he was to operate north of the Marne, on the 7th if he had to cross over to the south. French was not at Melun but visiting his troops twenty-five miles away. Murray was an unfortunate substitute. Not yet fully recovered from his collapse on the day of Le Cateau, he offered neither support nor enthusiasm. Without the agreement of the Field Marshal he could only show, in Galliéni's phrase, '*une grande repugnance à entrer dans nos vues*'. He undertook at least to convey Galliéni's proposals to Sir John French.

That morning another meeting had taken place at Bray-sur-Seine. Unlike Lanrezac, Franchet, within a few hours of assuming his command, knew that the time for private vendettas was over. He needed the BEF. France needed the BEF. He therefore invited Sir John French to meet him – in every sense – half-way. Instead – and it was a stroke of luck – it was Wilson who came, Wilson the Francophile, the friend of Foch, the champion of Plan XVII. With such a man Franchet could identify.

While waiting at Bray, Franchet received an urgent message from Joffre. How soon could Fifth Army be ready to join in a general offensive? The answer depended on the British.

By the time Wilson arrived Franchet had produced not simply a limited proposal for joint co-operation with the BEF, but a complete plan for the battle of the Marne. It had the merit of simplicity.

On the right, Foch would hold the exits from the marshes of St Gond against Hausen and Bülow, and then, as the main attack developed, push northward; Fifth Army would attack north-east, the gap between it and the BEF filled by Conneau's Cavalry Corps; the British would advance north towards the Marne at la Ferté-sous-Jouarre[21]; and Maunoury's Sixth Army, north of the Marne and the Ourcq, would strike east at Kluck's right flank and rear. The offensive would begin on 6 September.

---

[21] It should be remembered that when this meeting took place the BEF was still disposed astride the Grand Morin and level with Fifth Army.

Wilson consulted Macdonogh, the Chief Intelligence Officer who had accompanied him to Bray, and they agreed that Franchet's plan was entirely acceptable. Wilson, as Haig had done at Guise, added a rider that Sir John French's *imprimatur* would be necessary. No one at Bray was aware of Galliéni's visit to Melun, or of his much more limited proposal for the defence of Paris. No matter. Wise old Galliéni knew that he had put, as had been his intention, a lively cat among a flock of doubting pigeons.

Wilson returned to Melun, and, in spite of Murray, sent a telegram to Paris reporting the 'agreement' reached at Bray. At the same time Franchet informed Joffre at Bar-sur-Aube of his discussions, and of his readiness to move on the 6th. [22] 'The condition of my Army is not brilliant,' he added. But he was well aware that the condition of Kluck's and Bülow's Armies was probably even less brilliant. He was not aware that there was serious trouble in the German camp.

French returned from his visit to the troops that evening. There are several versions of what then happened, largely based on Joffre's insistence in his memoirs (with or without hindsight) that he would have liked to delay the offensive by a further day until the 7th. Standing on our bridge downstream, and knowing now the total confusion which existed on the other side of the hill, it is difficult to know whether in so doing he would have made a strategic rout out of a tactical victory. The evidence is against him. Galliéni, Franchet and Foch were straining too hard at the leash.

But not Sir John French. His last entry in his diary for 4 September was short and unequivocal:

> I have ordered the British Forces to retire some 12 miles towards Melun tonight *and have given no decided answer to the generals.* [23]

This further retreat would bring the BEF south of the Forest of Crécy on a line running east to west from Rozoy to Brie–Comte–Robert, and within ten miles of the Seine. It would expose the inner flanks of the French Fifth and Sixth Armies. It would invite no pursuit by Kluck. Operation Order No. 16, dated 4 September and timed 6.35 p.m., gives no reason. The men with whom French had spent that day were very angry indeed.

Even while French was writing this shameful instruction, Joffre was issuing his General Order for the battle of the Marne. It opened thus:

> The time has come to profit by the adventurous position of the German First Army and concentrate against that Army all the efforts of the Allied Armies of the extreme left.

Joffre went on to give precise details of the thrust of the great offensive – including that of the BEF – and he ended:

---

[22] Franchet's crucial report reached Joffre when, incredibly, he was entertaining two Japanese officers to dinner. *Sangfroid* could not go further.
[23] Author's italics.

These various Armies will take the offensive on the morning of the 6th of September.

During 5 September, while French was conducting a leisurely withdrawal towards the Seine, the eager Galliéni had jumped the gun and set Maunoury loose against the German flank guard on the Ourcq. Kluck's Chief of Staff, Kuhl, later admitted that *First Army* HQ had not the slightest inkling that Joffre was preparing a major offensive on his left flank. Indeed, during this day Kluck had continued his pursuit of Franchet's Fifth Army across the Grand Morin and had even pushed his own HQ as far forward as Rebais midway between Montmirail and Coulommiers. He was then twenty-five miles from Paris.

He had long since ceased to pay any attention to OHL, and it was not until the following morning that he learned that his fragile right flank had been attacked and driven in by Maunoury.

There now appeared upon the scene a kind of German Nolan in the person of Lt Col Hentsch, Moltke's chief Intelligence Officer. He was to appear once more, four days later, with even more dramatic effect. Now he brought news. All was not going well on the central and southern fronts. Despite great victories, the French had not been routed and destroyed. Indeed, OHL had evidence that substantial numbers of troops were being transferred from the French right to their left flank, something that Kluck had believed to be impossible. It was Kluck's fault. He had invented too many of his own communiqués and believed too many of OHL's. Hentsch's message was short and clinical. The main attack would now be made against the depleted French right flank, and the Kaiser was going to that sector, ready to make a triumphal entry into Nancy, a *grand geste* which Castelnau was going to deny him. Meanwhile the right-wing Armies would take up a defensive position facing Paris, and, if seriously threatened by a major attack against their vulnerable right wing, *would fall back behind the Marne*. [24]

Kluck was angry; but Kluck was no fool. Thus it was that two days later a patrol of the 4th DG on a ridge south of the Grand Morin saw the extraordinary sight of a long column of German infantry marching south, halt, face about, and start retreating whence they had come. But of all this Joffre was unaware on the morning of 5 September. He had another major problem on his hands.

The great German blunder had been made. Was it now to be redeemed by British perfidy? The decision to return to the offensive, the one decision which had obsessed Joffre ever since Charleroi, had been taken. Was it conceivable that Sir John French would quit the field at this critical moment? At 3 a.m. on 5 September Joffre sent, 'by hand of personal officer', a copy of his Order No. 6 – the order for the battle of the Marne – to Melun, by when the BEF had already started on the last leg of its retreat. Captain de Galbert, Joffre's emissary, returned, as Spears had so often

[24] Author's italics.

done before, with no more than a courteous promise of 'further consideration'. The time for consideration was past. The French machine had been set in motion. Only one man could engage the British gear-lever in the great forward drive.

Joffre, having carefully ensured that Sir John French would not absent himself, set out on the long drive to Melun. He arrived there at 2 p.m. What then happened is now history. Quietly, passionately, with – as an eye-witness recorded – 'an emotion of which I did not think him capable', Joffre told Sir John French what was at stake. It is a pity that there is no verbatim record of what he said. But he reduced a Field Marshal to tears. And he won his point. French's diary is brief:

> I have agreed to Joffre's plan provided my troops can rest all today and commence their move to get into position tomorrow [*the 6th*].

So the great retreat ended and the battle of the Marne began. Let Bob Barnard have the last word. 'And about bloody time too!'

CHAPTER 8

A Tale of Two Rivers: Marne and Aisne

There has long been a debate about the battle of the Marne. Who was its true architect? Was it a victory; and if not, why not? Was it, in fact, a 'battle' at all?

As to the architect, the rival factions have variously put forward Foch, Franchet, Galliéni and Joffre. No one has suggested French. And no one, curiously, has considered the possibility that it may even, by a perverse twist of chance, have been Kluck. Foch we can dismiss. His influence was peripheral, and then only after the action had been joined. Franchet certainly made the *decision* possible by his instant grasp of the situation which he inherited on 4 September, and by the powerful impact of his personality on an Army deeply infected by Lanrezac's defeatism.

The argument lies between Galliéni and Joffre. Galliéni was the first to understand the magnitude of Kluck's blunder, and thus the opportunity – perhaps the last one – to turn the tide. At the very least, his vision, his energy, his persistence forced Joffre's hand at a moment when time – and timing – were vital. The fact that Joffre decided to resume direct command of Maunoury's Sixth Army on 11 September, two days after OHL's decision to pull back the whole German right wing, is yet another instance of the pride and prejudice which were to bedevil the leaders on both sides throughout the war. Galliéni took it philosophically. As the tide flowed east, he could at least contemplate with pride the great city which he had defended *à outrance*.

The architect, in the last analysis, was Joffre, ably assisted by Kluck. It was he who kept his nerve when faced with the collapse of Plan XVII; it was he who recognized the mortal danger to his open flank and brilliantly improvised Maunoury's Sixth Army there; it was he who took the risk of weakening his right to bolster his left; and it was he who, by his iron resolution, held the Allied Armies together until the turn of the tide. To the end he believed that had the offensive been delayed by one more day, both Bülow and Kluck would have reached a point of no return. Perhaps. Hindsight is the first refuge not only of historians.

Was the Marne a victory? In the sense that it halted and then drove back the enemy right wing, and thus denied the Germans the chance of winning the war 'before the leaves fall', yes. But it was only a tactical victory. Had the great gap which opened up in the centre been exploited, and the pursuit pressed with a greater sense of urgency, nothing could have saved the Germans. In his memoirs Bülow had no doubts: '*First Army* could have been split and annihilated, and the right wing of *Second Army* enveloped.' It would be churlish to blame the men of the BEF and of Franchet's Fifth Army. The wonder is that, after two weeks of fighting and marching, exhausted in body and dispirited in mind, they found the resilience to turn upon their pursuers and drive them back fifty miles in ten days. One supreme act of leadership on 8 or 9 September, and there would have been no need for the battle of the Aisne. Therein lies the pity of war.

Was there, then, a 'battle of the Marne'? The answer is, no. Only on the extreme right where Foch fought a series of bitter engagements with Hausen and Bülow at St Gond, and on the extreme left where Maunoury stood firm against Kluck's counter-attacks on the Ourcq,[1] could it be said that battle was joined. In the centre, on the Marne itself, the German rearguards offered skilful and stubborn resistance. But there was no battle. Between 6 September and 10 September, total casualties in the entire BEF were 1,710, scarcely more than those of 3rd Division on the first day at Mons.

Joffre's signal for the great counter-stroke was brief, and innocent of rhetoric:

> At the moment when the battle upon which hangs the fate of the country is about to begin, all must remember that the time for looking back is past; every effort must be concentrated on attacking and throwing the enemy back.
>
> Troops which can no longer advance must at any cost keep the ground that has been won, and must die where they stand rather than give way.
>
> Under present conditions no weakness can be tolerated.

Franchet's order to his troops was more passionate, for he was a more emotional man. Indeed, he ended on a note which ironically echoes that of an English admiral at Trafalgar a century before: 'The country relies upon every man to do his duty.'

French was not given to heroics. He was, in a sense, caught in a corner of his own making, and therefore careful of the verdict of history. His Operation Order No. 17, timed 5.15 p.m. on the 5th, was laconic and revealing. It opens thus:

> The enemy has apparently [*sic*] abandoned the idea of advancing on Paris and is contracting his front and moving south-eastward [*Kluck*

---

[1] Both French and German sources refer to the fighting on this flank as the battle of the Ourcq.

had been moving south-eastward for five days].

The Army will advance eastward with a view to attacking.

Its left will be covered by the 6th French Army also marching east, and its right will be linked to the 5th French Army marching north.

The last sentence seems designed more for Kitchener's benefit than that of the Corps Commanders.

The men of the BEF could not believe the news when it reached them. 'Fancy marching towards the sunrise for a change!', said Charlie Borthwick of the KOSB. Micky Lay of 2/Oxford and Bucks L.I., who had been so disappointed at the lack of action near Frameries on 24 August, recorded:

> The decision to advance gave everyone a wonderful uplift. During the retreat there was a joke I remember which went: ''If they give us a medal for this it should have a pair of boots on it, and another pair given away as a present.'' We had marched over 200 miles, but such are the fortunes of war that it was not until *8 September* that the first man in the battalion was killed, in a patrol action. In the same scrap another man won the Médaille Militaire and was promoted corporal, our first decoration.

On 6 September French issued one of his rare Orders of the Day. Here are the two final paragraphs:

> Foiled in their attempt to invest Paris, the Germans have been driven to move in an easterly and south-easterly direction, with the apparent intention of falling in strength on the V French Army. In this operation they are exposing their right flank and their line of communication to an attack from the combined VI French Army and the British forces.
>
> I call upon the British Army in France to now show the enemy its power, and to push on vigorously to the attack beside the VI French Army. I am sure I shall not call upon them in vain, but that, on the contrary, by another manifestation of the magnificent spirit which they have shown in the past fortnight, they will fall on the enemy's flank with all their strength and in unison with their Allies drive them back.

At last the voice of authority and leadership. On the morning of 6 September no one was to know the panic which had seized OHL in general and Moltke in particular; nor the strange sequence of events which were to cause a gap of twenty miles (Montmirail–Lizy-sur-Ourcq) to open up between Bülow and Kluck; nor the dramatic intervention of a comparatively junior German officer which resulted in the retreat of the whole right wing north of the Aisne. It is the general verdict of history that the Allied advance was a chapter of lost opportunities; that if Fifth Army

149

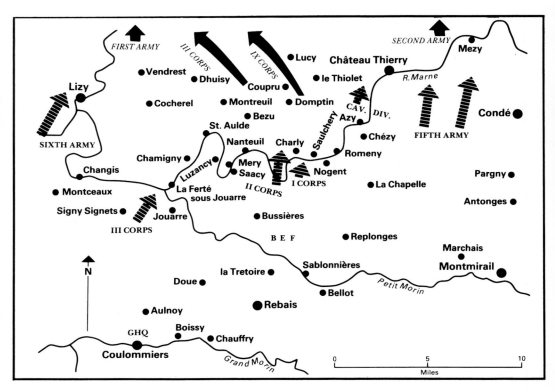

MAP 6. *The Marne*

and the BEF had 'pushed on vigorously', in French's phrase, especially when the great gap opened up, the Germans could have been defeated in detail and a tactical success turned into a strategic victory before the enemy had time to reinforce his line and regroup on the Chemin des Dames. This verdict is probably true, but it is easy to be wise after the event. Between 6 and 12 September the situation was as fluid as it had been during the retreat from Mons, and even more confused. Furthermore, between these days Kluck conducted an extremely skilful withdrawal, and by 9 September had put Maunoury's Sixth Army in great jeopardy.[2] It was Bülow whose moral cowardice, akin to that of Lanrezac, forced the issue.

On the morning of 6 September the Allied Armies of the left ran from Fère Champenoise to Nanteuil; on the right Foch's Ninth Army facing north at the exits to the marshes of St Gond; then, facing north-west, Franchet's Fifth Army, linked by Conneau's Cavalry Corps to the BEF, inclined slightly north-east near the Forest of Crécy; and on the left Maunoury's Sixth Army, north of the Marne from Meaux and facing east towards the Ourcq (see Map 6).

The issue of the next four days depended on whether the Germans could

[2] It was at a critical moment here on 7 September that there occurred the famous incident when Galliéni assembled 600 Paris taxis to rush his newly arrived IV Corps to reinforce Maunoury on the Ourcq.

defeat Foch and Maunoury on the wings before Franchet and French could create a decisive breakthrough in the centre. In the event Moltke contributed more than his fair share to the outcome, although it should be added that between 5 and 8 September no reports reached Luxembourg from the right-wing Armies and no orders were received by them from OHL (as late as 12 September Moltke had no idea where Kluck's *First Army* was).

Thus, assuming that the situation opposite Paris and the Seine was going according to his new plan, Moltke decided on 5 September to launch a major offensive by *Sixth* and *Seventh Armies* against the French fortress line in the south. So confident was he of success that the Kaiser was emboldened to travel to Prince Rupprecht's HQ, accompanied by a glittering escort, there to await a triumphal entry into Nancy. He travelled in vain. Despite the transfer of several of their divisions to Maunoury, Castelnau and Dubail not only held out, but stopped the German offensive in its tracks. On 8 September, still unaware of the dramatic developments on his northern front, Moltke called it off; and the following day, taking a leaf out of Joffre's book, he started moving *XV Corps* of *Seventh Army* and *7th Cavalry Division* of *Sixth Army* to his right flank, where they arrived just in time to fill the gap on the Aisne.

We need not concern ourselves in any detail with the French part in the advance to the Aisne; nor, except to explain the actions of Bülow and Kluck, with *First* and *Second Armies*. Instead the narrative now follows the BEF as it moved north to the Marne and then swung north-east to the Aisne, which it reached and then crossed on 12–13 September, just hours too late to establish itself on the northern escarpment. What might then have been?

When, on the morning of the 6th, the BEF turned to take the offensive it was – because of French's further retirement on the previous day – some fifteen miles behind the line from which Joffre had expected its advance to begin. In fact, this false alignment was to have the unintentional effect of resolving Bülow's dilemma for him; for it was air reconnaissance reports of five British columns entering the gap south of the Marne between Charly and la Ferté-sous-Jouarre on the 8th which finally decided him to pull *Second Army* right back.

On the 6th the BEF was disposed thus on a front of fifteen miles: on the right, covering the advance and in contact with Conneau's Cavalry Corps and Fifth Army, the Cavalry Division; then I Corps east of Rozoy; farther west II Corps approaching Coulommiers on the Grand Morin, covered by 3rd and 5th Cavalry Brigades;[3] and on the left, in touch with Maunoury, III Corps with the longest march coming up to Crécy, also on the Grand Morin.

[3] These two brigades were detached from Allenby and put under the command of General Hubert Gough. They are referred to in all orders as 'General Gough's Command' until 16 September, when they became 2nd Cavalry Division.

By that morning Kluck had reached the farthest point of his inward wheel with four Army Corps (*IX, III, IV* and *II*) and two cavalry divisions across the Marne, and with heads of columns across the Grand Morin. News of Maunoury's attack on his weak flank guard did not reach him until late the previous night, when he was entirely unaware of the counter-stroke which Joffre had prepared. He reacted immediately.

Tom Bridges of the 4th DG was privileged to witness an unusual sight. 'My squadron was advanced guard and from the village of Peçy [*five miles south-east of Rozoy*] we were able to see their infantry halted on the road. Then the phenomenon occurred. Under our eyes the enemy column began to wheel round in the road and retire to the north. It was the peak of Kluck's advance.' What he was seeing was the hasty withdrawal of *IV Corps* and *II Corps* to shore up the right flank and rear. For the first time Kluck, realizing that Maunoury represented not a diversion but a major threat, was seriously concerned, as the messages the following day which Bülow records (but Kluck does not) clearly show.

During the day Haig made only slow progress on the right, fearing – with a caution which he had already demonstrated – lest he should outrun Franchet or allow the enemy to infiltrate his left. There was little of French's 'vigorous' pursuit.

At 3.30 p.m. French ordered II and III Corps to close in on Haig's left. Smith-Dorrien, stubborn in retreat, now showed himself no less lively in advance, and by evening 3rd Division had reached the Grand Morin at Faremoutiers. Finding little opposition, 1/Wiltshires pressed on across the river, and by midnight had occupied the high ground at Le Charnois a mile farther north.

George Macklin was quite excited:

> First in at Mons and now first of the hunting pack! There had been a bit of a scrap while we were waiting to cross and I got a slight wound in the hand. But we were soon over and up the slope the other side. It was a moonlit night and we could see a few Germans scurrying away. We put out our picquets and settled down, feeling pretty pleased with ourselves. Then I remember clearly someone started singing 'You are the honeysuckle, I am the bee!' and everybody began laughing. Nothing strange about that until I realized it was a long time since we had had anything to laugh about. After that I slept like a log.

On the morning of 7 September the axis of the BEF's advance was shifted from east to north-east, and the day's objective was the crossing of the Grand Morin by all three Corps on a line running west from la Ferté Gaucher. Right-flank protection was provided by 2nd Cavalry Brigade, with 9th Lancers leading. Sgt James Taylor, whom we met earlier in Tidworth – where he was surprised to learn that he was off to fight the Germans and not the French – was about to have a unique experience:

> The regiment had been split up on various advanced guard duties. I was attached to Col. David Campbell's HQ with two troops of 'B' Sqn

– about forty of us in all, I'd say. About 9 a.m. we reached a place called Fretoy and crossing over a stream [*the Aubertin*] rode on towards the village of Moncel. The Colonel put us behind some haystacks and went on ahead with his trumpeter. The next thing we knew he was galloping back, and we could see why. About 500 yards away there was a line of German cavalry advancing towards us,[4] and I remember the Adjutant, Captain Reynolds, saying: 'By God, Colonel, they're going to charge us!' And they were!

I saw Colonel Campbell draw his sword [*in fact, his revolver*] and then he gave the order, very quiet and matter-of-fact: 'Follow me, gentlemen!' And off we went. I drew my sword [*sergeants and above did not carry lances*] and I had my heart in my mouth I can tell you! I didn't like the look of that row of lances one little bit. We hadn't had time to form a proper line – none of that knee-to-knee stuff – but we were going a much stronger gallop than the Germans and we met the left half of their line with a fair old clash. The Colonel and Captain Reynolds were down though I didn't see it. I did get a glimpse of two horses colliding and rearing up (I learned later this was Sgt Major Durant who was badly wounded as he lay on the ground). Then it was my turn. I made for a big German and I remember clearly thinking at the last moment: 'Come on, you're one of the Delhi Spearmen! [*the nickname of the 9th*]' Any road, he made a jab at me and I think he may have caught my horse. I certainly got him with my sword and fetched him out of the saddle.

Then there was a bit of a mêlée, horses neighing and a lot of yelling and shouting. The Germans soon galloped off towards the wood on our left and we galloped towards the village. I remember seeing Cpl Bolte run his lance right through a dismounted German who had his hands up and thinking that was a rather bad thing to do. Then suddenly I came to a sunken road with a six-foot drop. Somehow my horse scrambled down but as I turned to my right he came down on top of me. The next moment a German galloped along the lane and jabbed me in the back as he passed. I must have gone unconscious because the next thing I remember was being pulled out from under my horse by a youngster of 'B' Sqn called 'Cock' Warren and being put in a horse-ambulance with the Colonel, Capt. Reynolds, and four or five others.[5]

As the Germans retired to the north of the village, another squadron of *Dragoons* (the *4th Sqn*) made a bold attempt to ride down a dismounted flank guard of 18th Hussars, and was virtually wiped out in the process. By noon Moncel was firmly in British hands, and 2nd Cavalry Brigade was pressing on towards the Grand Morin. James Taylor was bumping his way back to the field dressing-station in the ambulance. He had helped to write a small paragraph in history, for the action at Moncel was the last lance-against-

---

[4] *2nd Squadron, 1st Guard Dragoon Regiment* of the *Guard Cavalry Division* (Richthofen). Their strength has been given variously between 70 and 120.
[5] 9th Lancers casualties at Moncel were 3 killed and 8 wounded.

lance charge in which any British cavalry regiment took part; and he was certainly the last British cavalryman to carry the scar of a lance-wound to his grave.

Only very rarely is it possible to match two opposing versions of a small action against each other. Apart from James Taylor's, there are five accounts of the charge at Moncel from the British side, including those of Colonel Campbell and of eye-witnesses like Frederic Coleman (see footnote on p. 14). The German account, as given in the history of the *1st Guard Dragoon Regiment*, is rather different, in both style and content:

> Major von Gayling forms the squadron into line and we move forward towards some haystacks. At that moment we suddenly see a mounted English squadron in a shallow dip. The blood quickens! Cavalry combat! There they sit in line, the English lancers, making no move, lances in their left hands, revolvers in their right [*sic*!].
>
> Why don't the English charge? Sitting there like that they have no chance. We cross two small ditches and then we are into them. There is a brief hand-to-hand fight, a mêlée of men and horses. A sergeant points his revolver but the bullet goes wide. The next moment horse and rider are down. Another lance-thrust tumbles an English lieutenant from the saddle. Several lancers throw themselves to the ground to escape from our relentless attack. Fallen horses, and riderless mounts, those of the Tommies who have been unhorsed. We shout 'Hurrah!' as the right wing of our squadron sweeps round to join the fight. The enemy gallops away in disorder. Pursuit! If we can drive them onto our other squadron, they are finished . . .

There follows a short note of the subsequent charge against the 18th

PLATE 21. *The 9th Lancers at Moncel, 7 September*

Hussars, and a list of casualties sustained by Gayling's squadron. These tell their own story.

8 September was a day of many decisions – and errors. That morning, all five cavalry brigades set off early. French's Operation Order No. 18 gave as his intention for the day's movement, 'to continue the pursuit in the direction of the Marne with the right of the Army on Nogent, attacking the enemy wherever met'. The main objective was the passage, by evening, of the Petit Morin, which would bring the BEF on a line about two miles south of the Marne. It was not a very ambitious target. And this is a convenient point to comment on the pace of the advance. [6]

Liddell Hart [7] has remarked upon its slowness, which in his view 'proved fatal to the chance of converting the German retreat into a disaster'. In part, this was due to the succession of river barriers which the Germans defended with great tenacity, even when the gap between *First* and *Second Armies* had opened up and the BEF and Franchet were opposed by little more than a thin cavalry screen. If proof were needed, it showed what could be achieved by the skilful use of machine-guns carefully sited to cover the river-crossings. But Liddell Hart goes on: 'In still greater part it was due to want of impulsion, and misguided direction. Sir John French seems to have had little faith in the prospect, and still less in his Allies' efforts. In consequence he trod on the brake rather than the accelerator.' The slowness of the advance is ascribed by Haig's chief of staff, Gough, to the fact that 'no attempt was made by GHQ to explain to the Corps and Divisional commanders the extraordinary opportunity now available for a decisive blow at the enemy'.

This last observation is naïve. Senior commanders should not need spoon-feeding. By 8 September it must have been clear that the Germans were pulling back fast. Although the weather was still hot, the men had not been subjected to exhausting marches, or to any pitched battles on the scale of, for example, Le Cateau. They were keen to push on, sensing – as their commanders seem not to have done – that a major victory was within their grasp. The main trouble lay on the right. Joe Clarke of the Connaughts was fed up. 'It was like travelling on a train that stopped at every station. We would do half a mile, then halt for an hour, and then move on for a bit. There was some shelling and machine-gun fire but nothing to worry about. I think we could have done a lot better.'

The truth was that one obsession had been replaced by another at GHQ. Whereas during the retreat the sole object had been to break off contact with the enemy by means of long marches day and night, so now the advance was governed by a determination to maintain a level alignment with Franchet's left wing and to avoid any risk of exposing either flank of the BEF. This was scarcely in keeping with either the spirit or the letter of French's Order of

[6]The average daily advances of the BEF were as follows: on the 6th, eleven miles; on the 7th, nine (including the crossing of the Grand Morin); on the 8th, ten (including the crossing of the Petit Morin); and on the 9th, seven (including the passage of the Marne).
[7]Liddell Hart: *History of the First World War*.

the Day. Furthermore, it seems that on the 8th neither Franchet nor French were aware of the gap that yawned in front of them. What is certain is that Allied caution on this day allowed Kluck to extricate the two remaining Corps of *First Army* and transfer them across the Marne to join the counter-attack on Maunoury's Sixth Army on the Ourcq.

None the less, by evening the BEF was safely across the Petit Morin and established on a line facing due north and within artillery range of the Marne, although by now all five cavalry brigades were actually *behind* the infantry. At 8.7 p.m. Joffre issued his Special Instruction No. 19 which drew attention to the fact that the right wing of the German Armies was now divided into two groups, separated by twenty miles and covered by only two cavalry divisions, four *Jäger* battalions and a hastily improvised force of all arms drawn from *5th Division* of *II Corps*. In the event, never was the chance of decisive victory so wantonly cast away.

It was a day of high drama on the German side. Early that morning Kluck recalled *IX* and *III Corps* – which, uncharacteristically, he had put under Bülow's command – and transferred them to his right flank. On this day he showed qualities of command which had been singularly lacking during the Allied retreat; for he was now convinced that not only could he simply hold Maunoury but that he could defeat him before a major breakthrough in the centre, and thus turn the Allied left wing. It was a calculated risk, and Kluck came very close to bringing it off. But he had reckoned without Bülow. More crucially, he had reckoned without Moltke.

At 7 a.m. on the 8th, Moltke sent Lt Col Hentsch on a second mission, this time to visit the HQ of all five Armies of the centre and right and bring back a clear idea of the situation. Why he picked so junior an officer (and one of the Intelligence rather than the Operations Section) has never been explained. More remarkably, Hentsch was given full powers (although no *written* instructions) to order, in the name of OHL, such movements *as he might decide on*[8] in order to co-ordinate the retreat 'should rearward movements have already been initiated'.

Hentsch drove first to *Fifth* and *Fourth Armies*. Here he found that there were no major problems, although it is likely that he felt it politic not to comment adversely, since these two Armies were commanded respectively by the Crown Prince and Grand Duke Albrecht of Württemberg. He went next to Châlons, where he met Hausen – as usual comfortably installed, and seemingly in command of the situation. That evening he arrived at the HQ of *Second Army*.

He found Bülow depressed and deeply anxious. He had never been by nature a very resolute character, but by now he seems to have convinced himself of impending disaster, and the agent of this conviction was the BEF as it advanced north into the gap. Neither he (nor Hentsch) knew – or troubled to find out – that Kluck was confident of inflicting a decisive defeat on Maunoury the following day.

There are so many conflicting versions of what now happened that it is

[8] Author's italics.

wiser to concentrate on the recorded views of the four men most closely involved (all, it should be said, had good reasons for establishing their own innocence).

Hentsch spent the night at Châlons. 'I discussed the situation thoroughly with General Bülow (and his chief staff officers). We weighed every possibility for avoiding a retreat. At 5.30 a.m. on 9 September, I examined the situation once again. After *First Army* had withdrawn *III* and *IX Corps* from the Marne to its right wing, there was no other possibility but to go back across the Marne at once.' Accordingly Hentsch set off without further delay to Kluck's HQ *'to order the retirement*[9] of *First Army* to the north-east'.

Bülow's version is subtly different, in that it put the onus for the retreat on Kluck. 'When early on the 9th September numerous enemy columns crossed the Marne . . . there was no doubt that the retreat of *First Army* was, for both tactical and strategical reasons, unavoidable, and that *Second Army* must also go back, in order not to have its right flank completely enveloped.' After ensuring in a message to OHL that the blame would lie with Kluck, Bülow ordered the retreat of *Second Army* at 1 p.m. on the 9th, and so informed his neighbour. There is no record of Kluck's immediate reaction.

Hentsch now motored on to *First Army* HQ (the sixty-mile journey took him seven hours because of 'panic behind the lines'), and arrived there at 12.30 p.m. Kluck was not available, so Hentsch had a long conference with his chief of staff, Kuhl. If Hentsch's own account is to be believed, he conducted himself with startling arrogance. After outlining the general situation along the whole front in the gloomiest terms – '*Second Army* is a mere remnant; the decision for its retreat behind the Marne cannot be altered' – he gave Kuhl his orders. '*First Army* must also retire – direction Soissons–Fère-en-Tardenois; and if absolutely necessary, still further, even as far as the line Laon–la Fère.'

Kuhl protested that *First Army* was already engaged in a major attack on Maunoury with every promise of success. Hentsch would not be budged. And so, according to Kuhl, orders for the retreat were issued at 2 p.m.[10] They were signed by him. Kluck seems not to have been consulted or even informed.

Moltke had one shot left in his locker. On 10 September he again put Kluck under Bülow's orders. That evening Bülow gave Kluck his instructions: '*First Army* on 11th September will retire behind the Aisne and, covered by the Aisne valley, *will close on the right*[11] of *Second Army*.'

The German withdrawal had become a full-scale retreat.

While Hentsch was busy 'commanding' the German Armies of the right on 9 September, OHL was given a sharp reminder of danger from another quarter.

[9] Author's italics.
[10] Hentsch later gave evidence, not challenged by Kluck, that the order to retreat had been given an hour *before* he reached *First Army* HQ.
[11] Author's italics.

Shortly after the Allied Armies began their advance, the Belgians in Antwerp learned that *IX Reserve Corps* and *6th Division* of *III Reserve Corps* (which Kluck had left behind to invest the fortress) were about to be replaced by *Landwehr* troops (as Schlieffen had originally intended) and transferred south to the main battlefield.[12] Accordingly King Albert ordered a second sortie in strength on the morning of the 9th. This operation had an immediate, if limited, success, for the Belgians recaptured Aerschot – scene of the first German atrocities – and even penetrated as far as Louvain, which had been sacked with clinical efficiency by *IX Reserve Corps* in August.

Always sensitive to the threat from Antwerp, OHL at once recalled *6th Division* (permanently), and also *IX Reserve Corps*. It went even further, for it also detrained *30th Division* of *XV Corps*, which was in transit from Alsace by way of Brussels.

This startled German reaction was considerably greater than the Belgians had expected, and on 13 September they withdrew inside the defensive perimeter of Antwerp. On such slender threads hang the fortunes of war; for had the Belgians managed to keep the Germans involved even for one more day, *IX Reserve Corps* and *XV Corps* would have reached the Aisne too late to fill the gaps.

In the event *IX Reserve Corps* was sent to Kluck's extreme right wing, where it helped to block Maunoury's outflanking movement. *XV Corps* became the nucleus of a new *Seventh Army*. To it were added *XII Corps* – transferred from Hausen – and *VII Reserve Corps*, which, released by the fall of Maubeuge on the 7th, arrived on the Chemin des Dames *just two hours* before Haig's I Corps could establish itself on the commanding heights north of the Aisne.

The Marne forms a wide arc from its source between Dijon and Langres to its confluence with the Seine just south of Paris. It flows for the most part through a wide valley dominated, like so many rivers in this part of France, by hills and by escarpments on its right bank. It was the one river common to all the Armies of both the Allied and German west flanks, and it is from this fact that the 'battle' takes its name. Had it not been for Moltke and Bülow, and the contagion which spread outward from their conviction of impending disaster, it could have provided a formidable defensive line; and in September 1914 history had not finished with the Marne.

From its source the river runs north-west to Vitry (Joffre's original HQ) and Châlons. Here it turns due west to Epernay and Château Thierry, and then follows a winding valley past Azy, Nogent, Charly, la Ferté-sous-Jouarre, Changis to a point just south of Lizy where it is joined by the Ourcq. Here it turns south-west to Meaux, and thence through open country to the Seine. It was Bülow's decision – after or even before Hentsch's visit – to pull back *Second Army* on either side of Epernay (thus

---

[12] There is no doubt that the absence of these formations contributed significantly to Kluck's problems on the Marne and the Ourcq.

dragging Hausen back on his left from Châlons), and Kluck's hurried recall of his *IX* and *III Corps* from south of the river on the 8th, which opened up the vital gap between Château Thierry and Lizy. It is an interesting footnote to this first phase of the war that the BEF's retreat followed a line *west* of the Ourcq, crossing the Marne downstream at Meaux, while the subsequent advance moved parallel to the retreat on the *east* bank of the Ourcq. It was not until 12 September that the BEF found itself on familiar ground near Soissons on the Aisne.

On the 8th the Allies were unaware of the crisis of confidence on the other side of the hill, although, as we have seen, Joffre's Special Instruction that evening confirmed the existence of the gap, although not yet the reason for it or the true significance of it. The BEF spent that night just south of the Marne, aligned with and in close contact with Franchet on its right and Maunoury on its left.

If it is possible to identify the most important of the several lost opportunities, it was here. Maunoury was locked in battle with *First Army* on the Ourcq, but the road lay open in front of the BEF and of Franchet's XVIII Corps at Château Thierry. Facing them were two tired cavalry divisions and a composite brigade hastily improvised from Kluck's *IX Corps*, thinly distributed. In the precipitate German withdrawal on the 8th, orders to blow all bridges across the Marne had been ignored, and only those at la Ferté and farther west had been destroyed (in the event, this was to delay Pulteney's III Corps on the left for over twelve hours). *But the road remained open*. The chance was lost – the chance to fall upon Kluck's rear and Bülow's right flank. It was an opportunity which would not present itself again. And the cautious advance north-east to the Aisne was, in Galliéni's phrase, 'always one corps too few and one day too late'.

Sir John French's Operation Order No. 19 issued at 7.30 on the 8th at Melun (GHQ moved to Coulommiers the following morning) reported the retirement of the enemy to the north and gave instructions for the advance to continue. There was no mention of the Marne, or of any general objective beyond a clear inference that the BEF should maintain strict alignment with the French on both flanks. The phrase 'press on regardless' was not in GHQ's canon, and while the pace of the advance was hampered by the thick woods on the north bank of the river and by sporadic rearguard actions, there was no attempt to exploit the enemy's disarray, and indeed the BEF had mixed fortunes on the 9th.

I Corps and II Corps bivouacked for the night little more than five miles north of the river, with the Cavalry Division and 5th Cavalry Brigade a mile to their *rear*. The idea of a night march or a night attack in concert with Franchet's XVIII Corps at Château Thierry seems not to have been considered, much to Kluck's relief.

III Corps on the left on either side of la Ferté-sous-Jouarre fared worse, for here the Germans had destroyed the road bridges and offered more serious resistance, especially by heavy artillery well sited on the high ground to the north. At this point the river is some eighty yards wide, and throughout the day the Royal Engineers worked with great skill and gallantry under constant fire. Eventually the passage was forced by way of the railway bridge two miles upstream at Chamigny, and 1/East Lancs and 1/Hampshires of 11th Infantry Brigade were ferried across by boat a mile to the west of the town. Charlie Watts did not enjoy the experience. 'We felt pretty naked, I can tell you, with shells plopping around us in the water and bullets whizzing about. Luckily we didn't have more than half a dozen casualties and we were relieved to reach the far bank and scuttle for cover. The sappers who took us over were great, cool as cucumbers seeing that they had to make the trip several times.'

None the less, by nightfall on the 9th more than half the infantry of III Corps was still south of the river. So was 3rd Cavalry Brigade.

Farther east, on the morning of the 9th, the Cavalry Division found the bridges at Azy, Nogent and Charly intact, and by 6 a.m. 1st and 4th Brigades had moved forward three miles, collecting some prisoners as they went. They were followed an hour later by 1st Division at Nogent and 2nd Division at Charly, and by noon the whole of I Corps was firmly established on the high ground to the north of the river. The passage of the Marne on the right flank had been virtually without incident, but when at 1 p.m. air reconaissance reported large bodies of German troops moving north-west from Château Thierry across Haig's front, and little more than a mile away from his advanced guards,[13] the order was given to I Corps and the Cavalry Division to halt. It was an inexplicable decision, for it was neither 'vigorous pursuit' nor 'attacking the enemy wherever met'. I Corps did not resume its advance until 3 p.m., and by then the chance had gone. The Germans were becoming as adept at 'slipping away' as the British had been. And equally fortunate.

II Corps, in the centre, also found the bridges at Nanteuil and Saacy intact and unprotected. 3rd Division was first across, with 9th Infantry Brigade leading, and by 10 a.m. was established on the high ground at Bezu two and a half miles north of the river, while 5th Division headed for Montreuil on the main road from Château Thierry to Lizy. There is no doubt that by now II Corps considered itself the fighting-cock of the BEF, and not without reason. It had borne the brunt of the fighting at Mons and Le Cateau, and up to 9 September had sustained over half the total of British casualties, especially among its officers and NCOs. By the time the advance began many of the gaps in its ranks had been filled, but it was still short of artillery and transport. None the less, it had acquired a splendid superiority complex, and it is at least arguable that this was largely due to the leadership of Smith-Dorrien. He had already become something of a legend, and his men loved him, which is more than could be said of their opinion of some of the directors; indeed – and one can only speculate – had he been in the driving seat (the word is explicit) at GHQ, the German retreat across the Marne would almost certainly have become a rout.

[13] *17th Division of IX Corps and 5th Cavalry Division of Richthofen's I Cavalry Corps.*

Thoroughbreds are not amenable to being ridden on too tight a rein.

None the less, II Corps had its problems on the 9th, for, advancing through thickly wooded country, it bumped into the composite brigade which Kluck had hastily cobbled together in the area of Montreuil. [14] The German artillery was particularly troublesome in front of 5th Division, and 14th Infantry Brigade could make only slow progress while its own divisional artillery searched the wooded area to its front.

Two men had rather different experiences this morning. Paddy Kett, Irish of the Irish, had his one and only chance to put his lance to good use.

> About 9 a.m. I was what we called the 'leading point' with a man named Macardy (who was killed at Ypres) when we bumped into a Uhlan on a country lane. He turned and made a bolt for it but he could hardly raise a canter and I soon caught up with him and stuck him between the shoulder-blades. I must have hit something pretty solid because I remember there was a terrific jar that nearly broke my wrist and as he went down he nearly pulled me out of the saddle with him.

Walter Wildgoose, Yorkshireman and English of the English, of 1/Lincolns had something else to write home about. About 11 a.m., when the German artillery was making life difficult for the leading battalions of 5th Division, General Shaw [15] sent two companies of the Lincolns to the west of Bezu to silence a particularly troublesome battery. Pte Wildgoose takes up the story.

> We worked our way up through the woods until we were not much more than 100 yards from their guns – so close, in fact, that we could hear the Germans talking. Then we opened up with everything and within a couple of minutes we had wiped them out, every man jack. Of course we then rushed forward but as we did so our own guns [65th Battery] opened up and caught us fair and square. I suppose they imagined we were Germans running away, but we lost twenty or thirty officers and men before we could get back under cover. And I'll tell you something interesting. The night before Mons we had been billeted in a convent. The Mother Superior had asked me to give her my cap badge and in return she gave me a rosary which I wore from then on. When we were running back for cover, one of our own shells landed no more than a yard from me. It was a dud and didn't go off. How I bless that rosary!

By dusk, Smith-Dorrien notwithstanding, II Corps had halted on a line east and west through Bezu and Montreuil, and extending Haig's left flank. By then, unknown to GHQ, Hentsch had completed his mission and the German right wing – indeed, the whole German line – was in full retreat.

---

[14] Two infantry regiments and six artillery batteries of *IX Corps*.
[15] Commander of 9th Infantry Brigade, 3rd Division.

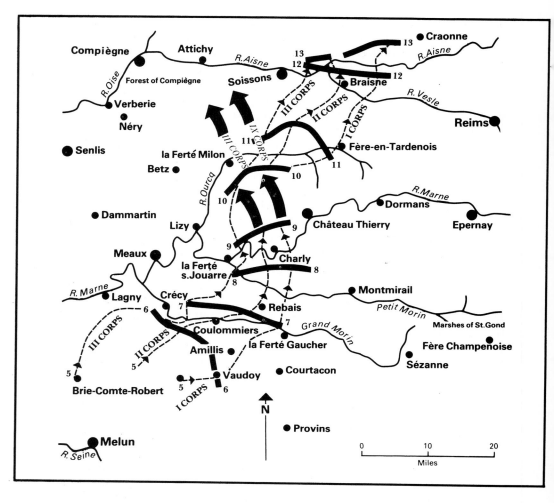

MAP 7. *The advance to the Aisne showing daily lines reached*

III Corps met greater resistance on the 9th, for its approach march brought it into contact with Kluck's rearguards on the Marne between la Ferté and Lizy-sur-Ourcq. The river here winds west through a broad valley, and the crossing-places could be enfiladed on both sides and also from the north bank. Here too all the bridges except the viaduct at Chamigny had been destroyed.

Most of the morning was spent in hazardous reconnaissance by the Royal Engineers while the divisional artillery unlimbered on the spur to the east of la Ferté and bombarded the German positions on the far bank. Frank Pusey with 31st (Howitzer) Battery had a grandstand seat.

We were on a spur that overlooked la Ferté and could see German shells falling on the town. Pretty heavy stuff it looked, but not all that much of it. Obviously they were trying to make things hot down there

162

on the river because they didn't answer back when we opened up. From the battery O.P. where I was, we could see our sappers working away near the bridge which the Germans had blown up, and during the afternoon they had managed to complete a pontoon bridge. It was a very brave piece of work. Shortly afterwards the column to which our Brigade was attached crossed the river farther up by a railway bridge at Chamigny, a very bumpy ride as the nearside wheels of the vehicles had to run over the railway sleepers.

By evening the French had occupied Château Thierry and air reconnaissance reported that all roads to the north-east of Lizy were full of marching columns of the enemy. Had the whole BEF succeeded in reaching the line of the main Château Thierry–Lizy road (which 9th Infantry Brigade had occupied during the morning) by noon and then pressed northward without the excessive caution which had marked the whole advance, it is extremely unlikely that Kluck would have escaped. But he did; and by midnight the battle of the Marne, the battle of lost opportunities, was over. All along the 100-mile front from Verdun to the Ourcq the German Armies were in retreat. The race was still on, the right-wing gap was still open, ahead lay the Aisne, the last great natural barrier. For both sides one factor dominated all others: time.

On 10 September the weather broke. It was a cruel twist of fortune after days of hot sunshine, for with the rain many roads soon became virtually impassable, and this effectively slowed the pace of the advance. The official History describes the movements of 10 and 11 September as 'the pursuit', but this is somewhat exaggerated. On the British right, Franchet – and

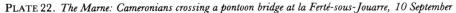

PLATE 22. *The Marne: Cameronians crossing a pontoon bridge at la Ferté-sous-Jouarre, 10 September*

especially Conneau's cavalry – was making steady progress and finding little opposition from *Second Army* as Bülow hastened to retreat behind the Aisne (the gap between Bülow and Kluck was still some fifteen miles wide, but as the axis of the retreat shifted east of north, it was now opposite Franchet's left wing.) On the 10th, however, the British advance was barely ten miles, with III Corps, after being delayed on the Marne, lagging behind the left flank. There were a number of rearguard actions, chiefly on the front of 2nd Infantry Brigade, but British casualties this day were fewer than 350, and more than 1,500 enemy prisoners were taken. Smith-Dorrien must have noted with satisfaction the other side of a coin he already knew well – the abandoned vehicles and equipment, the stragglers, the debris of an army in retreat. The evidence was not lost on his equally gratified men.

So, throughout a day of steady downpour, the BEF marched north and bivouacked for the night on a line three miles from the valley of the upper Ourcq, the Cavalry Division in touch with Conneau near Fère-en-Tardenois.

Joffre was in a hurry. His eyes were fixed not on the Aisne but farther north, on Laon and la Fère, on the open country where he could fight the decisive battle. He thus directed Maunoury on Soissons, and on an enveloping movement towards Noyon. To make room for Sixth Army, the BEF accordingly was inclined to the north-east, and in the process was allotted so narrow a front that there was considerable congestion on the few available roads; and still it rained ceaselessly.

French's orders for the 11th confirmed the change of direction and gave as the day's main objective the crossing of the Ourcq. Throughout this day the BEF met no opposition – a novel experience, and one with important implications which neither Joffre nor French seem to have grasped; for it meant that Kluck had succeeded in disengaging, and in so doing winning time to secure the high ground overlooking the Aisne and the opportunity to make his defensive preparations there. Joffre's Special Instruction No. 23 dated 12 September and French's Operation Order of the same day spoke only of 'pursuit' in the direction of Laon and la Fère, well to the north of the Aisne, with Franchet pressing forward on the right and Maunoury heading for Soissons, with his left swinging wide in a movement round Kluck's right wing at Noyon on the Oise. But the 11th and 12th were days of heavy cloud and no reconnaissance flights were possible. They would have provided food for thought, for they would have shown significant concentrations of German troops in the Laon area and columns moving south towards the Chemin des Dames. This was Heeringen's new *Seventh Army*[16] and *VII Reserve Corps* which, released by the fall of Maubeuge on the 7th, and after a forced march of forty miles in twenty-four hours, was hastening to fill the gap which still lay between Bülow and Kluck. The clock ticked on.

By midnight on the 12th the BEF had crossed the Vesle – a tributary of the Aisne – with little opposition, and lay facing slightly north-east, with its right three miles south of Bourg and one brigade of III Corps already

[16] *Seventh Army* was put under Bülow's command on 12 September.

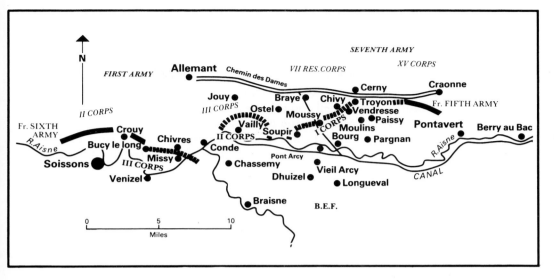

MAP 8. *The Aisne*

across the river near Bucy-le-Long, two miles east of Soissons. The scene
was set for the battle of the Aisne.

The Aisne battlefield (see Map 8) may best be likened to a hand with fingers
extended. The back of the hand is a high ridge running from Craonne in the
east to a point north of Soissons on the road to Laon, and traversed along its
length by the Chemin des Dames, which lies parallel to and about four miles
above the river. From here a series of sharp spurs, cut into by deep valleys,
run down towards the Aisne. There are seven main such 'fingers':
Paissy/Pargnan; Vendresse/Bourg; Chivy; Chavonne/Soupir; Vailly;
Chivres/Missy; Allemant/Bucy-le-Long. Across the valley the ground rises
again, although less sharply, and is cut through by the river Vesle which
meets the Aisne two miles east of Missy.

The Chemin des Dames ridge is a defensive position of exceptional
strength. As we shall see, the BEF came within hours of capturing it, and so
breaking through to the open country beyond. Both Franchet and
Maunoury could, before the Germans filled the gaps, have outflanked it. As
it was, the British line, throughout three weeks of stalemate, was one of the
most hazardous and improbable that any army has ever occupied.

The Aisne is a largely forgotten battle. This is very strange, for it was the
first 'situation' battle of the war, the first demonstration of the dominance of
defence over attack, the first indication of the role which artillery was to play
in a static confrontation, and the birthplace of trench warfare. After the
Aisne, both sides made one last attempt to exploit the only area left for
manœuvre, between the Oise and the sea. After the Aisne, only one
certainty remained: the war would last for a very long time indeed.

Statistics are often more revealing than their detractors would have

165

us believe. By 16 September[17] the strength of the BEF had grown to 163,897.[18] Between 12 September and the start of the transfer of the Army to Flanders on 3 October, casualties were 18,922. A larger proportion of this total was made up not from the cost of set-piece attacks, but by the daily wastage – like water dripping on a stone – from constant shelling, sniping, local patrol actions and occasional periods of frenzied activity. In such a situation a single shell could have fearful consequences. One such, falling on a farmyard south of the river at Longueval on 29 September, killed and wounded 39 officers and men of the 9th Lancers[19]. And a salvo from a British howitzer battery on the same day caused 83 German casualties near Courteçon.

Something else happened on the Aisne. Over the three weeks a new attitude to the war became apparent. Gone was the romantic ideal, the sense – even in retreat – of adventure. It is not easy for even the most stoical of men to enjoy living in waterlogged holes in the ground, pounded by shells and scraping up the remnants of shattered bodies. The spirit remained, because it was a very spirited old Army. But the humour had a bitter ring to it. 'I decided one morning to make a "book"', said Ted Henson of the Lincolns. 'Which of us would last another week? I couldn't get better than 10 to 1.' No underwriter would have accepted such odds.

14th September was to be the day of battle.[20] On the 13th, the BEF had advanced into the valley of the Aisne, its immediate objective the capture of the Chemin des Dames ridge and beyond that the line Laon–la Fère. 'The prospects of a break-through never were brighter than on this morning.'[21] This may have been true at the time, but certainly not in retrospect. The gap remained, partly opposite Franchet and partly in front of the BEF. Indeed, on the 13th Conneau's cavalry on Haig's right crossed the river and rode on unopposed as far as Sissonne, level with Laon, which meant that they were fifteen miles beyond Bülow's flank and *forty* miles north of Hausen's *Third Army*. But then, frightened by their own success, they turned and rode back to the safety of XVIII Corps' protective screen at Berry-au-Bac. Franchet was not amused. 'Had my whole Army had four legs on which to advance and not two, I should have slept that night in Bülow's château.'

The official History is severely critical of the BEF on this crucial day – 'a failure of the High Command to appreciate the situation . . . the divisions made a rather cautious and leisurely advance . . . in GHQ orders there was no hint whatever of the importance of time.' For once this criticism is unjust. It was on the 11th and 12th that the damage had been done.

[17] On this day, 6th Infantry Division, much delayed by the transfer of the main base to St Nazaire, joined the BEF.
[18] By the end of the first battle of Ypres in November it had reached 224,647; and by the end of May 1915, 601,000.
[19] *History of the 9th Lancers, 1715-1936.*
[20] It was also the day on which Moltke was dismissed as Chief of Staff at OHL. His place was taken by Falkenhayn, the then Minister of War.
[21] *Official History*, Vol I.

Throughout the 13th the weather was appalling, with driving rain and a wintry wind from the north-east. The British front, as the BEF approached the Aisne, was fifteen miles wide, from Bourg to Venizel. On this stretch of the river there were ten main crossing-places, all dominated by the main ridge and by the spurs running south. Unlike the very different situation on the Marne, Kluck had succeeded in destroying or severely damaging every bridge (except that at Condé, which was left as a trap) and in deploying a considerable concentration of artillery on the northern side. It is a remarkable fact that, thanks to the ingenuity of junior commanders and the devoted work of the Royal Engineers, almost the entire BEF, cavalry and artillery included, succeeded in crossing the river in full view of the enemy by way of one aqueduct, five pontoon bridges, three buckled girders, eight wooden planks, six rafts and twelve small boats. Before dawn on the 14th, the line had been established thus, right to left: Cavalry Division, 1st Division and 5th Infantry Brigade on the spurs between Paissy and Verneuil; five miles to the west at Vauxelles, 8th and 9th Infantry Brigades of the inevitable 3rd Division; and, after another gap of three miles, almost the whole of 5th Division and 4th Division between Missy and Crouy. There remained south of the river only three infantry brigades and 3rd and 5th Cavalry Brigades. It was a sufficient force to seize and occupy the Chemin des Dames ridge. But was it – however small the margin – too late?

The Germans were well aware that the issue would be decided not in days but in hours. On the 13th, Kluck's left (*III Corps*) held the ridge to the east of Soissons. Between him and Bülow's *VII Corps* there was still a gap of fifteen miles, held by three weak and exhausted cavalry divisions and all the artillery that he could muster. That gap was the Chemin des Dames, the key to the Aisne, even the key to defeat or victory. With Maunoury pressing on towards the Oise, Kluck could not extend his line farther east. If salvation were to come before the British reached the Chemin des Dames, it must come from elsewhere. It did. It came from the north. And it came with very little time to spare.

Haig has been criticized for the last lost opportunity. His critics should spend an hour on the Chemin des Dames (they should also spend another hour at Thiepval on the Somme); they should talk to some of the men who in both battles had to fight their way uphill; and they should remember that the Germans were very formidable opponents. Even then, during the bloody day of 14 September, the BEF came within yards of victory.

To fill the gap, OHL had created Heeringen's new *Seventh Army* which, as we have seen, was disrupted by the Belgian sortie from Antwerp. This Army, which for all immediate purposes consisted of *XV Corps* and *VII Reserve Corps*, was placed under the command of Bülow,[22] in whom Moltke seems to have had a touching faith scarcely justified by earlier events. *XV Corps* was directed south-east to counter the advance of Franchet's left

---

[22] Kluck had already been subordinated once more to Bülow. As before, he ignored or disobeyed all orders from that quarter.

wing. Thus it is with *VII Reserve Corps* that we are chiefly concerned.

This corps, commanded by Zwehl, had been released by the surrender of Maubeuge on the 7th. At first Moltke seems not to have known how or where to employ it, but on the morning of the 12th, as the British reached the Aisne opposite the gap which still separated Bülow and Kluck, Zwehl was ordered to make a forced march to Laon. He arrived there early on the 13th, having covered forty miles in twenty-four hours, during which one man in four had fallen out. After a rest of only three hours he pushed on towards Chavonne; but at 11 a.m. he received instructions to turn southeast to Berry-au-Bac on the French front. Zwehl, unlike Kluck, was a man who obeyed orders, but – and his decision was to cost the BEF dear – he felt himself too far committed already, and so ignored Bülow's cry for help. Had he not done so Haig and Allenby would have secured the unprotected Chemin des Dames ridge, and the road to Laon would have been open. Instead, *VII Reserve Corps* reached the Chemin des Dames on either side of Cerny at 2 p.m. At 4 p.m. 1st Division was less than two miles away. It had been a close-run thing.

The bitter fighting on 14 September – the real battle of the Aisne – raged along the entire front of the BEF. In fact, there were four distinct battles: Troyon, Verneuil, Soupir and Chivres. Of these Troyon was the most successful, and also the most bloody. By that night the BEF occupied an extraordinary line running from the Chemin des Dames on the right and then south-west over the succession of spurs and across the valleys to Missy on the river bank, and thence to Crouy two miles north-east of Soissons (see Map 8). Despite repeated attacks and counter-attacks this hazardous line remained virtually unchanged throughout the next three weeks.[23] At the end an entirely new concept of warfare had developed out of stalemate; and on 3 October the BEF began to move north to a very different kind of stage where a new name was to dominate all others: Ypres.

There is a repetitive character about the fighting on the Aisne. This does not imply inactivity or any lack of savagery. On the contrary, it was a battle of attrition, dominated by artillery and by bloody hand-to-hand fighting. None the less, the story can best be told by concentrating on two very different aspects of the battle at opposite ends of the line, each seen through very different eyes.

First Troyon. The morning of 14 September was wet and misty. Haig's immediate objective was the Chemin des Dames. He was not aware that the ridge had been occupied and already entrenched by Zwehl's *VII Reserve Corps*.

2nd Infantry Brigade[24] set off at dawn from Moulins and marched to Vendresse. Here the three leading battalions climbed the ridge to their right

---

[23] 6th Infantry Division reached the Aisne on 16 September. Instead of joining III Corps, its three brigades (16th, 17th and 18th) were attached separately to the three Army Corps.
[24] 2/Royal Sussex, 1/Loyal North Lancs, 1/Northamptons, 2/KRRC.

and deployed thus, right to left: Northamptons, KRRC, Royal Sussex. Beyond the Northamptons was 1/Coldstream, detached from 1st (Guards) Brigade. Two hours later the remaining three battalions of this brigade reached Vendresse and moved on up the left-hand spur towards Cerny. During the forenoon 3rd Infantry Brigade reached the head of the valley as Divisional reserve.

The objective of 2nd Infantry Brigade was the sugar-factory at the cross-roads north of Troyon. Here the Germans had established a strong position with many machine-guns, two batteries of artillery, and trenches which enfiladed the approaches on either side of the factory. Farther to the rear was a formidable battery of 8-inch howitzers which far outgunned 116th Battery, deployed on the plateau near Paissy (this battery actually found itself in front of the infantry positions during the battle).

First into action were the Royal Sussex, who attacked the German trenches on the Chivy road. Here is Pte Pelling's diary:

> On reaching a village we were ordered to open out in Artillery formation (something we had practiced a good deal at home) and advanced up the hill. Half way up the Germans gave us all they had got. All those troops who used to turn out on Sundays in their Reds and Bands were now lying on the ground killed, badly wounded, or wounded, though a lot of course survived. I think I escaped by being well forward, the shells and bullets going over and beyond. We lost a lot of people we have had as pals for so long . . . One shocking sight was a field gun drawn by six horses, and with a boy trumpeter, being bowled over by a direct hit and rolling over and over like a big toy.

PLATE 23. *Troyon. 'We attacked up the slope.' View from the old sugar factory on the Chemin des Dames*

During the morning the Royal Sussex lost 9 officers and 255 rank and file. Later in the day the battalion actually reached the factory, where its machine-gun section under Lt Dashwood did great execution to the German batteries, and to their infantry east of the cross-roads. Indeed, when the latter decided to surrender they were summarily dealt with by their own guns.

Towards noon the Loyals were sent up in support of the attack. Let Pte Sam Owen tell his story – and that of the days that followed. His account has the quality of understatement and good humour which are the hallmark of so many men of the old Army:

> On the morning of the 14th we were marching up a road which the Germans had under fire. I was with a party under my Company officer, Capt. Body, who was aside of me most of the time. We attacked up the slope and things were rather hot as the Germans were firing their field guns down the slope. I looked back but could not see the Capt. I think that a shell must have hit him and blew him to pieces as we never found a trace of him. We took the position and settled down for the night. [25]
>
> We were in full view of the sugar factory. I went out there and helped a wounded man back to a dressing-station. When I got back to the line I reported to Capt. Allison. . . . In the morning Capt. Allison said that Mr Carew and him was going to the mess-cart to get something to eat, but they were unfortunate. A shell dropped by the mess-cart and killed both of them. They were very much liked by the troops.
>
> We sorted ourselves out [*the old phrase again*] and rejoined our Companies the next morning. It was a bit hot as the enemy was enfilading us from his trench. We were working hard to improve our own trench when a shell landed on top and buried Sgt Cawthorne and myself. They dug us out and carried us down to a cave and laid us on some straw. The M.O. (who was a real pig) came to look at us but never attempted to see what injuries we had sustained. So we decided to get back to the trenches. I told the Company officer we may as well get killed in the trenches as starve in a cave. He asked if I still had my hair-cutting tools as the men looked like a lot of French prostitutes, so I used what time I could in making them tidy.
>
> After a few days a Regt [1/*East Yorks*] came to relieve us. They looked very clean and smart, as they had only just arrived, and they were a bit cocky. A little later Jerry attacked their trenches and we had to go back and regain the position. The new lot didn't have much to say! . . .
>
> Eventually we were relieved by the French and went off to Ypres. Things had been fairly quiet until the French arrived, but they made so much noise that Jerry thought we were going to attack. It was the French that caught it and had a lot of casualties.

[25] 'Settled down for the night.' The Loyals' casualties at Troyon were 14 officers and 514 rank and file.

PLATE 24. *The Aisne at Missy*

Sam Owen thus took his leave of Troyon. He had contributed to a desperate battle which had come close to being a decisive victory. He had been an old soldier when he came to France. He was now also a wiser one.

Away to the south-west on the river bank, a very different kind of battle had been joined. Here the East Surreys and the Manchesters had crossed to Ste Marguerite by raft. Lt Roupell's diary provides a vivid picture of the fighting here and at Missy during the next few days. It is not least interesting for its candour, its often unconventional comments, its sadness and its humour. It is not surprising that such a man was to win the Victoria Cross six months later.

George Roupell's story is best told in a series of verbal snapshots, but these cannot properly convey the constant mental and physical strain to which he and his men were subjected. Not all were able to stand that strain. To them George Roupell shows both compassion and criticism.

First, let us set the scene. 14th Infantry Brigade crossed the Aisne opposite the villages of Ste Marguerite and Missy. Less than half a mile in front of them lay the dominating spur of Chivres (George Roupell's 'hill'), which overlooked the river and which guarded any further advance to the Chemin des Dames. It was heavily protected by infantry and artillery, and it was to torment the East Surreys for three melancholy weeks. It was never captured. George Roupell's camera begins to record:

> We crossed by a board raft with a rope attached which was pulled backwards and forwards like a ferry boat. It only held about fifteen men, but company by company we moved across, rather surprised that we hadn't been shelled.

The Colonel's idea was to get to the hill before night and hope for the

PLATE 25. *Missy: the Chivres spur, only 350 yards above the village*

best in the morning [*the 14th*]. Some hope! It was a nasty position; we were on top of the ridge without any idea where the enemy were.

By morning the battalion had been forced to retire to Missy.

The range from the hill was only 350 yards and we couldn't see the enemy on account of the trees. It seemed a cheery prospect and I suppose if I hadn't got into such a fixed state of mind, I should have pointed out various difficulties or else burst into tears and refused to move! Fortunately I did neither.

There were other problems. His Company commander, for example.

T's nerves were getting terribly bad at this time and I was practically assuming command of the company, but his presence made things difficult and it was a very bad time for the men.

Each entry underlines the growing strain; and each records, almost laconically, the steady drain from casualties; an artillery shell here, a sniper's bullet there.

Since our fight at Mons on August 23rd we had not had a single day's rest. When we were not fighting, we were marching as hard as we could. Men were physically weak from the long marches and mentally weak from the continual strain of never being out of reach of the enemy's guns. . . . It is scarcely surprising that under these conditions traces of panic and of loss of self-control appeared.

Then a slightly uncharacteristic, rather Victorian comment:

172

It is on these occasions (and it always will be as long as the same type of officer is obtained) that the officer stands out so far above the NCO and man. . . . The few remaining officers did *everything*. NCO's were there but could not be relied on to do anything but the most simple and unmistakeable directions. . . . The NCOs and men were all brave enough, but the strain by now destroyed all their initiative.

It is a view that many other officers would not have shared; and many men would have had their own views about some of their officers. One man, George Roupell's CSM, Woolger, killed by a random shell on the 16th, was beyond criticism:

He looked after the men well and kept up strict discipline at a time when discipline was very liable to become slack. He and I used to compare the men's conduct on active service and under fire with what it had been in peacetime. On the whole one had judged pretty accurately what men would do well in a scrap. As far as I was concerned, Sitch was my only mistake. Woolger was right about him. In peacetime he had been before me time after time for petty crimes; very seldom anything but a series of rotten little offences that one got very tired of: laughing on parade, talking and not paying attention on parade, dirty, etc. On active service he turned out first-rate. He was always cheery, never lost his head, and was a man I could rely on to do any job he was told to do. He was a typical casual cockney and always saw the bright side of everything, an invaluable man in the company.

Life was not all grey and humourless. Thus there was convened a rather unusual court-martial at Missy on 19 September, where George Roupell found himself the defending officer. The accused was alleged – and he was not alone – of having 'absented himself from duty' (a euphemism for desertion).

The court was convened in a small house next door to the church, a favourite target of one of the German heavy batteries at Chivres. Witnesses were duly called; but it was a godless little house, for it contained no bible. Undaunted, Lt Roupell administered the oath on a handsomely bound French cookery book. And when the Germans fired off their periodic salvoes, the court duly adjourned until the noise subsided. The court-martial lasted six hours. The accused, rather fancying a long period of detention far away from the firing-line, was sentenced to be returned to the most exposed and perilous trenches. It was not the defending officer's finest forensic triumph.

So – twenty miles apart – two different men lived out their different weeks on the Aisne.

Change of Scene: An Interlude

Towards the end of September, both sides realized that they had reached a situation of stalemate on the Aisne. [1] The Allies had failed to make the vital breakthrough towards Laon, and the Germans, despite massive attacks on the 24th and 25th, had been unable to dislodge the BEF from its precarious position between the river and the Chemin des Dames. 'Given forces fairly equally matched,' wrote Sir John French later, 'you can "bend" but you cannot "break" your enemy's trench line.' This was to remain true for four long years: at 'first Ypres'; at 'second Ypres'; at Loos; at Aubers; on the Somme; at Verdun; at Passchendaele; even in Ludendorff's final offensives of 1918. When, in August of that year, Haig succeeded where others had failed, fresh factors had arisen to confound the truth of French's view. 'I don't think the war ended,' said a veteran. 'I think it just died of old age.'

Both sides had their problems, not least of which was a growing shortage of artillery ammunition for which neither had catered. Incredibly, they were also faced by a shortage of men. Both Schlieffen and Plan XVII had assumed a short and comprehensive victory. Kitchener's accurate assessment of a long war was only too right, but it would take time to raise a citizen army adequately trained and equipped to match the challenge. In September – still adamant that his 14 Territorial divisions and 14 Yeomanry brigades were not competent to take the field – he had at his disposal fewer than 250,000 men.

At OHL a new mind was at work. Falkenhayn was not a Kaiser's toady; nor was he interested in the princely standing of some of his Army commanders. [2] He was concerned in achieving the victory which Moltke had wantonly cast away.

That victory was not to be won on the Moselle, or on the centre of his front, although he kept his eyes fixed on Verdun. If it was to be won before winter, and while he still had freedom of manœuvre, then the one empty battleground lay to the north between the Oise and the coast; and to this proposition he now addressed himself.

---

[1] Between 16 September and 1 October GHQ issued no daily Operation Orders.
[2] In fact, Prince Rupprecht and Grand Duke Albrecht were to command *Sixth* and *Fourth Armies* at Ypres.

So did Joffre. If he could not break through on the Aisne, then his answer lay in a wide outflanking movement north of Maunoury's Sixth Army opposite Noyon. Perhaps at Bapaume. Perhaps at Arras. Perhaps at Lille. And always – especially at OHL – there was the thorn in the German side: Antwerp.

Thus there began the series of attempts to envelop the open west flanks of both armies. It has been called 'the race to the sea'. That was not the original intention of either Joffre or Falkenhayn. Both sought a decision long before reaching the Flanders plain. But the sea was of special interest to a third party: the British. And the British now intervened.

French was concerned. As he watched the growing movement to extend the line farther north he saw the BEF becoming a mere adjunct to Joffre's plan, a kind of solid hinge on which GQG could swing either a defensive gate or a battering-ram. And that if Joffre failed, the BEF would once again be called upon to bail him out. He also knew – and this was to prove a trump card – that Kitchener and his co-directors in London were planning a combined operation designed to secure Antwerp from German attack and turn Falkenhayn's right flank by a major sea-borne landing on the coast. Almost for the first time (and French may be forgiven for reminding the War Cabinet of his advocacy of the Antwerp project as far back as 5 August), the British realized that a great naval power can exercise equally great military pressure.

On 27 September, Churchill visited French at Fère-en-Tardenois. French described the occasion thus:

> My friend Winston Churchill paid me a visit (when) we first discussed together the advisability of joint action by the Army and Navy. It was then that we sketched out plans for an offensive with one flank towards the sea which, although the (later) fall of Antwerp effected a drastic change in the conditions, were the same in principle as those which took substantial shape and form. [3]

Neither French's diary nor Churchill's papers elaborate upon this meeting; but from it were to be born the Antwerp disaster, the transfer of the BEF, and the first battle of Ypres. Neither man has any responsibility for the fall of Antwerp, which by 1 October had become a lost cause. It is to the lasting credit of Sir John French that he saw the true danger; that he persuaded Joffre; and that by saving the Channel ports he averted a crisis even greater than that which Joffre had faced at the gates of Paris. The price was the virtual destruction of the old Regular Army.

On 29 September, French addressed himself to Joffre. His note expressed his wish 'to regain my original position on the left flank of the French Armies' (a wish for which Henry Wilson later took an entirely unsubstantiated credit).

[3] French: *1914*.

> Now that the position of affairs has become clearly defined and that the immediate future can be forecasted with some confidence [*bold words indeed*], I wish to press the proposal with all the power and insistence which are at my disposal.[4]

French then went on to tell Joffre of the imminent arrival of 7th Infantry Division, 3rd Cavalry Division and the Indian Corps. He did not mention Churchill's Naval Division.

> There remains the question of *when* this move should take place. I submit that *now* is the time. We are all sedentary armies and movements and changes are easily [*sic*] made. It is for these reasons that I advocate the transfer of my force from its present position to the extreme left of the line and I advocate that the change should be made now.[4]

In French's note there was no mention of Antwerp (always a curious blind spot with Joffre), or of the Channel ports (which were anything but a blind spot). Joffre had plenty of evidence of French's earlier flirtation with an evacuation from Le Havre and even St Nazaire, and the idea of moving the BEF to an area convenient for a quick departure gave him good reason to hesitate.

None the less, he replied to French the following day (30 September). After rehearsing French's arguments, he went on: 'For nearly 15 days the Armies of the centre have been *accrochées* to the ground without making any real advance.' Joffre felt very doubtful about so major a change in policy, and gave his reasons at some length (the most important of which was the limited railway facilities, since he was busy transferring whole Armies across French's rear). Tactful as ever, he ended thus: 'To sum up, the Commander-in-Chief shares Marshal French's view but cannot be entirely of the same opinion as to the time at which this movement should be carried out.[5]

By 30 September, French had made his mind up. He was leaving the Aisne, whatever Joffre said or whatever his reasons for saying so. It is to Joffre's credit – for he had massive problems of his own as far north as Arras – that he did not simply refuse French any transport facilities. On receipt of Joffre's reply of the 30th, French informed him that his 2nd Cavalry Division ('Gough's Command') would leave the Aisne sector by road on 3 October. Joffre informed him that rail transport would be available to uplift II Corps at Pont St Maxence near Compiègne on 5 October. So the BEF began its move to Flanders. With hindsight, it would probably have wished it had stayed in its primitive little trenches on the Aisne.

---

[4] French: *op. cit.*
[5] It was broadly agreed that the BEF should be concentrated at Lille. It did not get there until *17 October 1918.*

Before we summarize briefly the timetable of this momentous move ('the best week of the war', said Albert Whitelock of the Bays. 'Lovely autumn weather and we rode along slowly, resting by day and really enjoying ourselves'), it is instructive to look a little further into the mind of Sir John French, because that mind was about to be severely tested.

In his memoirs he complained that Kitchener (drowned in 1916, and therefore not able to speak for himself) 'did not make things easy for me'. He particularly resented Kitchener's 'stream of directions' and the fact that Rawlinson's force (7th Infantry Division and 3rd Cavalry Division) would be an independent command.

> I regret I must record my deliberate opinion that the best which could have been done was *not* done, owing entirely to Lord Kitchener's endeavour to unite in himself the separate and distinct roles of a Cabinet Minister in London, and a Commander-in-Chief in France. [6]

Here a month later, and at a new crisis in the war, is an echo of that angry meeting in the British Embassy in Paris on 1 September. Even five years afterwards, Sir John French could neither forgive nor forget.

The BEF moved off with remarkable efficiency, and – since it was in close contact with a numerous enemy – remarkable secrecy. Indeed, as late as 8 October, when all but I Corps had left, the Germans were still reporting that all six British infantry divisions were in front of them. Movement was during the hours of darkness, and any excessive noise was masked by lively displays of fireworks from the gunners. Joe Temple was not too pleased. 'I went through the whole war without a scratch except that when we were coming back across the river near Vailly, they dropped one short and I got a chip through my arm. My mate alongside of me, who was glad we were going back, laughed his head off!'

The 'order of release' went thus (infantry formations by rail from the Compiègne area, the two cavalry divisions by road). [7]

First away on the night of 2/3 October was 2nd Cavalry Division, which reached St Pol on the 9th. It was followed, a day's march in rear, by 1st Cavalry Division. II Corps entrained on 5 October and arrived at Abbeville on the 8th and 9th. III Corps (now including 6th Infantry Division) detrained and concentrated in the area of St Omer and Hazebrouck on the 11th, followed a week later by I Corps, which reached Hazebrouck on the 19th and from there marched on Ypres. GHQ moved to Abbeville on 8 October, and five days later to St Omer.

The British were not to see the Aisne again until May 1918, and then in circumstances far removed from stalemate.

---

[6] French: *op. cit.*
[7] How the different formations came into action on arrival we shall see in the next chapter.

CHAPTER 9

Antwerp. 'Enter left, the BEF'

The Belgian sortie on 9 September had achieved a modest success by diverting enemy troops from the Marne battlefield. In the longer term, however, the elimination of Antwerp as a potential threat to German communications through Liège and Brussels was imperative, and when Falkenhayn succeeded Moltke on the 14th this became one of his chief priorities. With stalemate on the Aisne and the successive attempts by the French and German High Commands to outflank each other to the north of the Oise, the fate of Antwerp became a matter of vital importance, not least to the British with their eyes now fixed on Flanders and the Channel ports.

On 28 September the German bombardment began. For the reduction of the fortress Falkenhayn assembled *III Reserve Corps, 4th Ersatz Division*, a *Marine Division* and three *Landwehr Brigades*, under General Beseler. The chief agents of destruction were a formidable arsenal of 160 heavy and 13 super-heavy guns, the largest of which were of 16·2-inch and 12-inch calibre. This force was concentrated on the south-east defences of the city. As so often before, the key factor was time.

As we have seen, Churchill visited Sir John French at Fère-en-Tardenois on 27 September and there discussed with him proposals for reinforcing Antwerp, and for a major sea-borne landing at Zeebrugge or Ostend designed both to turn the German right flank and to block any attempt by the enemy to capture Calais and Boulogne. Out of this discussion came the decision to move the BEF from the Aisne to Flanders.

Churchill, however, was already off the mark. On 20 September a Royal Marine Brigade of four battalions had been landed at Dunkirk, accompanied by a few guns and by 82 motor vehicles, intended to give the impression of a formidable invasion. Here it was joined by the celebrated Commander Samson, RN, who had stayed ashore with his 3-pdr armoured cars after the brief demonstration in August, and since then had made the Pas de Calais his private parish, terrorizing any enemy cavalry patrols he met with that mildly lunatic enthusiasm which has long distinguished the British attitude to war from that of the Germans.[1]

The RM Brigade was a Churchillian improvisation, little more than

[1] 'He was, in fact,' said Capt. Hardwick of the Royal Dragoons, 'a bloody nuisance.'

2,000 strong. It consisted largely of reservists with over twenty-one years' service and some seven hundred recruits with no service at all, who had never fired a rifle.[2] Its officers were, for the most part, the very old and the very young.

None the less, the Brigade had an interesting time.[3] Its orders (it was under Admiralty direction) were 'to make its presence felt'. This it did by assuming a military aspect and travelling around the Pas de Calais without the remotest idea of its function. Lt Chater rather enjoyed himself. After landing at Dunkirk, his battalion was sent to Cassel, sixteen miles to the south. Cassel — which was to play a significant role in the great battles presently to develop — is a tall, volcanic hill which rises out of the Flanders plain. Here Lt Chater sat in considerable comfort and surveyed the scene. 'The sun shone,' he wrote. 'We could see some movement to the east. But for all the world, I might as well have been at home.'

Lt (later Major-General) Jamieson, of the 'Portsmouth' Battalion, had a rather different experience. On the 28th, at the request of the civic authorities, he and his men were sent to Lille. It was no more than a gesture, for the battalion was scarcely 500 strong and there was no information about any German presence in the area. In fact, on this date the new French Tenth Army and the German *Sixth Army* were locked in battle at Arras in what was to prove the last of the many efforts at envelopment before the arrival of the BEF in Flanders. North of Arras, operating with extreme caution towards Ypres, was *IV Cavalry Corps*, fearful of a British landing in strength on the coast.

Jamieson's battalion, like Birnam Wood advancing on Dunsinane, created a great deal of panic on the German side. A brush with a Uhlan patrol just east of Lille caused the commander of *6th Cavalry Division* to report that he had been 'heavily attacked by a force of all arms'. The Marines, at least as apprehensive as the enemy and with a good deal more reason, patrolled the suburbs of Lille and awaited developments.

Those developments were already taking place in Antwerp, where the German attack on the outer perimeter of forts was making headway. By 3 October the Belgian High Command informed the British Government that if it could not be assured of substantial reinforcements within three days, it would be obliged to evacuate the city and withdraw the Field Army (six under-strength infantry divisions and a cavalry division) and the fortress troops to the Ostend area. Mindful of the vital importance of Antwerp in the context of the redeployment of the BEF, the British replied that they would despatch two Naval Brigades[4] at once, and by 7 October the 7th Infantry Division and the 3rd Cavalry Division,[5] the latter at least to occupy Ghent and so cover any withdrawal down the coast. But first the Royal Marine Brigade was sent by train from Cassel and Lille to Vieux

---

[2] 'One platoon, when the brigade went to Antwerp, is said to have consisted entirely of pensioner sergeants and colour-sergeants.' *Official History*, Vol II.
[3] Its commander, General Aston, was replaced by General Paris on 29 September.
[4] These two Brigades consisted of totally untrained naval reservists and, improbably, some 2,000 volunteer soldiers from Durham and Northumberland who had never fired a rifle.
[5] 'Rawlinson's Force.'

PLATE 26. *7th Infantry Division landing at Zeebrugge, 6 October*

Dieu within the inner perimeter of the Antwerp forts, where they arrived early on the morning of 4 October. There was a surprise awaiting them. 'At 9 o'clock,' noted Lt Jamieson, 'we fell in prior to moving up to Lierre on the south-east perimeter and found ourselves marching past Winston Churchill in his Trinity House uniform!' The First Lord of the Admiralty was not going to be denied his share of the action. [6]

The reader may wonder how it was possible for the British to have road and rail access to Antwerp from the Belgian Channel ports six weeks after the Germans had occupied Brussels. The answer, as has been noted earlier, is that for all their resources the Germans were short of men. The Scheldt, running west from Antwerp to its junction with the Lys at Ghent, provides a natural barrier and a corridor of some fifteen miles between it, the Dutch frontier and then the sea. If the river could be held and Ghent occupied, this corridor, with two railway lines, was adequate to give access to the city or, if necessary, provide an escape route from it. Fortunately, the Germans were too slow to realize this. Their true objective should have been not Antwerp but Ghent. It is sometimes cheaper to starve a garrison into surrender than bombard it into ruins.

None the less, Antwerp was doomed. We need not concern ourselves here with the detailed process of its reduction. The key date was 8 October, by when Rawlinson's Force [7] had occupied Bruges, and Admiral Ronarc'h's Naval Brigade [8] Ghent. The French 87th Territorial Division was also detraining at Poperinghe.

[6] Later that day Churchill telegraphed Asquith, suggesting that he should take command of all British forces in Antwerp. His proposal was hurriedly declined and he returned to London on the 5th.
[7] On 9 October, 7th Infantry Division and 3rd Cavalry Division were transferred from Kitchener's direct control to Sir John French, and were constituted as IV Corps.
[8] Admiral Ronarc'h's Naval Brigade consisted of 6,500 petty officers and sailors, mostly reservists. More importantly it had no fewer than 40 machine-guns, nearly twice as many as a British infantry *division*.

180

The withdrawal could now begin. It was conducted throughout the days and nights of 8 and 9 October, and despite German attempts to cut the railway lines at Moerbeke and Selsaete west of Antwerp, the entire Belgian Field Army and the garrison troops made good their escape to a line running south from Ostend. By 15 October they had established their position on the Yser from Nieuport to Dixmude, from which the Germans were never to dislodge them.

The British fared less well. All – or nearly all – the Naval Division managed to get away. At Moerbeke the Germans intercepted a trainload of Marines, sailors and refugees. There was a brisk engagement in the dark, but many of the troops were taken prisoner before the remainder managed to fight their way through to Selsaete, where, providentially, they found another train to take them to Bruges. The survivors arrived there at 3 p.m. on 10 October, at last under the protection of 7th Division.

But back in Antwerp there had occurred once more a familiar story. Two battalions of 1st Naval Brigade on the eastern perimeter never received the order to withdraw. Driven into a corner by the German assault, their commander marched them across the frontier into Holland, where they were disarmed and interned.[9]

The Antwerp expedition was in a sense a disaster, but given the modest military capability of the force involved, it provided precious time for the Belgians to make good their escape, and for the BEF to reach the main battlefield. It also demonstrated an extraordinary lack of initiative and determination on the German side. When General Beseler accepted the surrender of Antwerp on 10 October the only prisoners he could report from the burning town were four city councillors.

There is a footnote. Hidden away in a pile of papers,[10] there is this bitter comment by an anonymous naval survivor interned in Groningen in Holland:

> The Expedition seems to have been a huge crime from start to finish – men, most of whom couldn't shoot, officered by men who proved themselves totally incapable, probably because they had had no military training.

The 7th Division and the 3rd Cavalry Division – both Regular – differed from the formations of the original BEF. For the most part they consisted of units recalled from overseas stations (the Royals and the 10th Hussars, for example, from South Africa; 2/Royal Scots Fusiliers and 2/Wiltshires from Gibraltar; and so on). As a result, like all units serving abroad, they were virtually up to strength and required very few reservists to complete to war establishment. Average length of service was five years. It is one of the brutal ironies of war that, although they were the last Regular divisions to

---

[9]The casualties of the Naval Division, including the internees and the prisoners taken at Moerbeke, were 2,610, of which only 57 were killed. On 11 October the Division was re-embarked to Dover. It did not reappear until Gallipoli in 1915.
[10]Liddle Archives.

join the BEF before 22 November, they were to sustain by far the highest level of casualties. This was pure chance. Inserted in the line on the right of I Corps as the battle for Ypres started on 21 October, they took the full brunt of the main German efforts to effect a decisive break-through. When one month later 7th Division was withdrawn from the salient it had been reduced to less than a quarter of its original infantry strength. No single division suffered so fearful a drain on its effectives until the morning of 1 July 1916 on the Somme.

The original commander of this Force – General Rawlinson – had briefly taken over 4th Division on the Aisne at the end of September. And it is more than a coincidence that early in October three of the four Corps Commanders of the BEF – Haig, Smith-Dorrien and Rawlinson – had served under Kitchener at Omdurman, a point not lost on Sir John French.

Until 9 October, when IV Corps was formed and transferred to French's command, Rawlinson received his orders direct from Kitchener. The first of these, dated 5 October, [11] was carefully worded and defined his task as 'assisting and supporting the Belgian Army defending Antwerp, which place is besieged by the Germans'. His force numbered some 30,000 men.

As we now know, Rawlinson's two divisions – perhaps fortunately – were too late to reach Antwerp. He therefore adopted an alternative contingency plan and moved his force to Bruges and sent two infantry brigades south-east to join Ronarc'h's contingent at Ghent, thus providing a strong flank protection to cover the Belgian and British withdrawal down the coast. Back at Antwerp Beseler did not realize until the 10th that the Belgians and British had escaped, and belatedly, on the following day, he ordered *III Reserve Corps* and *4th Ersatz Division* to move westward on Ostend.

Jack Cusack, [12] a regimental scout with the Royals of 6th Cavalry Brigade, was in his element. A Scot of independent mind, he had a roving commission covering the advance to Bruges:

> My only disappointment was that I couldn't find any Germans. But I got on well with the locals and soon my French was pretty good. Well, let's say I got by with about twenty words! I still had my Basuto pony from South Africa, a tough little character who stood up to his work much better than some of our Irish bloodstock. Occasionally I saw some French cavalry in fancy dress and they would show me dents in their breastplates which they said were bullet marks. I also saw Belgian machine-guns being pulled on little carts by dogs. The story went that when any shelling started the dogs took fright and ran back into the German lines with their bloody guns.

---

[11] The previous day the War Office had already issued orders direct to General Capper, GOC of 7th Division. Capper was killed in action in 1915.
[12] Cusack was probably the only man to have served variously with all three regiments of the old Union Brigade: the Royals, the Greys and the 'Skins'.

PLATE 27. *The Royal Dragoons (3rd Cavalry Division) entering Ypres, 13 October*

While Rawlinson was manœuvring around Ghent, and Beseler's force was moving cautiously towards him, the stage was being set farther west. By 9 October Smith-Dorrien's II Corps, arriving from the Aisne, had detrained at Abbeville, and by the 11th had reached the area of Béthune with the two Cavalry Divisions[13] covering its left flank. Four days earlier the German *IV Cavalry Corps* had entered Ypres and was reconnoitring in the direction of Hazebrouck. Here it suddenly discovered the presence of the British in some strength, and hastily withdrew to the area of Bailleul. Slowly the battle-lines were being drawn.

On 11 October[14] Sir John French, judging that the Belgians and the Naval Division had made good their escape along the coastal corridor, ordered Rawlinson's Force – now IV Corps – to retire on Ypres. On the 13th, 3rd Cavalry Division entered the town, and the following day 7th Division took up its position on an arc facing south-east astride the Menin road. Across four blood-soaked years the Germans never again succeeded in setting foot in Ypres. An air photograph taken on 11 November 1918 shows a scene of utter destruction as great as at Hiroshima on 6 August 1945. The only difference is that the process took longer.

Ypres. The name stands beside Mons, the Somme and Passchendaele (itself part of the long agony) in the dreadful litany of British experience in

---

[13] On 9 October 1st and 2nd Cavalry Divisions were formed into the Cavalry Corps under Allenby.
[14] On this day Joffre appointed Foch 'Commander of the Northern Group of Armies' – that is to say, those between the Oise and the sea. He had no authority over Sir John French, but he was to exercise a formidable influence.

the Great War. It was not *one* battle. With the exception of 1916, when the directors on both sides chose two other slaughter-houses at Verdun and on the Somme, Ypres was in constant ferment, never a 'quiet' sector, never a place of refuge.

There were four great climaxes, not all at or near the town itself: 'First Ypres' in the autumn of 1914, with which we are here concerned; 'Second Ypres' in the spring of 1915, where the Germans first introduced poison gas, and which 'spawned' the related battles of Neuve Chapelle, Festubert and Loos[15]; 'Third Ypres', culminating in the mud of Passchendaele in November 1917; and – though rarely so described – 'Fourth Ypres', which started with Ludendorff's massive and desperate attack on the Lys on 9 April 1918 and his last attempt to reach the Channel ports. By another of those strange ironies of history this final offensive was halted just short of Hazebrouck, where four years earlier *IV Cavalry Corps* had turned back as the BEF arrived from the Aisne.

We shall never know the cost of Ypres. There are statistics, certainly. But they are incomplete, and – in a bitter sense – academic. For four years it remained an insatiable glutton which devoured everything and everyone provided to satisfy its appetite. It is said that on 11 November 1918 there remained on this battleground – measuring no more than thirty miles square – not one single living tree and not one single undamaged building. The cemeteries speak for themselves.

Why Ypres? There are three answers: first, as the most westerly town of Belgian Flanders, it was a vital centre of communications. Whoever held Ypres held the key to Calais and Boulogne. But as the years wore on it became at once an obsession and a symbol: for the Germans, an obsession that here lay the shortest route to that victory which Bülow and Kluck had so wantonly cast away on the Marne; and for the Allies, a symbol of defiance. If Pétain did indeed say at Verdun, 'They shall not pass!', how more profoundly true is this of the Allied defence of Ypres?

The first battle of Ypres should more accurately be described as 'the first *battles for* Ypres'. They lasted from 10 October to 22 November, overlapping both in terms of time and of place; and subsequent chapters will show how the different battles interacted on each other.

First, however, it is necessary to have a clear picture of the battlefield, for its topography largely dictated the shape of each successive confrontation and the tactical intentions of both sides.

To the west of the Belgian frontier (that is to say, west of a line running north from Arras to the sea at Dunkirk) lies 'French' Flanders. It is rich, arable country, 'not,' in the words of the official History, 'unlike the Weald of Kent' except that it is dominated by a series of tall features such as Cassel, Mont des Cats, and – on the eastern edge – Kemmel, which give an uninterrupted view over the Flanders plain. These features were to play an

[15] It was the battle of Loos which finally convinced Kitchener that French should be replaced as C-in-C by Haig.

184

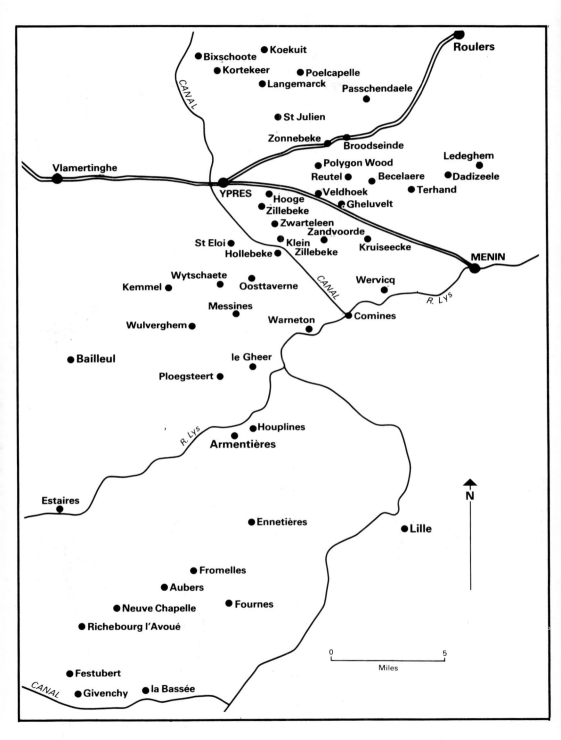

MAP 9. *Flanders: the British Sector*

important part in the long series of battles for Ypres, but in 1914 they remained in Allied hands.

The plain is watered by two main rivers: the Yser, which flows north-east and then north to the coast at Nieuport and is connected to Ypres by a canal which joins the river at Dixmude; and the Lys, which runs roughly west from Ghent to Armentières, and which was to be the southern boundary of the last phase of 'First Ypres'.

'Belgian' Flanders is quite different in character. When the men of II Corps arrived at Béthune they were dismayed by what they saw. Suffolk-born Jim Cannon, who had taken such an instinctive dislike to the slag-heaps and mining villages around Frameries, was appalled when he surveyed the prospect. 'After Mons, I had hoped we had seen the last of coal-pits.' In fact he need not have been too concerned, for here the mining-belt runs for only a few miles from Lens to la Bassée. But there were other, equally unattractive features.

It is – and was – a countryside of small farms and hedges intersected by a network of canals and dykes which connected the rivers and provided the chief means of transportation. The water-table here is so high that any trench-digging, even in dry seasons, resulted in waterlogging. The cynical view of the canal system was that if it was essential to travel by water, then canals were preferable to roads. The effect of months of sustained artillery bombardment was to destroy the drainage system of the low ground and to convert the battlefield into a quagmire. If the survivors have any single memory of Flanders it is summed up in one word: mud.

Belgian Flanders is flat; but not *entirely* flat. Ypres itself lies at the centre of a shallow saucer. The battles of the next four years were to be battles for the control of the eastern and southern rims of this saucer.

East of Kemmel there runs a ridge starting from Messines and Wytschaete. Then it follows a wide north-easterly curve through remembered names like Hollebeke, Zillebeke, Zwarteleen, Herenthage and Sanctuary Woods, Hill 60, Gheluvelt and Veldhoek, Nonne Bosschen and Polygon Woods, Broodseinde and Passchendaele, where – as the BEF threw its left flank back through Langemarck to Bixschoote – the famous Salient was formed. From Bixschoote along the Yser canal to Dixmude, and thence along the Yser itself to the sea at Nieuport, the land is a swampy desolation of ditches, much of it at or below sea-level. Throughout, this part of the line was held by the French and the Belgians.

The Flanders ridge is a very modest one, rising gently to no more than 200 feet, and at its nearest point only three miles from Ypres. But it was to be an artillery battle, and artillery battles are about observation. Thus 'First Ypres' was to be a series of battles for this long ridge. It was to have two moments of supreme crisis: at Gheluvelt on 31 October, and at Nonne Bosschen on 11 November – a prophetic date indeed.

The fighting that took place in the British sector between 10 October and 22 November was complex and extremely confused. It spread north as the formations of the BEF reached Flanders successively from the Aisne (IV Corps, as we have seen, reached Ypres on 13–14 October as it retired from Bruges and Ghent; and by 17 October, 7th Division had advanced east across the Menin road and had reached Kruiseecke, within four miles of Menin itself. This was to be the apex of the salient, although not for long.) The only 'constant' element in a British line which stretched for thirty-one miles lay on its extreme right, where throughout the fighting the boundary between the British II Corps (and later the Indian Corps) and the French was the la Bassée Canal. The British held Givenchy (just west of la Bassée) and the French XXI Corps (of Maud'huy's Tenth Army), Vermelles.[16] For the rest it was a great tidal battle, more ebb than flow, as the Germans flung nine Army Corps[17] and four Cavalry Corps against the Allied line, always with a numerical superiority of two to one, and often as great as six to one.

For the reader to have a clear picture of this confrontation it is best to show the Allied line as it was on the morning of 21 October when Haig's I Corps, the last to arrive from the Aisne, had entered the line on the left of IV Corps[18] at Ypres (see Map 11). This map illustrates the shape of the original salient and the southern line astride the Lys.

There are some important comments to add before continuing the general narrative.

First, there were four 'official' battles:

    1 *La Bassée*:   10 October to 2 November

    2 *Armentières*:   13 October to 2 November

    3 *Messines*:   12 October to 2 November

    4 *Ypres*:   19 October to 22 November
        a) Langemarck: 21-24 October
        b) Gheluvelt: 29-31 October
        c) Nonne Bosschen: 11 November

These are only 'dates of convenience'. They do not mean formal beginnings and tidy conclusions. They can be described, in musical terms, as a 'theme and variations'. The fighting did not stop south of the Lys on 2 November. Here the 'variations' continued until the end. The 'theme' was stated and restated *fortissimo*, until the finale, at Ypres.

Secondly, the battles in Flanders were quite unlike those of the earlier weeks of retreat and advance; Mons, Marne and Aisne, where formations kept their identity and operated without, so to speak, cross-pollination. In Flanders there were no neat compartments, no strict divisional boundaries,

---

[16] Temporarily lost on 11 October.
[17] Right to left. *Fourth Army* (*III, XXII, XXIII, XXVI* and *XXVII Reserve Corps*) and *Sixth Army* (*XIX, XIII, VII* and *XIV Corps*).
[18] On 27 October, 7th Infantry Division and 3rd Cavalry Division came under command of I Corps, and Rawlinson returned to England to organize 8th Infantry Division, the last of the Regular formations.

only a series of desperate expedients to fill gaps with men of any unit that a commander could find to 'putty up' the holes.

Thirdly, the cavalry. By 10 October they had seen the last of their horses. They were now infantry, and despite their lack of numbers, they demonstrated their legendary musketry skill at Messines and Hollebeke; and against everything that the Germans threw at them they held the line. The four German Cavalry Corps opposed to them were brave, but greatly inferior in the art of dismounted action.

Finally, the infantry. What is there left to say about the infantry? In the following narrative there are references to 'battalions' and 'companies'. These are simply terms of reference. At the crisis of 'First Ypres' a battalion meant at best 300 men, and a company 80. Sometimes, a handful. Sometimes, nothing. In the great battles for Ypres forty-seven battalion commanders[19] were killed, thirty-one were wounded, and history does not record the casualties among those officers who found themselves the only survivors, and therefore the only commissioned leaders left. Nor does it record the remnants who were left in the charge of senior NCOs, and even private soldiers. 'They were' – and Zwehl's words were never more true – 'very exceptional soldiers.'

An example will suffice. On 29 October, 1/Coldstream were overwhelmed south of Gheluvelt. Chippy Carpenter, the Colonel's bugler, remembers it well.

> The Germans came at us in a solid block. We fired away and knocked them down but they kept on coming. I remember Capt. Evelyn Gibbs firing his revolver, then chucking his cap at the Jerries and shouting: 'Every man for himself!' He was taken prisoner. The rest of us managed to get away and that night we joined up with 4th (Guards) Brigade.[20] I think there were about 160 of us. We had lost all our officers.

---

[19] 1/Loyals alone lost three commanding officers between the Marne and Ypres.
[20] The survivors of 1/Coldstream joined up with 2/Coldstream and 3/Coldstream near Polygon Wood. It is the only time all three battalions were together.

CHAPTER 10

La Bassée: Armentières

It had to be II Corps, the fighting-cocks of the BEF. An uncharitable explanation might be that Smith-Dorrien was still being made to expiate his crime of disobedience at Le Cateau, but in fact II Corps had been the easiest, and therefore the first, formation to be withdrawn from the Aisne, and thus reached Abbeville a day ahead of the two Cavalry Divisions which were making their way north by road.

Sir John French, after a meeting with Foch, decided not to wait until the whole BEF was concentrated in its new area but, as the German cavalry screen fell back into Belgium, to push forward in the direction of Roulers (on the 13th Foch wrote to Joffre: 'The marshal wishes at all costs to go to Brussels. I shall not hold him back.'). Unfortunately, French's enthusiasm was short-lived. As II Corps and then III Corps met strong and growing resistance, and long before the arrival of I Corps, he was seriously considering withdrawing the entire BEF into a vast entrenched camp at Boulogne, just as he had flirted with the idea of a similar withdrawal to Le Havre after the battle of Mons. Then he had been talked out of the preposterous proposal by Kitchener and Wilson. Now – and not for the last time – it took all Foch's tact and *élan* to dissuade him. Indeed, it is no exaggeration to say that Foch's main problem from now on was to revive French's flagging spirits, not least on the dark day of 31 October. How French could swing from the heights to the depths we shall presently see. The black despair was part of his volatile character. The moments of elation were Foch's doing.

Meanwhile the Germans had not been idle. During the first week of October a new *Sixth Army* had been created by the transfer of *XIX, XIII, VII* and *XIV Corps* from the southern sectors, and these, based on Lille, now began to deploy towards the north-west in the path of the British II and III Corps.

On their extreme right, in the coastal corridor, Beseler's *III Reserve Corps* and his other troops released by the fall of Antwerp were facing the Belgian Field Army on the line of the Yser between Dixmude and the sea, and this line was extended south by the French towards Bixschoote. But Beseler was the vanguard of a much more formidable (and largely unexpected) force.

This was another new Army – the *Fourth* – drawn from divisions created on 16 August. [1] It consisted of *XXII, XXIII, XXVI* and *XXVII Reserve Corps*, and its allotted sector was to extend the front on the right of *Sixth Army* from Menin to the sea. These *Reserve Corps* consisted largely of semi-trained volunteers – students, teachers, artisans, retired officers and other ranks – with a stiffening of professional soldiers from active formations. If they fought without great skill, they demonstrated fanatical courage and suffered very heavy casualties; but they had an immense numerical superiority, and were supported by several hundred guns of heavy and medium calibre.

In the words of the official German monograph on the battles for Ypres, [2] Falkenhayn's intention was short and to the point: 'To close successfully with the enemy and to gain Calais was the aim and object of the 1914 campaign.' The Germans never understood how they failed to achieve this object, despite repeatedly reinforcing their already massive front-line strength. Again and again the monograph uses the word *Durchbruch* (breakthrough). Finally there comes this admission: 'No break-through of the enemy's lines had been accomplished. . . . We had not succeeded in making the decisive break-through, and the dream[3] of ending the campaign in the west in our favour had to be consigned to its grave.'

We, standing on our bridge downstream, know now why the German dream ended in disillusion. There were perilous moments, many of them. But the Germans, for all their numbers, failed repeatedly to exploit success, apparently convinced – as many of their prisoners testified – that behind the Allied line a vast army lay concealed waiting to lure them to their doom. We know that this was not so; and so did the Germans. This phantom army was their only alibi for an otherwise incomprehensible failure.

The BEF and its allies needed no alibis. Even when battalions had been wiped out or reduced to remnants, when whole batteries of guns had been destroyed, when cooks and drivers and orderlies – 'a wafer here, a wafer there,' said Foch – had been sent to fill the gaps, the line somehow stood firm. Some modern cynics affect to believe that the defence of Ypres has become an exaggerated part of British folk-history. To such there is a simple answer. Had it not been for 'the first seven divisions' and the British cavalry, for d'Urbal and Dubois, for King Albert and his Belgians, there would be no modern cynics to disparage a passage of arms as improbable as it is immortal.

On 10 October – the official date on which the battle of la Bassée began – Sir John French issued his Operation Order No. 33 at Abbeville (GHQ moved two days later to St Omer). 'It is the intention of the Commander-in-Chief to advance to meet the enemy, prolonging the French left.' This phrase – with minor variations – was to be repeated daily until 20

---

[1] Since the Schlieffen Plan envisaged the total defeat of France within thirty-nine days of mobilization, it is difficult to understand why these 'volunteer' divisions were required, except as occupation troops.
[2] *Ypres, 1914.*
[3] French, with much less reason, was repeatedly dreaming the same dream in reverse.

October, when suddenly the accent and the emphasis changed. 'The Commander-in-Chief intends to *contain*[4] the enemy with the II, III and Cavalry Corps, and the 7th Division of IV Corps *and to attack vigorously with the I Corps.*'[4]

What then had happened between 10 and 20 October? It is not possible in a single book covering so wide a stage to deal with every action, whether large or small (and there were dozens of both). But during this period a pattern emerged. In a sense it was not unlike the first day on the Mons canal, where the fighting spread like a slow fuse from right to left. There were two significant differences. First, the scale was altogether greater. Secondly, the BEF was now attacking, not – at least at first – defending.[5]

First into action, as we have seen, was II Corps astride the la Bassée canal, although this time in reverse order with 5th Division on the right and 3rd Division on the left. Bob Barnard and Tom Bradley were still there. To both of them the canal salient at Mons seemed a lifetime away. Six weeks in war can be an eternity. Thus Barnard, in reflective mood: 'I don't know when all this talk about *estaminets* and brothels and high jinks behind the lines began. It must have been a lot later because I don't remember anything like that in the early days. In fact I didn't get any home leave until 1915, and I'd been wounded twice by then. Funny thing, but I wasn't all that keen on going home. It was the coming back I didn't like.'

As the fighting developed in Flanders, the 'eye of the storm' moved northward from la Bassée (which neither the British nor later the Indians succeeded in capturing) to the Ypres salient, where the great series of battles raged from Messines to Bixschoote. By 11 November – and this is often forgotten – two-thirds of the salient was held by the French, for no other reason than that Haig, who had met and defeated the German offensive which was launched on 29 October, had neither the men nor the resources left.

It is impossible to reconstruct the daily – and nightly – events at every point along this constantly changing line; or to mention every unit of the BEF involved;[6] or to rehearse the dreadful catalogue of casualties. For that the reader must turn to the official History. The story is most simply told as a series of different scenes, some occupying the centre of the stage, others being played out simultaneously, or in the wings – the whole combining to create a single drama.

The drama opened with a prologue – 'the advance on Menin' – which involved 5th, 3rd and 6th[7] Divisions in the south and 7th Division in the north. This prologue was short-lived. In the south, 6th Division actually reached a point within four miles of Lille on 19 October, but heavily

[4]Author's italics.
[5]By early October, casualties were being replaced by a steady stream of reinforcements. None the less a subaltern of 1/Queen's, wounded during the retreat, did not recognize one single officer when he rejoined his battalion early in November.
[6]Excluding the Indian Corps, there took part in 'First Ypres': 22 cavalry regiments, 4 Yeomanry regiments, 88 Regular infantry battalions, 7 Territorial battalions, and 95 batteries of artillery.
[7]Between 3rd and 6th Divisions came Conneau's cavalry.

attacked on that day by the newly arrived *XIII Corps* and *VII Corps*, the whole line was driven back virtually to its starting-point on a front of some fifteen miles running from Givenchy, thence to Neuve Chapelle, and so to Armentières, where it linked up with 4th Infantry Division. This line was to be held until the end.

From 24 October until 22 November there were no more advances, only desperate defence and heroic counter-attack. The real tragedy is that right up to the day of Gheluvelt both French and Foch were convinced that they were winning a battle which they were in extreme danger of losing; French, because he did not trouble to discover the truth, and Foch, because with him the wish was always father to the thought, and he felt it imperative to imbue French with his own optimism. GHQ's Operation Orders up to 29 October are peppered with phrases like 'attack of I Corps progressing favourably', 'I Corps and IV Corps . . . will attack vigorously to-morrow.' Haig, who was fighting for his life near Ypres, knew better, and so ignored orders which he could not conceivably carry out.

The extent of French's euphoria is illustrated by his daily reports to Kitchener in London:

24 October: 'The battle is practically won.'

25 October: 'The situation is growing more favourable every hour.'

26 October: 'The Germans are quite incapable of making any strong and sustained attack.'

27 October: 'I am confident and very hopeful. It is only necessary to press the enemy hard in order to ensure complete success and victory.'

On 28 October French ordered that 'the offensive should be continued'. On 29 October the 'incapable' Germans launched a tremendous assault on the apex of the salient.

What Kitchener's reaction was to French's daily diet of optimism we do not know.[8] If, when the truth became brutally apparent, he considered the time had come to replace the C-in-C, he does not seem to have been able to carry the War Cabinet with him. In any event the crisis in the salient was such that the removal of French would have been politically impossible, and his likely successor, Haig, was otherwise occupied at his HQ in the White Château.

The advance of II Corps began on 13 October. Opposed to it, and screening the main enemy concentration in the area of Lille, were the two *Cavalry Corps* which had faced the BEF first on the Marne and again on the Aisne. *Jäger* battalions occupied la Bassée.

[8] The volume of French's private diary covering the period from 21 October to 22 November cannot be traced.

5th Division lay astride the canal with 13th Brigade on the right in touch with the French, 15th Brigade in the centre at Givenchy, and 14th Brigade on the left, the line being continued northward by 3rd Division, their old comrades-in-arms at Mons. Early on a morning thick with mist the Germans began a heavy bombardment of Givenchy, which was held by the Bedfordshires and the Dorsets. 'We'd never experienced anything like it before,' recalls Pte Kennedy. 'The stuff just rained down and soon the place was in flames and our casualties were very heavy. One platoon of 'B' Company was just wiped out by two shells one after the other, and by noon we'd lost all our officers.'

During the afternoon, after bitter hand-to-hand fighting, the Bedfords were driven out of the village[9] and 11th Battery, RFA, lost two guns, although another section, firing down the village street like machine-guns, managed to get away. This left the Dorsets totally exposed and enfiladed on the canal on two sides. They withdrew to a position just west of the canal bridge, but not before they had suffered over 400 casualties.[10]

Farther north, 3rd Division and Conneau's 7th Cavalry Division made slow progress, impeded by the difficult ground and by stubborn enemy resistance. It is a measure of the price that the BEF was about to pay that on the 13th, a day of comparatively minor activity, the casualties in II Corps alone were 987. Here both Bob Barnard and Tom Bradley were wounded, but neither seriously enough to warrant a ticket to 'Blighty'. Meanwhile, still farther north, III Corps was coming into line between Aubers, of evil memory, and Armentières.

George Roupell was north of Givenchy with 14th Brigade on 13 October near the village of Richebourg l'Avoué. Here – and during the next two days – the fighting, though less severe, was still costly. Once again his diary, with its laconic style, tells us more about the nature of war than many of the dramatic and highly coloured accounts. The entries for this period are subtly different from those at Mons and on the Aisne. First, it was already a different war, and it was being fought on a very different stage which by its character broke up the action into small, sporadic engagements. Secondly, the BEF was – however slowly – advancing. Thirdly, German tactics had started to change with the introduction of night attacks. And finally, George Roupell himself had changed, although he seems not to have realized it.

The entries are shorter, for there was little opportunity to sit and scribble. There are many references to food and sleep, those two subjects closest to the heart of every fighting man. And by now there was a steady supply of letters and parcels from home. The war was falling into shape.

Yet still the entries record, with a monotony which is at once moving and matter-of-fact, the dreadful daily cost. Here is one:

> Retired to trenches on right of village in rear of 'D' company. A shell
> hit a few of my men. Bullen and self dug ourselves in. Bridgeland killed

[9] It was recaptured on the 16th.
[10] There occurred here one of several alleged instances of pretended surrender by German troops and of the abuse of a white flag.

in front trench. Sat in little pits on the road side. In the evening the church was burnt down. Retired at night to a position behind the distillery and dug ourselves in. Carpenter wounded.

And again:

I remember one field on this advance literally sprinkled with large tins of bully beef! Too much even for the strong men. They threw away the tins, in spite of the fact that away went their food for the whole day and that of a number of other men. . . . Several killed, who wouldn't be wanting bully beef any more.

And still the anodyne sense of humour:

Private Templer [*who was to carry Roupell out of action at Hill 60*] has just bagged a fowl from the HQ farm, and explains that 'he found it hanging on a tree'; the usual excuse is that the bird attacked them and they had to kill it in self-defence!

During 14–15 October II Corps dug in on a line running north from Givenchy through Festubert to Estaires, with Conneau's cavalry on its left. Air reconnaissance showed a considerable enemy build-up around Lille, and Smith-Dorrien felt that he should await Pulteney's arrival on his left and then make an enveloping attack before the Germans could deploy in strength. [11]

French's Operation Order for the forward movement on 16 October opens with a familiar ring. 'It is the intention of the C-in-C to advance eastwards, attacking the enemy wherever met.' So far as GHQ was concerned, the total German strength facing the Allies north of la Bassée consisted of two (possibly three) Army corps in the area of Lille, two cavalry corps retiring east of Armentières, and Beseler's Antwerp force in the coastal corridor. Not for the first time, this was a gigantic under-estimate. Falkenhayn had carefully and deliberately intended that it should be so.

French's line of advance, right to left, was briefly thus: [12] II Corps to advance on Lille; III Corps to occupy Armentières and move eastward with its two divisions astride the Lys; Cavalry Corps to cover the left flank and the eventual junction between III Corps and IV Corps at Menin; IV Corps itself to advance eastward, 7th Division aiming between Courtrai and Roulers, ten miles north-east of Ypres with its left flank protected by 3rd Cavalry Division. North of Ypres on the Yser canal and on the Yser itself the French and the Belgians would attack, or at least contain, Beseler's *III Reserve Corps. Provided that GHQ's appreciation of enemy strength and location was correct*, 16 October held out the promise of that decisive envelopment which

[11] In the event, it was Rawlinson's 7th Division at Ypres which nearly succeeded in reaching Roulers, II Corps' original objective.
[12] On 16 October I Corps was still in transit from the Aisne.

both sides had sought ever since the stalemate on the Aisne.

16 October proved to be a false dawn. Unknown to GHQ, Courtrai and Roulers, the objectives of Rawlinson's 7th Division, were already occupied by Falkenhayn's newly formed *Fourth Army* of four Reserve Corps. South of Menin the German *Sixth Army* consisted not of two, but of *four* Active Corps. It was the story of Mons all over again. At least Henry Wilson was not responsible this time for GHQ's gross error of judgment. Nor was Sir John French. The culprit was Foch.

If 16 October proved to be a false dawn, it was also the day which began to shape 'First Ypres'. Falkenhayn at first held his hand. The farther he could entice the BEF forward, the greater would be the effect of his counter-stroke. On this day, only II Corps and 6th Division of III Corps made any significant progress, to which we will return. By 21 October, when I Corps had taken over the sector north-east of Ypres, the salient had been created[13] and the British line ran roughly thus, right to left:[14]

II Corps: From Givenchy to Aubers.

III Corps: Astride the Lys, east of Armentières.

Cavalry Corps: From Messines to Hollebeke.

IV Corps: From Hollebeke to Zonnebeke.

I Corps: From Zonnebeke to Bixschoote.

This is an over-simplification of a series of battles where advances were measured in yards, and villages and woods – even hedges and farmyards – constantly changed hands. Zandvoorde was lost. Gheluvelt was lost, won, and lost again. So too were Messines and Wytschaete. But when, on 11 November, the Germans made their last great effort in 1914 to secure Ypres at Polygon Wood and then at Nonne Bosschen, they won neither. And by that night the old salient, battered and dented, was much as it had been on 21 October. No German was within three miles of Ypres.

On the night of 15–16 October *I Cavalry Corps* opposite 5th Division and *II Cavalry Corps* farther north were relieved by *VII Corps* (*13th* and *14th Divisions*).[15]

At this point the Flanders battlefield began to assume a clearly defined pattern which *in essence* was to remain unchanged throughout the next four weeks; in essence, because it was in reality *two* battlefields, one north and the other south of the river Lys. Of these the northern was to be the scene of the fiercest fighting and of the greatest moments of crisis, if only because at its centre lay Ypres. By the end of October the Germans had abandoned

[13] 7th Division had reached – or had been allowed to reach – as far east as the Menin–Roulers road on 18 October.
[14] See Map 9.
[15] The German line was extended during the next two days by the arrival of *XIII Corps* and *XIX Corps*, covering roughly the line of the Lys from Houplines to Menin.

any attempt at a decisive break-through in the south, and also on the French and Belgian sector between Ypres and the sea.

It may therefore help the reader to have as a point of reference the general dispositions on the two battlefields as 'First Ypres' began. This table does not attempt to show detailed location of units or movements of formations from one battlefield to another; nor does it give precise boundaries. There was nothing precise about 'First Ypres', which was a succession of 'tidal waves'. But the dividing line between north and south remained unchanged.

The reader should constantly keep in mind the course of the river Lys, which runs west and then south-west from Menin to Armentières, a distance of roughly fourteen miles. It flows through Wervicq, Comines, Warneton and Frelinghien (two miles east of Armentières). All these places were throughout in German hands, and Comines – at the centre, and connected by a canal – is eight miles from Ypres. Between lie the ridges and spurs of the northern battlefield which were to dictate the tidal flow.

The opposing sides were broadly disposed thus:

South of the Lys (from British right to left)

British:	5th Division, 3rd Division, 19th Brigade, 6th Division, 4th Division (part), and later five Indian Infantry Brigades.
German:	*Sixth Army:* *XIV Corps* (part), *VII Corps, XIII Corps, XIX Corps* (part).

North of the Lys

British:	4th Division (part), 1st Cavalry Division, 2nd Cavalry Division, 7th Division, 3rd Cavalry Division, 2nd Division, 1st Division.
German:	*XIX Corps* (part), *I, IV* and *V Cavalry Corps* *Fourth Army:* *XXVII Reserve Corps, XXVI Reserve Corps.* *XXIII Reserve Corps* and later *III Reserve Corps*

When the great offensive was launched on 29 October *Army Group Fabeck* was inserted at the junction between *Sixth Army* and *Fourth Army* on the Lys.

This table takes no account of subsidiary German formations or of French divisions fighting alongside or within the BEF line. But on a simple, if rough, arithmetical count it shows 16 German infantry divisions and 6 cavalry divisions opposed to 7⅓ British infantry divisions, 3 cavalry divisions and 5 Indian brigades. The introduction of *Army Group Fabeck* on 29 October added at least a further 6 infantry divisions to the German strength. The BEF had *no* reserves. Any fair-minded referee would have declared it 'no contest'. He would have been wrong.

With the recapture of Givenchy on the 16th,[16] Smith-Dorrien ordered II Corps to wheel south of east with its right flank on the la Bassée canal, and its left at Fauquissart six miles to the north. Beyond Fauquissart came Conneau's Cavalry Corps, now reduced to two divisions by the transfer of half his force to de Mitry north of Ypres; and by the following morning Pulteney's III Corps had occupied Armentières and had secured the crossings of the Lys as far east as Houplines, with 6th Division south of the river and 4th Division north by le Gheer to Ploegsteert Wood. The plan, as described in French's Operation Order No. 37 issued at St Omer on the 16th, was for an enveloping movement round the German right wing designed to capture Menin and then – by inference – to invest and capture Lille. This plan had one fatal flaw. It totally disregarded the strength and disposition of Prince Rupprecht's *Sixth Army* on and south of the river. In fact, by the evening of the 16th the Germans already had a two to one superiority on the 'southern' battlefield, and Rupprecht had offensive intentions of his own.

French's Operation Order of the 16th instructed II Corps to capture la Bassée (it never did) and to advance eastward in touch with Conneau. III Corps was to push forward on either side of the Lys, its left protected by Allenby's cavalry. IV Corps was to attack Menin from the direction of Ypres. There was neither hint nor suggestion of the impending appearance of *Fourth Army* on the 'northern' battlefield.

At first the British advance made steady progress south of Armentières, despite many casualties and growing enemy resistance which seems to have been treated with little concern at GHQ. French was in his most euphoric mood.

On the 17th, 15th Brigade captured Violaines, a mile north of la Bassée, and 14th Brigade, still farther east, occupied Lorgies. On the left 3rd Division captured the Aubers ridge, and at dusk 9th Brigade took Herlies by a bayonet charge, led by 1/Lincolns. Pte Wildgoose was there, still wearing his rosary: 'It was my first bayonet charge and a proper bloodthirsty affair it was. I can't remember whether I got home with the point. I do know that the Germans didn't like the taste of steel and they soon made a bolt for it. I can't say I blame them. A bayonet is a wicked weapon.' The prisoners taken at Herlies provided an unpleasant surprise, for they were identified as part of *VII Corps (14th Division)*, whose presence in the line was at that date entirely unexpected.

During the following two days II Corps, Conneau's cavalry, and 6th Division of III Corps continued to advance slowly, and by the evening of the 19th the general line ran north-east from Givenchy, thus:

II Corps: 5th Division, from Givenchy, east of Violaines to the western outskirts of le Transloy (4 miles).
3rd Division, thence just west of Illies to (inclusive) Herlies and le Pilly.

[16]On this date IV Corps, on the 'northern' battlefield, began its advance towards the Menin–Roulers road.

197

Conneau:	North of le Pilly, by Grand Riez to Fromelles and thence to le Maisnil.
III Corps:	6th Division, from Radinghem north-east to Ennetières,[17] thence to Premesques and Epinette.
	4th Division, astride the Lys from Epinette, thence east of Houplines and Armentières to le Gheer and Ploegsteert Wood.

As we have seen, the tone of Sir John French's Operation Orders changed abruptly on 20 October with the introduction of the words 'to contain' along the line of the Lys and south to la Bassée, and the arrival of Haig's I Corps as the offensive instrument north and north-east of Ypres. For the first time, on this day there were guarded suggestions that the Germans might be in the process of conjuring a very large rabbit out of the hat in the area of Courtrai and Roulers, although there was little indication of this in French's directive to Haig on the 19th (see p. 208).

Foch, dedicated to the proposition of a decisive battle against the 'vulnerable' German flank and strongly supported by Joffre, was using all his powers of flattery and persuasion to keep Sir John French from looking too cautiously over his shoulder at the inviting prospect of Calais and Boulogne. Foch knew that in Henry Wilson he still had a powerful advocate at GHQ. There is no doubt that to achieve his purpose he deliberately and repeatedly deceived French. In the last analysis, it was just as well. The cost to the BEF was bitter indeed; but the dividend was substantial. It was nothing less than improbable victory out of the prospect of certain defeat. Foch acknowledged this debt by agreeing to the relief of the remnants of the BEF from the Ypres salient on 15 November.

French's change of mind on 20 October was due to a simple decision on the other side of the hill. On this day Falkenhayn decided that, having collected his resources and done his sums, the time had come to spring the trap. Accordingly, he set in train a series of counter-attacks along his entire front from la Bassée to the sea. We shall concern ourselves here with the 'southern' battlefield – with what have come to be known as the battles of la Bassée and Armentières. Lest the reader may think that these were subsidiary actions compared with those of the 'northern' battlefield, a simple statistic should suffice: between 14 October and 22 November the casualties suffered by II Corps, III Corps, the Indian Corps, and 19th Infantry Brigade were, so far as it is possible to be precise, 615 officers and 26,150 other ranks. It was scarcely a sideshow.

The German attack in the south developed simultaneously on the fronts of both II and III Corps. It started with a disaster comparable to that of the Gordons at Audencourt and the Munsters at Etreux.

On the 19th, 2/Royal Irish of 3rd Division occupied the village of le Pilly

---

[17] This was the most easterly point reached in the advance. Here III Corps was little more than three miles from Lille.

on the Aubers ridge, midway between Herlies (already captured by 9th Brigade) and Fournes (which was Conneau's objective for that day). In fact, despite several false reports of success, the French never reached Fournes. The Royal Irish, believing their position to be covered, stood fast; and when on the 20th Smith-Dorrien began to pull back his left the Royal Irish were isolated and surrounded. Subjected to a heavy bombardment during the morning, they were attacked by three battalions of *14th Division*. There could be only one outcome, but it was not until 3 p.m. that the survivors, nearly all wounded, were forced to surrender. In the two days covering the capture and subsequent loss of le Pilly the battalion lost 17 officers and 561 other ranks. Only 30 other ranks escaped to rejoin their lines that night.

The loss of the Royal Irish was a matter of anger and sadness among the men of 8th Brigade, for the battalion had fought with great distinction from the first day of action. Tom Bradley of 4/Middlesex was particularly upset: 'My mind went back to the morning at Mons when the Irish came up into the salient and covered our withdrawal without regard to their own losses. Not many of those original lads were still around in October, but if it hadn't been for them, I wouldn't be here to tell the tale. It always seemed to be the same. The best bunch always seemed to be in the thick of things.' Very true. Some battalions – 'the best bunch' – had won a particular reputation for reliability and fighting quality, and their unenviable reward was to be given the most dangerous tasks. None the less, most of the disasters which befell the BEF owed as much to human error as to regimental pride.

The *Sixth Army* offensive against the southern sector, timed to coincide with the *Fourth Army* attack against the northern, may be summarized thus. First, on the front of II Corps. Here the main effort was concentrated on 3rd Division, and by the 22nd it had been forced back to the line Lorgies–Aubers. On its left, Conneau's cavalry had been withdrawn and replaced by 19th Infantry Brigade of III Corps, leaving a dangerous gap west of Fromelles, which had been evacuated by Conneau. (This gap was filled on the 23rd by the Jullundur Brigade of the Lahore Division. On this and the following six days 1/Manchesters and 47th Sikhs particularly distinguished themselves.) Yet as before, and as they would again, the Germans failed to exploit their success, for instead of concentrating their main effort against 3rd Division they at once committed their *13th Division* against 5th Division on the right of II Corps.

Faced by envelopment on his left, Smith-Dorrien had already begun preparing a reserve position which was virtually the same as that from which the original advance had started on the 15th. With hindsight, it can now be seen that the move forward had been precipitate, for the BEF was committed – as the Germans had so often been – piecemeal, and Intelligence estimates of German strength had been criminally inaccurate. This cannot have been the fault of Macdonogh, who had learned his lesson at Mons. If anything, it was the product of a euphoria carefully fostered by Foch and shared for a short while by French.

Smith-Dorrien (and, for that matter, Pulteney) had never wanted to embark on *l'offensive à outrance* – not, at least, without proper preparation and a clear picture of the prospect before him. Lille was an inviting prize, and tantalizingly close. But might it not be possible that the same idea had also occurred to Falkenhayn? Not so, said GHQ.

Thus Smith-Dorrien, no stranger to retreat, decided to pull back; but this time there was no question of the 'stopping-blow' of Le Cateau. It was to be a matter of a fighting withdrawal and a series of desperate defensive actions, too numerous to record. Once more the BEF succeeded in slipping away, for in the words of the official History, 'the retirement of II Corps on the night of 22/23 October to the new line was carried out without the slightest interference, though next day at least one German regiment stormed the villages that had been abandoned'.

On 24 October, II Corps lay thus, right to left: Givenchy, thence east of Festubert, Richebourg l'Avoué, east of Neuve Chapelle, Fauquissart, Rouges Bancs.[18] This line was to be held until the end of the battle of la Bassée, with one exception. On 26 October the Germans launched a major assault on Neuve Chapelle, which lay roughly at the junction between 5th Division and 3rd Division.

The battle lasted for four days. Why the Germans should have expended so much costly effort (six infantry regiments and two *Jäger* battalions, with twice the normal artillery support) to gain an objective of little tactical importance is difficult to understand; and more difficult still when, after an unsuccessful counter-attack on the 28th, a British patrol entered the ruined village at 3 a.m. the following morning, only to find that it had been evacuated by the enemy.

The German military mind is not always easy to understand. The fighting had cost them well over 5,000 casualties. The official records do not even mention Neuve Chapelle, neither its capture nor its evacuation, which suggests that the Germans considered the action to have been a failure. A more probable answer is that on 29 October the battle of Gheluvelt – the battle to end all battles – began. We know, for example, that all the heavy artillery of *Sixth Army* was withdrawn from the front of II and III Corps on the 29th to support Fabeck's *Army Group*; and on 30 October *26th Division*, which had taken a major part in the battle for Neuve Chapelle, was north of the Lys and about to join in the attack on the Messines–Wytschaete ridge. Not even the Germans could sustain a major offensive along the entire front.

On the British side, the order of battle at Neuve Chapelle reads very much like that on the canal at Mons: 7th, 8th and 9th Infantry Brigades of 3rd Division, and 14th Infantry Brigade of 5th Division, to which were added such additional units as Smith-Dorrien could beg or borrow from Allenby and from the Lahore Division. Distinctions are invidious, but in the forefront of the fighting were our old friends from Obourg and Nimy, 4/Middlesex and 4/Royal Fusiliers; 1/Northumberland Fusiliers and

---

[18] These names were not to be allowed a decent anonymity; for it was here and hereabouts that 'Second Ypres' was to be fought in 1915.

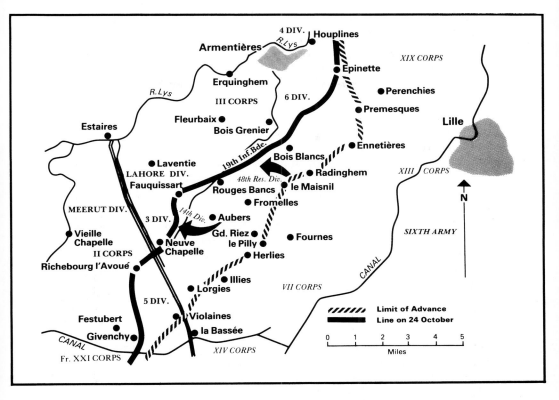

MAP 10. *La Bassée*

1/Lincolns; 1/Wiltshires; and above all, 1/Royal West Kents (Harry Bell was severely wounded here), which by the 29th had been reduced to 328 men commanded by two newly joined subalterns and two sergeant-majors. 'Once more', says the official History, 'the British troops had shown a superiority over the enemy in fortitude and endurance . . . and once more fire discipline had, in his eyes, multiplied the force opposing him into immense superiority of numbers.'

While Smith-Dorrien was thus engaged Pulteney was fighting the battle of Armentières. As II Corps fell back on the hinge of Givenchy, so 19th Infantry Brigade and 6th Division were obliged to conform. By the 22nd it had been necessary to evacuate what had suddenly become a dangerous salient formed by the line of the previous advance: Fromelles–Radingham –Ennetières–Premesques. On the 23rd, III Corps was holding a front of twelve miles from Rouges Bancs to Epinette and thence to Houplines, le Gheer and St Yves, where 4th Division was in touch with Allenby's Cavalry Corps, itself under increasing pressure between Messines and Hollebeke. Facing Pulteney were the greater part of *XIII Corps*, *48th Reserve Division*, *XIX Corps* and *I Cavalry Corps*.

Yet curiously the Germans, with this immense superiority, did not press their attacks with anything like the ferocity experienced by 3rd Division farther south, even though Armentières was an immeasurably more important objective than Neuve Chapelle. Indeed, it was not until the 30th (by when battle had been joined in earnest at Gheluvelt) that 4th Division, north of the Lys, was subjected to a major infantry attack.[19] After the inevitable dawn bombardment an assault was made in great strength on 1/Hampshires of 11th Brigade, holding a one-mile front east of Ploegsteert Wood.

Charlie Watts was kept very busy.

> I thought things had been pretty hot first time round at Le Cateau, but this was much hotter. As fast as we knocked the Jerries down they kept on coming and God knows how many dead and wounded were lying out in front of our trenches, many of them only 50 yards away. I believe they actually got into a trench away on our right and wiped out a whole platoon. Just in time the Somersets came up in support and Jerry decided he had had enough. By then my rifle was so hot I could scarcely touch it. Someone said we'd fired a thousand rounds apiece. I shouldn't wonder.

Farther south 6th Division, less well tempered on the anvil of war, and 19th Brigade, veterans of the earliest days, withstood ceaseless bombardment and a series of uncoordinated infantry attacks, chiefly against 16th and 18th Brigades. These were met with devastating effect by – in particular – 1/Leicesters, 1/East Yorks and 2/Durham L.I. It is difficult to be precise, but over a period of four days these three units were attacked by upward of ten German battalions, by when the newcomers of 6th Division had been blooded in every sense. They had also learned the art of self-defence in a brutally uncompromising school. Jim Wyles of the Leicesters, who had not fired a shot on the Aisne, remembers his first experience of action:

> Our trenches weren't up to much, but they gave us a bit of protection. We had two companies in the line with a machine-gun at each end firing at an angle across our front. To the Germans it must have seemed like a wall of lead. I remember an officer walking along behind us, cool as you like, giving fire orders like on the ranges. But this wasn't the ranges and he was knocked out within a few minutes. If I remember one thing clearly, it was the dreadful cries of the wounded Germans out in front of us. That really upset me. It was something I was to hear many times again.

By 30 October the German attacks south of the Lys had begun perceptibly to slacken. If III Corps had seemed to be less involved than II Corps, let the reader not be deceived. Between 15 and 31 October, its casualties were 207 officers and 5,572 other ranks, of which two-thirds were

[19] 4th Division had even been able to send most of 10th Brigade south of the river to support 6th Division.

PLATE 28. *Into battle*

incurred by 6th Division. By now every survivor in the BEF was a battle-hardened veteran.

The official end of the battles of la Bassée and Armentières is 2 November. In fact, the battles in Flanders never ended. What the record means is that from that date the Germans abandoned any idea of a major offensive south of the Lys. What then of II Corps and III Corps?

On 29 and 30 October II Corps, which had been in constant action since 23 August and was worn out by casualties and fatigue, was relieved by the Lahore and Meerut Divisions of the Indian Corps. It went back into billets to lick its wounds and recharge its batteries. It was promised ten days' rest. Ten days? By *1 November* its weary battalions were being sent back into the line in succession to plug the gaps in Haig's hard-pressed sector north of the river. There were no complaints. The men shouldered their packs, kissed their rifles, uttered a prayer, and returned to duty. At least they went in comparative style, for the most part in London buses.

III Corps stayed where it was; but not for long. As the great battle for the Messines ridge was joined, so it sucked into it every available reserve. III Corps was all that remained. Battalion by battalion, it took its leave of the comparative peace and quiet of Armentières and soldiered on in new and inhospitable trenches.

Givenchy and Festubert. Neuve Chapelle and Aubers. For all too short a time they were forgotten. One name now transcended all others: Ypres.

CHAPTER 11

Ypres and the Salient: Crisis and Climax

19 October is the point of departure. Not until that evening did the geometry of 'First Ypres' begin to assume the broad outline which was to dictate the course of the battle throughout the next four weeks. That outline, as we have seen, followed the ridges – the 'saucer's rim' – running to the south and east of the town. It was for these ridges, almost imperceptible to the eye as major features, that the great battle was fought, yard by yard, copse by copse, farm by farm. On no single day between 19 October and 22 November did the salient line remain intact. It was breached at Langemarck, near Zonnebeke and Polygon Wood, at Gheluvelt, Zandvoorde, Hollebeke.[1] It was restored again – and again – and again. And through the salient there ran, south-east to north-west, like a vital artery, the Menin road. And like an artery, it bled greatly whenever it was cut. There is small virtue in measuring one level of blood-letting against another; but the Menin road – and the woods and ridges on either side – was the scene of long and sanguinary conflict.

Before the story of the salient starts, there are a number of random observations which may serve to explain or illustrate certain aspects of 'First Ypres' (but see also p. 186).

First the battleground. When the BEF arrived in Flanders in October it was as yet untouched by war. It was a farming countryside of villages and small-holdings, broken by hedges and ditches, with many copses and larger woods. It looked then almost exactly as it looks to-day. Even after the bitter battles of First Ypres, there were many houses and farms still standing, and the woods which covered the long ridge were not greatly damaged. They continued to provide a considerable degree of cover, and indeed the German practice of bombarding the forward edges created a series of natural barricades of fallen tree-trunks which served the defenders well, and greatly impeded the attacking infantry. It was not until the end of 1917, when the drainage system had been destroyed, that the salient came to resemble a lunar landscape.[2]

[1] The battle for the Messines ridge has its own, later place in the narrative.
[2] On 7 June 1917 British Tunnelling Companies exploded nineteen gigantic mines under Messines and Wytschaete which literally blew off the entire top of the ridge.

PLATE 29. *The old Menin road*

Next, the trenches. 'First Ypres' certainly saw the growth of the trench-system which was to become a permanent feature of the Western Front, but throughout October and November the phrase 'digging in' often meant little more than the hasty construction of rifle-pits or occasionally a more continuous line without revetment or overhead protection. The Germans with their immense preponderance of heavy artillery firing high-explosive projectiles[3] gave their opponents no respite, and therefore no time to construct elaborate defences, but the official monograph refers repeatedly to the British ingenuity in the use of ground and the improvisation of strong-points.

During these early days there were no communication trenches, and this made it virtually impossible to evacuate the wounded except at night. George Roupell's diary dwells at some length on this problem:

> One could not face some of the sights in the trenches with any squeamish sentiment . . . When a man was wounded, the cry went up 'where's the officer, a man hit.' It was the officer's job to put on iodine and bandage up the wound, and one saw some pretty unpleasant sights. The officers were supplied with hypodermic syringes and morphia tablets to keep men quiet till we could get them away, but on the whole the men were wonderfully good, and it was only in the more serious cases that one used drugs.

By now the men had grown a kind of carapace – a mixture of resignation and black humour. George Roupell quotes an instance:

> As an example of how callous all the men got I remember one section of the line which we took over about this time, in which the French had

[3] The first 'experimental' 18-pdr HE shells were sent to France on 19 October, but none were fired at Ypres until the morning of 31 October. The BEF had neither trench mortars nor hand-grenades during 'First Ypres'. Five primitive Very-light pistols were issued to I Corps on 13 November.

suffered a number of casualties and had apparently buried them locally. At any rate there were lots of bits lying about, and in one part of our parapet a hand stuck out into the trench. We couldn't remove the corpse without breaking down a long bit of parapet, so there it stayed and when we were relieved from that section all the men shook hands with this grim relic and said 'good-bye' in a cheerful way as they hurried out of the front line!

Then there was the weather. The winter of 1914–15 was the worst in living memory. The rain was bad enough, for rain in Flanders meant mud, and the men in the line, tested to the limit of endurance by unceasing enemy attacks, had also to survive the misery of constant downpours and waterlogged trenches. 'We used to look at those lovely woods,' recalls George Medhurst, 'and wished we were there. Not because they were safer, but at least they were dry!' In November the weather turned bitterly cold, with heavy frost and even driving snow. And it is interesting to note that when the Germans finally accepted defeat at the gates of Ypres their official communiqués – day after day – resorted to blaming their failure in phrases like 'the fighting in West Flanders continues, hindered during the last few days by rainy and stormy weather. . . . The fighting on the right flank yesterday also, in consequence of unfavourable weather, showed only trifling progress.' Mud and snow can be great levellers.

Finally, there is something of which the reader must never lose sight. The narrative refers – for there is no other means of reference – to divisions and brigades, to battalions and companies. These references are in fact meaningless. Certainly after the major attack of Fabeck's *Army Group* on 29 October a 'battalion' meant perhaps 300 effectives, a 'company' as little as 80 or 50 or 30 or – sometimes – none. From October onward, there was a steady stream of reinforcements to fill the gaps. But Kitchener remained stubbornly and dangerously adamant that Haldane's Territorial Army was not fit to fight. A few – only seven – Territorial battalions were committed to battle at 'First Ypres'. They conducted themselves with a distinction that put Kitchener to shame. The old Regular Army did not help. By November what was left of it took a very jaundiced view of the reinforcements being sent out from home. 'No young recruits were sent, and many of the men were the dregs of the depots, old worn drunken wasters'.[4] In the autumn of 1914 1/Bedfords received 169 serving soldiers, 43 reservists, 745 Special reservists and 34 re-enlisted old (i.e. 'South Africa') soldiers.[5] It does not greatly matter. These 'dregs of the depots' fought bravely and died bravely. Old Contemptibles they may have been. Contemptible they were not.

While II Corps, III Corps and the Cavalry Corps were pushing slowly forward towards Lille and Menin, IV Corps, on 19 October, extended the line by advancing south-east of Ypres along the Menin road, while on its left

---

[4] *Official History*, Vol II.
[5] *Official History*, Vol II.

de Mitry's four French cavalry divisions, the Belgian cavalry division, and the 87th Territorial Division moved steadily east. De Mitry's force actually reached Roulers on this day, but there its advance was abruptly halted – for two reasons.

First, it found itself confronted by a formidable obstruction in the shape of the new German *Fourth Army*. Secondly, on the morning of the 19th, Beseler's *III Reserve Corps*, lying over de Mitry's left shoulder, began the battle of the Yser. This attack, against the Belgian Army, was the ultimate attempt at envelopment of the Allied left, and it came very close to succeeding. The battle hung in the balance until at the moment of supreme crisis the Belgians enlisted the aid of an ally more powerful than all the French and British divisions put together. On the evening of 28 October their engineers succeeded, at the second attempt, in opening the gates of the Furnes lock at Nieuport and letting in the sea between the Yser and the Ypres railway. Gradually this inundation spread as far south as Dixmude and created an impassable barrier. The race to the sea was over. The sea had won. The battles for Ypres began.

Rawlinson's IV Corps Operation Order of 18 October, issued at Poperinghe at 11 p.m., said this: 'IV Corps will advance to-morrow (the 19th) to attack the enemy in the neighbourhood of Menin.' The right flank of 7th Infantry Division would be covered by Allenby's 2nd Cavalry Division, the left flank by 3rd Cavalry Division which, *tout simple*, 'will occupy Roulers' [*which de Mitry was about to evacuate!*]. There was no single mention of the enemy, his disposition or his strength. Small wonder. Neither IV Corps nor GHQ had the slightest knowledge of either, as we shall presently see.

7th Division marched off down the Menin road. It was in fact marching straight at *two* German Army Corps. Falkenhayn held his hand. He could afford to. Capper's right-hand brigade, the 20th, reached Kruiseecke, two miles south-east of Gheluvelt, on one of the low spurs running from the main ridge. There it was only four miles from Menin. It was at the apex of the salient; and it did not stay there long. On 26 August it was driven back to the crossroads near Gheluvelt.

Pte Rooney of 2/Border Regiment, a former miner from Whitehaven who had joined the Army 'because shift-work interfered with my courting', and who in his last days looked exactly like the original model for Bairnsfather's Old Bill, remembers the reception his battalion received as they arrived at Kruiseecke:

We had no idea where the enemy was, but when we reached the village they opened up with everything they'd got. We had no time to dig in or do anything and during that evening and following days we lost at least 300 men.[6] It was my first day in action and I was really only a kid. Looking back, I enjoyed it in a funny sort of way. Not the killing and the dreadful noise, but the excitement and the fact that we were in the middle of a real battle.

[6] In fact, more than 550. By the 26th, 20th Brigade had lost 46 officers and 1,402 men.

207

While 20th Infantry Brigade was thus dangerously exposed at Kruiseecke the rest of 7th Division and the two brigades of 3rd Cavalry Division pushed farther east in accordance with the general – and excessively optimistic – plan agreed between Foch and Sir John French, despite growing evidence of a massive German build-up from Lille and round Courtrai and Roulers. Falkenhayn still held his hand, and apart from strong resistance opposite Kruiseecke, there was at first little enemy activity, a fact which should surely have aroused suspicions at GHQ.

To the left of 20th Brigade, 21st Brigade reached Terhand two miles north of the Menin road, and beyond them 22nd Brigade were a mile farther east near Dadizeele, at which point they were actually within sight of Menin. They were also within full view of the German outpost line and artillery, which now began to react sharply. It was 10 a.m., and during the next two hours 1/Royal Welsh Fusiliers was subjected to a violent bombardment and suffered severe casualties. 7th Division had reached the limit of its advance.

Farther left, 3rd Cavalry Division did even better. 10th Hussars of 6th Cavalry Brigade reached Ledeghem on the parallel road and railway from Menin to Roulers. It was the most easterly point the British were to reach for four years. To the north 6th Cavalry Brigade occupied Moorslede and Passchendaele, by when there was significant increase in enemy resistance.

Suddenly, just after 1 p.m., General Capper was ordered to abandon the attack on Menin. No reason was given, but the reasons are not far to seek. First, the truth had dawned on GHQ that IV Corps was being enticed into a formidable mousetrap. Secondly, de Mitry's precipitate withdrawal from Roulers had uncovered the left flank of Byng's 3rd Cavalry Division. French thus found himself in much the same position as he had been on the morning of 23 August at Mons, but with a significant difference. He was now faced not by one German *Army* but by two. Accordingly IV Corps began to pull back its centre and left, leaving 20th Brigade at Kruiseecke, thus as it were creating a small salient projecting from a longer one. By evening 7th Division occupied a line from Zandvoorde eastward to Kruiseecke, whence it turned north across the Menin road, passing west of Becelaere to Zonnebeke, where it joined 3rd Cavalry Division.

That evening French had a meeting with Haig, whose I Corps had now reached Flanders from the Aisne. He gave him these instructions:

> The enemy's strength on the front *Menin–Ostend*[7] is estimated at *about a corps and no more.*[7] I Corps will advance via Thourout with the object of capturing Bruges. The enemy is to be attacked and driven on Ghent.

The instructions left Haig free to attack north of Ypres or east towards Courtrai. He would have de Mitry's cavalry on his left and 3rd Cavalry Division on his right.

---

[7]Author's italics.

The reader may well feel that he has been here before – at 5.30 a.m. on 23 August at Smith-Dorrien's HQ at Sars-la-Bruyère. There is the same inexplicable euphoria, the same incomprehensible underestimate of German strength, this time compounded threefold, if not fourfold. Much had happened before that evening meeting on the 19th. Beseler had launched the battle of the Yser. IV Corps had run into trouble along its whole line. De Mitry was in full retreat from Roulers. Air reconnaissance had reported column after column of German troops moving west into the very path of Haig's proposed victory march. How then was it possible to speak of 'about a corps and no more'?

We shall never know. But two things are certain. First, Sir John French correctly committed I Corps to the Ypres salient when he had a second option astride the Lys, and therefore along the shortest route to Menin and Lille. This may have been gambler's luck, but on the 19th French was convinced that he – and his Allied opposite number, d'Urbal – had a golden opportunity to roll up the German right. Secondly, French now had a new Svengali – Foch. 'The marshal wishes at all costs to go to Brussels.' Foch's words have a hollow ring in the light of what was now to happen. He was still living in the dream-world of Plan XVII, for he had only one military philosophy: *l'offensive à outrance*. He could not give orders to French; but he could work on him. And work on him he did. He went a great deal further than that. He encouraged him. He carried a permanent hypodermic syringe of adrenalin. And at critical moments – of which there were to be many – he provided French troops, which he could ill spare, to fill the gaps and hold the line. Like all Frenchmen, he could be devious; but unlike some Frenchmen, he was dedicated to the simple proposition that if victory was not possible, defeat was not an inevitable alternative. He was a considerable soldier.

So to Haig; another considerable soldier. When, on 19 October, I Corps went forth to do battle his brief was simple: capture Bruges and Ghent and finish the war. The Germans had other ideas. From the opening battle of Langemarck until the final relief of the BEF in the salient four weeks later, Haig fought the battles for Ypres virtually single-handed, as Smith-Dorrien had fought the battles of Mons and Le Cateau. This is no criticism of Sir John French. When the great crises occurred GHQ, with no reserves left, had to leave Haig – and his brave and resourceful subordinate commanders, to say nothing of his incomparable men – to fight to the finish. They did. And once the great battle was joined there was nothing GHQ could do except pray. There is a marvellous vignette of Haig, on the desperate day of Gheluvelt, *riding* with his staff up the Menin road, watching the ever-closer fall of shells and noting the growing number of retreating stragglers. If Mons and Le Cateau belong to Smith-Dorrien, 'First Ypres' is Haig's memorial.

As I Corps moved forward, the salient took shape. It was, as we have seen, to change day by day, with the French taking over this sector and that. But 21 October provides a clear visual picture.

On that day the salient resembled – as well it might – a large question mark (see Map 11). At its northern end it ran from Bixschoote on the Yser canal, thence in a wide semicircle following the rim of ridges through Langemarck, west of Poelcapelle and Passchendaele, thence to Zonnebeke, east of Polygon Wood, through Gheluvelt, Kruiseecke, Zandvoorde, and so to the bend in the Ypres–Comines canal near Hollebeke. Here it turned south along the Wytschaete–Messines ridge, east of Ploegsteert, to the river Lys at Armentières.

This neat geographical shape was not destined to last for long. As first the German *Sixth Army* and then the *Fourth Army* was flung against this thinly held sixteen-mile front, so it began to buckle; first in the north and north-east, then on either side of the Ypres–Menin road, at Hollebeke, and along the Messines ridge. Throughout 'First Ypres' only Armentières, Ploegsteert, Wulverghem, Klein Zillebeke, Zillebeke and Bixschoote remained continuously in Allied hands; and, of course, Ypres itself. Elsewhere along the salient the line ebbed and flowed in repeated attack and counter-attack. The two great crises were those of 31 October and 11 November. On both these days the Germans attacked furiously north and south of the Menin road, for in 1914 the German High Command remained obsessed with the town of Ypres. When in 1918 Ludendorff made one last supreme effort to reach Calais he chose the line of the Lys. It always was, always had been, the right road to victory; but by then it was too late.

The first German attack on the north-eastern part of the salient was made on 21 October[8] against 7th Division by troops of *XXVI Reserve Corps*. Even as late as this day the existence or at least the true size of *Fourth Army* was not known at French and British HQ. Such information as they had encouraged Foch and French to dismiss the *Reserve* formations as poor-quality.

It was a dangerous assumption. Even if the volunteers (the very word was a military novelty in Germany) of the new *Reserve Corps* were short on training, they were long on courage to the point of fanaticism. If they were indifferently led, they were themselves indifferent to death; and they were very numerous. It was their misfortune to be committed at the outset against the most professional of all soldiers, bravely led, and uniquely expert in the use of their limited range of weapons. In a special Order of the Day on the crucial 29 October, the Kaiser dismissed these men as 'trash'; 'feeble adversaries who surrender in mass if they are attacked with vigour'. If Foch misjudged the patriotic fervour of the young German volunteers, the Kaiser was guilty of a more dangerous mistake – that of standing history on its head. The British soldier was accustomed to abuse, but he did not take kindly to the charge of cowardice. Furthermore, the Germans never did – perhaps never will – understand the British mind. When, during the confused fighting in Polygon Wood on 24 October, bullets were flying in all directions, some of the cross-fire was contributed by gunner officers indulging in a private hare-shoot.[9]

[8] But see below for the earlier situation at Hollebeke.
[9] The Northumberland Hussars – the first Territorial unit to go into action – were engaged in this fighting in Polygon Wood.

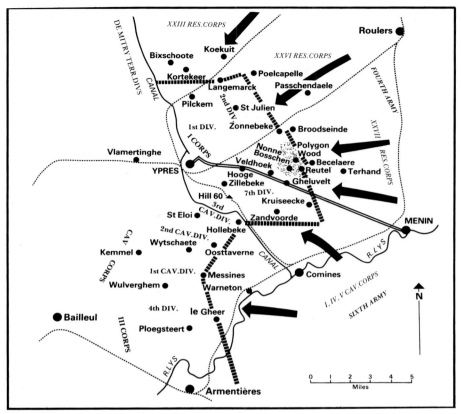

MAP 11. *The Salient, 21 October*

On the morning of the 21st the front of IV Corps ran from Zandvoorde, east to Kruiseecke, and then four miles north to Zonnebeke, the left of 7th Division covered by 3rd Cavalry Division. Between Zandvoorde and Hollebeke (2nd Cavalry Division) there was a gap of almost two miles, of which the Germans fortunately seem not to have been aware. Indeed, throughout this day the enemy attacks, although supported by the heavy and persistent bombardment which was to continue day and night during the next three weeks and along the whole salient,[10] were uncoordinated. There is no doubt that the German High Command was deceived by the accuracy and volume of British artillery and rifle fire into thinking that the opposition was far more formidable than was the case. In fact, until the entry of I Corps into the battle during the evening of the 21st German superiority east of Ypres was of the order of six to one. It was scarcely less on the southern flank.

At 8 a.m., after an hour's heavy enfilade fire from the Passchendaele ridge which overlooked its trenches near Zonnebeke, 22nd Brigade was attacked in strength by infantry of *52nd Reserve Division*. They came forward

---

[10] By 11 November, when British batteries were rationed to six rounds per gun per day, the Germans were also experiencing an acute shortage of artillery ammunition.

in massed formation, 'singing and waving their rifles in the air', according to one account. 'As fast as we shot them down, others took their place. Even when their own artillery barrage caught them by mistake, they kept on advancing. They were incredibly, ridiculously brave.'

That evening Lt Furze of 2/Queen's recorded in his diary:

> I left my trench and found Major C. in a state of panic. He said in as many words that the enemy was on top of us [*he was not far wrong*] and 'B' Coy had to retire as speedily as possible. Bullets were now flying in all directions and the whole thing seemed to be a chaos.
>
> I couldn't see why I should retire but I got my platoon out and told them to run for their lives to the main road (about 400 yards in rear). Never have I run so hard or felt so exhausted. Several of my men were bowled over and how I escaped myself is more than a marvel.

By evening the Queen's had lost 7 officers and 171 other ranks; but they had not been overrun, and it was not until 4th (Guards) Brigade of 2nd Division relieved Byng's cavalry on its left at 5.30 p.m. that the battalion was withdrawn into the ruins of Zonnebeke. The line of 22nd Brigade then ran thence to the east of Polygon Wood, joining the left of 21st Brigade at Reutel. This modest retirement was the only German success of the day, for a strong attack by *54th Reserve Division* farther south towards Gheluvelt was repulsed with heavy loss by 21st Brigade. Thus on 21 October two much-depleted brigades had withstood two full-strength enemy divisions. It is small wonder that the Germans could not believe the evidence of their own eyes. And it was a story which was about to be repeated again and again.

Before passing to the entry of I Corps into the salient, it is important to turn back the clock and describe briefly the situation which had developed on the southern flank, for here the Germans, had they but known it, gave up an opportunity (which they would only have once again) of making a decisive break-through to Ypres along the line of the Comines canal.

On the night of 20–21 October the salient ran from Messines north-east to Oosttaverne and Hollebeke, and this line was held by 1st and 2nd Cavalry Divisions. Between Hollebeke and Zandvoorde there was the previously mentioned gap of almost two miles. Beyond this, 20th Brigade of 7th Division extended the line to Kruiseecke. Even ignoring the existence of the gap, the line was perilously thin.

By midnight on the 20th the Germans had moved no fewer than six cavalry divisions[11] across the Lys between Menin and Warneton, thus underlining the 'northern' and 'southern' halves of the battlefield. It is no disrespect to Allenby's men to say that they were lucky that the cards of war fell as they did. German cavalry training – as the BEF had discovered during the retreat – was still rooted in the tradition of the Franco-Prussian War. Mounted, the numerous divisions were a positive impediment, and largely useless against the fire-power of modern weapons. Dismounted,

[11] *V, IV* and *I Cavalry Corps.*

German cavalrymen were lacking in basic infantry skills and – above all – far inferior to their British counterparts in musketry. They also undoubtedly lacked the *furor Teutonicus* of the young volunteers of *Fourth Army*. If two *Reserve Corps* had been committed against the southern flank of the salient, it is probable that the British line, for all its resolution, could not have withstood the shock.

During the morning of the 21st – although not under serious attack by the *Bavarian Cavalry Division* facing it – 3rd Cavalry Brigade at Hollebeke was ordered (the official History charitably speaks of a 'misunderstanding') to withdraw from the village and the neighbouring château to St Eloi to the north-west, only three miles from Ypres, thus widening the already critical gap. Realizing both the error and the danger, Hubert Gough at once ordered that the line must be restored. It was[12] – and at a cost of only fifteen casualties, which is sufficient commentary on the Germans' failure to grasp their golden opportunity this day. Indeed, by that evening, with the arrival of I Corps on his left at Zonnebeke, Rawlinson felt able to send 6th Cavalry Brigade to plug the gap west of Zandvoorde and move 7th Cavalry Brigade into reserve (a rare and precious word) between Hooge and Zillebeke. The first of many crises had been met. The German monograph does not mention any fighting at the village and château of Hollebeke on the 21st, beyond saying that the *Bavarian Cavalry Division* did not come 'within 2000 metres of Hollebeke', even though it had occupied the château. Silence, however, is not always golden. The following day the Divisional Commander was summarily dismissed. Joffre was not the only man to send unsuccessful generals packing.[13]

On 21 October, I Corps – desperately late – arrived in the salient. It did not, however, arrive to repel any growing threat to Ypres from the north-east. On the contrary. As we have seen, Sir John French's Operation Order for 20 October spoke of 'containing the enemy with the II, III and Cavalry Corps, and the 7th Division of IV Corps and *to attack vigorously with the I Corps*'.[14] The Order went on: 'The I Corps will march in the direction of Thourout [*halfway to Bruges and of singularly little importance*].' Foch was working busily on French, and French was back in one of his periodic bouts of euphoria. Luckily for the BEF, the arrival of I Corps brought with it a salutary injection of realism in the person of Douglas Haig. There was no further mention of Thourout. Only of Ypres.

On the 21st, 2nd Division moved forward to the line of the Zonnebeke–Langemarck road, and by that evening had relieved the left of Rawlinson's IV Corps. It had been Haig's intention to occupy the Passchendaele–Poelkapelle ridge, but de Mitry's withdrawal and growing enemy strength (*XXVI* and *XXIII Reserve Corps*) halted his advance. Passchendaele was to remain in German hands for three years. Its final

---

[12] The château itself was not recaptured until the following day. It was lost again on 30 October.
[13] The British, with insular tact, did not use words like *limogés*. The recurrent phrase in the official History is: 'Invalided home.'
[14] Author's italics.

capture in 1917 (by when it had largely ceased to be of any military value) left an indelible mark and an unforgettable name on the record of British arms.

At 3 p.m. Haig ordered I Corps to dig in on the line which it had reached, and thus the northern hinge of the salient was formed. At midnight this line ran as follows:

2nd Division (with a brigade in reserve at St Jean): from Zonnebeke to a point one mile east of Langemarck.

1st Division (with a brigade in reserve at Pilckem): from Langemarck to Koekuit, thence due west to Kortekeer and Bixschoote, its left in touch with de Mitry's Territorial divisions on the Yser canal.

The salient – now sharply defined – was continued south by 7th Division (Zonnebeke – Reutel – Kruiseecke – Zandvoorde), then by 6th Cavalry Brigade to Hollebeke and by the Cavalry Corps from Hollebeke to Messines. At midnight 3 British infantry divisions and 2½ cavalry divisions faced at least 6 German infantry divisions and 6 cavalry divisions. Apart from 2½ brigades in reserve near Ypres, Sir John French had committed his entire resources. He had no option.

On the morning of the 22nd a strong position lay to our immediate front. It followed a line Bixschoote – Langemarck – Zonnebeke – Reutel – Gheluvelt, and I and IV British as well as the French IX Corps,[15] all picked troops, had been located there. They had dug a well-planned maze of trenches behind barbed-wire entanglements before a single German shell arrived to disturb their work.[16]

This is, of course, nonsense. The 'maze of trenches' were hastily dug, and averaged little more than three feet deep. They were not continuous. There were no supports and no traverses. There was no wire. German shells had effectively 'disturbed their work' for two days. The monograph – for by no means the only time – is here seeking to excuse the German failure to overwhelm a vastly inferior opponent – inferior, that is, only in numbers. The BEF in this sector did not consist of 'picked troops'. They were the only troops available. They simply happened to be very expert and very resolute.

Throughout the 22nd the Germans attacked the face of the salient, the main efforts being against 5th Infantry Brigade (2/Worcesters, 2/Oxford and Bucks L.I., 2/HLI) near Langemarck, and at the junction between 21st and 22nd Infantry Brigades[17] farther south. Both proved to be costly failures. Micky Lay remembers 'a rampart of dead and wounded no more

[15] Dubois's IX Corps did not take over 1st Division's sector until the afternoon of the 23rd.
[16] Ypres, 1914.
[17] 22nd Infantry Brigade had been forced to evacuate Zonnebeke that morning.

than 50 yards in front of our trenches'. At Reutel *54th Reserve Division* attacked 21st Infantry Brigade in great strength, but, caught in the open by the guns of 2nd Division in support, and by the machine-guns of 2/Green Howards and 2/RSF, the massed infantry was decimated within minutes, and when the survivors bravely came forward again they were driven back by the concentrated rifle-fire of the left-flank battalion, 2/Wiltshires.

On the northern face of the salient 1st Division was driven out of Kortekeer, but this loss was offset on the southern face by the recapture of Hollebeke Château by a single squadron of the Royals (6th Cavalry Brigade) which routed a regiment of the *Bavarian Cavalry Division*. The château was to be the scene of bitter fighting for several days. 'I can't think why,' said Herbert Jeffreys of the Royals. 'There was nothing left of it. I suppose it had become a bit of a symbol.'

The fighting on the 22nd marked the beginning of a new tactical approach, accentuated by the break-up of IV Corps on 27 October when 7th Division was attached to I Corps and 3rd Cavalry Division to Allenby's Cavalry Corps. With the salient now defined, and enemy pressure constantly switching from one sector to another in search of a weak joint, Haig abandoned any idea of a formal battle order. Such reserves as there were became in effect a general I Corps reserve, and battalions and batteries were moved outside their own divisions and brigades to stiffen the line at the most critical points. The process was known as 'puttying-up', and it was this brilliant improvisation which – apart from the stamina and fortitude of the men – made possible the victory of 'First Ypres'. For example: on the 22nd, 6th Infantry Brigade (the reserve of 2nd Division) was used to support first 7th Division and then 1st Division; during the battle of Gheluvelt, two groups under General Bulfin (2nd Infantry Brigade) and General Lord Cavan (4th Guards Brigade) were sent to plug the gap near Klein Zillebeke; on the same day the line of *3rd* Infantry Brigade was extended by 2/RSF of *21st* Infantry Brigade; and the decisive counter-attack to restore the line of *3rd* Infantry Brigade after the German break-through was made by 2/Worcesters, the reserve battalion – indeed, the only real reserve – of *2nd* Division.[18]

There is one aspect of this battle which has not been much considered; and it is as important as it is remarkable. The fighting during the great German offensive which began on 29 October was extremely confused and fluid. All normal forms of communication were disrupted. 'The ground rocked under the constant bombardment,' says one report, 'and to show oneself was to invite instant elimination.' Yet remarkably Haig and his subordinate commanders succeeded in maintaining control and somehow 'reading' the battle. The Germans did not; otherwise they would never have lost Gheluvelt – and with it perhaps the war. It was the same story during the simultaneous battle for the Messines ridge.

The answer is that senior British commanders *commanded*. Not from remote châteaux (the tragedy at Hooge will presently be described), but by close personal involvement, with generals and brigadiers far forward in the

[18] Reference to the Order of Battle on p. 245 will show what these improvisations implied.

eye of the storm; with brave and efficient staff officers; and with the great unsung heroes, the battalion 'runners'. At no stage was Haig out of the picture. It may not have been a very pretty picture, but at the White Château he could watch the ebb and flow. And rightly judge the proper process of 'puttying-up'.

Foch could also read the battle. As we know, the idea of a defensive posture was anathema to him. Now, on 23 October, with a splendid disregard of reality, he ordered General d'Urbal, commander of the new Eighth Army, to launch an offensive along the whole French line north of Ypres. In a letter to the British C-in-C, Foch asked that *the whole British Army* [19] 'should support the French attack by acting offensively *along its whole front,* [19] the left moving on Courtrai'. D'Urbal issued his orders early on the 23rd. In the words of the official History, 'they could not be taken seriously'. Sir John French took them seriously, even enthusiastically, as his telegrams to Kitchener daily confirmed. Foch could read French like a book, and if there were any blank pages he could rely on Henry Wilson to fill them in.

Fortunately, Haig was not given to such excesses of enthusiasm. He was barely holding his own in the salient, and while the directors at Doullens, St Omer and Poperinghe were assembling their actors for a grand finale, he was in a sense manning the footlights, well aware that he was confronted by a large and hostile audience.

D'Urbal's offensive predictably stuttered and stopped. But Foch had not been playing to the gallery. He had been busy coaching Sir John French. Thus on 23 and 24 October two important things happened.

First, on the afternoon of the 23rd, Dubois's IX Corps (17th and 18th Divisions) took over the whole BEF sector from Bixschoote to Zonnebeke. As a result, 1st Division was withdrawn into I Corps reserve in time to meet the challenge which was shortly to come astride the Menin road; and 2nd Division was able to close up to 7th Division on its right, south of Zonnebeke, and so stiffen the hard-pressed line between Becelaere and Gheluvelt. It is difficult to imagine the superhuman strain to which these men were subjected; bombarded day and night, constantly under fire, often up to their knees in water, sleeping when they could, fed when it was possible. As the earth has salt, these were the salt of the earth.

But secondly, the Germans had arrived at a moment of truth.

> With the failure of the *46th Reserve Division* to gain a decisive victory between Bixschoote and Langemarck, the fate of *XXVI* and *XXVII Reserve Corps* was also settled. For the time being, any further thought of a break-through was out of the question. They had suffered heavily in the contest against a war-experienced and *numerically superior opponent entrenched in strongly fortified positions.* [20]

So the first scene ended. The next was to be savage – and decisive.

---

[19] Author's italics.
[20] *Ypres, 1914.* The italicization is by the present author.

216

By the evening of 24 October the commanders of both the German *Fourth* and *Sixth Armies* recognized that their efforts to break the British line had met with little or no success; the former north-east of Ypres on either side of Zonnebeke, the latter on the front held by II and III Corps between Givenchy and St Yves to the north of Armentières. Despite their immense superiority in men and material, they had failed – as they had failed at Mons and Le Cateau – to overcome resolute, highly professional defenders. They had also – and this applies to all the battles for Ypres – been outfought at every command-level from general to NCO; and never was this to be more clearly illustrated than during the storm which was about to break on the BEF, when majors would find themselves commanding the remnants of brigades and sergeants all that was left of battalions. If there is one single reason why the Germans failed to achieve victory between 29 October and 2 November this is it. They were not afraid to die. They seem to have been afraid to take the critical decisions which alone win battles.

On 27 October OHL elected to stake everything on a single, mighty blow delivered on a seven-mile front between Gheluvelt and Messines. The target was Ypres. The intention was the destruction and defeat of the BEF.

The instrument of this great attack was to be *Army Group Fabeck*, commanded by General Fabeck of *XIII Corps* (then opposite Armentières) and consisting of *XV Corps* from the Aisne, *II Bavarian Corps* from Péronne, *6th Bavarian Reserve Division* and *26th Reserve Division*, supported by six cavalry divisions and the equivalent of six infantry brigades. North of the Menin road the attack would be made by *XXVII Reserve Corps* of *Fourth Army*. Fabeck's group consisted of fresh, full-strength formations. More crucially,

PLATE 30. *Roll-call of 2/Scots Guards, 27 October. Twelve officers and 460 men answered*

217

there were assembled, as Fabeck's battering-ram, 262 heavy guns and 484 artillery pieces of smaller calibre. The starting-pistol would be fired at dawn on 29 October, and despite his earlier disappointment at Nancy, the Kaiser arrived at Prince Rupprecht's *Sixth Army* HQ on the 31st to preside over the destruction of the BEF and the capture of Ypres. He was to be disappointed again.

Facing this formidable group, the BEF lay thus on the night of 28 October: II Corps (which was not involved) from the la Bassée canal to Rouges Bancs, three miles from Armentières; III Corps and 19th Infantry Brigade, astride the Lys, from Rouges Bancs to St Yves a little south of Messines; Cavalry Corps (three divisions) thence to Hollebeke and Zandvoorde; I Corps (now including 7th Infantry Division) from Zandvoorde to Zonnebeke with five out of nine infantry brigades in the line. To match Fabeck's assembly of artillery, the BEF could offer exactly 44 guns of a calibre greater than 18-pdr. But the performance of the divisional artillery in the coming battle was to match that at Le Cateau, with batteries pushed forward and on several occasions even ahead of the infantry trenches. Frank Flood remembers firing at a mass of German infantry near Zandvoorde at a range of no more than 500 yards. 'It was incredible. We simply cut them to bits, but still they came on and if it hadn't been for some infantry on our right, they would have been on top of us. The only reason they stopped coming forward was that there were none left to keep coming.'

Before the curtain rises on Gheluvelt, there are two notes to add. Little has been said of the part played by the Royal Engineers, other than their signal contribution on the Mons Canal and during the advance to the Aisne. Now, in Flanders, with little bridging work, their main task was to help the infantry in digging and improving trenches and in constructing strong-points.[21] But the sappers were also well trained in musketry. On 2 November, 23rd and 26th Field Companies, pressed into the line as the only infantry reserve, did noble work west of the Menin road; and their contribution was matched elsewhere. Finally, at the risk of repetition, the reader should remember that words like 'brigade' and 'battalion' had become meaningless. When 1/Coldstream went into action at the crossroads south of Gheluvelt on the 29th, its total strength was *then* only 350. It withdrew by evening 160 strong; and with no officers. If it were possible to arrive at the strength of an average infantry battalion in the line at the start of the battle of Gheluvelt – or, indeed, elsewhere – then a reasonable estimate would be five officers and 300 other ranks.[22]

Fabeck's *Army Group* was disposed thus at midnight on 28 October. The right of *XV Corps* (*30th Division*) lay facing north-west along the Menin road. Its left (*39th Division*) was opposite the Zandvoorde ridge. Farther left came *II Bavarian Corps*; and opposite Messines *26th Infantry Division*. Finally, in touch with *XIX Corps* north of the Lys and facing part of 4th Infantry

[21] In 1914 signals communication was the responsibility of the Royal Engineers. The present Royal Corps of Signals did not then exist.
[22] On the morning of 1 November, the total survivors of 1/Loyals were one officer and thirty-five men (including Sam Owen from Troyon).

Division and 19th Infantry Brigade at St Yves and Ploegsteert were two cavalry divisions and five *Jäger* battalions.

The Allied line – for the BEF was to be progressively reinforced by the French, especially in the sector Wytschaete–Oosttaverne–St Eloi (where the Germans came within three miles of Ypres)[23] – is not so easily defined, for by the 29th many divisional and brigade formations had been broken up into *ad hoc* groups. For example, as we have seen, two such groups consisting of battalions from 2nd Division's only available reserves were formed under the command of Generals Bulfin and Lord Cavan, and these effectively plugged the gap caused by the loss of Zandvoorde and Hollebeke.

The battle of Gheluvelt was to prove not only an extraordinary feat of arms but also a lasting tribute to Allied co-operation, which was not to be the most signal feature of the years that followed. Above all, it was a master-piece of improvisation which the Germans could not match. In the words of the official History:

> The Germans were very cautious, perhaps as a result of their earlier losses, and failed to follow up success at once. At critical moments the infantry seemed to stop, possibly owing to heavy losses in officers; in any case the hesitation of Fabeck's *Army Group* was in striking contrast to the reckless bravery of the new *Reserve Corps* earlier in the battle.

There is an answer. Fabeck's attack, for all its weight (fifty-two battalions or more against a notional thirty, and massive artillery superiority) was in a sense speculative. Instead of concentrating on a single, decisive break-through, it dissipated its strength, never certain whether the fate of Ypres depended on the Menin road, on Zandvoorde and Hollebeke, or on the Messines ridge; and this lack of decision made it possible for Haig, in card-playing terms, to lead from weakness and still trump each ace that Fabeck held.

The official German monograph is particularly interesting. It ignores the recapture of Gheluvelt by 2/Worcesters on the afternoon of 31 October. Instead it says: 'We now come to the most vital point of the battle: who was to be the victor in the fight for the Wytschaete–Messines ridge?' The Germans were to be the victors; but it was an empty victory. The German General Staff knew this, for on 11 November it made one final attempt to reach Ypres along the Menin road.

This monograph is a record of self-inflicted frustration. It is extremely inaccurate, because it dared not tell the truth; and it is therefore a very re-vealing document. Again and again it speaks of Allied numerical superi-ority; of woods and villages 'fortified by numerous trenches, strong-points and wire'; of a seemingly endless stream of fresh reinforcements. *All* this is untrue. The answer was more simple. The men of the BEF were 'very ex-ceptional soldiers'. They were ordered to resist to the last; and they did.

---

[23] Three times between 29 October and 3 November Dubois, whose IX Corps extended Haig's line from Zonnebeke to Poelcapelle, proved a trusty friend by providing part of his reserve to fill vital gaps.

With their musketry skill, platoons seemed to the Germans like battalions. Individual guns, always short of ammunition, performed like batteries. They were not all heroes, for they were ordinary men, and ordinary men are not by nature heroic. But the British can be very bloody-minded; and this the Germans discovered. Just once, as we shall see, the monograph had no alternative but to tell the truth.

The morning of 29 October was, like almost every other morning, very foggy. The previous evening, Sir John French had given Haig orders for an attack by 2nd Division east of Zonnebeke in concert with Dubois's IX Corps. It was the last such order. There were to be no more attacks for a long time; only desperate defence and counter-attack.

By midnight Haig was well aware that the Germans were preparing a major offensive, and that the likely effort would be in the area of the cross-roads one mile south of Gheluvelt and farther west in front of Zandvoorde and Hollebeke – perhaps even as far as the Messines ridge held by Allenby's Cavalry Corps and an Indian brigade.

The British line at the Gheluvelt crossroads was at the junction between 7th Division and 1st Division (in both cases 'Brigade' would be a more accurate description). South of the road was the remnant of 20th Infantry Brigade which had taken such a battering at Kruiseecke; right to left 2/Gordons and 1/Grenadiers, with in support 2/Scots Guards and 2/Borders. Alf Matthews remembers only that he was almost too tired to keep his eyes open. 'When later that morning the enemy infantry attacked us – hundreds of them, it seemed – they made a target you couldn't miss even with your eyes shut, and I think mine were shut once or twice, in spite of the racket. By then I was firing away almost by force of habit.'

The German attack, in fact, was launched unexpectedly (at 5.30 a.m.) against 1st (Guards) Brigade to the *north* of the crossroads. It was made by three battalions of *6th Bavarian Reserve Division*,[24] and was carried out with the same reckless courage which had been shown by the young volunteer troops of *Fourth Army*. Here the British line was thinly held by 1/Cold-stream, two companies of 1/Black Watch and the machine-gun section of 1/Gloucesters (from 3rd Brigade). There was no preliminary bombard-ment. Under cover of the fog, the leading enemy infantry reached the right-hand trenches of 1st Brigade unnoticed, and finding no opposition on the main road worked round to the rear. Heavily outnumbered, two companies of the Coldstream and one of the Black Watch were overwhelmed, and after a bitter hand-to-hand fight in the trenches they were killed or captured to a man. Farther left, the remaining three companies in the line beat off a series of heavy attacks. It was now 6.30 a.m., and not for the last time the Germans seem not to have known how to exploit their success. At 7 a.m., when news of the German break-in at the crossroads reached General Fitz-Clarence[25] (1st Brigade) at Gheluvelt, he sent up 1/Gloucesters (on loan to

---

[24] Two days later this division had been switched to the left flank for the attack on Wytschaete.
[25] This outstanding officer – holder of the VC – was killed in action early on 12 November only hours after the decisive defeat of the Prussian Guard at Nonne Bosschen.

him from 3rd Brigade). There is little doubt that the intervention of this battalion – and ineffective German leadership – prevented an even greater disaster.

Remarkably, the men of 7th Division to the south of the Menin road were unaware of the fate of their comrades to the north, for they were not in touch with the Coldstream, and their view was severely limited by the fog and by farm buildings. This was lucky for the enemy infantry, for they would have provided an easy target as they moved confidently down the road in column of fours. 1/Grenadiers were congratulating themselves that reports of a German attack were a false alarm. They were shortly to be disabused of any such notion.

At 7.30 a.m. as the fog began to clear, the Germans opened a heavy bombardment on the two forward battalions of 20th Brigade, followed at once by an infantry attack in great strength. Heavily outnumbered and with their scattered trenches infiltrated by the enemy, the Grenadiers were slowly driven back, despite two brave attempts by 2/Gordons on their right to restore the situation. By noon they were holding a ditch (which passed for a trench) south of the Menin road near Gheluvelt, supported by 2/Borders in Brigade reserve. That night the battalion mustered five officers and 192 men. It had lost 470. Pat Wilson remembers only a day of confused fighting and mutual slaughter, 'much of it hand-to-hand and dead and wounded lying everywhere'. The sacrifice had not been in vain. The Germans, despite their success, did not attempt to exploit it. Throughout the following days, when virtually nothing stood between them and Ypres, they repeatedly failed to press home one break-through after another. There is no rational explanation except that Gheluvelt and Messines were irrational battles, and that the Germans not only dissipated their overwhelming strength but also convinced themselves – or were convinced by the exemplary determination of their stricken opponents – that a massive army lay waiting for them on the other side of the hill.

When news reached General Capper at 10.15 a.m. that his line had been broken south of the Menin road he was unaware of the equally desperate situation north of the crossroads. Here General Lomax (1st Division) had already set in train a plan to restore the situation. His chosen instrument was 3rd Infantry Brigade – General Landon – who first sent 1/Gloucesters forward to support (ineffectually as it proved) the remnants of 1st (Guards) Brigade. He then moved up his three remaining battalions from Veldhoek on the Menin road with instructions to secure Gheluvelt and to retake the trenches lost by 1/Coldstream and 1/Black Watch. They were too late to carry out the second part of this instruction, for shortly after 10 a.m. the surviving companies of the Coldstream and Black Watch were overwhelmed. Complete disaster was avoided by two companies of 1/Scots Guards on the left of 1st Brigade which counter-attacked the Germans, drove them out of the British trenches, and prevented an enveloping movement which threatened to engulf the whole brigade.

So, by the evening of the 29th, 3rd Brigade was disposed thus south-east of Gheluvelt astride the Menin road, right to left: 1/Queens to the south,

2/Welch and 2/South Wales Borderers to the north, with 1/Gloucesters withdrawn into reserve at Veldhoek. The reader will do well to remember these battalions, for they were shortly to be involved in the most critical battle of 'First Ypres'. And they should never be forgotten.

It is time to turn away briefly from the Menin road and consider the other flanks of the salient.

On the 29th neither Foch nor French had the slightest knowledge of the assembly of Fabeck's *Army Group* ('the break-through', said the Kaiser's Order of the Day, 'will be of decisive importance. We must settle for ever . . . with our most detested enemy [*the British*].') The intention was therefore clear. The great offensive would be aimed at the sector between Gheluvelt and Messines. But when?

The fighting in this sector on the 29th should have been warning enough that a major storm was brewing. Yet, taking their cue from Foch, both d'Urbal and French issued orders on the evening of the 29th for 'a continuation of the offensive' towards Roulers (i.e., *north-east* of Ypres). Dubois duly instructed IX Corps (17th, 18th and 31st Divisions) to secure Poelcapelle as a preliminary to a further advance. In fact, during this day IX Corps advanced more than a mile, reaching the outskirts of Poelcapelle, recapturing Zonnebeke, and establishing a foothold on the Passchendaele ridge, while farther left de Mitry occupied Bixschoote and Kortekeer. Haig, more alive to the true situation to the south, sounded a cautionary note: 'Orders as to the resumption of the offensive will be issued in the morning when the situation is clearer than it is at present.' None the less during the 29th the left flank of 2nd Division (6th Infantry Brigade) pushed forward in touch with Dubois and captured Broodseinde, a mile north-east of Zonnebeke at the crossroads halfway between Roulers and Ypres. It was to be the limit of the advance in this sector. Indeed, before many hours were out Haig would be calling on Dubois for help.

During the 29th there was little pressure on the Cavalry Corps, for (unknown to Haig and Allenby) the German cavalry on that front was in the process of being relieved by Fabeck's troops. Haig, however, was rightly concerned at the gap between Hollebeke and Zandvoorde, and throughout the day there was a considerable shifting and regrouping of units within the salient as Haig sought to create a flexible reserve, or series of reserves, to meet any of several contingencies.[26] Enemy activity here during the 29th consisted of persistent bombardment of the southern face of the salient, clearly designed to mask the deployment of Fabeck's *Army Group*. But there was another significant straw in the wind. Early this day the Germans began the systematic air and artillery bombardment of the town of Ypres. It has been suggested that this was wanton destruction, or even a mark of frustration. This is possible, but very unlikely. All roads led from Ypres. Any attempt to reinforce the salient, or transfer major bodies of troops from

[26] On the 28th Haig had moved his HQ from Hooge Château to the White Château at Hellfire Corner just east of Ypres. As we shall see, this may have saved his life.

PLATE 31. *Haig's Headquarters. The White Château as it was in early October, 1914*

north to south or vice versa, or maintain the flow of supplies and ammunition would have to be made through this bottleneck. Ypres was a legitimate target. And a ruthless enemy who had burned down the great library at Louvain for no conceivable military reason would be unlikely to worry too much about the destruction of the historic Cloth Hall.

Fabeck's next attack was launched at dawn on 30 October. Despite the earlier assault on the Gheluvelt crossroads, it was unexpectedly concentrated on the sector Zandvoorde–Messines, and was made by (right to left) *39th Division* (*XV Corps*); *3rd* and *4th Divisions* (*II Bavarian Corps*) and *6th Bavarian Reserve Division*; and *26th Division* (*XII Corps*), supported by most of Fabeck's numerous heavy artillery. Facing this formidable array of fresh troops were (left to right): five battalions of 7th Division; six battalions of Bulfin's composite force;[27] part of 3rd Cavalry Division; 2nd Cavalry Division; 1st Cavalry Division; and fewer than 100 guns. The German intention was clear: to capture the Messines ridge and to break through to Ypres between Zandvoorde and Hollebeke astride the Comines canal.

The battle was now in the hands of Haig (above all) and Allenby. Between the evening of 29 October and 3 November, when the immediate crisis was over, no Operation Orders were issued by GHQ. There was little that French could do beyond switching exhausted units of Smith-Dorrien's II Corps north after their relief by the Indian Corps, and calling upon Foch for help, as Haig was obliged to call on Dubois. Fortunately, their calls did not go unheeded.

The battle on the 30th opened with a tremendous bombardment by Fabeck's heaviest guns concentrated on the Zandvoorde ridge, occupied by 7th Cavalry Brigade, and farther east on the trenches of 22nd Infantry Brigade lying on a forward spur. After an hour's heavy shelling – during

[27] 2/Grenadiers, 2/Oxford and Bucks L.I., 1/Northamptons, 2/Royal Sussex, 2/Gordons, 1/Irish Guards; all at or below half-strength.

223

PLATE 32. *Ypres: The Cloth Hall* (Above) *1912;* (centre) *1 November 1914;* (bottom) *1 December 1918*

which 1st and 2nd Life Guards suffered severe casualties – the infantry of *39th Infantry Division* came forward in great numbers, but with great caution. Ernest Hook describes the scene:

> We had no protection from the shelling as our trenches were on the forward slope and in full view of the enemy and although our gunners [*105th and 106th Batteries*] put up a great show, they were no match for Jerry's heavy stuff. We could see their infantry in great masses about 1000 yards away. Just about then I was hit by a shell that nearly took my left arm off and my officer sent me to the rear. It was the end of the war for me. I believe that later on one of our squadrons was surrounded and completely wiped out [*it was*].

Shortly after 8 a.m. 7th Cavalry Brigade – or what remained of it – was withdrawn to a reserve line from Klein Zillebeke north-east to Herenthage Wood, and thence towards Gheluvelt. By 10 a.m. Zandvoorde was in enemy hands, and during the morning 22nd Infantry Brigade, enfiladed from two sides, was compelled to retire to the new support line. [28] Yet again the German infantry, unwilling to face too much of their opponents' fire, halted on the ridge. It is inconceivable that a more resolute enemy more resolutely handled could not have pressed forward to Klein Zillebeke and beyond. At Hill 60, less than a mile to the north, he would have been within sight of Ypres. It was to be five months before he captured that vital feature; and a month later he had lost it again. And George Roupell had won his VC.

Haig's problem now was to contain Fabeck's *Group*, the strength of which he had begun to measure. Fortunately for him – and inexplicably – the enemy did not press his attack along the Menin road this day. Nor did Fabeck co-ordinate the attack of *39th Division* with that of *4th Bavarian Division* on its left. The reserve line running east from Klein Zillebeke, if extremely insecure, was not being seriously pressed. The next danger lay astride the Comines canal and at Hollebeke, where the château was still held by a squadron of the Royals.

To blunt the impending attack by *4th Bavarian Division* on the canal Haig boldly, if unwisely, decided to pre-empt Fabeck's option by a counter-attack to recover Zandvoorde. Although it was a brave intention by a commander with dwindling and overstretched resources, [29] such an attack was little more than a desperate bluff; and to that extent it succeeded. The Bavarians, imagining themselves to be confronted by fresh troops in large numbers, advanced cautiously. In fact Haig's 'phantom army' consisted of the squadron of Royals at Hollebeke Château; the remainder of 6th Cavalry Brigade; three cavalry regiments (the Greys, 3rd Hussars and 4th Hussars) loaned to Haig by Allenby; two infantry battalions from Bulfin's

[28] During this withdrawal 1/Royal Welsh Fusiliers, the rearguard, was virtually destroyed. Only the Quartermaster and 86 other ranks survived.
[29] Realizing his growing lack of reserves, Haig called on Dubois for help. Dubois, aware – if d'Urbal was not – that his own 'offensive' was making small progress, at once sent a cavalry brigade and three battalions of his Corps reserve to the Hooge–Zillebeke area.

force; and two battalions from 7th Divisional reserve; supported by the artillery of 7th Division. It was probably adequate for the relief of Kimberley; but never for the recapture of Zandvoorde. Tom Frere of the 3rd Hussars was mildly amused. 'We were so thin on the ground that the German artillery simply wasted their ammunition trying to find us. They would probably have done better with a few well-placed snipers.'

At 10.30 a.m. the two divisions of *II Bavarian Corps* attacked on either side of the Comines canal. They made little initial progress while their guns constantly searched, as Tom Frere suggested, for needles in haystacks.

But there were not enough needles. As the *3rd Bavarian Division* advanced on the left of the *4th*, 2nd Cavalry Division, reduced to six regiments, was forced to swing back its northern flank until by evening the Cavalry Corps lay roughly along the line of the Messines–Wytschaete ridge and thence north-east. At 2.30 p.m. the Royals evacuated Hollebeke Château, and by 5 p.m. the village was in German hands. 'We went back in good order,' said Jack Cusack, no longer the cheerful regimental scout of two weeks earlier. 'We fired a few parting shots as we went but I don't think there were any Germans within 1,000 yards. We had three or four wounded and we took them with us, leaving Jerry an empty heap of rubble.'

During the afternoon Haig issued orders that the line from the bend in the canal north of Hollebeke to Gheluvelt was to be held at all costs. But it was so thin a line that he was forced to juggle with his slender reserves. Part of 2/KRRC and 1/Loyals (2nd Brigade) were sent up to join 1/Queen's and 2/RSF south of the Menin road, [30] while three out of the five available battalions of 2nd Divisional reserve were sent to join Bulfin at Klein Zillebeke. Towards 8 p.m. the London Scottish of I Corps reserve at Hooge – the first Territorial infantry battalion to enter the battle – was sent to support 2nd Cavalry Division at St Eloi.

It had been a day of mixed fortunes; and the day was not yet over. Zandvoorde and Hollebeke had been lost. Casualties had been great, and the men were exhausted by the strain of battle. The Cavalry Corps had been forced back to its last true line of defence, and 7th Division had been reduced to half its effective strength. Foch, realizing that the true crisis was yet to come, had promised to send his 32nd Division the next day to plug the gap astride the Comines canal. Haig needed all the men and all the time he could get. Men were one thing; time was at the enemy's disposal.

Yet throughout this day Fabeck had achieved no real success. His costly attacks had pushed the southern face of the salient back nearly two miles but he had failed to break the line, and his troops had shown little determination to do so. Against his massive infantry strength, Haig had only twenty-one depleted battalions in the line; [31] and this the enemy did not know, for if it were true it made nonsense of both logic and arithmetic.

---

[30] See Diagram E.
[31] Four battalions – 1/Grenadiers, 1/Coldstream, 1/RWF and 2/Wiltshires – no longer existed as effective units.

PLATE 33. (Above) *London comes to Ypres*
       (Below) *'Semper fidelis . . .'*

Fabeck's plan was ambitious – in the event, too ambitious. It entailed cracking the whole southern salient like a nut between the pincers of Messines and Gheluvelt: by storming the Messines ridge on his left and then seizing the Kemmel heights beyond; and by a simultaneous and decisive breakthrough to Ypres along the Menin road. How near he came to achieving this grandiose plan we shall now see.

At 10 p.m. on the night of the 30th, *26th Division* began the attack on Messines. The battle for the ridge was to last four days – in fact, four years. But before it reached its climax there was to be a greater crisis on the 31st. We will therefore first turn eastward – to Gheluvelt.

Gheluvelt is a small village (even smaller in 1914) which lies almost exactly halfway between Ypres and Menin. It stands on a tiny spur running south-east from Veldhoek on the main Ypres ridge, as does Kruiseecke a mile farther on. It provided such forward observation as there was, but with the loss of Becelaere and Zandvoorde to the north and south it was itself both overlooked and enfiladed. But above all, it was on the Menin road; and the Menin road led to Ypres.

It is curious that the name Gheluvelt is forgotten, if indeed it was ever long remembered except by those who were there; for here, in this unremarkable village, was fought a battle as vital as Waterloo and as bloody as Malplaquet. On the fate of Gheluvelt hung the fate of Ypres; and on the fate of Ypres hung the outcome of the War. Battalions of twelve infantry regiments were involved in the fighting; seven of them were in the tenuous line defending the south-east approaches to the village; and one – 2/Worcesters – was to win a lasting glory by its counter-attack during the afternoon, which drove the Germans out of Gheluvelt, recaptured the ruined village, and so re-established the line which had been broken earlier in the day.

By the end of the action 1/Queen's had been reduced to two officers and twelve other ranks; 2/KRRC that night could muster only 150; of 1/Loyals only one officer and thirty-five men remained, and of 2/RSF only 151 men. 2/Worcesters, whose gallant counter-attack saved the day, lost 187 all ranks killed and wounded out of fewer than 400 who took part.

The German record scarcely mentions Gheluvelt, and no casualty figures are given. But the official monograph, which is rarely accurate or truthful, has this to say:

> The fact that neither the enemy's commanders nor their troops gave way under the strong pressure we put on them, but continued to fight the battle, though their situation was most perilous, gives us an opportunity to acknowledge that there were men of real worth opposed to us who did their duty thoroughly.

This is a sufficient epitaph for the men who fought at Gheluvelt.

The morning of 31 October was fine, with little of the usual mist and cloud. There was minor German activity early on. The British line lay across the Menin road, just east of Gheluvelt, thus: [32] On the right, 1,000 yards south-west of Gheluvelt, was all that remained of 2/RSF (21st Brigade). On their left were two companies of 1/Loyals and a company of 1/Queen's.

Here, due south of the village, there was a sharp salient held by two companies of 2/KRRC and the other companies of 1/Queen's. This was the 'orchard' salient. It was to prove both a death-trap and a graveyard.

Behind this line – 1,000 yards in rear on the Menin road – was Landon's reserve: two companies each of 1/Loyals and 2/KRRC. Their strength – which should have been more than 1,000 – was, in fact, 522.

Continuing east, the line was extended by 3rd Infantry Brigade: astride the road, 2/Welch in and forward of the village; on their left across the front of Gheluvelt Château, 1/South Wales Borderers; from there 1/Scots Guards continued the line north towards the other battalions of 1st (Guards) Brigade, 1/Camerons and 1/Black Watch. The total strength in and near the village was fewer than 2,000 men.

The attack against the Gheluvelt position was made north of the road by *54th Reserve Division (XXVII Reserve Corps)* and south of it by *30th Division (XV Corps)* with twenty or more battalions in the line and a further 7 or 8 in reserve. It was launched at 6 a.m. along the whole front, but without success except for the capture of the orchard opposite the salient occupied by the Queen's and the KRRC. Despite several counter-attacks it proved impossible to dislodge the enemy, and as further troops came forward, both the salient and the trenches of the Loyals and RSF farther west came under heavy enfilade fire along the immediate front and from Zandvoorde.

None the less, this first attack made little progress, and at 8 a.m. there began a sustained artillery bombardment of a violence and accuracy never yet encountered by these experienced troops. Within two hours the right-hand company of the Welch in front of the village had been 'simply blown out of its trenches' and the battalion, leaving one company forward, was forced to retire to a shallow depression 500 yards to the north and thence towards Veldhoek. The line had been broken; [33] and north and south of the road the flanks of both the Queen's and SWB were exposed. By now communications to the rear had broken down and every runner sent back to report was killed. Gheluvelt was at the mercy of the enemy.

At 10 a.m. the Germans launched a converging attack with four battalions of *54th Reserve Division* north of the road and three battalions of *30th Division* south, while three further battalions engaged the remnants of the KRRC in the salient. For the moment – but not for long – the Loyals and RSF on the extreme right were not subjected to infantry assault but were pinned down by intense artillery and machine-gun fire. And still the defenders stood their ground, even when the KRRC were driven back to

[32] See Diagram E.
[33] A company of 1/Gloucesters sent up from Brigade reserve to fill the gap was virtually wiped out and its 13 survivors taken prisoner.

the support line on the road. For over an hour they held at bay an enemy more than ten times their number. And it was here that the German monograph recorded: 'Over every bush, hedge and fragment of wall floated a film of smoke, betraying a machine-gun rattling out bullets.' In fact by 11 a.m. the defenders of Gheluvelt had only five machine-guns still in action, and virtually no ammunition for those guns. Once again the Germans discovered what British rifle-fire was like. When they learned the truth, they did not believe it. This – and inferior leadership – alone can explain their fatal hesitation later in the day.

Gheluvelt – that is to say, the heap of rubble to which the village had been reduced – was captured by the Germans about 11.30 a.m. To the north, in the area of the château, 1/SWB and 1/Scots Guards were still holding out strongly, protected from the close attention of German artillery by a number of small copses. But the Queen's, still in their salient, were doomed. Surrounded by the enemy, they were, in the words of the official History, 'shot down from front, flank and rear'. As we have seen, only two officers and twelve other ranks escaped. It is an indication of the Germans' own casualties and of their sense of frustration that the British prisoners were treated with extreme brutality.

It was now the turn of the Loyals and the RSF. Isolated and with no hope of reinforcement or relief, they fought literally to the death; but they held on for nearly two hours and exacted so great a toll on the enemy that the gap in the line was contained. It was a moment of supreme crisis, but not of total disaster. It was to be a memorable afternoon.

North of the village, the remaining company of 2/Welch had been over-whelmed, and by 11.45 a.m. the thirty-seven survivors, with only sixteen rifles still firing, were captured. At noon the SWB and Scots Guards had been forced back into the grounds of the château where a spirited bayonet charge sent the Germans tumbling back to the safety of the near-by copses. There was a short lull.

Back at the White Château, Haig heard that Gheluvelt had been lost, although he was not yet aware of the true gravity of the crisis. The battle was now in the hands of his Divisional Commanders – Lomax (1st Division) and Monro (2nd Division). He had no real Corps reserve. He could rely only on the courage of his men and the errors of the enemy. He was to have ample proof of both, but during the morning he was also concerned to create a last-ditch line of defence east of Ypres in the event of a decisive German break-through (during the battle of Gheluvelt, Bulfin's force at Klein Zillebeke was also under strong attack).

During the morning Lomax and Monro consulted together and Monro put 2/Worcesters at the disposal of 1st Division. It was to be an inspired decision. There was some consideration of reinforcing the line at Gheluvelt with other troops of 2nd Division reserve, but this was wisely abandoned. Neither commander could have foreseen the coming course of events, at once tragic and triumphant.

At 1 p.m. General FitzClarence (1st Guards Brigade) rode over to the

PLATE 34. *Hooge Château, scene of the disaster to the staffs of 1st and 2nd Divisions on 31 October*

Battalion HQ of the Worcesters at Polygon Wood and ordered Major Hankey 'to advance without delay and deliver a counter-attack with the utmost vigour against the enemy who was in possession of Gheluvelt, and to re-establish our line there'. It has been called an act of desperation. So it was. But it was also a supreme example of the true exercise of command.

As FitzClarence was visiting Hankey, Lomax rode back to Hooge Château, which housed the HQ of both First and Second Divisions since Haig's move to the White Château on the 28th. It was not a wise arrangement, but it is easy to be wise after the event. There Lomax told Monro that his line had been broken and Gheluvelt lost. Half an hour later a salvo of shells fell in the grounds of the château, three of which struck the building, mortally wounding Lomax, stunning Monro, and killing or wounding all except one of the assembled staff officers. It was a black moment in an already black day, but it is a mark of the extraordinary resilience of this Army that within an hour the command structure had been restored; and by then good news – incredible news – was on the way.

During the morning one company of 2/Worcesters had been sent forward to a reserve position behind 1/SWB. Thus when he received his orders from FitzClarence Hankey had only three companies at his disposal. One of the twelve officers who took part in the forthcoming action described their state:

> Every single soul dog tired, cold, wet, and plastered with mud, had been unwashed and unshaven for days on end. Our hair had grown to an incredible length, and beards were of such varied types and sizes that it was only with difficulty that some of us could be recognized. There we were – a pretty picture indeed.

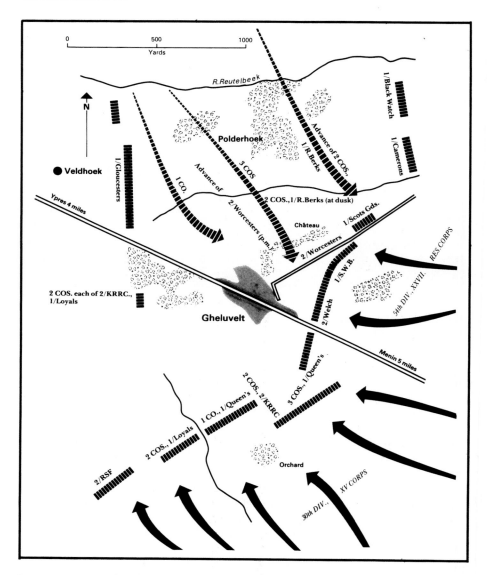

DIAGRAM E. *Gheluvelt, 31 October*

At 2 p.m. Hankey set out, after off-loading packs, issuing extra ammunition, and fixing bayonets. The first part of the advance was screened by trees, but as they reached the Polderhoek ridge, and deployed into line, Hankey and his men were greeted by a formidable prospect. A thousand yards ahead lay the burning rubble of Gheluvelt. The open ground between, swept by artillery fire, was littered with dead and wounded, and a steady stream of stragglers was coming back.

Hankey decided that the only way of crossing this deadly stretch was by one long rush; and so the Worcesters charged. 'Men fell at every pace, and in the space of a few minutes over a hundred of the battalion were killed or

232

wounded. Those who still could dashed forward.' Suddenly they saw the château in front of them. The Germans, milling aimlessly around the grounds and still engaged at close quarters with the SWB, were not expecting visitors. Capt. Clarke, the Adjutant, goes on:

> There was the Hun alright, but we had surprised him . . . There was a cheer and we charged as best we could over the last open ground. He began to withdraw, but his fight at such close quarters was feeble. A few Germans were bayonetted, though most were shot at point-blank range, but we hastened his retirement, cleared the château grounds, and pushed on to the sunken road with our right on Gheluvelt church.

It is impossible to say how many Germans fled before this irresistible attack, but four battalions would not be an exaggeration. By 4 p.m. Gheluvelt had been recaptured and the line had been restored. It was a famous victory; and the Germans, fearing that the Worcesters might be the first rather than the last British reinforcements, kept their distance.

The news of the recapture of Gheluvelt reached Haig when Sir John French was visiting his HQ. It came, as one of Haig's staff officers recorded, like a reprieve – 'as if we had all been under sentence of death and most suddenly received a free pardon'.

French was less sanguine, for even if the recapture of Gheluvelt was true, the situation remained extremely critical with strong attacks against Bulfin's force at Klein Zillebeke and a growing threat to Allenby's Cavalry Corps at Messines. On his way back to St Omer, French met Foch by chance at Vlamertinghe. He spoke of retreat, even to the gates of Ypres, and (according to Foch) said 'there is nothing left for me to do save to go up and be killed with I Corps'. Foch, the great Pangloss, was horrified. 'You must not speak of dying, but of winning,' he said. 'I shall attack to right and left' – and he promised further reinforcements in the Hollebeke sector and an offensive by Dubois to the north the following day. We do not know from French's diary what he really believed at this moment, but he seems to have been overwhelmed by events. Fortunately, Foch was not. After suggesting to French what orders he might properly give to Haig, he applied himself to his own cheerfully offensive preparations; and French returned to St Omer.

Haig needed no orders. All he received was a copy of Foch's comments and a note from French which said, superfluously: 'It is of the *utmost importance* to hold the ground you are on now. It is useless for me to say this, because I know you will do it if it is humanly possible', and ending: 'I will finally arrange with Foch *what* our future role will be.' Haig could have told him in one word: survival.

While the senior directors were thus indulging in military semantics at Vlamertinghe, Haig had spent the evening of the 31st adjusting his battered line. Gheluvelt had been recaptured. But with increasing pressure farther south, Gheluvelt was no longer of tactical importance. Thus after dark the men of 1st Division and 2/Worcesters were withdrawn to a new line running across the Menin road in front of Veldhoek to the south-eastern edge of Polygon Wood. The Germans did not interfere; and it was not until dawn on 1 November that they cautiously reoccupied Gheluvelt. It had been a memorable day, and in the event a decisive one. It is difficult to trace any personal recollections of the fighting. Not many men survived the battle. Of those who did time has taken its toll. The few who remain may not remember the date on which they first dug their little trenches and prepared to face the storm. It was St Crispin's Day.

As one crisis came and went, another took its place. The scene now changes to Messines and to the ridge which Fabeck – perhaps with hind-sight – believed held the key to Ypres. [34]

On the night of 29–30 October – that is to say, after Fabeck's initial attack at Gheluvelt crossroads – the British line at the southern hinge of the salient ran thus: at Ploegsteert Wood and St Yves, 11th Infantry Brigade of Pulteney's 4th Division (this Division was soon to be drawn into the battle for the ridge, as were battalions of 5th Division farther south); farther left came 57th Wilde's Rifles of the Lahore Division; Messines itself was held by 1st Cavalry Brigade, whence the line ran north-east towards Hollebeke (the remainder of 1st Cavalry Division and 2nd Cavalry Division) and the junction with 3rd Cavalry Division on the Comines canal.

There was virtually *no* reserve except by drawing on the depleted units of II Corps, which had only that day been relieved by the Indian Corps. Other help was on the way as Foch diverted his 32nd Division and 9th Cavalry Division to strengthen the sagging line from Wytschaete to the canal. [35] But like Blücher, in another moment of crisis, would he be in time?

During the 29th there was no major infantry attack on this southern hinge, but with the loss of Zandvoorde and Hollebeke, Allenby was compelled to pull back his left flank; and heavy artillery bombardment of the ridge was clear evidence that Fabeck's plan of attack was not confined to the Menin road and the Zandvoorde ridge alone. By 30 October the Cavalry Corps lay forward of the line Messines–Wytschaete–St Eloi, with 3rd Cavalry Division and Bulfin's force on its left. The noose around Ypres was being tightened. To the north-east all was quiet.

By the 30th, Fabeck had deployed *3rd Bavarian Division*, and *26th Division* (soon to be joined by *6th Reserve Bavarian Division*) supported on his left – opposite Ploegsteert – by *40th Division* of *XIX Corps*. There was the usual massive arsenal of guns in attendance. Messines was heavily shelled, and towards evening, there was a determined infantry attack up the ridge. It achieved nothing, even though the German account speaks of 'the capture of Wambeke' about a mile east of Messines, a village which the British had never occupied. This lack of success marked a sudden change in German

---

[34] *Ypres, 1914.*
[35] By 6 November the French had taken over the entire sector from Wulverghem to Klein Zillebeke with Grossetti's XVI Corps (32nd, 39th and 43rd Divisions and two cavalry divisions). Dubois's battalions were still at Hooge.

PLATE 35. *The parapet*

tactics. Throughout the rest of the battle for the ridge the pattern was largely one of ceaseless bombardment by day and infantry attacks by night (it was a period of full moon). In a sense it was a confession of weakness, for German infantry had not been trained in night-fighting, and even when they achieved success they seemed once again not to know how to exploit it; and the infantry attacking the ridge were not the raw volunteers of *Fourth Army*.

At 1.45 a.m. two battalions of *26th Division* attacked the British trenches in front of Messines. This attack may be considered as the beginning of a bitter and confused battle which was to last for four days.[36] It was met by a small but resolute defence – a squadron of 9th Lancers, the Queen's Bays, two squadrons of 5th DG, and the 57th Rifles (attacked again before dawn while they were being relieved by 2/Inniskilling Fusiliers from 12th Brigade).

It was to be a very different battle from that at Gheluvelt, but no less critical. At no time did Allenby have more than 2,000 rifles on the ridge, and fewer than 80 guns behind it. The ridge was lost, regained and lost once more. But, as has been said, it was an empty victory for the Germans. Their objective was Kemmel two miles to the west. It was nearly four years before they reached it, at what cost we shall never know.

'The fighting round Messines was really weird,' recalls Albert Whitelock of the Bays.

> The German infantry seemed to wander forward not knowing where to go, while their guns kept on firing, not seeming to care whether they hit friend or foe. There were six of us in a small cottage and we simply picked them off as they came up the slope. But they kept coming and finally we had to dodge back into the village.

[36] The German monograph notes with astonishment that throughout the battle the local villagers refused to leave their shattered homes, even at the height of the fighting.

But numbers tell. By early morning on the 31st, 1,000 British cavalrymen faced six times that number of German infantry; and at noon these unequal opponents were fighting house by house for the possession of Messines. It was here that the London Scottish was sent forward. It went into action 750 strong, and within hours its losses were 321 as it advanced through 4th Cavalry Brigade (6th Dragoon Guards) to the eastern slope of the ridge. When the following day the battalion was withdrawn to Wulverghem it had given Kitchener a conclusive answer to his stubborn prejudice against 'amateur' soldiers. [37]

While the drama was reaching its climax at the centre of the stage a directors' meeting was held at Dunkirk. Here, on 1 November, Kitchener met Poincaré, Joffre and Foch. There was one notable absentee. French was unable (unwilling?) to attend, and conveyed his apologies through his Military Secretary. He was certainly deeply involved in a battle for survival (so was Foch), but it is equally probable that he had no great wish to meet Kitchener at this moment. The Secretary of State, however, had not come either to praise or to bury Caesar.

Although he was again wearing his Field Marshal's uniform, he had donned his political hat; and he had come to reassure his Allies. The war, he told them, was destined to be long and bitter (as indeed he had believed ever since the first meeting of the War Council on 5 August). In no circumstance would Britain forsake France, but it would take time to raise and train his New Armies. Not until the spring of 1915 would a steady and growing flow of new divisions be ready; by 1917 the flow would have become a flood. He kept his word, even if he did not survive to witness what happened to that flood. Perhaps it was as well. Kitchener the soldier would not easily have suffered Lloyd George the arch-politician. None the less, Poincaré and his colleagues were duly reassured. 'Only survive the winter,' Kitchener is reported to have said. 'Then all will be well.' The directors bade each other adieu and departed to their several stations.

We left the Messines ridge as the German attack was growing in intensity. It is not possible – as, for example, at Gheluvelt – to follow the fighting on 1 and 2 November hour by hour, shell by shell, or bullet by bullet. By midnight on the 2nd the Germans had occupied the ridge, and were still attacking the southern flank of the salient at Klein Zillebeke. But the attack – by (right to left) *3rd Bavarian Division*, *6th Reserve Bavarian Division*, *3rd Division* (of the new *II Corps*), and *26th Division* – had spent itself, crippled by casualties and by the exhaustion of the men. Prisoners taken on 2 November said they had had no food for three days, and little sleep for five. So much for Schlieffen. So much for the degradation of the human spirit. 'Do you know something?' said Ernie Hunt of the Loyals. 'There's

[37] In keeping with its 'second-class' status the Territorial Army was still equipped with the old and inefficient Lee-Metford rifle.

nothing special about Germans. They bleed like the rest of us when they're hit.'

The loss of the ridge went thus.

Two miles separate Messines from Wytschaete. It is still possible to drive through both villages without noticing them, so insignificant are they. But even now the ridge, later battered and blown asunder, commands the Flanders plain. Yet its highest point is little more than 200 feet.

During the afternoon of 31 October, 4th Cavalry Brigade and the London Scottish were driven off the gap between the two villages and fell back on the Wulverghem ridge a mile to the west. In Messines a desperate battle was joined in the village. Here, at 4 p.m. the line – if it can be so called – ran through the main square wth squadrons of four different cavalry regiments engaged by eight German battalions. North and south of the village 2/KOYLI and 2/KOSB (or what remained of them) had been rushed up from what 13th Infantry Brigade had fondly believed to be a 'rest area' near Estaires.[38] 'It was a rough day,' recorded Joe Green, a 'South Africa' man of the 5th DG, in his diary. 'We were firing at each other across streets and down streets, and the gunners on both sides were belting away as if we didn't exist. I didn't join the cavalry for *this*!'

It could not last. When it was clear that the thin line on the centre of the ridge had been driven back General de Lisle withdrew his troops from Messines at 9 a.m. on 1 November, covered by the fire of the London Scottish. But by then Wytschaete had also been lost. At 2.45 a.m. the Germans – now concentrating on night attacks – pushed forward in great strength and occupied the eastern half of the village. General Gough (2nd Cavalry Division) at once called forward the reserve battalions of II Corps from Kemmel (1/Lincolns and 1/Northumberland Fusiliers). He could well have spared those weary men another day, but days no longer counted. Walter Wildgoose was quite philosophical. 'I had had a night's sleep and a proper clean-up. Back we went.' Back they went – and by noon 1/Lincolns had lost another 8 officers and 293 other ranks. And they had not saved Wytschaete. There was no way of saving Wytschaete. Or was there?

At 8 a.m., supported by the newly arrived French 32nd Division, Gough's cavalry attacked the village. The German explanation is that their own artillery 'compelled the colonel of *17th Bavarian Reserve Regiment* to withdraw his victorious troops temporarily'. Throughout this day the battle for Wytschaete continued. Early in the morning, with the Germans aiming at the gap on the ridge, 12th Lancers and a squadron of 20th Hussars ('very exciting and very frightening', says Jim Saunders) stormed the village with troops of the French 32nd Division and recaptured it. There they stayed; but not for long.

2 November, a fine, sunny day, was to be the climax and – although no one then knew – the end of the first and second crises of 'First Ypres'. By

[38] It is tiny movements like this which convinced the Germans that the British had unlimited reserves.

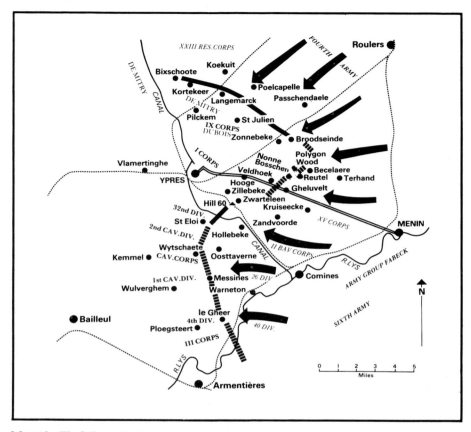

MAP 12. *The Salient, 31 October*

morning the French had arrived in strength and 2nd Cavalry Division had
been withdrawn into reserve. The French held some five miles of the salient
between the ridge and Zandvoorde. And by that evening the Germans had
recaptured Wytschaete. Fabeck had his ridge. But he had before him an
unbroken enemy, and the road to Ypres along the Comines canal – his
only other option – was still held. There had been problems and disasters
along the salient; but the salient had held firm. Throughout the 2nd the
enemy continued his attacks against the southern face from St Eloi to the
Menin road, where *30th Division* managed to reach Veldhoek and the north-
eastern corner of Herenthage Wood before being driven back by a
determined Anglo-French counter-attack. In the centre *39th Division*
attempted – for the last time, as it proved – to break through at Klein
Zillebeke and Zwarteleen towards Hill 60. Somehow the line still held.

On this day scarcely one battalion – or more accurately, *company* – was
fighting with its original brigade or division, and the 7th Division had been
reduced to one-fifth of its original strength. Of Pte Rooney's company in
2/Borders, which had first come into action at Kruiseecke on the 19th ('it
seemed years ago' he recalled), only eleven men remained. And when
during the afternoon of the 2nd, General Ruggles-Brise of 20th Brigade was

238

severely wounded, command devolved on his Brigade Major. By then every senior field officer had been killed or wounded. The brigade had lost 106 of its original 124 officers. One battalion was in the charge of a sergeant.

Yet 2 November marks the climax of 'First Ypres'. In a sense, Falkenhayn threw in the towel. There was to be one more supreme effort and one more crisis, but this day is given in the final record as the end of the battles of la Bassée, Armentières and Messines. Only along the Menin road the battle of Gheluvelt, the last of the great battles for Ypres, continued with unabated ferocity. Indeed, during the evening of the 2nd, OHL was contemplating the withdrawal of divisions from Flanders to restore the situation on the Eastern Front after Hindenburg's crushing defeat before Warsaw; and in his memoirs Falkenhayn recorded that on that same evening the High Command debated whether the Ypres offensive should not be stopped and some other front in France attacked. In the event, it was decided to make one last effort.

In the official History and the German monograph there is only one identical sentence: 'During the next three days, the 3rd, 4th and 5th November, there was little change in the situation at the front.' Bill Martyn remembers the 3rd. 'It was the first day for two weeks that not a single German shell arrived. It was the first morning when you could hear yourself speak without shouting. And it was the first day that the battalion had no casualties. It was certainly a day to remember.'

So was 5 November; for on this day 7th Division and 3rd Infantry Brigade (of Gheluvelt fame) were relieved. A few went to Ypres while the rest were withdrawn to the sanctuary of Locre and Bailleul behind the Kemmel heights. The men could hardly believe their luck. Bill Martyn goes on: 'I had to learn what a proper night's sleep meant all over again! We had long since forgotten what a hot meal was like. But in a couple of days, after a decent wash and brush-up, we looked like real soldiers again. Only one thing we missed, our friends and comrades who had not been so lucky.'

PLATE 36. *'It seemed that out of battle I escaped . . .'* (Wilfred Owen)

II Corps was also not so lucky. On the night of 29–30 October it had been relieved by the Indian Corps. Since then five battalions had been sent up to the Messines ridge. Now, after only a few days' rest, ten battalions were sent back into the line near Hooge to replace 7th Division. By 6 November Smith-Dorrien was in effect a Corps Commander without a Corps.

The last crisis – and the last climax – came on a prophetic date: 11 November. During the five previous days the enemy had made a series of small attacks designed to disrupt Allied defensive preparations and the reinforcement of the salient. But the veteran fighting-men and their commanders were not deceived. The German is a creature of habit; and he was up to his old habits again. First the calm; then the storm. A violent storm was indeed brewing.

OHL had decided on one final attempt to reach Ypres.[39] The main blow was to fall on the British astride the Menin road north of Gheluvelt between Herenthage, Veldhoek, Nonne Bosschen Wood and Polygon Wood. The battle presently to be joined, the last scene of the long-running battle of Gheluvelt and the final one of 'First Ypres', is known officially as 'Nonne Bosschen'. We shall see why.

For this offensive OHL created a formidable new instrument under General Linsingen, commander of *II Corps*. It consisted of General Plettenberg's *4th Division* and Winckler's *Composite Guard Division* (*1st* and *4th Guard Brigades*). Here if ever was an élite force, at full strength and supported by 228 guns. If the Kaiser were to make a theatrical entry into Ypres, he would do so in style at the head of his finest troops.

The German plan for 11 November directed Fabeck's *XV Corps* to attack on Plettenberg's left and *XXVII Reserve Corps* on his right. The intention, therefore, was to isolate the British centre from any outside support. The British were not greatly concerned. The men had weathered the same storms before; and by now one German soldier was much the same as another. The BEF, short of sleep, short of food, increasingly short of ammunition, was not interested in the lessons of history. It had never heard of St Privat or Gravelotte. What it did not know was that against it, from Messines to Polygon Wood, a front of nine miles, the Germans had assembled 12½ divisions.

'The morning was grey and foggy: mist hung about all the forenoon, and a light wind carried it with the smoke of battle towards the enemy.' Thus the official History. When at 6 p.m. the rain came, both the battle and the crisis were over.

At 6.30 a.m. the Germans opened the most violent bombardment yet experienced along the nine-mile front from Messines to Reutel; but the greatest weight was concentrated on the newly arrived battalions of II Corps. By a cruel irony, their order of battle reads almost exactly like that

[39] The offensive was timed for 10 November, but was postponed for twenty-four hours due to bad weather. No one troubled to tell *Fourth Army*, which by launching its attack between Langemarck and Dixmude on the 10th destroyed any element of surprise.

240

on the Mons canal on 23 August, even if many names and faces had changed. But Bob Barnard – wounded here for the second time – was still there. 'It was absolute hell. The shelling went on for over two hours, all sorts, ''Black Marias'', ''Jack Johnsons'', the lot. Much of it was falling on our left, but one shell landed right on a small trench with three men in it and simply blew them to bits.'

At 9 a.m., with punctual German regularity, came the infantry. It has been suggested that Nonne Bosschen was a battle of Guards against Guards. This is not so. And indeed, the first German attack on the Allied right was marked by a significant lack of resolution. It was soon clear that the enemy had no stomach for the fire of British and French artillery massed near Kemmel and at Ploegsteert. Here the Germans made no progress at all. Indeed, Allenby felt able to send off 1st Cavalry Division to assist Haig.

Farther left, the French, holding the canal sector near Verbranden-molen, were attacked by no fewer than five German divisions of *Army Group Fabeck*. By noon the enemy was within 3,000 yards of Ypres, and within reach of Hill 60. But, as in every crisis of 'First Ypres', a tiny injection saved the patient. Allenby could not help. Haig could not help. But the ever-willing Dubois sent his 7th Hussars from St Jean. It was enough. The tide flowed back.

'It was on the British centre that the fiercest German attack fell.' This line, held by General Wing's composite Division, ran from Shrewsbury Forest to Herenthage Wood, thence across the Menin road to Veldhoek Château, Glencorse Wood, Nonne Bosschen, and so to the south-west corner of Polygon Wood. Even to-day the place-names read like a litany. They are quiet now; but not on that day of battle.

Wing's Division (it seems strangely proper that II Corps should be in at the death) held this line (126 officers and 4,188 men and a company of French Zouaves) up to the Menin road. Thence, to Veldhoek, were 2/Duke of Wellington's in some strength. Across the face of Nonne Bosschen to Polygon Wood, a dangerous distance of 1,000 yards, was the remnant of FitzClarence's 1st (Guards) Brigade, now entirely Scottish. [40] It numbered 812 all ranks. Haig's reserve was derisory. It included, significantly, three Field Companies of the Royal Engineers (17th, 56th and 59th) employed as infantry; and it also included – the only reserve battalion of 2nd Division – 2/Oxford and Bucks L.I.

South of the road *4th Division* attacked 'without enthusiasm and in a sort of dazed way, as if they were drugged'. Broken by artillery and rifle fire, they were driven back, battalions reduced to companies and scarcely an officer surviving. The two groups of II Corps – McCracken's and Gleichen's – veterans of Le Cateau, scarcely considered themselves to have been disturbed. Though they did not know it, they had been attacked by more than 7,000 German infantry. 'It was quite a nice morning,' recalls George McClelland, of Royal Irish Rifles. 'We even had time to clean our

[40] 1/Scots Guards, 1/Camerons, 1/Black Watch.

rifles and have a bit of bully. When the Germans had another go in the evening [*4 p.m.*], we gave them another dose, and off they went. I can only say that the ground in front of us looked like a slaughter-house.'

North of the Menin road, the picture was different. Here *4th Guard Brigade* attacked astride the road (how often has that phrase occurred?) against 1/Lincolns and 2/Duke of Wellington's. The German monograph tells what happened. '*4th Guard Grenadier Regiment* at once suffered such heavy losses that the first two attacks made no headway.' But farther east *2nd Guard Grenadier Regiment* succeeded in breaking into General Shaw's line, and despite counter-attacks by 2/Royal Sussex and 1/RSF, a dangerous salient had been created. Was this to be another – and this time decisive – Gheluvelt? It was not.

The climax was to come east of the road where 1st (Guards) Brigade – or what remained of it – faced the German *1st Guard Brigade*: indeed, in Wilfred Owen's words, a 'strange meeting'.

The two regiments of *1st Guard Brigade* had orders to advance north-westward into the gap between Polygon Wood and the Veldhoek woods. Success here would have carried them straight through to Hooge. Beyond lay Ypres.

Here the Germans came very close to the decisive break-through. Indeed, they would have achieved it, had not *1st* and *3rd Foot Guard Regiments* been directed on divergent lines, and if *XXVII Reserve Corps* on the extreme right had not seemingly decided to opt out of the battle. By noon the Germans had created a gap of half a mile in their own front.

On their right *3rd Foot Guard Regiment* attacked 1/King's on the south-east

PLATE 37. *Nonne Bosschen, 11 November. Defeat of the Prussian Guard by 2/Oxford and Bucks L.I.*

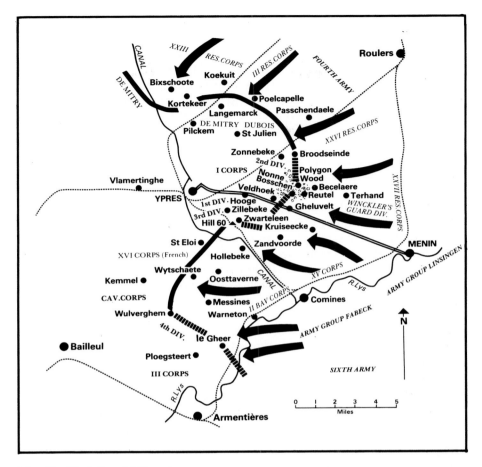

MAP 13. *The Salient, 11 November*

edge of Polygon Wood. 'The men of the King's from their holes could see that what they first thought was a second attack was in reality a continuous wall of German dead and wounded, lying several deep twenty-five to seventy yards away in a turnip field.'

But still the Prussian Guard came on, numerous and brave; and Fitz-Clarence's Brigade fought its way back, equally brave but much less numerous. From the corner of Polygon Wood, 1/King's continued to do great execution; but by noon parties of Prussian Guard had forced their way into Nonne Bosschen, a large copse between Polygon Wood and the Menin road. Let Micky Lay of 2/Oxford and Bucks L.I. take up the story:

> On the morning of 11 November we were in reserve. After breakfast (a real treat those days), the Regiment was ordered to move, which we did, again in a hurry, to Nonne Bosschen wood, in some slight shelling. The edge of the wood was held by some Gunners [*XLI Brigade*] armed with rifles. 'A' and 'B' Companies advanced through the wood

and drove the advancing Germans back. They were Prussian Guards, not one under six-feet tall . . . 'C' Company came up to hold the edge of the wood with 'D' Company and RHQ in a farm behind them. The Germans ran back and by dusk we held the whole of Nonne Bosschen. Our casualties were light. It had been a rapid advance. A few days later we were relieved by the French and marched to a timber yard in Ypres. And on 18 November we went to billets in Bailleul. Hard boards and two blankets for sleeping was sheer luxury.

In the German account there is no mention of the attack of Winckler's *Guard Division* or of its repulse. Small wonder.

So ended Nonne Bosschen. So ended 'First Ypres'. During the following days there was desultory fighting along the salient. But the Germans had no longer the heart or strength to pursue what was now a lost cause. They retired to lick their considerable wounds and manufacture their excuses. They had not captured Ypres. If they had any cause for congratulation, it was this: they had destroyed the old Regular Army.

Foch, for all his cheerful optimism, had watched with pride and admiration the conduct of the BEF in adversity. Now, as the Germans' last offensive foundered on the rifles of perhaps 10,000 weary men, he agreed to take over the salient.

Between 15 November and 22 November the relief of I Corps and the reorganization of the British line took place, and the French assumed responsibility for the salient until early the following year. The last two British units to leave were 115th and 116th Batteries of 1st Division. By midnight on the 22nd, the BEF was established on a front of twenty-one miles from Givenchy to Kemmel, two miles west of Wytschaete. By a strange coincidence, this was exactly the same frontage as that held by Smith-Dorrien's II Corps at Mons three months to the day earlier.

Between 12 October and 22 November when the curtain fell, British and Indian casualties amounted to 58,155, of which the highest proportion had been sustained by 7th, 3rd and 1st Divisions. [41]

'In the British battalions which fought from Mons to Ypres there scarcely remained with the colours an average of one officer and thirty men of those who had landed in August, 1914. The old British Army was gone beyond recall.' [42]

Beside the road at Sanctuary Wood there is a single grave. It is that of a subaltern, aged twenty. He lies there because, when the war was over, his sergeant brought the young man's parents to show them where the officer – 'my officer' – fell.

There is no more to be said.

[41] During the same period German casualties are stated as 134,315.
[42] *Official History*, Vol II.

Order of Battle

BRITISH EXPEDITIONARY FORCE
(5 Aug.–22 Nov. 1914)
(excluding ancillary services)

Commander-in-Chief:	**Field Marshal Sir John French**
Chief of Staff:	Lt Gen. Sir Archibald Murray
Sub-Chief of Staff:	Maj. Gen. Henry Wilson
QMG:	Maj. Gen. Sir William Robertson
AG:	Maj. Gen. Sir Nevil Macready
GSO 1 (Intelligence):	Col G. M. W. Macdonogh

Cavalry Division (Allenby)

1ST CAVALRY BRIGADE
2nd Dragoon Guards (The Bays)
5th Dragoon Guards
11th Hussars

2ND CAVALRY BRIGADE
4th Dragoon Guards
9th Lancers
18th Hussars

3RD CAVALRY BRIGADE
4th Hussars
5th Lancers
16th Lancers

4TH CAVALRY BRIGADE
Composite Regt, Household Cavalry
6th Dragoon Guards
3rd Hussars

RHA: III Bde ('D' and 'E' Btys)
VII Bde ('I' and 'L' Btys)
RE: 1st Field Squadron

5TH (INDEPENDENT) CAVALRY BRIGADE
2nd Dragoons (The Royal Scots Greys)
12th Lancers
20th Hussars

RHA: 'J' Bty
RE: 4th Field Troop

I CORPS (Haig)

1st Division (Lomax)

1ST (GUARDS) BRIGADE
1/Coldstream Guards
1/Scots Guards
1/Black Watch
1/Royal Munsters

2nd Division (Monro)

4TH (GUARDS) BRIGADE
2/Grenadier Guards
2/Coldstream Guards
3/Coldstream Guards
1/Irish Guards

2ND INFANTRY BRIGADE
2/Royal Sussex
1/Loyal North Lancs
1/Northamptons
2/KRRC

3RD INFANTRY BRIGADE
1/Queen's
2/South Wales Borderers
1/Gloucesters
2/Welch Regt

CAVALRY: 'C' Sqn, 15th Hussars
RFA: XXV Bde (113, 114, 115 Btys)
XXVI Bde (116, 117, 118 Btys)
XXXIX Bde (46, 51, 54 Btys)
XLIII (How) Bde (30, 40, 57 Btys)
RGA: 26 Heavy Bty
RE: 23rd and 26th Field Coys

5TH INFANTRY BRIGADE
2/Worcesters
2/Oxford and Bucks L.I.
2/HLI
2/Connaught Rangers

6TH INFANTRY BRIGADE
1/King's (Liverpool)
2/South Staffords
1/Royal Berkshires
1/KRRC

CAVALRY: 'B' Sqn, 15th Hussars
RFA: XXXIV Bde (22, 50, 70 Btys)
XXXVI Bde (15, 48, 71 Btys)
XLI Bde (9, 16, 17 Btys)
XLIV (How) Bde (47, 56, 60 Btys)
RGA: 35 Heavy Bty
RE: 5th and 11th Field Coys

II CORPS (Grierson; then Smith-Dorrien)

3rd Division (Hubert Hamilton)

5th Division (Fergusson)

7TH INFANTRY BRIGADE
3/Worcesters
2/South Lancs
1/Wiltshires
2/Royal Irish Rifles

8TH INFANTRY BRIGADE
2/Royal Scots
2/Royal Irish Regt
4/Middlesex
1/Gordons

9TH INFANTRY BRIGADE
1/Northumberland Fusiliers
4/Royal Fusiliers
1/Lincolns
1/Royal Scots Fusiliers

CAVALRY: 'A' Sqn, 15th Hussars
RFA: XXIII Bde (107, 108, 109 Btys)
XL Bde (6, 23, 49 Btys)
XLII Bde (29, 21, 45 Btys)
XXX (How) Bde (128, 129, 130 Btys)
RGA: 48 Heavy Bty
RE: 56th and 57th Field Coys

13TH INFANTRY BRIGADE
2/KOSB
2/Duke of Wellington's
1/Royal West Kents
2/KOYLI

14TH INFANTRY BRIGADE
2/Suffolks
1/East Surreys
1/DCLI
2/Manchesters

15TH INFANTRY BRIGADE
1/Norfolks
1/Bedfordshires
1/Cheshires
1/Dorsets

CAVALRY: 'A' Sqn, 19th Hussars
RFA: XV Bde (11, 52, 80 Btys)
XXVII Bde (119, 120, 121 Btys)
XXVIII Bde (122, 123, 124 Btys)
VIII(How) Bde (37, 61, 65 Btys)

RGA: 108 Heavy Bty
RE: 17th and 59th Field Coys

19TH INFANTRY BRIGADE
(formed at Valenciennes, 22 August)
2/Royal Welsh Fusiliers
1/Cameronians
1/Middlesex
2/Argylls

L. OF C BATTALION
1/Devons (to 8th Infantry Brigade in September)

GHQ TROOPS
North Irish Horse
South Irish Horse

Royal Flying Corps: 2nd, 3rd, 4th, 5th and 6th Aeroplane Squadrons

III CORPS (Pulteney)
(formed in France 31 August)

4th Division (Snow)	**6th Division (Keir)**
(reached Le Cateau 24 August)	*(reached the Aisne 16 September)*

10TH INFANTRY BRIGADE
1/Royal Warwicks
2/Seaforths
1/Royal Irish Fusiliers
2/Royal Dublin Fusiliers

16TH INFANTRY BRIGADE
1/The Buffs
1/Leicesters
1/KSLI
1/York and Lancaster

11TH INFANTRY BRIGADE
1/Somerset L.I.
1/East Lancs
1/Hampshires
1/Rifle Brigade

17TH INFANTRY BRIGADE
1/Royal Fusiliers
1/North Staffords
2/Leinsters
3/Rifle Brigade

12TH INFANTRY BRIGADE
1/King's Own
2/Lancashire Fusiliers
2/Royal Inniskilling Fusiliers
2/Essex

18TH INFANTRY BRIGADE
1/West Yorks
1/East Yorks
2/Sherwood Foresters
2/Durham L.I.

CAVALRY: 'B' Sqn, 19th Hussars
RFA: XIV Bde (39, 68, 88 Btys)
XXIX Bde (125, 126, 127 Btys)
XXXII Bde (27, 134, 135 Btys)
XXXVII (How) Bde (31, 35, 55 Btys)
RGA: 31 Heavy Bty
RE: 7th and 9th Field Coys

CAVALRY: 'C' Sqn, 19th Hussars
RFA: II Bde (21, 42, 53 Btys)
XXIV Bde (110, 111, 112 Btys)
XXXVIII Bde (24, 34, 72 Btys)
XII (How) Bde (43, 86, 87 Btys)
RGA: 24 Heavy Bty
RE: 12th and 38th Field Coys

IV CORPS (Rawlinson)
(but see text passim)

7th Division (Capper)	**3rd Cavalry Division (Byng)**
(landed Zeebrugge 6 October)	*(landed Zeebrugge 7 October)*

7th Division (Capper)
(landed Zeebrugge 6 October)

20TH INFANTRY BRIGADE
1/Grenadier Guards
2/Scots Guards
2/Border Regt
2/Gordons

21ST INFANTRY BRIGADE
2/Bedfordshires
2/Green Howards
2/Royal Scots Fusiliers
2/Wiltshires

22ND INFANTRY BRIGADE
2/Queen's
2/Royal Warwicks
1/Royal Welsh Fusiliers
1/South Staffords

3rd Cavalry Division (Byng)
(landed Zeebrugge 7 October)

6TH CAVALRY BRIGADE
3rd Dragoon Guards
1st Royal Dragoons
10th Hussars

7TH CAVALRY BRIGADE
1st Life Guards
2nd Life Guards
Royal Horse Guards

RHA: 'K' Bty
RE: 3rd Field Squadron

CAVALRY: Northumberland Hussars
RHA: XIV Bde ('C', 'F', 'T' Btys)
RFA: XXII Bde (104, 105, 106 Btys)
XXXV Bde (12, 25, 58 Btys)
RGA: III (Heavy) Bde (111, 112 Btys)
RE: 54th and 55th Field Coys

NOTES

1   8th Infantry Division arrived in France on 6 November but, except for a small contingent, did not enter the fighting area until after 22 November.

2   The Indian Corps began disembarking at Marseilles on 30 September, but only the following formations were in action in France and Flanders by 22 November: the Ferozepore and Jullundur Brigades of the Lahore Division; all three Brigades of the Meerut Division; the Secunderabad Cavalry Brigade; and the Jodhpur Lancers.

3   The Antwerp Force consisted of two Royal Naval Brigades and one Royal Marine Brigade.

4   The following Yeomanry and Territorial units were serving in the line by 22 November: Oxfordshire Hussars, Northumberland Hussars, Leicestershire Yeomanry and North Somerset Yeomanry; 14th London Regt (London Scottish), 1/HAC, 8/Royal Scots, 16th London Regt (Queen's Westminster Rifles), 5/Cameronians, 5th London Regt (London Rifle Brigade), 1/Hertfordshires. By December 1914 and January 1915 the picture had changed dramatically, for by then the old Army had been bled white.

5   Finally, it should be remembered that in the savage fighting of the first battle of Ypres many units virtually ceased to exist, while others were transferred from one formation to another. This Order of Battle is therefore as accurate a record as possible of the fighting men who qualified for the Mons Star. Let it be remembered that so did many men of the RASC, RAMC, Military Police and others whose units are not recorded here. It was not necessary to be in a front-line trench to be under fire.